# Revelations & the Bible Decoded by Enoch

*"The hubris of intellect decries that which is foreign to its concepts"*

*William C. Henry Sr.*

# *Disclaimer*

**46 St. Books**
Published by 46 St. Books
46 St. Books USA Inc.,
Philadelphia, PA 19144, USA

Copyright © William C. Henry Sr., 2012 - Updated 5/2013

All rights reserved under International and Pan-American Copyright Conventions.

ISBN # 978-0-615-73178-0

Library of Congress Cataloging-in-Publication Data
LCCN#2012954449

Henry Sr., William.
Revelations & the Bible Decoded by Enoch

PRINTED IN THE UNITED STATES OF AMERICA

PUBLISHER'S NOTE
This book is a work of non-fictional based on archival scriptures, texts, and documents. All images used are either owned, work for hire, acquired works, use with permission, and from the Library of Congress.

BOOKS ARE AVAILABLE AT QUANTITY DISCOUNTS WHEN USED TO PROMOTE PRODUCTS OR SERVICES. FOR INFORMATION PLEASE WRITE 46 ST. BOOKS, 55 WEST PENN ST, PHILADELPHIA, PA 19144 OR VISIT OUR WEBSITE AT WWW.46STBOOKS.COM

# *Dedication*

*This book is dedicated to all that was, to all that is, and to all that is to come! We as human beings are at a crucial point in our development and understanding as spiritual beings. The small inconsequential differences that we have allowed to fester and separate us will fall away as a veil when we truly begin to understand. I dedicate this to one and all, great and small, for I am no greater than my sister, and no smaller than my brother.*

*This book is dedicated to the memory of my mother, my firstborn son, and to my best friend. You are all extremely loved and missed, but, I know without a doubt that we shall meet again!*

*I leave a special dedication to Immanuel Velikofsky. You have tilled the soil for us to harvest the understanding of that which is still to be reaped.*

Will Henry

*Missing you more each day T* ☹

*Jeremiah 48: 8 And the spoiler (Destroyer) shall come upon every city, and no city shall escape: the valley also shall perish, and the plain shall be destroyed, as the LORD hath spoken*.

*"the tribes of the desert have become Egyptians everywhere."*
*Ipuwer – Lament for Ipuwer*

# Table of Contents

Introduction – pg. 9

Astronomy Glossary – pg.11

Apocryphal Book of Enoch Decoded (400-160 BCE)– pg. 27

The Exodus Decoded (300 BCE)– pg. 51

Hebrew Scapegoat – pg. 73

Ipuwer Papyrus Decoded (1300 BCE) – pg. 75

Lament for Sumer and Urim (2000 BCE) – pg. 79

Jubilees Decoded (100 BCE)– pg. 83

Job Decoded (600-400 BCE)– pg. 95

Tabu-utul-bel – The Pious Sufferer (1500 BCE) – pg. 107

Apocalypse of Peter Decoded (1-76 CE)– pg. 111

Ezekiel Decoded (600 BCE) – pg. 115

Revelations to St. John Decoded (70-95 CE) – pg. 121

Essene Revelations (150-80 BCE) – pg. 167

Enki and the Sumerian Cylinder Seals Decoded (3100-1000 BCE) – pg. 179

The Sacred Number 40 – pg. 211

The Sacred Number 7 – pg. 213

Zodiac & Biblical Theology – pg. 221

Angels and Demons – pg. 227

El's in the Bible – pg. 229

Biblical Word Frequencies – pg. 231

Zodiac Wheels around the globe – pg. 233

Obelisks, Steeples, Minarets, Jacob's Ladder, and Spires – pg. 235

Aztec/Maya World Sun Connection – pg. 243

Lord Krishna, Mahabharata, Ophicuchus, and Kali Yuga – pg. 247

Egyptian Kings List of note – pg. 249

Conclusions – pg. 253

Addendum I – The Celestial Vault of Pope Paul III – pg. 269

Addendum II – Earth's Global Geomagnetic Field – pg. 275

Addendum III – Ezekiel the Prophet – Tammuz – pg.277

*Contest Extra – pg. 281*

*References – pg. 283*

# *Introduction*

This project came upon me out of the proverbial blue. There seemed to be a door upon a door opening up, each revealing another tantalizing clue. As these clues and doors opened, veils began to drop that showed me other possibilities. The paradigm of our present reality began to take on another form, as misinterpretations, lies, and half-truths become clear and evident. I have taken every opportunity to handle the subject matter in a manner sensitive to others beliefs, and still present the material in an honest and easy to interpret manner. Each and every person born into Creation has a Divine right to worship as their soul sees fit. Wherever our souls return to on the day that we pass on, we all return to the same Divine progenitor. I know without doubt that there is a single source that connects and binds us one to the other. I love and respect all that has come into Creation, and I am humbled constantly by one and all.

I grew up in Philadelphia, Pennsylvania, to a mother that would become an ordained minister in the Pentecostal church. We at one time lived next door to the church, and if you got sick they would carry you to service for prayer. As a child, my mother and I would have philosophical discussions on the Bible and a myriad of topics. I was constantly amazed by her intellect, as she was one of the few people that I have seen that able to complete a New York Times crossword puzzle in one sitting. It takes me a week to do one to this day, and there still may be some blank spots. My mother taught me to constantly expand my horizons and to question all presented before me. I spent every weekend at the beautiful main branch of the Philadelphia Public Library, sprawled out on the floor of the edifice from opening to close. This was where I went to escape into the world of Roman, Greek, and Norse mythology, and whatever topic piqued my interest. This expanding intellect often collided in Sunday school with questions that could not be answered, and the worst thing that an adult can do is to try and fit their square answer into a child's round peg! I was thereafter quietly excused from Sunday school responsibilities, and this left time to enjoy my beloved Philadelphia Eagles.

I am an eternal student of religion, history, mythology, architecture, language, arts, astronomy, music, sports, and more. I find our existence to be such a beautiful and terrifying thing. We presently sit at a crossroads in understanding our place in Creation. There are hints of civilizations that were here on Earth before our present memory accounts for. We must begin to rethink many of the ways that we worship and what we worship. I do believe that there is True Divinity awaiting us. This is not about New Age or Space Age. I have never attended a Masonic meeting and have no affiliations with any organization at all! I am not here to further anyone's agenda, but to present the documents in an unbiased manner. I will never tell anyone who, how, or what to believe in. Presented within this book is simply what was found once some of the language of the ancients was understood. I will show where there has been a complete synthesis of astronomy, astrology, deities, theology, rites, rituals, and more.

The Apocryphal Book of Enoch has been bandied about these past few years as being a book of mysticism, magic, and spurious texts. I guess that it took someone equally spurious to understand it, such as myself. Once we begin to understand the language and theology that Enoch used, it becomes crystal clear what he speaks of. By understanding Enoch, we understand the other narratives of; Revelations, Exodus, Ezekiel, Peter, Paul, and the Sibylline Oracles along with many others have borrowed, or wholly rewrote Enoch out of the Bible!

Enoch was adored by the early Hebrews and Christians, although his book was not included in the Torah, Tanakh or King James Bible. This curious exclusion of the first Prophet has been debated by theologians and researchers alike. The Books of Enoch date from around 300 BCE, and have survived into the present time in an Ethiopian and Greek version. I had never read much of the Book of Enoch, until one day I decided to pick it up. When I looked at the books that I had left alone prior, I was astounded! The language that Enoch used jumped off the pages at me. I will show with painful clarity why Enoch was not included in the Bible, and just what Enoch was so enraptured with as well as many others!

There will be a small segment that instantly see what is there and understand that truth. There will be some that will not examine it at all, and others that may get angered. We all must remember that we have a seminal right of free expression and understanding. I am not here to tear anything down, my hope is to build something up. I truly have love for one and all.

# *Glossary of Astronomy Terms*

This will in all probability be the first book in publishing history to lead with the glossary. And it will probably be the last one to do so. You may wonder why I chose to lead with the astronomy glossary? This question bears an excellent explanation. This is your first lesson in understanding the language of Enoch. Once we understand that Enoch is astronomy mixed with theology, it is easy to understand his astronomical observations, prophecies, and parables. In Genesis, Enoch was the 7th in line from Adam, the son of Jared, the father of Methuselah, the grandfather of Lamech, and the great grandfather of Noah. Enoch lived sixty-five years, walked with God three-hundred years, and then was no more. The only man said to have walked with God bears only a one line mention after he leaves us with a 364 day calendar year. When Enoch speaks of gates, windows, portals, mansions, houses, chariots, shepherds, parabolic and more, he is talking in the astronomy terms of the time. The later writers of Sacred or Biblical texts, their prophecies and theology become transparent once we truly understand what has been improperly relayed all of these millennia. It is important to look at our Biblical texts with open and unbiased eyes.

*Aberration of Starlight* - The angular shift in the apparent direction of a star caused by the orbital motion of the Earth

*Absolute Magnitude* - The apparent magnitude a star would have if it were at a distance of 10 parsecs (pc)

*Absorption Line* - A dark line superimposed on a continuous spectrum when a gas absorbs light from a continuous source that is hotter than the absorbing gas

*Acceleration* - The rate of change of velocity. An acceleration may involve a change of speed, direction of motion, or both

*Acceleration of Gravity* - The acceleration of a body, equal to 9.8 meters per second per second (m/s2), caused by the force of gravity near the surface of the Earth

*Accretion* - The growth in the mass of a body by the infall of matter gravitationally attracted to the body

*Accretion Disk* - A disk of gas and dust spiraling inward toward a star or toward the nucleus of a galaxy

*Accretional Heating* - The heating of a body by the impacts that occur as it grows by adding infalling material

*Achondrite* - A stony meteorite lacking chondrules

*Active Galactic Nucleus* - The nucleus of an active galaxy

*Active Galaxy* - A galaxy whose nucleus is unusually bright and small. Seyfert galaxies, BL Lacertae objects, and quasars are examples of active galaxies

*Active Region* - A region of the Sun's surface layers that has a large magnetic field and in which sunspots, flares, and prominences preferentially occur

*Adaptive Optics* - A system for modifying the shape of the mirror of a telescope to compensate for atmospheric seeing and to produce sharp images

*Ae and Be Stars* - Pre-main sequence stars more massive than 3 solar masses

*Aerosol* - Liquid droplets and solids suspended in the atmosphere of a planet or satellite

*Aesthenosphere* - A layer of plastic, deformable rock located in the upper mantle of a planet directly below the lithosphere

*Albedo* - The ratio of the light reflected in all directions by a surface to the light incident on it. A perfectly reflecting surface has an albedo of 1, a perfectly absorbing surface has an albedo of 0

*Alpha Particle* - The nucleus of a helium atom, consisting of two protons and two neutrons

*Altitude* - The angular distance between the direction to an object and the horizon. Altitude ranges from 0 degrees for an object on the horizon to 90 degrees for an object directly overhead

*Amino Acid* - A carbon-based molecule from which protein molecules are assembled

*Amor Asteroid* - A member of a class of asteroids having orbits that cross the orbital distance of the Earth

*Angular Momentum* - The momentum of a body associated with its rotation or revolution. For a body in a circular orbit, angular momentum is the product of orbital distance, orbital speed, and mass. When two bodies collide or interact, angular momentum is conserved

*Annihilation* - The mutual destruction of a matter-antimatter pair of particles. The charges on the two particles cancel and the mass of the particles is entirely converted to energy

*Annular eclipse* - A solar eclipse in which the Moon is too far from the Earth to block the entire Sun from view and a thin ring of sunlight appears around the Moon

*Antapex* - The direction in the sky away from which the Sun is moving. Because of the Sun's motion, nearby stars appear to converge toward the antapex

*Antimatter* - A type of matter which annihilates ordinary matter on contact. For every particle, there is a corresponding antimatter particle. For example, the antimatter counterpart of the proton is the antiproton

*Apex* - The direction in the sky toward which the Sun is moving. Because of the Sun's motion, nearby stars appear to diverge from the apex

Aphelion - The point in the orbit of a solar system body where it is farthest from the Sun
Apollo Asteroid - A member of a class of asteroids having orbits that cross the orbital distance of the Earth
Apparent Brightness - The observed brightness of a celestial body
Apparent Magnitude - The observed magnitude of a celestial body
Apparent Solar Day - The amount of time that passes between successive appearances of the Sun on the meridian. The apparent solar day varies in length throughout the year
Apparent Solar Time - Time kept according to the actual position of the Sun in the sky. Apparent solar noon occurs when the Sun crosses an observer's meridian
Arachnoid - A circular feature on the surface of Venus connected to other similar features by a web of fractures
Ascending Node - The point in the Moon's orbit where it crosses the ecliptic from south to north
Association - A group of stars whose gravity is insufficient to hold it together but has not yet had time to disperse
Asteroid - A small, planet-like solar system body. Most asteroids are rocky in makeup and have orbits of low eccentricity and inclination
Asteroid Belt - The region of the solar system lying between 2.1 and 3.3 astronomical units (AU) from the Sun. The great majority of asteroids are found in the asteroid belt
Astrology - A pseudoscience that holds that people and events are influenced by the configurations of the Sun, Moon, and planets with respect to each other and the stars
Astronomical Unit (AU) - The average distance between the Earth and the Sun
Asymptotic Giant Branch (AGB) - The portion of the H-R diagram occupied by enormous, cool stars with helium-burning shells
Aten Asteroid - An asteroid having an orbit with semi-major axis smaller than 1 AU
Atom - A particle consisting of a nucleus and one or more surrounding electrons
Atomic Number - The number of protons in the nucleus of an atom. Unless the atom is ionized, the atomic number is also the number of electrons orbiting the nucleus of the atom
Aurora Australis - Light emitted by atoms and ions in the upper atmosphere near the south magnetic pole. The emission occurs when atoms and ions are struck by energetic particles from the Sun
Aurora Borealis - Light emitted by atoms and ions in the upper atmosphere near the north magnetic pole. The emission occurs when atoms and ions are struck by energetic particles from the Sun
Autumnal Equinox - The point in the sky where the Sun appears to cross the celestial equator moving from north to south. This happens on approximately September 22
Azimuth - The angular distance between the north point on the horizon eastward around the horizon to the point on the horizon nearest to the direction to a celestial body
Baily's Beads - Points of light around the limb of the Moon just before and just after a total eclipse of the Sun. Baily's beads are caused by sunlight shining through valleys on the Moon's limb
Balmer Series - A series of absorption or emission lines of hydrogen seen in the visible part of the spectrum
Barred Spiral Galaxy - A spiral galaxy in which the nucleus is crossed by a bar. The spiral arms start at the ends of the bar
Basalt - An igneous rock often produced in volcanic eruptions
Big Bang - The explosive event at the beginning of the universe. The expansion produced the Big Bang that continues today
Binary Accretion Theory - A theory of the origin of the Moon that holds that the Moon and the Earth formed at about the same time out of the same swarm or cloud of material
Binary Star System - A pair of stars that orbit each other under their mutual gravitational attraction
Bipolar Outflow - Relatively narrow beams of matter ejected in opposite directions by a protostar
Black Hole - A region of space from which no matter or radiation can escape. A black hole is a result of the extreme curvature of space by a massive compact body
Blackbody - An object that is a perfect absorber of radiation falling on it
Blackbody Radiation - The electromagnetic radiation emitted by a blackbody. The spectrum and intensity of blackbody radiation are controlled by the temperature of the blackbody. Many stars and other celestial bodies approximate blackbodies
Blazar - A type of active galaxy named for BL Lacertae, the first of the type discovered. Blazars show rapid, unpredictable variations in brightness
Bow Shock - The region where the solar wind is slowed as it impinges on the Earth's magnetosphere
Broad Line Region - The high-density region in a quasar where broad emission lines are formed
Brown Dwarf - A star with too low a mass for nuclear fusion to begin in its core
C-type Asteroid - One of a class of very dark asteroids whose reflectance spectra show no absorption features due to the presence of minerals
Capture Theory - The theory of the origin of the Moon that holds that the Moon formed elsewhere in the solar system and then was captured into orbit about the Earth

*Carbonaceous Chondrite* - A stony meteorite that contains carbon-rich material. Carbonaceous chondrites are thought to be primitive samples of material from the early solar system
*Cassini's Division* - A conspicuous 1800 kilometer (km) wide gap between the outermost rings of Saturn
*Celestial Equator* - The circle where the Earth's equator, if extended outward into space, would intersect the celestial sphere
*Celestial Horizon* - The circle on the celestial sphere which is 90 degrees from the zenith. The celestial horizon is approximately the boundary between the Earth and sky
*Celestial Mechanics* - The part of physics and astronomy that deals with the motions of celestial bodies under the influence of their mutual gravitational attraction
*Celestial Sphere* - An imaginary sphere surrounding the Earth. The celestial bodies appear to carry out their motions on the celestial sphere
*Cell* - The smallest structural unit of an organism that is capable of independent functioning, consisting of one or more nuclei, cytoplasm, and various organelles, all surrounded by a semipermeable cell membrane
*Central Force* - A force directed at the center of motion of a body. Gravity is the central force that accounts for the orbital motion of solar system bodies
*Centripetal Acceleration* - The acceleration toward the center of motion, that causes the path of an orbiting body to continually bend away from a straight line path
*Centripetal Force* - The central force that produces centripetal acceleration
*Cepheid Variable* - A member of a class of yellow pulsating stars that vary in brightness as they expand and contract. The period of a Cepheid is related to its luminosity
*Chandrasekhar Limit* - The maximum mass, about 1.4 solar masses, that a white dwarf star can have.
*Charge Coupled Device (CCD)* - An array of photosensitive electronic elements that can be used to record an image falling on it
*Chondrite* - A meteorite containing chondrules
*Chondrule* - A small, spherical body embedded in a meteorite. Chondrules are composed of iron, aluminum, and magnesium silicate rock
*Chromosphere* - The part of the Sun's atmosphere between the photosphere and the corona
*Circle* - A curve on which all points are equidistant from the center
*Circular Speed* - The speed that causes an orbiting body to have a circular orbit rather than an elliptic one
*Circumpolar* - A body is close enough to a celestial pole that its diurnal circle is always above the horizon. Circumpolar stars neither rise nor set
*Close Pair* - A binary system in which the two stars are close enough together that they transfer matter to one another during some stages of their evolution
*Cloud Core* - The dense part of molecular cloud where star formation takes place
*Cluster of Galaxies* - A group of galaxies held together by their mutual gravitational attraction
*Cluster of Stars* - A group of stars held together by their mutual gravitational attraction
*CNO Cycle* - The series of reactions by means of which massive stars fuse hydrogen into helium
*Collision Fragment* - A satellite which probably is a fragment of a larger satellite broken apart by a collision with a meteoroid
*Coma* - A spherical gaseous region that surrounds the nucleus of a comet. The coma of a comet may be 100,000 kilometers (km) or more in diameter
*Comet* - A small, icy body in orbit about the Sun. When a comet is near the Sun, it displays a coma and a tail
*Common Envelope* - A stage in the evolution of a close pair of stars in which matter shed by one of the stars fills the region just outside the Roche lobes of the two stars
*Conduction* - The transfer of heat by means of direct collisions between adjacent atoms, molecules, or ions
*Conic Section* - One of four kinds of curves (circle, ellipse, hyperbola, and parabola) that can be formed by slicing a right circular cone with a plane
*Conjunction* - The appearance of two celestial bodies, often a planet and the Sun, in approximately the same direction
*Conucleation* - A possible explanation for the origin of a wide binary pair of stars in which the two cloud fragments that become the stars are already in orbit about one another when they form
*Constellation* - One of 88 regions into which the celestial sphere is divided
*Continuous Spectrum* - A spectrum containing neither emission nor absorption lines
*Convection* - The process of energy transport in which heat is carried by hot, rising and cool, falling currents or bubbles of liquid or gas
*Convection Zone* - The outer part of the Sun's interior in which convection occurs
*Coordinate System* - A system in which numbers are used to give the location of a body or event. The longitude-latitude system is an example of a coordinate system used to locate things on the Earth's surface
*Coordinates* - The numbers used in a coordinate system. Longitude and latitude are examples of coordinates
*Core* - The innermost region of the interior of the Earth or another planet

*Coriolis Effect* - The acceleration which a body experiences when it moves across the surface of a rotating body. The acceleration results in a westward deflection of projectiles and currents of air or water when they move toward the Earth's equator and an eastward deflection when they move away from the equator

*Corona* - The outermost layer of the Sun's atmosphere. Gases in the corona are tenuous and hot

*Corona* - A circular feature on the surface of Venus. Coronae appear to be collapsed volcanic domes and can be as much as several hundred kilometers across

*Corona* - A type of surface feature of Uranus's satellite Miranda. Coronae consist of parallel ridges and troughs producing a striped appearance. Coronae have sharp boundaries.

*Coronal Hole* - A low density, dim region in the Sun's corona. Coronal holes occur in regions of open magnetic field lines where gases can flow freely away from the Sun to form the solar wind

*Coronal Mass Ejection* - A blast of gas moving outward through the Sun's corona and into interplanetary space following the eruption of a prominence

*Cosmic Background Radiation (CBR)* - Radiation observed to have almost perfectly uniform brightness in all directions in the sky. The CBR is highly redshifted radiation produced about a million years after the universe began to expand

*Cosmic Ray* - Extremely energetic ions and electrons that travel through space almost at the speed of light. Most cosmic rays come from great distances and may be produced in supernovas and pulsars

*Cosmic Ray Exposure Age* - The length of time that has passed since a meteorite broke off from a larger body and became exposed to radiation damage from cosmic rays

*Cosmological Principle* - The assumption that all observers in the Universe at a given time would observe the Universe to have the same essential features and large-scale structure

*Cosmology* - The study of the Universe as a whole

*Crater* - A roughly circular feature on the surface of a solar system body caused by the impact of an asteroid or comet

*Crater Density* - The number of craters of a given size per unit area of the surface of a solar system body

*Crater Saturatlon* - The maximum crater density a solar system body can have. Once saturation is reached, new craters can only be produced by eradicating old ones

*Crescent Phase* - The phase of the moon at which only a small, crescent-shaped portion of the near side of the Moon is illuminated by sunlight. Crescent phase occurs just before and after new moon

*Critical Density* - The value that the average density of the Universe must equal or exceed if the universe is closed. If the density of the Universe is less than the critical density, the Universe will continue to expand forever

*Crust* - The outermost layer of the interior of a planet or satellite

*Dark Matter* - Matter that cannot be detected or has not yet been detected by the radiation it emits. The presence of dark matter can be deduced from its gravitational interaction with other bodies

*Dark Nebula* - A dense, interstellar cloud containing enough gas and dust to block the light of background stars. The dimming of background stars gives the appearance of a region with no stars

*Declination* - The angular distance of a celestial body north or south of the celestial equator. Declination is analogous to latitude in the terrestrial coordinate system

*Decoupling Epoch* - The time about a million years after the expansion of the universe began when the universe became transparent and light could, for the first time, travel great distances before being absorbed or scattered. The cosmic background radiation was produced at the decoupling epoch

*Deferent* - One of the circles on which a planet moved according to the Ptolemaic model of the solar system

*Degenerate Gas* - A gas in which a type of particle (electrons or neutrons) are as tightly packed as permitted by the Pauli exclusion principle. In a degenerate gas, temperature has essentially no influence on pressure

*Degree* - A unit used to measured angles. There are 360 degrees in a circle

*Density* - The mass of a body divided by its volume

*Density Wave Theory* - A theory to account for the spiral arms of spiral galaxies. According to the density wave theory, spiral arms are the crests of waves moving through a galaxy like water waves move through water

*Descending Node* - The point in the Moon's orbit where it crosses the ecliptic from north to south

*Detector* - A device used to measure light once it has been brought into focus by a telescope

*Deuterium* - An isotope of hydrogen. The nucleus of a deuterium atom is a deuteron

*Deuteron* - A nucleus of deuterium, an isotope of hydrogen. A deuteron contains one proton and one neutron

*Diamond Ring* - The last of Baily's beads, which seems to shine with special brilliance just before a solar eclipse becomes total

*Differential Rotation* - Rotation in which the rotation period of a body varies with latitude. Differential rotation occurs for gaseous bodies like the Sun or for planets with thick atmospheres

*Differentiation* - The gravitational separation of the interior of a planet into layers according to density. When differentiation occurs inside a molten body, the heavier materials sink to the center and the light materials rise to the surface

*Direct Motion* - The eastward apparent motion of a solar system body with respect to the stars. Direct motion is interrupted by regular episodes of retrograde (westward) motion

*Disk Instability* - A possible explanation for the origin of a close binary pair of stars in which one star forms within the disk of gas and dust orbiting another, newly formed star

*Dispersion* - The separation of white light according to wavelength. Dispersion produces a rainbow-like spectrum

*Diurnal* - Daily

*Diurnal Circle* - The circular path that a celestial body traces out as it appears to move across the sky during an entire day. Diurnal circles are centered on the north and south celestial poles Doppler Effect - The change in the frequency of a wave (such as electromagnetic radiation) caused by the motion of the source and observer toward or away from each other

*Dust Tail* - A comet tail that is luminous because it contains dust that reflects sunlight. The dust in a comet tail is expelled from the nucleus of the comet

*Dwarf* - A main sequence star

*Dynamo* - A process in which electric currents within a rotating, convective body produce a magnetic field

*Eccentricity* - A measure of the extent to which an orbit departs from circularity. Eccentricity ranges from 0.0 for a circle to 1.0 for a parabola

*Eclipse* - The obscuration of the light from the Sun when the observer enters the Moon's shadow or the Moon when it enters the Earth's shadow. Also, the obscuration of a star when it passes behind its binary companion

*Eclipse Seasons* - The times, separated by about 5 1/2 months, when eclipses of the Sun and Moon are possible

*Eclipse Track* - The path of the Moon's shadow across the Earth during a solar eclipse

*Eclipse Year* - The interval of time (346.6 days) from one passage of the Sun through a node of the Moon's orbit to the next passage through the same node

*Eclipsing Binary* - Binary star systems for which the orbital plane of the stars lies so nearly in the line of sight that two stars alternately pass in front of one another, causing eclipses

*Ecliptic* - The plane of the Earth's orbit about the Sun. As a result of the Earth's motion, the Sun appears to move among the stars, following a path that is also called the ecliptic

*Eddington Luminosity* - The maximum luminosity that a body could emit without driving away surrounding material

*Einstein Ring* - The ring or near ring into which the image of a distant quasar is distorted if the quasar lies directly behind a galaxy or cluster of galaxies producing a gravitational lens

*Electromagnetic Wave* - A periodic electrical and magnetic disturbance that propagates through space and transparent materials at the speed of light. Light is an example of an electromagnetic wave

*Electron* - A low-mass, negatively charged particle that can either orbit a nucleus as part of an atom, or exist independently as part of a plasma

*Element* - A substance that cannot be broken down into a simpler chemical substance. Oxygen, nitrogen, and silicon are examples of the approximately 100 known elements

*Ellipse* - A closed, elongated curve describing the shape of the orbit that one body follows about another

*Elliptical Galaxy* - A galaxy having an ellipsoidal shape and lacking spiral arms

*Emission Line* - A narrow, bright region of the spectrum. Emission lines are produced when electrons in atoms jump from one energy level to lower energy level

*Energy Flux* - The rate at which a wave carries energy through a given area Energy Level - Any of the many energy states that an atom may have. Different energy levels correspond to different distances of the electron from the nucleus

*Epicycle* - One of the circles upon which a planet moved according to the Ptolemaic (geocentric) model of the solar system. The center of the epicycle moved on a larger circle, called the deferent

*Equant* - In the Ptolemaic system, the point from which the motion of the epicycle around the deferent is uniform

*Equation of State* - The relationship among pressure, density, and temperature for a gas or fluid. The ideal gas law, for which pressure is proportional to the product of temperature and density, is an example of an equation of state

*Equator* - The line around the surface of a rotating body that is midway between the rotational poles. The equator divides the body into northern and southern hemispheres

*Equatorial Jet* - The high-speed, eastward, zonal wind in the equatorial region of Jupiter's atmosphere

*Equatorial System* - A coordinate system, using right ascension and declination as coordinates, used to describe the angular location of bodies in the sky

*Equipotential* - A line or surface of equal potential energy. On the Earth, a line of equal elevation is approximately an equipotential

*Escape Velocity* - The speed that an object must have to achieve a parabolic trajectory and escape from its parent body

*Event Horizon* - The boundary of a black hole. No matter or radiation can escape from within the event horizon

*Evolutionary Track* - The path in an H-R diagram followed by the point representing the changing luminosity and temperature of a star as it evolves

*Exosphere* - The outer part of the thermosphere. Atoms and ions can escape from the exosphere directly into space

*Explosion Model* - A model for the formation of clusters of galaxies in which the clusters form at the intersections of expanding shells of matter driven outward by gigantic explosions

*Extinction* - The dimming of starlight due to absorption and scattering by interstellar dust particles.

*Fabry- Perot Etalon* - A nonabsorbing, multireflecting device, similar in design to the Fabry-Perot interferometer, that serves as a multilayer, narrow-bandpass filter.

*Fabry-Perot interferometer* - A plane-parallel interferometer that yields extremely high contrast over a wide range of finesse values without significantly reducing transmission.

*Filament* - A dark line on the Sun's surface when a prominence is seen projected against the solar disk

*Fireball* - An especially bright streak of light in the sky produced when an interplanetary dust particle enters the Earth's atmosphere, vaporizing the particle and heating the atmosphere

*Fission* - A nuclear reaction in which a nucleus splits to produce two less massive nuclei

*Fission* - A possible explanation for the origin of a close binary pair of stars in which a star splits into two pieces, each of which becomes a star

*Fission Theory* - A theory for the origin of the Moon in which the Moon consists of matter that was flung from the primitive Earth because of the Earth's rapid rotation

*Flare* - A brief, sudden brightening of a region of the Sun's atmosphere, probably caused by the abrupt release of magnetic energy

*Focal Length* - The distance between a mirror or lens and the point at which the lens or mirror brings light to a focus

*Focal Plane* - The surface where the objective lens or mirror of a telescope forms the image of an extended object

*Focal Point* - The spot where parallel beams of light striking a lens or mirror are brought to a focus

*Focus* - One of two points from which an ellipse is generated. For all points on the ellipse, the sum of the distances to the two foci is the same

*Force* - A push or a pull

*Fragmentation* - A possible explanation for the origin of a close binary pair of stars in which a collapsing cloud breaks into several pieces, each of which becomes a star

*Frequency* - The number of oscillations per second of a wave

*Full Phase* - The phase of the moon at which the bright side of the Moon is the face turned toward the Earth

*Fusion* - A nuclear reaction in which two nuclei merge to form a more massive nucleus

*Galactic Bulge* - A somewhat flattened distribution of stars, about 6 kiloparsecs (kpc) in diameter, surrounding the nucleus of the Milky Way

*Galactic Cannibalism* - The capture and disruption of one galaxy by another

*Galactic Disk* - A disk of matter, about 30 kiloparsecs (kpc) in diameter and 2 kiloparsecs thick, containing most of the stars and interstellar matter in the Milky Way

*Galactic Equator* - The great circle around the sky that corresponds approximately to the center of the glowing band of the Milky Way

*Galactic Halo* - The roughly spherical outermost component of the Milky Way, reaching to at least 30 to 40 kiloparsecs (kpc) from the center

*Galactic Latitude* - The angular distance of a body above or below the galactic equator

*Galactic Longitude* - The angular distance, measured eastward around the galactic equator, from the galactic center to the point on the equator nearest the direction to a body

*Galactic Nucleus* - The central region of the Milky Way

*Galaxy* - A massive system of stars, gas, and dark matter held together by its own gravity

*Gamma Ray* - The part of the electromagnetic spectrum having the shortest wavelengths

*Geocentric* - Centered on the Earth. In a geocentric model of the solar system, the planets moved about the Earth

*Geodesic* - The path in spacetime followed by a light beam or a freely moving object

*Giant* - A star larger and more luminous than a main sequence star (dwarf) of the same temperature and spectral type

*Giant Impact Theory* - The theory of the origin of the Moon that holds that the Moon formed from debris blasted into orbit when the Earth was struck by a Mars-size body

*Giant Molecular Cloud* - An unusually large molecular cloud that may contain as much as 1 million solar masses

*Gibbous Phase* - The phase of the moon at which the near side of the Moon is more than half illuminated by sunlight. Gibbous phase occurs just before and after full moon

*Globular Cluster* - A tightly packed, spherically shaped group of thousands to millions of old stars

*Granule* - A bright convective cell or current of gas in the Sun's photosphere. Granules appear bright because they are hotter than the descending gas that separates them

*Gravitational Lens* - A massive body that bends light passing near it. A gravitational lens can distort or focus the light of background sources of electromagnetic radiation

*Gravitational Potential Energy* - The energy stored in a body subject to the gravitational attraction of another body. As the body falls, its gravitational potential energy decreases and is converted into kinetic energy

*Gravitational Redshift* - The increase in the wavelength of electromagnetic radiation that occurs when the radiation travels outward through the gravitational field of a body

*Gravity* - The force of attraction between two bodies generated by their masses

*Great Attractor* - A great concentration of mass toward which everything in our part of the universe apparently is being pulled

*Great Circle* - A circle that bisects a sphere. The celestial equator and ecliptic are examples of great circles

*Great Red Spot* - A reddish elliptical spot about 40,000 km by 15,000 km in size in the southern hemisphere of the atmosphere of Jupiter. The Red Spot has existed for at least 3 1/2 centuries

*Greatest Elongation* - The position of Mercury or Venus when it has the greatest angular distance from the Sun

*Greenhouse Effect* - The blocking of infrared radiation by a planet's atmospheric gases. Because its atmosphere blocks the outward passage of infrared radiation emitted by the ground and lower atmosphere, the planet cannot cool itself effectively and becomes hotter than it would be without an atmosphere

*Ground State* - The lowest energy level of an atom

*HII Region* - A region of ionized hydrogen surrounding a hot star. Ultraviolet radiation from the star keeps the gas in the HII region ionized

*Habitable Zone* - The range of distances from a star within which liquid water can exist on the surface of an Earth-like planet

*Half-life* - The time required for half of the atoms of a radioactive substance to disintegrate

*Heliocentric* - Centered on the Sun. In the heliocentric model of the solar system, the planets move about the Sun

*Heliopause* - The boundary of the heliosphere, where the solar wind merges into the interstellar gas

*Helioseismology* - A technique used to study the internal structure of the Sun by measuring and analyzing oscillations of the Sun's surface layers

*Heliosphere* - The region of space dominated by the solar wind and the Sun's magnetic field

*Helium Flash* - The explosive consumption of helium in the core of a star when helium fusion begins in a degenerate gas in which pressure doesn't rise as energy is produced and temperature increases

*Herbig-Haro Object* - A clump of gas illuminated by a jet of matter streaming away from a young star

*Hertzsprung-Russell Diagram (H-R diagram)* - A plot of luminosities of stars against their temperatures. Magnitude may be used in place of luminosity and spectral type in place of temperature

*Hierarchical Clustering Model* - A model for the formation of clusters of galaxies in which individual galaxies form and then begin to collect into clusters

*Horizon System* - A coordinate system, using altitude and azimuth as coordinates, used to locate the positions of objects in the sky

*Horizontal Branch Star* - A star which is undergoing helium fusion in its core and hydrogen fusion in a shell surrounding the core

*Hubble Time* - An estimate of the age of the universe obtained by taking the inverse of Hubble's constant. The estimate is only valid if there has been no acceleration or deceleration of the expansion of the universe

*Hubble's Constant (H)* - The rate at which the recession speeds of galaxies increase with distance. Current estimates of Hubble's constant range from 50 to 100 kilometers per second per megaparsec (km/s per Mpc)

*Hubble's Law* - The linear relationship between the recession speeds of galaxies and their distances. The slope of Hubble's law is Hubble's constant

*Hydrostatic Equilibrium* - The balance between the inward directed gravitational force and the outward directed pressure force within a celestial body

*Hyperbola* - A curved path that does not close on itself. A body moving with a speed greater than escape velocity follows a hyperbola

*Ideal Gas Law* - The equation of state for a low-density gas in which pressure is proportional to the product of density and temperature

*Igneous Rock* - A rock formed by solidification of molten material

*Impetus* - A theory of motion, developed in the fourteenth and fifteenth centuries, that motion could continue only so long as a force was at work

*Inclination* - The tilt of the rotation axis or orbital plane of a body

*Index of Refraction* - The ratio of the speed of light in a vacuum to the speed of light in a particular substance. The index of refraction, which always has a value greater than 1.0, describes how much a beam of light is bent on entering or emerging from the substance

*Inertia* - The tendency of a body at rest to remain at rest and a body in motion to remain in motion at a constant speed and in constant direction

*Inertial Motion* - Motion in a straight line at constant speed followed by a body when there are no unbalanced forces acting on it

*Inferior Planet* - A planet whose orbit lies inside the Earth's orbit

*Inflation* - A brief period of extremely rapid and enormous expansion that may have occurred very early in the history of the universe

*Infrared* - The part of the electromagnetic spectrum having wavelengths longer than visible light but shorter than radio waves

*Instability Strip* - A region of the H-R diagram occupied by pulsating stars, including Cepheid variables and RR Lyrae stars

*Intercrater Plain* - Smooth portions of the surface of Mercury that lie between and around clusters of large craters

*Interferometry* - The use of two or more telescopes connected together to operate as a single instrument. Interferometers can achieve high angular resolution if the individual telescopes of which they are made are widely separated

*Interstellar Matter* - Gas and dust in the space between the stars

*Interstellar Reddening* - The obscuration, by interstellar dust particles, of blue starlight more strongly than red starlight

*Ion* - An atom from which one or more electrons has been removed

*Ionization* - The removal of one or more electrons from an atom

*Ionosphere* - The lower part of the thermosphere of a planet in which many atoms have been ionized by ultraviolet solar photons

*Iron Meteorite* - A meteorite composed primarily of iron and nickel

*Irregular Cluster* - A cluster of galaxies that lacks a symmetrical shape and structure

*Irregular Galaxy* - A galaxy having an amorphous shape and lacking symmetry

*Isochrone* - Lines in an H-R diagram occupied by stars of different masses but the same age

*Isotopes* - Nuclei with the same number of protons but different numbers of neutrons

*Isotropic* - Looking the same in all directions

*Jet* - A narrow beam of gas ejected from a star or the nucleus of an active galaxy

*Kelvin-Helmholtz Time* - The time it would take a star to contract from infinite diameter down to the main sequence while radiating away the gravitational energy released during contraction

*Kepler's Laws of Planetary Motion* - Three laws, discovered by Kepler, that describe the motions of the planets around the Sun

*Kiloparsec (kpc)* - A unit of distance, equal to 1000 parsecs (pc), often used to describe distances within the Milky Way or the Local Group of galaxies

*Kinetic Energy* - Energy of motion. Kinetic energy is given by one half the product of a body's mass and the square of its speed

*Kirchhoff's Laws* - Three "laws" that describe how continuous, bright line, and dark line spectra are produced

*Kuiper Belt* - A region beyond Neptune within which a large number of comets are believed to orbit the Sun. Short period comets are thought to originated in the Kuiper belt

*L1* - The point between two stars in a binary system where matter may flow from one star to the other

*Latitude* - The angular distance of a point north or south of the equator of a body as measured by a hypothetical observer at the center of a body

*Lava* - Molten rock at the surface of a planet or satellite

*Leap year* - A year in which there are 366 days

*Light* - The visible form of electromagnetic radiation

*Light Curve* - A plot of the brightness of a body versus time

*Light-Gathering Power* - A number, proportional to the area of the principal lens or mirror of a telescope, that describes the amount of light that is collected and focused by the telescope

*Light Year* - The distance that light travels in a year

*Limb* - The apparent edge of the disk of a celestial body

*Limb Darkening* - The relative faintness of the edge of the Sun's disk (limb) compared with the center of the Sun's disk

*Line of Nodes* - The line connecting the two nodes of the Moon's orbit around the Earth

*Lithosphere* - The rigid outer layer of a planet or satellite, composed of the crust and upper mantle

*Local Group* - The small cluster of galaxies of which the Milky Way is a member

*Local Hour Angle* - The angle, measured westward around the celestial equator, between the meridian and the point on the equator nearest a particular celestial object

*Long-period Comet* - A comet with an orbital period of 200 years or longer

*Longitude* - The angular distance around the equator of a body from a zero point to the place on the equator nearest a particular point as measured by a hypothetical observer at the center of a body

*Lookback Time* - The length of time that has elapsed since the light we are now receiving from a distant object was emitted

*Luminosity* - The rate of total radiant energy output of a body

*Luminosity Class* - The classification of a star's spectrum according to luminosity for a given spectral type. Luminosity class ranges from I for a supergiant to V for a dwarf (main sequence star)

*Luminosity Function* - The distribution of stars or galaxies according to their luminosities. A luminosity function is often expressed as the number of objects per unit volume of space that are brighter than a given absolute magnitude or luminosity.
*Lunar Eclipse* - The darkening of the Moon that occurs when the Moon enters the Earth's shadow.
*Lyman A Forest* - The large number of absorption lines seen at wavelengths just longer than the wavelength of the Lyman a line of hydrogen in the spectrum of a quasar. The Lyman a forest is caused by absorption by gas clouds lying between the quasar and the Earth
*Lyman Series* - A series of absorption or emission lines of hydrogen lying in the ultraviolet part of the spectrum
*M-type Asteroid* - One of a class of asteroids that have reflectance spectra like those of metallic iron and nickel
*Magellanic Clouds* - Two irregular galaxies that are among the nearest neighbors of the Milky Way
*Magma* - Molten rock within a planet or satellite
*Magnetopause* - The outer boundary of the magnetosphere of planet
*Magnetosphere* - The outermost part of the atmosphere of a planet, within which a very thin plasma is dominated by the planet's magnetic field
*Magnetotail* - The part of the magnetosphere of a planet stretched behind the planet by the force of the solar wind
*Magnitude* - A number, based on a logarithmic scale, used to describe the brightness of a star or other luminous body. Apparent magnitude describes the brightness of a star as we see it. Absolute magnitude describes the intrinsic brightness of a star
*Main Sequence* - The region in an H-R diagram occupied by stars that are fusing hydrogen into helium in their cores. The main sequence runs from hot, luminous stars to cool, dim stars
*Main Sequence Lifetime* - The length of time that a star spends as a main sequence star
*Major Axis* - The axis of an ellipse that passes through both foci. The major axis is the longest straight line that can be drawn inside an ellipse
*Mantle* - The part of a planet lying between its crust and its core
*Maria* - A dark, smooth region on the Moon formed by flows of basaltic lava
*Mascon* - A concentration of mass below the surface of the Moon that slightly alters the orbit of a spacecraft orbiting the Moon
*Mass* - A measure of the amount of matter a body contains. Mass is also a measure of the inertia of a body
*Mass Number* - A measure of the mass of a nucleus given by the total number of protons and neutrons in the nucleus
*Mass-Luminosity Relation* - The relationship between luminosity and mass for stars. More massive stars have greater luminosities
*Maunder Minimum* - A period of few sunspots and low solar activity that occurred between 1640 and 1700
*Mean Solar Time* - Time kept according to the average length of the solar day
*Megaparsec (Mpc)* - A unit of distance, equal to 1 million parsecs, often used to describe the distances of objects beyond the Local Group
*Meridian* - The great circle passing through an observer's zenith and the north and south celestial poles
*Mesopause* - The upper boundary of the mesosphere layer of the atmosphere of a planet
*Mesosphere* - The layer of a planet's atmosphere above the stratosphere. The mesosphere is heated by absorbing solar radiation
*Messier Objects* - Deep sky objects list by Charles Messier (1730-1817). Charles Messier was a French Astronomer whose work on the discovery of comets led to the compilation of the Messier Catalogue of nebulae and star clusters. The reason Messier compiled this catalogue was to save time while comet hunting. It takes time for a comet hunter to check each suspected comet (by checking for motion). With his small instrument (2 or 3 inch diameter refractor), even star clusters would look fuzzy like comets. (Check this by observing some of the M objects using binoculars.) By using his catalogue, Messier could see whether a comet suspect was actually a nebulae that he had previously observed. In all Messier has his name on 12 comets between 1760 and 1798. Actually, he independently discovered at least 15 comets, but did not get credit for all of his discoveries - in some cases they had been previously discovered. (Remember that communications were very slow in those days.) Louis XV gave Messier the nickname "Comet Ferret." Messier compiled an initial list of 103 objects. Of the seven other objects, M104 was added in 1921 by Camilille Flammarion who found it on Messier's copy of his 1781 catalogue; M105 through M107 were observed by Messier's chief comet hunting rival, Pierre Mechain (1744-1804) and were added in 1947; M108 and M109 were mentioned by Messier in his description of M97 and were added in 1960; and M110 was on Messier's map of M31. M110 was added in 1966. Note that not all the objects are real - some are clearly mistakes.
*Metallic Hydrogen* - A form of hydrogen in which the atoms have been forced into a lattice structure typical of metals. In the solar system, the pressures and temperatures required for metallic hydrogen to exist only occur in the cores of Jupiter and Saturn
*Metamorphic Rock* - A rock that has been altered by heat and pressure
*Meteor* - A streak of light produced by meteoroid moving rapidly through the Earth's atmosphere. Friction vaporizes the meteoroid and heats atmospheric gases along the path of the meteoroid

*Meteor Shower* - A temporary increase in the normal rate at which meteors occur. Meteor showers last for a few hours or days and occur on about the same date each year
*Meteorite* - The portion of a meteoroid that reaches the Earth's surface
*Meteoroid* - A solid interplanetary particle passing through the Earth's atmosphere
*Microlensing event* - The temporary brightening of a distant object that occurs because its light is focused on the Earth by the gravitational lensing of a nearer body
*Micrometeorite* - A meteoritic particle less than a 50 millionths of a meter in diameter. Micrometeorites are slowed by atmospheric gas before they can be vaporized, so they drift slowly to the ground
*Milky Way* - The galaxy to which the Sun and Earth belong. Seen as a pale, glowing band across the sky
*Mineral* - A solid chemical compound
*Minimum* - The time of minimum light in a light curve
*Minor Planet* - Another name for asteroid
*Minute of Arc* - A unit of angular measurement equal to 1/60 of a degree
*Mode of Oscillation* - A particular pattern of vibration of the Sun
*Molecular Cloud* - A relatively dense, cool interstellar cloud in which molecules are common
*Momentum* - A quantity, equal to the product of a body's mass and velocity, used to describe the motion of the body. When two bodies collide or otherwise interact, the sum of their momenta is conserved
*Narrow Line Region* - The low density region in a quasar where narrow emission lines are formed
*Neap Tide* - An unusually low high tide and unusually high low tide that occur when the tidal forces of the Sun and Moon act at right angles to one another
*Neutral Gas* - A gas containing atoms and molecules but essentially no ions or free electrons
*Neutrino* - A particle with no charge and probably no mass that is produced in nuclear reactions. Neutrinos pass freely through matter and travel at or near the speed of light
*Neutron* - A nuclear particle with no electric charge
*Neutron Star* - A star composed primarily of neutrons and supported by the degenerate pressure of the neutrons
*Neutronization* - A process by which, during the collapse of the core of a star, protons and electrons are forced together to make neutrons
*New Comet* - A comet that has entered the inner solar system for the first time
*New Phase* - The phase of the moon in which none or almost none of the near side of the Moon is illuminated by sunlight, so the near side appears dark
*Nodes* - The points in the orbit of the Moon where the Moon crosses the ecliptic plane
*Normal Spiral Galaxy* - A galaxy in which the spiral arms emerge from the nucleus
*North Celestial Pole* - The point above the Earth's north pole where the Earth's polar axis, if extended outward into space, would intersect the celestial sphere. The diurnal circles of stars in the northern hemisphere are centered on the north celestial pole
*North Circumpolar Region* - The region of the northern sky within which the diurnal circles of stars do not dip below the horizon. The size of the north circumpolar region varies with the latitude of the observer
*Nova* - An explosion on the surface of a white dwarf star in which hydrogen is abruptly converted into helium
*Nucleic Acid* - A long chain of nucleotides. DNA and RNA are nucleic acids
*Nucleosynthesis* - The building up of more massive elements from less massive elements through nuclear reactions in stars
*Nucleoitide* - The class of organic molecules of which nucleic acids are composed
*Nucleus* - The massive, positively charged core of an atom. The nucleus of an atom is surrounded by one or more electrons. A nucleus missing one or more accompanying electrons is called an ion
*Nucleus* - An irregularly shaped, loosely packed lump of dirty ice several kilometers across that is the permanent part of a comet
*Number Density* - The number of particles in a given volume of space
*Objective* - The main lens or mirror of a telescope
*Oblateness* - A departure from spherical shape of a body in which the body's polar diameter is smaller than its equatorial diameter
*Occultation* - Occultations occur when a moving object, such as a planet or the moon, blocks the light coming from a more distant object, such as a star.
*Oort Cloud* - The region beyond the planetary system, extending to 100,000 AU or more, within which a vast number of comets orbit the Sun. When comets from the Oort cloud enter the inner solar system, they become new comets
*Opacity* - The ability of a substance to absorb radiation. The higher the opacity, the less transparent the substance is
*Opposition* - The configuration of a planet or other body when it appears opposite the Sun in the sky
*Orbit* - The elliptical or circular path followed by a body that is bound to another body by their mutual gravitational attraction
*Organic molecule* - A molecule containing carbon
*Outflow channel* - A Martian valley with few tributaries probably formed by the sudden melting and runoff of sub-surface water

*Outgassing* - The release of gas from the interior of a planet or satellite
*Ozone* - A molecule consisting of three oxygen atoms. Ozone molecules are responsible for the absorption of solar ultraviolet radiation in the Earth's atmosphere
*Pair Production* - A process in which gamma rays are transformed into a particle and its antiparticle (such as an electron and a positron)
*Pancake Model* - A model for the formation of clusters of galaxies in which protoclusters form first and then fragment into individual galaxies
*Parabola* - A geometric curve followed by a body that moves with a speed exactly equal to escape velocity (parabolic trajectory)
*Parallax* - The shift in the direction of a star caused by the change in the position of the Earth as it moves about the Sun
*Parsec* - The distance at which a star has a parallax of 1 second of arc. At a distance of 1 parsec (pc), an AU fills an angle of one second of arc
*Patera* - A type of Martian volcano that resembles shield volcanos, but has even more gentle slopes
*Pauli Exclusion Principle* - A physical law that limits the number of particles of a particular kind that can be placed in a given volume. A gas in which that limit is reached is degenerate
*Penumbra* - The outer part of the shadow of a body where sunlight is partially blocked by the body
*Perihelion* - The point in the orbit of a body when it is closest to the Sun
*Period* - The time it takes for a regularly repeated process to repeat itself
*Period-luminosity Relationship* - The relationship between the period of brightness variation and the luminosity of a Cepheid variable star. The longer the period of a Cepheid is, the more luminous the Cepheid
*Perturbation* - A deviation of the orbit of a solar system body from a perfect ellipse due to the gravitational attraction of one of the planets
*Phase Change* - A change in the physical state of a substance. The boiling, freezing, and melting of water are examples of phase changes
*Photon* - A massless particle of electromagnetic energy
*Photosphere* - The visible region of the atmosphere of the Sun or another star
*Pixel* - A "picture element," consisting of an individual detector in an array of detectors used to capture an image
*Planet* - One of the nine major bodies in orbit around the Sun
*Planetary Nebula* - A luminous shell surrounding a hot star. The gas in a planetary nebula was ejected from the star while it was a red giant
*Planetesimal* - A primordial solar system body of intermediate size that accreted with other planetesimals to form planets and satellites
*Planetology* - The comparative study of the properties of planets
*Plasma* - A fully or partially ionized gas
*Plasma Tail* - A narrow, ionized comet tail pointing directly away from the Sun
*Plate* - A section of the Earth's lithosphere pushed about by convective currents within the mantle
*Plate Tectonics* - The hypothesis that the features of the Earth's crust such as mountains and trenches are caused by the slow movement of crustal plates
*Plerion* - A supernova remnant, like the Crab Nebula, which has a filled center rather than being a shell
*Plume* - A rising column of gas over a hot region in the interior or atmosphere of a body
*Polarity* - The property of a magnet that causes it to have north and south magnetic regions
*Precession* - The slow, periodic conical motion of the rotation axis of the Earth or another rotating body
*Pressure* - The force exerted per unit area
*Primary Distance Indicator* - A type of object, such a Cepheid variable, for which we know the size or brightness by observing them in the Milky Way
*Prime Meridian* - The circle on the Earth's surface that runs from pole to pole through Greenwich, England. The zero point of longitude occurs where the prime meridian intersects the Earth's equator
*Primeval Atmosphere* - The original atmosphere of a planet
*Prograde Motion* - The eastward (normal) revolution of a solar system body.
*Prograde Rotation* - The eastward rotation of a solar system body
*Prominence* - A region of cool gas embedded in the corona. Prominences are bright when seen above the Sun's limb, but appear as dark filaments when seen against the Sun's disk
*Proper Motion* - The rate at which a star appears to move across the celestial sphere with respect to very distant objects
*Protein* - A large molecule, consisting of a chain of amino acids, that makes up the bodies of organisms
*Proton* - A positively charged nuclear particle
*Proton-proton Cycle* - A series of nuclear reactions through which stars like the Sun produce energy by converting hydrogen to helium. Named because the first reaction in the series is the reaction of one proton with another

*Protostar* - A star in the process of formation
*Pulsar* - A rotating neutron star with beams of radiation emerging from its magnetic poles. When the beams sweep past the Earth, we see "pulses" of radiation
*Quarter phase* - The phase of the moon in which half of the near side of the Moon is illuminated by the Sun
*Quasar* - A distant galaxy, seen as it was in the remote past, with a very small, luminous nucleus
*R-process* - The process of building up massive nuclei in which neutrons are captured at a rate faster than the newly produced nuclei can undergo radioactive decay
*Radial Velocity* - The part of the velocity of a body that is directed toward or away from an observer. The radial velocity of a body can be determined by the Doppler shift of its spectral lines
*Radiant* - The point in the sky from which the meteors in a meteor shower seem to originate
*Radiation Era* - The period of time, before about 1 million years after the expansion of the universe began, when radiation rather than matter was the dominant constituent of the universe
*Radiative Transfer* - The transport of energy by electromagnetic radiation
*Radio Galaxy* - A galaxy that is a strong source of radio radiation
*Radioactivity* - The spontaneous disintegration of an unstable nucleus of an atom
*Rays* - Long, narrow light streaks on the Moon and other bodies that radiate from relatively young craters. Rays consist of material ejected from a crater at the time it was formed by an impact
*Recession Speed* - The rate of movement of a galaxy away from the Milky Way caused by the expansion of the universe
*Recombination Epoch* - The time, about 1 million years after the expansion of the universe began, when most of the ions and electrons in the universe combined to form atoms
*Recurrent Nova* - A binary system in which the white dwarf star undergoes repeated nova outbursts
*Reflectance Spectrum* - The reflectivity of a body as a function of wavelength
*Reflection* - The bouncing of a wave from a surface
*Reflection Nebulae* - A cloud of interstellar gas and dust that is luminous because the dust it contains reflects the light of a nearby star
*Reflectivity* - The ability of a surface to reflect electromagnetic waves. The reflectivity of a surface ranges from 0% for a surface that reflects no light to 100% for a surface that reflects all the light falling on it
*Reflector* - A telescope in which the objective is a mirror
*Refraction* - The bending of light when it passes from a material having one index of refraction to another material having a different index of refraction
*Refractor* - A telescope in which the objective is a lens
*Regolith* - The surface layer of dust and fragmented rock, caused by meteoritic impacts, on a planet, satellite, or asteroid
*Regular Cluster* - A cluster of galaxies that has roughly spherical symmetry
*Regular Satellites* - Regularly spaced satellites with nearly circular orbits that form miniature "solar systems" about their parent planets
*Resolution* - The ability of a telescope to distinguish fine details of an image
*Resonance* - The repetitive gravitational tug of one body on another when the orbital period of one is a multiple of the orbital period of the other
*Retrograde Motion* - The westward revolution of a solar system body around the Sun
*Retrograde Rotation* - The westward rotation of a solar system body
*Richness* - A measure of the number of galaxies in a cluster. The more galaxies there are, the greater the richness
*Right Ascension* - Angular distance of a body along the celestial equator from the vernal equinox eastward to the point on the equator nearest the body. Right ascension is analogous to longitude in the terrestrial coordinate system
*Rille* - A lunar valley, probably the result of volcanic activity
*Roche distance* - The distance from a planet or other celestial body within which tidal forces from the body would disintegrate a smaller object
*Roche lobe* - The region around a star in a binary system in which the gravity of that star dominates
*Rock* - A solid aggregation of grains of one or more minerals
*Rotation Curve* - A plot of the speed of revolution of the stars and gas in a galaxy versus distance from the center of the galaxy
*RR Lyrae Star* - A member of a class of giant pulsating stars, all of which have pulsation periods of about 1 day
*Runoff Channel* - One of a network of Martian valleys that probably were formed by the collection of widespread rainfall
*S-process* - The process of building up massive nuclei in which neutrons are captured at a rate slower than the newly produced nuclei can undergo radioactive decay
*S-type Asteroid* - One of a class of asteroids whose reflectance spectra show an absorption feature due to the mineral olivine
*Saros* - The length of time between one member of a series of similar eclipses and the next (6585 1/3 days)

*Scarp* - A cliff produced by vertical movement of a section of the crust of a planet or satellite

*Scattering* - The redirection of light in random directions when it strikes atoms, molecules, or solid particles

*Schwarzschild Radius* - The radius of the event horizon of a black hole

*Sea Floor Spreading* - The splitting of the oceanic crust where magma forces the existing crust apart, creating new ocean floor

*Second of Arc* - A unit of angular measurement equal to 1/60 of a minute of arc or 1/3600 of a degree

*Secondary Atmosphere* - The atmosphere that forms after a planet has lost any original atmosphere it had

*Secondary Distance Indicator* - A type of object for which we know the size or brightness because objects of that type have been found in nearby galaxies

*Sedimentary Rock* - A rock formed by the accumulation of small mineral grains carried by wind, water, or ice to the spot where they were deposited

*Seeing* - A measure of the blurring of the image of an astronomical object caused by turbulence in the Earth's atmosphere

*Seismic Wave* - Waves that travel through the interior of a planet or satellite and are produced by earthquakes or their equivalent

*Seismometers* - Sensitive devices used to measure the strengths and arrival times of seismic waves

*Semi-major Axis* - Half of the major axis of an ellipse. Also equal to the average distance from the focus of a body moving on an elliptical orbit

*Seyfert Galaxy* - A barred or normal spiral galaxy with a small, very bright nucleus

*SETI* - The search for extraterrestrial intelligence

*Sgr A\** - A small, bright source of radio emission, possibly the accretion disk of a black hole, that probably marks the exact center of the Milky Way

*Shield Volcano* - A broad, gently sloped volcano built up by the repeated eruption of very fluid lava

*Short-period Comet* - A comet with an orbital period shorter than 200 years

*Sidereal Clock* - A clock that marks the local hour angle of the vernal equinox

*Sidereal Day* - The length of time (23 hours, 56 minutes, 4.091 seconds) between successive appearances of a star on the meridian

*Sidereal Month* - The length of time required for the Moon to return to the same apparent position among the stars

*Sidereal Period* - The time it takes for a planet or satellite to complete one full orbit about the Sun or its parent planet

*Silicate* - A mineral whose crystalline structure is dominated by silicon and oxygen atoms

*Sinuous Rille* - A winding lunar valley possibly caused by the collapse of a lava tube

*Smooth Plains* - Widespread sparsely cratered regions of the surface of Mercury possibly having a volcanic origin

*Solar Constant* - The solar energy received by a square meter of surface oriented at right angles to the direction to the Sun at the Earth's average distance (1 AU) from the Sun. The value of the solar constant is 1,372 watts per square meter

*Solar Flare* - An explosive release of solar magnetic energy

*Solar Motion* - The motion of the Sun with respect to the nearby stars

*Solar Nebula* - The rotating disk of gas and dust, surrounding the newly formed Sun, from which planets and smaller solar system bodies formed

*Solar Wind* - The hot plasma that flows outward from the Sun

*Solidification Age* - The amount of time that has passed since a meteorite solidified from the molten state

*South Celestial Pole* - The point above the Earth's South Pole where the Earth's polar axis, if extended outward into space, would intersect the celestial sphere. The diurnal circles of stars in the southern hemisphere are centered on the south celestial pole

*Spacelike Trip* - A path in spacetime that would require motion at a speed faster than the speed of light

*Spacetime* - The combination of three spatial coordinates and one time coordinate that we use to locate an event

*Spacetime Diagram* - A diagram showing one spatial coordinate against time, in which the paths of bodies and beams of light can be plotted

*Spectral Class* - A categorization, based on the pattern of spectral lines of stars, that groups stars according to their surface temperatures

*Spectrograph* - A device used to produce and record a spectrum

*Spectroscopic Binary* - A pair of stars whose binary nature can be detected by observing the periodic Doppler shifts of their spectral lines as they move about one another

*Spectroscopy* - The recording and analysis of spectra

*Spicule* - A hot jet of gas moving outward through the Sun's chromosphere

*Spiral Arm* - A long narrow feature of a spiral galaxy in which interstellar gas, young stars, and other young objects are found

*Spiral Galaxy* - A flattened galaxy in which hot stars, interstellar clouds, and other young objects form a spiral pattern

*Spokes* - Dark, short-lived radial streaks in Saturn's rings

Spring Tide - An unusually high, high tide and unusually low, low tide that occur when the tidal forces of the Sun and Moon are aligned. This occurs at full moon and new moon
Star - A massive gaseous body that has used, is using, or will use nuclear fusion to produce the bulk of the energy it radiates into space
Starburst Galaxy - A galaxy in which a very large number of stars have recently formed
Steady State Theory - A cosmological theory in which the universe always remains the same in its essential features, such as average density. In order to maintain constant density while expanding, the steady state theory required the continual creation of new matter
Stefan-Boltzmann Law - The relationship between the temperature of a blackbody and the rate at which it emits radiant energy
Stellar Occultation - The obstruction of the light from a star when a solar system body passes between the star and the observer
Stellar Parallax - The shift in the direction of a star caused by the change in the position of the Earth as it moves about the Sun
Stellar Population - A group of stars that are similar in spatial distribution, chemical composition, and age
Stony Meteorite - A meteorite made of silicate rock
Stony-iron Meteorite - A meteorite made partially of stone and partially of iron and other metals
Stratosphere - The region of the atmosphere of a planet immediately above the troposphere
Subduction - The process through which lithospheric plates of a planet or satellite are forced downward into the mantle
Summer Solstice - The point on the ecliptic where the Sun's declination is most northerly. The time when the Sun is at the summer solstice, around June 21, marks the beginning of summer
Sunspot - A region of the Sun's photosphere that appears darker than its surroundings because it is cooler
Sunspot Cycle - The regular waxing and waning of the number of spots on the Sun. The amount of time between one sunspot maximum and the next is about 11 years
Sunspot Group - A cluster of sunspots
Supergiant - An extremely luminous star of large size and mass
Supergranulation - The pattern of very large (15,000 to 30,000 km in diameter) convective cells in the Sun's photosphere
Superior Planet - A planet whose orbit lies outside the Earth's orbit
Superluminal Motion - The apparent separation of components of a quasar at speeds faster than the speed of light
Supernova - An explosion in which a star's brightness temporarily increases by as much as 1 billion times. Type I supernovas are caused by the rapid fusion of carbon and oxygen within a white dwarf. Type II supernovas are produced by the collapse of the core of a star
Supernova Remnant - The luminous, expanding region of gas driven outward by a supernova explosion
Synchronous Rotation - Rotation for which the period of rotation is equal to the period of revolution. An example of synchronous rotation is the Moon, for which the period of rotation and the period of revolution about the Earth are both 1 month
Synchrotron Emission - Electromagnetic radiation, usually observed in the radio region of the spectrum, produced by energetic electrons spiraling about magnetic field lines
Synodic Month - The length of time (29.53 days) between successive occurrences of the same phase of the Moon
Synodic Period - The length of time it takes a solar system body to return to the same configuration (opposition to opposition, for example) with respect to the Earth and the Sun
T Tauri Star - A pre-main sequence star, less massive than about 3 solar masses, showing intense emission lines
Terminal Velocity - The speed with which a body falls through the atmosphere of a planet when the force of gravity pulling it downward is balanced by the force of air resistance
Terrae - The light-colored, ancient, heavily cratered portions of the surface of the Moon
Terrestrial Planet - A rocky planet located in the inner solar system
Thermal Equilibrium - The condition in which a body or a portion of a body gains energy (by generating it or absorbing it) at the same rate at which energy is transported away from it
Thermal Pulse - The rapid consumption of helium in a shell within an asymptotic giant branch star
Thermosphere - The layer of the atmosphere of a planet lying above the mesosphere. The lower thermosphere is the ionosphere. The upper thermosphere is the exosphere
Tidal Capture - A possible explanation for the origin of a wide binary pair of stars in which two cloud fragments tidally interact with and capture one another
Tidal Force - The differences in gravity in a body being attracted by another body
Tidal Heating - The frictional heating of the interior of a satellite as it is flexed and released by a variable tidal force due to its parent planet
Tides - Distortions in a body's shape resulting from tidal forces
Timelike Trip - A path in spacetime that can be followed by a body moving slower than the speed of light
Transform Fault - The boundary between two of the Earth's crustal plates that are sliding past each other

*Transverse Velocity* - The part of the orbital speed of a body perpendicular to the Sun between the body and the Sun
*Triple A Process* - A pair of nuclear reactions through which three helium nuclei (alpha particles) are transformed into a carbon nucleus
*Trojan Asteroid* - One of a group of asteroids that orbit the Sun at Jupiter's distance and lie 60 degrees ahead of or behind Jupiter in its orbit
*Tropical Year* - The interval of time, equal to 365.242 solar days, between successive appearances of the Sun at the vernal equinox
*Tropopause* - The upper boundary of the troposphere of the atmosphere of a planet
*Troposphere* - The lowest layer of the atmosphere of a planet, within which convection produces weather
*Type Ia Supernova* - An extremely energetic explosion produced by the abrupt fusion of carbon and oxygen in the interior of a collapsing white dwarf star
*Type II Supernova* - An extremely energetic explosion that occurs when the core of a massive star collapses, probably producing a neutron star or black hole
*Ultraviolet* - The part of the electromagnetic spectrum with wavelengths longer than X rays, but shorter than visible light
*Umbra* - The inner portion of the shadow of a body, within which sunlight is completely blocked
*Umbra* - The dark central portion of a sunspot
*Universe* - All the matter and space there is
*V-type Asteroid* - The asteroid Vesta, which is unique in having a reflectance spectra resembling those of basaltic lava flows
*V/Vmax Test* - A statistical method used to determine whether quasars have changed over time
*Van Allen Belts* - Two doughnut-shaped regions in the Earth's magnetosphere within which many energetic ions and electrons are trapped
*Velocity* - A physical quantity that gives the speed of a body and the direction in which it is moving
*Vernal Equinox* - The point in the sky where the Sun appears to cross the celestial equator moving from south to north. This happens approximately on March 21
*Visual Binary Star* - A pair of stars orbiting a common center of mass in which the images of the components can be distinguished using a telescope and which have detectable orbital motion
*Vogt-Russell Theorem* - The concept that the original mass and chemical composition of an isolated star completely determine the course of its evolution
*Voids* - Immense volumes of space in which few galaxies, and clusters of galaxies can be found
*Volatile* - Element or compound that vaporizes at low temperature. Water and carbon dioxide are examples of volatiles
*Waning Crescent* - The Moon's crescent phase that occurs just before new moon
*Wave* - A regular series of disturbances that moves through a material medium or through empty space
*Wavelength* - The distance between crests of a wave. For visible light, wavelength determines color
*Waxing Crescent* - The Moon's crescent phase that occurs just after new moon
*Weight* - The gravitational force exerted on a body by the Earth (or another astronomical object)
*White Dwarf* - A small, dense star that is supported against gravity by the degenerate pressure of its electrons
*Wide Pair* - A binary star system in which the components are so distant from one another that they evolve independently
*Wien's Law* - The relationship between the temperature of a blackbody and the wavelength at which its emission is brightest
*Winter Solstice* - The point on the ecliptic where the Sun has the most southerly declination. The time when the Sun is at the winter solstice, around December 22, marks the beginning of winter
*X Ray* - The part of the electromagnetic spectrum with wavelengths longer than gamma rays but shorter than ultraviolet
*X-ray burst* - Sporadic burst of X rays originating in the rapid consumption of nuclear fuels on the surface of the neutron star in a binary system
*X-ray pulsar* - A neutron star from which periodic bursts of X rays are observed
*Year* - The length of time required for the Earth to orbit the Sun
*Zeeman Effect* - The splitting of a spectral line into two or more components when the atoms or molecules emitting the line are located in a magnetic field
*Zenith* - The point on the celestial sphere directly above an observer
*Zero Point* - The point from which the coordinates in a coordinate system are measured. For example, the vernal equinox is the zero point of right ascension and declination in the celestial coordinate system
*Zodiacal Constellations* - The band of constellations along the ecliptic. The Sun appears to move through the 12 zodiacal constellations during a year
*Zodiacal Light* - The faint glow extending away from the Sun caused by the scattering of sunlight by interplanetary dust particles lying in and near the ecliptic
*Zonal Winds* - The pattern of winds in the atmosphere of a planet in which the pattern of wind speeds varies with latitude

*Zone of Convergence* - According to plate tectonics, a plate boundary at which the crustal plates of a planet are moving toward one another. Crust is destroyed in zones of convergence

*Zone of Divergence* - According to plate tectonics, a plate boundary at which the crustal plates of a planet are moving away from one another. Crust is created in zones of divergence

# *The Apocryphal Book of Enoch Decoded – written @ 300 BCE*

**From-The Apocrypha and Pseudepigrapha of the Old Testament**

**Chapter 1**

1 The words of the blessing of Enoch, wherewith he blessed the elect and righteous, who will be

2 living in the day of tribulation, when all the wicked and godless are to be removed. And he took up his parable and said -Enoch a righteous man, whose eyes were opened by God, saw the vision of the Holy One in the heavens, which the angels showed me, and from them I heard everything, and from them I understood as I saw, but not for this generation, but for a remote one which is

*Eloquently stated!*

6 And the high mountains shall be shaken, And the high hills shall be made low, And shall melt like wax before the flame

7 And the earth shall be wholly rent in sunder, And all that is upon the earth shall perish, And there shall be a judgment upon all (men).

*The cosmic catastrophe of Noah @ 2344 BCE.*

9 And behold! He cometh with ten thousands of His holy ones To execute judgment upon all, And to destroy all the ungodly: And to convict all flesh Of all the works of their ungodliness which they have ungodly committed,
And of all the hard things which ungodly sinners have spoken against Him.

*This is a reference to the coming catastrophe that the comet/proto-planet Venus will bring along with her meteoric debris (ten thousand holy ones - meteor train - cockatrice).*

**Chapter 2**

1 Observe ye everything that takes place in the heaven, how they do not change their orbits, and the luminaries which are in the heaven, how they all rise and set in order each in its season, and

2 transgress not against their appointed order.

*Enoch/Enkime begins to give us an astronomy lesson, as planets sinned in the transgression of their parabolic trajectory.*

**Chapter 6**

1 And it came to pass when the children of men had multiplied that in those days were born unto

2 them beautiful and comely daughters. And the angels, the children of the heaven, saw and lusted after them, and said to one another: 'Come, let us choose us wives from among the children of men

3 and beget us children.' And Semjaza, who was their leader, said unto them: 'I fear ye will not

4 indeed agree to do this deed, and I alone shall have to pay the penalty of a great sin.' And they all answered him and said: 'Let us all swear an oath, and all bind ourselves by mutual imprecations

5 not to abandon this plan but to do this thing.' Then sware they all together and bound themselves

6 by mutual imprecations upon it. And they were in all two hundred; who descended in the days of Jared on the summit of Mount Hermon, and they called it Mount Hermon, because they had sworn

7 and bound themselves by mutual imprecations upon it. And these are the names of their leaders: Samlazaz, their leader, Araklba, Rameel, Kokablel, Tamlel, Ramlel, Danel, Ezeqeel, Baraqijal,

8 Asael, Armaros, Batarel, Ananel, Zaqiel, Samsapeel, Satarel, Turel, Jomjael, Sariel. These are their chiefs of tens.

*6:1 to 6:8 is an accounting of how and when the fallen angels (meteors/comets) (Angel = An & El) took wives from the daughters of men. This union is one made of a metaphor that I will elaborate on later. They swear an oath and are bound (star grouping) on Mount Hermon which sits in a direct line with the Jordan-Gihon fault line that runs down to the Gulf of Aqqaba.*

*Anunnaki = Meteorites of Uranus    An/Anu = Uranus    El = Saturn    Spirits = Planets    Lord of /Hosts = Sun*

*Nephilim (Genesis 6:4) = Neph/Stone  ilim/fallen - When you have kidney stones you go to see a NEPHrologist!*

**Chapter 7**

1 And all the others together with them took unto themselves wives, and each chose for himself one, and they began to go in unto them and to defile themselves with them, and they taught them charms

2 and enchantments, and the cutting of roots, and made them acquainted with plants. And they

3 became pregnant, and they bare great giants, whose height was three thousand ells: Who consumed

*Enoch 7:1 to 7:3 gives us a better understanding of the tone of the text. When Enoch/Enkime speaks of them taking wives and defiling themselves, the meteors deposited iron sulfide and other mutagenic agents. There are plenty of examples on the books of groundwater, radiation, silver and gold mines, as well as iron and other metals causing diseases and afflictions to humans and animals exposed to contaminated water. These contaminants may have led to an explosion of tall (giants – 7' to 15') human births in affected regions. The three thousand ells is a massive amount as they would soar into the atmosphere at 4,500' in height. This is clearly a phenomenon that is occurring in the atmosphere from the cosmic heavens above, as we know there have been no persons born that stood .85 miles in height. The devil is in the language, and truly intuiting and understanding what the ancient writers were trying to portray. We tend to look at documents to support our position, or to exclude another's as opposed to allowing the document to speak its truth to us.*

<u>SCALE</u>

*U.S. Male Avg. Ht/Wt  2010 = 70"(5' 10") and 165lbs*

*Enoch/Enkime's Giants Avg. Ht/Wt = 4,500' and 126,938.5lbs*

*U.S. Male Avg. Stride Distance = @ 20" – 2,640 strides per mile – New York to Los Angeles 7.92 million strides – 4 Miles per hour non-stop – 750 hours (31.25 days)*

*Enoch/Enkime's Giants Avg. Stride Distance = 1,285' – 4.11 strides per mile – New York to Los Angeles  12,330 strides – 257 Miles per hour non-stop – 11.67 hours*

*Ell: The Scottish ell was 37 inches in length. I have used 36 inches as a standard. An ellwand was a rod of length used for measurement. The 3 stars (3 Kings) in the Belt of Orion were called the "King's Ellwand," in Scotland.*

4 all the acquisitions of men. And when men could no longer sustain them, the giants turned against

5 them and devoured mankind. And they began to sin against birds, and beasts, and reptiles, and

6 fish, and to devour one another's flesh, and drink the blood. Then the earth laid accusation against the lawless ones.

*Enoch 7:4 to 7:6 The disasters brought by the meteors begin to kill the fish in the water (iron sulfide) and the animals on land and air, bringing with it drought and plague. The mutated giants in their own enclaves may have turned to cannibalizing unwary travelers, as is noted in documents and texts around the globe.*

Chapter 8

1 And **Azazel** taught men to make swords, and knives, and shields, and breastplates, and made known to them the metals of the earth and the art of working them, and bracelets, and ornaments, and the use of antimony, and the beautifying of the eyelids, and all kinds of costly stones, and all

2 colouring tinctures. And there arose much godlessness, and they committed fornication, and they

*Enoch 8:1 & 8:2 Azazel (Comet/Venus) brought in the Iron Age with the heavy meteoric distribution. Men learned to fashion this new stronger metal for swords, knives, shields, and breastplates. The tensile strength of this new metal would make one going to battle feel assured of Divine victory (God's Armor). The same iron was used to make jewelry and makeup (arsenic/poison?) that appealed to men and caused more sexual enticement to flourish.*

3 were led astray, and became corrupt in all their ways. **Semjaza** taught enchantments, and root-cuttings, **'Armaros** the resolving of enchantments, **Baraqijal** (taught) astrology, **Kokabel** the constellations, **Ezeqeel** the knowledge of the clouds, **Araqiel** the signs of the earth, **Shamsiel** the signs of the sun, and **Sariel** the course of the moon. And as men perished, they cried, and their cry went up to heaven . . .

*Root cutting, enchantments, astrology (1$^{st}$ mention), constellations, clouds, signs, sun, and moon.*

Chapter 10

4 and his seed may be preserved for all the generations of the world.' And again the Lord said to Raphael: 'Bind Azazel hand and foot, and cast him into the darkness: and make an opening

5 in the desert, which is in Dudael, and cast him therein. And place upon him rough and jagged rocks, and cover him with darkness, and let him abide there for ever, and cover his face that he may

6 &7 not see light. And on the day of the great judgment he shall be cast into the fire. And heal the earth which the angels have corrupted, and proclaim the healing of the earth, that they may heal the plague, and that all the children of men may not perish through all the secret things that the

*Enoch 10:4 to 10:7 When Raphael is instructed to bind Azazel and to cast him into darkness, an opening in the desert Dudael, and to cast him therein, this is a common term in astronomy for "binding" of star groups to create the zodiac characters. The trajectory of the comet/Venus must have taken it on a path over the desert as it descended into hell. The comet/proto-planet Venus curiously wound up being bound, as it has settled in (maybe?) as a civilized citizen.*

*\*NASA imaging taken in 2013 shows that when the solar winds die down, Venus begins to form a tail and assumes the shape of a comet.*

Chapter 12

1 Before these things Enoch was hidden, and no one of the children of men knew where he was

2 hidden, and where he abode, and what had become of him. And his activities had to do with the Watchers, and his days were with the holy ones.

*Enoch/Enkime is in protective custody.*

Chapter 14

8 written. And the **vision** was shown to me thus: Behold, in the vision **clouds** invited me and a **mist** summoned me, and the **course** of the **stars** and the **lightnings** sped and hastened me, and the **winds** in

9 the vision caused me to **fly** and lifted me **upward**, and bore me into **heaven**. And I went in till I drew nigh to a **wall** which is **built** of **crystals** and surrounded by **tongues** of fire: and it began to affright

10 me. And I went into the tongues of **fire** and drew **nigh** to a **large house** which was built of **crystals**: and the **walls** of the house were like a **tesselated floor** (made) of **crystals**, and its groundwork was

11 of crystal. Its **ceiling** was like the **path** of the **stars** and the **lightnings**, and between them were

12 fiery **cherubim**, and their **heaven** was (clear as) water. A flaming fire surrounded the walls, and its

13 portals blazed with fire. And I entered into that **house**, and it was hot as fire and cold as ice: there

14 were no delights of life therein: fear covered me, and trembling got hold upon me. And as I quaked

15 and trembled, I fell upon my face. And I beheld a **vision**, And lo! there was a **second house**, greater

16 than the former, and the entire **portal** stood open before me, and it was built of flames of fire. And in every respect it so excelled in splendour and magnificence and extent that I cannot describe to

17 you its splendour and its extent. And its floor was of **fire**, and above it were **lightnings** and the path

18 of the **stars**, and its ceiling also was flaming fire. And I looked and saw therein a **lofty throne**: its appearance was as **crystal**, and the **wheels** thereof as the **shining sun**, and there was the vision of

*This reply has elicited many responses from a cross section of society. The theologian believes that Enoch/Enkime has been raptured to the throne of God. The UFO community believes that Enoch/Enkime was abducted by aliens, and that his description is that of a flying saucer. I have actually seen it from both perspectives, but when I looked at Enoch's/Enkime's words again, they stood out! Enoch is describing a zodiac wheel of celestial design. When Enoch/Enkime speaks of houses, it is a reference to the paths that light and stars take as they enter an astronomical observatory. The ceiling being as the path of the stars and lightnings speak of the stars of the zodiac constellation being overhead of the complex. The ancients understanding was that the Earth was basically situated in a snow globe like structure with houses or windows to allow rain to pass through - Firmaments!*

*Windows, clouds, clouds, mist, course, stars, lightnings, winds, fly, upward, heaven, wall, built, crystals, tongues, fire, nigh, large house, crystals, walls, tesselated floors, crystals, ceiling, path, stars, lightnings, cherubim, heaven, house, vision, second house, portal, fire, lightnings, stars, lofty throne, crystal wheels, shining sun! - FIRMAMENTS*

 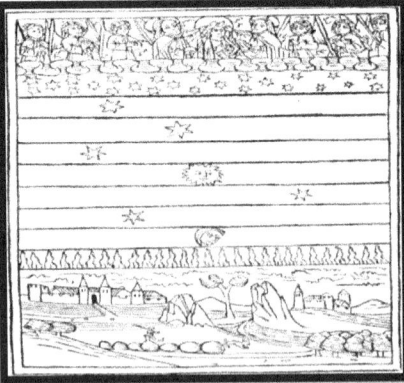 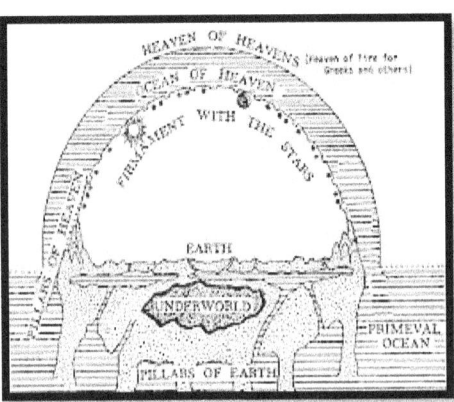

**Firmaments woodcut 1888**    **Firmaments 1475**    **Hebrew Cosmology**

19 **cherubim**. And from underneath the **throne** came **streams** of flaming **fire** so that I could not look

20 thereon. And the **Great Glory** sat thereon, and His **raiment** shone more **brightly** than the **sun** and

21 was **whiter** than any **snow**. None of the **angels** could enter and could behold His face by reason

22 of the **magnificence** and glory and no flesh could behold Him. The flaming **fire** was **round** about **Him**, and a **great** fire stood before Him, and none around could draw nigh Him: **ten thousand times**

23 **ten thousand (stood) before Him**, yet He needed no **counselor**. And the most **holy ones** who were

24 nigh to Him did not **leave** by night nor depart from Him. And until then I had been **prostrate** on my face, **trembling**: and the Lord called me with His own mouth, and said to me: ' Come hither,

25 **Enoch**, and hear my word.' And one of the **holy ones** came to me and waked me, and He made me **rise** up and approach the door: and I **bowed** my face **downwards**.

*Enoch 14:19 to 14:25 I believe to be a direct reference to the coming Age of Aries, as Enoch/Enkime represented the Age of Taurus. The comet would cause blindness and cataracts if you were to look directly at it in close orbit. This was in all likelihood a common practice of lowering ones eyes upon the comet's flybys. We know today not to look directly into the sun ,eclipse, or a nuclear reaction. There are curious cases of people being cured of blindness in the Bible, and the comet may have been the cause and the cure?*

### Chapter 18

1 I saw the treasuries of all the winds: I saw how He had furnished with them the whole creation

2 and the firm foundations of the earth. And I saw the corner-stone of the earth: I saw the four

3 winds which bear [the earth and] the firmament of the heaven. And I saw how the winds stretch out the vaults of heaven, and have their station between heaven and earth: these are the pillars

*Enoch 18:1 to 18:3 Enoch/Enkime shows a clear understanding of the layers of the atmosphere and how the four winds are distributed by them.*

4 of the heaven. I saw the winds of heaven which turn and bring the circumference of the sun and

5 all the stars to their setting. I saw the winds on the earth carrying the clouds: I saw the paths

6 of the angels. I saw at the end of the earth the firmament of the heaven above. And I proceeded and saw a place which burns day and night, where there are seven mountains of magnificent stones,

7 three towards the east, and three towards the south. And as for those towards the east, was of coloured stone, and one of pearl, and one of jacinth, and those towards the south of red stone.

*I believe this to be a reference to the seven stars of the Pleiades (7 sisters).*

12 the height and towards the depth. And beyond that abyss I saw a place which had no firmament of the heaven above, and no firmly founded earth beneath it: there was no water upon it, and no

13 birds, but it was a waste and horrible place. I saw there seven stars like great burning mountains,

*Enoch/Enkime talks about a black hole in this declaration.*

## Chapter 20

3 over the world and over Tartarus. Raphael, one of the holy angels, who is over the spirits of men.

*This statement gives the angel Uriel (Uranus) dominion over Tartarus (Hell/Hyades/Taurus constellation?), and the angel Raphael (Venus) over mankind.*

## Chapter 21

6 dost thou ask, and why art thou eager for the truth? These are of the number of the stars of heaven, which have transgressed the commandment of the Lord, and are bound here till ten thousand years,

*The stars that transgress their appointed orbits are cast into a black hole for ten-thousand years. No one knows what takes place inside a black hole past the event horizon beyond the singularity. We may discover one day that Enoch/Enkime knew! The ten thousand years speak of a Kali Yuga Age.*

## Chapter 23

4 I asked saying: 'What is this which **rests not?**' Then **Raguel**, one of the **holy angels** who was with me, answered me and said unto me: 'This **course** of fire which thou hast seen is the **fire** in the **west** which **persecutes all the luminaries of heaven**.'

*Venus!*

## Chapter 33

1 And from thence I went to the ends of the earth and saw there great beasts, and each differed from the other; and (I saw) birds also differing in appearance and beauty and voice, the one differing from the other. And to the east of those beasts I saw the ends of the earth whereon the heaven

*The great beasts and birds different in appearance, beauty and voice, are the constellations:*

*Beasts: Beast (Lupus), Sea Monster (Cetus), and Water Serpent (Hydra)*

*Birds: Eagle (Aquila), Swan (Cygnus), and Crow (Raven)*

2 rests, and the portals of the heaven open. And I saw how the stars of heaven come forth, and

3 I counted the portals out of which they proceed, and wrote down all their outlets, of each individual star by itself, according to their number and their names, their courses and their positions, and their

4 times and their months, as Uriel the holy angel who was with me showed me. He showed all things to me and wrote them down for me: also their names he wrote for me, and their laws and their companies.

*Enoch 33:2 to 33:4 gives us an astronomy lesson on the portals out of which the stars, sun, and moon proceed, and their outlets.*

## Chapter 36

1 And from thence I went to the south to the ends of the earth, and saw there three open portals

2 of the heaven: and thence there come dew, rain, and wind. And from thence I went to the east to the ends of the heaven, and saw here the three eastern portals of heaven open and small portals

3 above them. Through each of these small portals pass the stars of heaven and run their course to the west on the path which is shown to them. And as often as I saw I blessed always the Lord of Glory, and I continued to bless the Lord of Glory who has wrought great and glorious wonders, to show the greatness of His work to the angels and to spirits and to men, that they might praise His work and all His creation: that they might see the work of His might and praise the great work of His hands and bless Him for ever.

*Enoch 361:1 to 36:3 gives clear proof of what Enoch's/Enkime's theology encompasses. The large portals and small portals are windows through which the sun, moon, and stars travel along an observatory like Stonehenge. The celestial observatories typically have a large outer ring with two smaller rings within and a sacrificial altar. The ancients were able to realign the stars to track the path of the equinox and solstices.*

## Section II. Chapters XXXVII-LXXI
## The Parables (Parabolics?)

Chapter 40

1 And after that I saw thousands of thousands and ten thousand times ten thousand, I saw a multitude

*Millions of meteorites (barads).*

2 beyond number and reckoning, who stood before the Lord of Spirits. And on the four sides of the Lord of Spirits I saw **four presences**, different from those that sleep not, and I learnt their names: for the angel that went with me made known to me their names, and showed me all the hidden things.

3 And I heard the voices of those **four presences** as they uttered praises before the Lord of glory.

4,5 The first voice blesses the Lord of Spirits for ever and ever. And the second voice I heard blessing

6 the Elect One and the elect ones who hang upon the Lord of Spirits. And the third voice I heard pray and intercede for those who dwell on the earth and supplicate in the name of the **Lord of Spirits**.

7 And I heard the fourth voice fending off the Satans and forbidding them to come before the Lord

8 of Spirits to accuse them who dwell on the earth. After that I asked the angel of peace who went with me, who showed me everything that is hidden: 'Who are these four presences which I have

9 seen and whose words I have heard and written down?' And he said to me: 'This first is Michael, the merciful and long-suffering: and the second, who is set over all the diseases and all the wounds of the children of men, is Raphael: and the third, who is set over all the powers, is Gabriel: and the fourth, who is set over the repentance unto hope of those who inherit eternal life, is named Phanuel.'

10 And these are the four angels of the Lord of Spirits and the four voices I heard in those days.

*Enoch 40:2 to 40:10 These four presences form the basis of John's Four Horseman in the Book of Revelations. We know that Michael symbolizes the planet Mars, the anthropomorphism is representative of the planets as Angels. Gabriel (Gibril/Gabriel/Horus/Mummu) is Mercury, Raphael represent Venus, and Phanuel (The Face of God) represents the Moon.*

Chapter 41

1 And after that I saw all the secrets of the heavens, and how the kingdom is divided, and how the

*Enoch/Enkime's gives his clear and total commitment to astrotheology! We were just given an astronomy lesson by Enoch in regard to the secrets of the heavens and how the kingdom is divided. This has long been confused to be the Heaven that mankind goes to upon their death. Enoch/Enkime in his manner is telling us that the Kingdom of God is in the heavens above us.*

2 actions of men are weighed in the balance. And there I saw the mansions of the elect and the mansions of the holy, and mine eyes saw there all the sinners being driven from thence which deny the name of the Lord of Spirits, and being dragged off: and they could not abide because of the punishment which proceeds from the Lord of Spirits.

*Again; mansions, houses, rooms, windows, portals, columns, and posts, are astronomy based terms that Enoch/Enkime uses.*

5 beginning of the world. And I saw the chambers of the sun and moon, whence they proceed and whither they come again, and their glorious return, and how one is superior to the other, and their stately orbit, and how they do not leave their orbit, and they add nothing to their orbit and they take nothing from it, and they keep faith with each other, in accordance with the oath by which they

6 are bound together. And first the sun goes forth and traverses his path according to the commandment

*Enoch 41:5 & 41:6 shows that Enoch understands that we revolve around the Sun, and how the Moons orbit is fixed.*

7 of the Lord of Spirits, and mighty is His name for ever and ever. And after that I saw the hidden and the visible path of the moon, and she accomplishes the course of her path in that place by day and by night-the one holding a position opposite to the other before the Lord of Spirits. And they give thanks and praise and rest not; For unto them is their thanksgiving rest.

*Enoch/Enkime understands that we see the same side of the moons face, and that it does not rotate.*

**Chapter 43**

1 And I saw other lightnings and the stars of heaven, and I saw how He called them all by their

*The lightnings that Enoch/Enkime often speaks of are comets, and the planets/stars are angels.*

2 names and they hearkened unto Him. And I saw how they are weighed in a righteous balance according to their proportions of light: (I saw) the width of their spaces and the day of their appearing, and how their revolution produces lightning: and (I saw) their revolution according to the

*The planets are named and again we have references to light proportions, width of spaces (apertures), days of appearance, and how their revolutions generate lightning. This is completely astronomy based terminology.*

3 **number of the angels, and (how) they keep faith with each other. And I asked the angel who went**

*Enoch/Enkime teaches us that based on the number of planets (angels) their revolution is dictated by this grouping, and how they keep faith (gravity/dark matter/order) with each other.*

4 with me who showed me what was hidden: 'What are these?' And he said to me: 'The Lord of Spirits hath showed thee their **parabolic** meaning (lit. 'their parable'): these are the names of the holy who dwell on the earth and believe in the name of the Lord of Spirits for ever and ever.'

*The translator of the text believes that Enoch/Enkime meant "parable" when it translated as "parabolic." Enoch knows what he speaks of! Enoch/Enkime just gave an exhaustive astronomy lesson, and he is speaking of a "parabolic trajectory!" In astrodynamics or celestial mechanics a parabolic trajectory is a" Kepler Orbit." When moving away from a source it is called an escape orbit or capture orbit. Enoch/Enkime is not speaking in parables at this time, and a parabolic trajectory fits perfectly as he leads into Chapter 44 and one of the most revealing statements in all of his text.*

*\*Jesus spoke to the people and disciples in PARABLES, as he could not speak to them in PARABOLICS!*

**Chapter 44**

Also another phenomenon I saw in regard to the lightnings: how some of the stars arise and become lightnings and cannot part with their new form.

*WOW! I believe that my point has been proven by Enoch's/Enkime's own words. Another phenomenon in regard to the lightnings, and how some stars arise and become lightnings and cannot part with this new form! The theory that Venus started as a comet/proto-planet was put forth most notably by Mr. Velikofsky, and these theories are being borne out over time. I feel that Enoch/Enkime discovered or was taught that stars are sometimes born as comets and never lose the coma or tail. Venus ping-ponged through our neighborhood with ferocious devastation. The Earth, Mercury, and the Moon have negative polarities, but Venus and Mars have positive polarities. Venus has left us plenty of proof of the sword that she wielded. One need only look at our Grand Canyon and Valles Marinaris on Mars for evidence. Once we are able to peer through the shroud that Venus has, we may begin to see many scars on her surface, as she curiously has a completely new surface! The plasma discharge from Venus ejected millions of square miles of dirt and rock into orbit, as well as causing the electrically scalloped features of those topsoil denuded planets. These canyons can be found on other bodies in our neighborhood as well.*

**Chapter 46**

1 And there I saw One who had a head of days, And His head was white like wool, And with Him was another being whose countenance had the appearance of a man, And his face was full of graciousness, like one of the holy angels.

*The Head of Days with white hair like wool is a reference to the Sun/Aquarius (Galzu). The man whose face was full of graciousness is a reference to the age that follows Aries, the Age of Pisces. The bulk of Enoch's/Enkime's references to the cosmos are in our own backyard.*

**Chapter 65**

1, 2 And in those days Noah saw the earth that it had sunk down and its destruction was nigh. And he arose from thence and went to the ends of the earth, and cried aloud to his grandfather Enoch:

*Noah/Ziusudrah obviously understands that the pole of the Earth has shifted (or dropped below the celestial plane), and had begun to cause disasters. Noah cries out to a great grandfather that left (raptured?) seventy-five years before his birth. Enoch/Enkime lived sixty-five years, walked with God three-hundred years, and then was no more. We curiously have a three-hundred and sixty-five day calendar year. In the Sumerian tradition Ziusudra/Utnum Napishtu (Noah) calls out to the Lord Enki at this point for help. The Sumerian epic predates the Hebrew accounting of the Great Flood by several hundred years. The character of Enoch was fashioned from the Sumerian King Enkime, and reworked into the Biblical figure we have come to know. I believe it safe to say that Enoch never existed as a human being.*

3 and Noah said **three** times with an embittered voice: Hear me, hear me, hear me.' And I said unto him: ' Tell me what it is that is **falling** out on the earth that the earth is in **such evil plight**

*Meteorites AKA Barads!*

**Chapter 71**

1 And it came to pass after this that my spirit was translated And it ascended into the heavens: And I saw the holy sons of God. They were stepping on flames of fire: Their garments were white [and their raiment], And their faces shone like snow.

2 And I saw two streams of fire, And the light of that fire shone like hyacinth, And I fell on my face before the Lord of Spirits.

3 And the angel Michael [one of the archangels] seized me by my right hand, And lifted me up and led me forth into all the secrets, And he showed me all the secrets of righteousness.

4 And he showed me all the secrets of the ends of the heaven, And all the chambers of all the stars, and all the luminaries, Whence they proceed before the face of the holy ones.

6 And my spirit saw the girdle which girt that house of fire, And on its four sides were streams full of living fire, And they girt that house.

8 And I saw angels who could not be counted, A thousand thousands, and ten thousand times ten thousand, Encircling that house. And Michael, and Raphael, and Gabriel, and Phanuel, And the holy angels who are above the heavens, Go in and out of that house.

9 And they came forth from that house, And Michael and Gabriel, Raphael and Phanuel, And many holy angels without number.

10 And with them the Head of Days, His head white and pure as wool, And His raiment indescribable.

*Enoch 71:8 to 71:10 – 10,000 x 10,000 (meteorites), Head of Days (Sun/Aquarius/Galzu), Gabriel, Raphael, Michael, and Phanuel!*

## Section I I I. Chapters LXXII-LXXXII
## The Book of the Heavenly Luminaries (Stars, Planets, and Zodiac)

**Chapter 72**

1 The book of the courses of the luminaries of the heaven, the relations of each, according to their classes, their dominion and their seasons, according to their names and places of origin, and according to their months, which Uriel, the holy angel, who was with me, who is their guide, showed me; and he showed me all their laws exactly as they are, and how it is with regard to all the years of the world

2 and unto eternity, till the new creation is accomplished which dureth till eternity. And this is the first law of the luminaries: the luminary the Sun has its rising in the eastern portals of the heaven,

3 and its setting in the western portals of the heaven. And I saw six portals in which the sun rises, and six portals in which the sun sets and the moon rises and sets in these portals, and the leaders of the stars and those whom they lead: six in the east and six in the west, and all following each other

4 in accurately corresponding order: also many windows to the right and left of these portals. And first there goes forth the great luminary, named the Sun, and his circumference is like the

5 circumference of the heaven, and he is quite filled with illuminating and heating fire. The chariot on which he ascends, the wind drives, and the sun goes down from the heaven and returns through the north in order to reach the east, and is so guided that he comes to the appropriate (lit. ' that ') portal and

6 shines in the face of the heaven. In this way he rises in the first month in the great portal, which

7 is the fourth [those six portals in the cast]. And in that fourth portal from which the sun rises in the first month are twelve window-openings, from which proceed a flame when they are opened in

8 their season. When the sun rises in the heaven, he comes forth through that fourth portal thirty,

9 mornings in succession, and sets accurately in the fourth portal in the west of the heaven. And during this period the day becomes daily longer and the night nightly shorter to the thirtieth

10 morning. On that day the day is longer than the night by a ninth part, and the day amounts exactly to ten parts and the night to eight parts. And the sun rises from that fourth portal, and sets in the fourth and returns to the fifth portal of the east thirty mornings, and rises from it and sets in the fifth

12 portal. And then the day becomes longer by two parts and amounts to eleven parts, and the night

13 becomes shorter and amounts to seven parts. And it returns to the east and enters into the sixth

14 portal, and rises and sets in the sixth portal one-and-thirty mornings on account of its sign. On that day the day becomes longer than the night, and the day becomes double the night, and the day

15 becomes twelve parts, and the night is shortened and becomes six parts. And the sun mounts up to make the day shorter and the night longer, and the sun returns to the east and enters into the

16 sixth portal, and rises from it and sets thirty mornings. And when thirty mornings are accomplished,

17 the day decreases by exactly one part, and becomes eleven parts, and the night seven. And the sun goes forth from that sixth portal in the west, and goes to the east and rises in the fifth portal for

18 thirty mornings, and sets in the west again in the fifth western portal. On that day the day decreases by two parts, and amounts to ten parts and the night to eight parts. And the sun goes forth from that fifth portal and sets in the fifth portal of the west, and rises in the fourth portal for one-

20 and-thirty mornings on account of its sign, and sets in the west. On that day the day is equalized with the night, [and becomes of equal length], and the night amounts to nine parts and the day to

*Chapter 72 is one big astronomy lesson from Enoch. Chapters 73 and 74 were not shown, but contain the same astronomy lessons.*

**Chapter 75**

1 And the **leaders** of the **heads** of the thousands, who are placed over the whole **creation** and **over** all the **stars**, have also to do with the four intercalary days, being **inseparable** from their **office**, according to the reckoning of the year, and these render service on the **four** days which are not

*Enoch's/Enkime's fixed calendar has long been scrutinized as having been flawed. His calendar only has 360-days, with four 90-day periods being separated by a transition day for a total of 364 calendar days. With our present orbit, rotation, and axis, we are given a 365-day calendar year.*

2 **reckoned** in the **reckoning** of the year. And **owing** to them **men** go **wrong** therein, for those **luminaries** truly render **service** on the **world-stations**, one in the first **portal**, one in the third **portal** of the **heaven**, one in the fourth **portal**, and one in the sixth **portal**, and the **exactness** of the **year** is

*If mankind does not reckon the four intercalary days their calendar will be off track. Enoch constantly relates luminaries, stations, and portals of heaven, as their understanding was of a domed firmament in the sky.*

3 accomplished through its separate **three hundred and sixty-four stations**. For the **signs** and the **times** and the **years** and the **days** the angel Uriel showed to me, whom the Lord of glory hath set for ever **over** all the **luminaries** of the **heaven**, in the heaven and in the world, that they should **rule** on the face of the heaven and be seen on the **earth**, and be leaders for the **day** and the **night**, i.e. the **sun, moon, and stars**, and all the **ministering creatures** which make their **revolution** in all the **chariots**

*Enoch/Enkime shows that the Earth passes through 364 stations (days/houses). The signs, times, years, and days! This is an area where astronomy has become fully blended with theology, as Enoch/Enkime speaks of the luminaries of heaven and that the world should rule on the face of heaven. This speaks of the Egyptian philosophy of, "As above, So below." The ministering creatures that make their revolution in all the chariots of heaven are the creatures of the zodiac constellations. The chariots in the heavens revolves at 1° per celestial portion (72yrs). A full revolution of 360° through the zodiac takes 25,920 years, which is a complete zodiac cycle or age (or 365 x 72 = 26,280yrs). The human life span/portion and celestial portion are one and the same – 72 years!*

**Chapter 78**

1, 2 And the names of the **sun** are the following: the first **Orjares**, and the second **Tomas**. And the **moon** has four names: the first name is **Asonja**, the second **Ebla**, the third **Benase**, and the fourth

3 Erae. These are the **two great luminaries**: their **circumference** is like the **circumference** of the

4 **heaven**, and the **size** of the circumference of both is alike.

*Enoch/Enkime has already begun or continued the practice of deities and stars having multiple names. The Sun has 2 names and the Moon has 4 names, and Enoch clearly understands their shape and circumference.*

## Chapter 80

2 And in the days of the sinners the years shall be shortened, - **Post comet effect**
And their seed shall be tardy on their lands and fields, - **Stunted crops**
And all things on the earth shall alter,
And shall not appear in their time: - **Seasons and crops will not follow their schedule**
And the rain shall be kept back - **Droughts caused by the comets desertification effects**
And the heaven shall withhold (it).
3 And in those times the fruits of the earth shall be backward,
And shall not grow in their time,
And the fruits of the trees shall be withheld in their time.
4 And the moon shall alter her order,
And not appear at her time. – **An extended period of daylight**
5 [And in those days the sun shall be seen and he shall journey in the evening on the extremity of the great chariot in the west]
And shall shine more brightly than accords with the order of light. – **Venus – The Evening Star! Total astrotheology!**
6 And many chiefs of the stars shall transgress the order (prescribed).
And these shall alter their orbits and tasks,
And not appear at the seasons prescribed to them. – **Planets and their satellites will be thrown from their normal orbits**
7 And the whole order of the stars shall be concealed from the sinners, - **The skies will change their order due to the pole shift**
And the thoughts of those on the earth shall err concerning them,
[And they shall be altered from all their ways],
Yea, they shall err and take them to be gods. – **Venus, Mars, Moon, Mercury, Jupiter, Saturn, and the Sun**
8 And evil shall be multiplied upon them,
And punishment shall come upon them So as to destroy all.'

## Chapter 82

4 Blessed are all the righteous, blessed are all those who walk In the way of righteousness and sin not as the sinners, in the reckoning of all their days in which the sun traverses the heaven, entering into and departing from the portals for thirty days with the heads of thousands of the order of the stars, together with the four which are intercalated which divide the four portions of the year, which

*The righteous blessings, walking in the way of righteousness, and not sinning, are in perspective to the heavenly bodies and not the sins of man! Planets (righteous) that do not transgress (sin) their orbit, is the manner in which we would expect this statement to read. This is wholly an astrological statement blended with theology.*

*\* Sin (Nannar Sin) is a name for the Moon, as she was captured by the Earth at some point in a cosmic upheaval and "sinned," against her appointed order. People would have sex mainly at night under the Moon, and so they sinned with this practice.*

5 lead them and enter with them four days. Owing to them men shall be at fault and not reckon them in the whole reckoning of the year: yea, men shall be at fault, and not recognize them

6 accurately.

*Men will not reckon the seasons and days as the stars will shift (throne/order) and the seasons will be delayed.*

8 Lord of the whole creation of the world hath subjected the host of heaven. And he has power over night and day in the heaven to cause the light to give light to men -sun, moon, and stars,

9 and all the powers of the heaven which revolve in their circular chariots. And these are the orders of the stars, which set in their places, and in their seasons and festivals and months.

*Enoch/Enkime speaks of the host of heaven, Sun, Moon, stars, and all the powers of the heaven which revolve in their circular chariot! The zodiac constellations (Band of Animals) revolve in the round above us in a circular chariot.*

## ASTRONOMY 101

10 And these are the names of those who **lead** them, who watch that they enter at their **times**, in their **orders**, in their **seasons**, in their **months**, in their **periods** of **dominion**, and in their **positions**. Their four leaders who **divide** the four parts of the **year** enter first; and after them the **twelve** leaders of the orders who divide the months; and for the **three hundred and sixty (days)** there are **heads** over thousands who divide the days; and for the four **intercalary** days there are the leaders which sunder

12 the four parts of the year. And these heads over thousands are intercalated between

13 **leader** and **leader**, each behind a **station**, but their leaders make the **division**. And these are the names of the leaders who divide the **four parts** of the **year** which are ordained: **Milki'el, Hel'emmelek,** and **Mel'ejal,**

14 and **Narel**. And the names of those who lead them: **Adnar'el,** and **Ijasusa'el,** and **'Elome'el**- these three follow the leaders of the orders, and there is one that follows the three leaders of the orders which follow those leaders of stations that divide the four parts of the year. In the beginning of the year **Melkejal** rises first and rules, who is named **Tam'aini** and sun, and

16 all the days of his **dominion** whilst he bears rule are **ninety-one days**. And these are the **signs** of the days which are to be **seen** on **earth** in the days of his dominion: **sweat**, and **heat**, and calms; and all the trees bear fruit, and leaves are produced on all the trees, and the **harvest** of **wheat**, and the rose-flowers, and all the **flowers** which come forth in the field, but the trees of the winter season become withered. And these are the names of the leaders which are under them: **Berka'el, Zelebs'el,** and another who is added a head of a thousand, called **Hilujaseph**: and the days of the dominion of this (leader) are at an end.

18 The next leader after him is **Hel'emmelek,** whom one names **the shining sun**, and all the days

19 of his light are ninety-one days. And these are the **signs** of (his) days on the earth: glowing heat and dryness, and the **trees ripen** their fruits and produce all their fruits ripe and ready, and the **sheep pair** and become **pregnant**, and all the fruits of the earth are gathered in, and everything that is

20 in the fields, and the winepress: these things take place in the days of his dominion. These are the names, and the orders, and the leaders of those heads of thousands: **Gida'ljal, Ke'el,** and **He'el,** and the name of the head of a thousand which is added to them, **Asfa'el**: and the days of his dominion are at an end.

*Milki' el – Spring / Hel' emmelek – Summer / Mel' ejal – Fall / Narel – Winter*

*4 Seasons – 12 Months – 364 Calendar days*

**CORRESPONDING SEASONS**

<u>Milki' el – Spring</u>

*Hebrew Calendar: Abib, Zif, Sivan – March 14 Purim (Feast of Esther), April 1 New Years Day for reign of Kings, April 10 Passover Lamb chosen, April 14 Passover Lamb sacrificed, April 15 First Day of Passover "Feast of Unleavened Bread," April 16 Offering of First Fruits, April 21 Seventh day of Passover*

*United States: March, April, May – March 17 St. Patrick's day, April 1 April Fool's day, April 15 Tax day, April 22 Earth day*

<u>Hel' emmelek – Summer</u>

Hebrew Calendar: Tammuz, Ab, Elul – Feast of First Fruits (Passover, Weeks, Shabouth) 49 days from the onset of Passover equals 49 days

United States: June, July, August – July 4 Independence Day

<u>Mel' ejal – Fall</u>

Hebrew Calendar: Tishri, Heshvan, Kislev – September 1 New Years Day (Rosh Hashana, Feast of Trumpets), September 10 Day of Atonement (Yom Kippur (Ur)) September 15 Feast of Tabernacles first day (Sukkoth), September 22 Eight day Feast of Tabernacles (Great Day of Feast)

United States: September, October, November – September Labor Day, October 31 Halloween, November – Thanksgiving

<u>Narel – Winter</u>

Hebrew Calendar: Tebet, Shabat, Adar – December 25 Hanukkah 8 days

United States: December, January, February – December 25 Christmas, January 1 New Years Day, February 2 Groundhog Day, February 14 Valentine's Day

| Babylonian Calendar | Hebrew Calendar | Babylonian Deity | Zodiac Sign | Gregorian Calendar |
|---|---|---|---|---|
| Arah Nisanu | Nisan | Anu & Bel | Aries | March/April |
| Arah Aru | Iyar | Ea |  | April/May |
| Arah Simanu | Sivan | Sin | Gemini | May/June |
| Arah Dumuzu | Tammuz | Tammuz |  | June/July |
| Arah Abu | Av | Aru | Leo | July/August |
| Arah Ululu | Elul | Ishtar |  | August/September |
| Arah Tisritum | Tishrei | Shamash | Libra | September/October |
| Arah Samna | Chesvan | Marduk | Scorpio | October/November |
| Arah Kislimu | Kislev | Nergal | Sagittarius | November/December |
| Arah Tebetum | Tebet | Pap-sokkal | Capricorn | December/January |
| Arah Sabatu | Shebat |  | Aquarius | January/February |
| Arah Addaru/Arah Adar | Adar | Erra | Pisces | February/March |

The Babylonian calendar was a luni-solar calendar of twelve months, each beginning when a new crescent moon was sighted low on the western horizon. In the 6$^{th}$ century BCE the Hebrews adopted the Babylonian names into the Hebrew calendar. We need just look at the similarities in words to see that these terms were derived from one source. The Hebrews lived among the Babylonians for years, and there is always an exchange of culture, marriages, practices, and beliefs.

Nisan / Nisanu = Anu (Anubis) & Bel (Bel & the Dragon)      Simanu / Sivan = Sim/Anu & Sin

Dumuzu = Tammuz (they weep for Tammuz)      Ululu / Elul = Bull      Tisritum / Tishrei

Kislimu /Kislev (Kiev?)      Tebetum / Tebet (Tibet?)      Sabatu / Shebat (Sheba)

Adar / Addaru – Adar is taken from the Akkadian adaru

Section IV. Chapters LXXXIII-XC.
The Dream-Visions.

Chapter 83

3 vision. And regarding them I prayed to the Lord. I had laid me down in the house of my grandfather Mahalalel, (when) I saw in a vision how the heaven collapsed and was borne off and fell to

4 the earth. And when it fell to the earth I saw how the earth was swallowed up in a great abyss, and mountains were suspended on mountains, and hills sank down on hills, and high trees were rent

5 from their stems, and hurled down and sunk in the abyss. And thereupon a word fell into my mouth,

8 a great destruction. And now, my son, arise and make petition to the Lord of glory, since thou art a believer, that a remnant may remain on the earth, and that He may not destroy the whole

*Mahaleel encourages Enoch/Enkime to make a plea for the salvation of mankind.*

9 earth. My son, from **heaven** all this will come upon the earth, and upon the earth there will be great

10 destruction. After that I arose and prayed and implored and besought, and wrote down my prayer for the generations of the world, and I will show everything to thee, my son Methuselah. And when I had gone forth below and seen the heaven, and the **sun** rising in the **east**, and the **moon** setting in the **west**, and a few **stars**, and the whole **earth**, and everything as He had known it in the beginning, then I blessed the Lord of judgment and extolled Him because He had made the sun to go forth from the **windows** of the east, and he ascended and rose on the face of the heaven, and set out and kept **traversing** the **path** shown unto him.

*Heaven, Sun, east, Moon, west, stars, windows, and paths!*

Chapter 85

*"Bulls Parable" or the "Flood of Noah/Ziusudra"*

1,2 And after this I saw another dream, and I will show the whole dream to thee, my son. And Enoch lifted up (his voice) and spake to his son Methuselah: ' To thee, my son, will I speak: hear my words-incline thine ear to the dream-vision of thy father. Before I took thy mother Edna, I saw in a vision on my bed, and behold a bull came forth from the earth, and that bull was white; and after it came forth a heifer, and along with this (latter) came forth two bulls, one of them black and

4 the other red. And that black bull gored the red one and pursued him over the earth, and thereupon

*The White Bull (Comet) came forth from the Earth, then a Heifer (Moon), and 1 Black Bull (Venus) and 1 Red Bull (Mars). The Black Bull gores the Red Bull (planetary collision/plasma discharge).*

> *The first red bull, born of the (cloud) womb, born of wind and clouds, comes on thundering with rain. "Atharva Veda – 1000 BCE" verse 12:1 Prayer to lightning! This shows how the symbolism was common for those periods. The Revelation to John was written @ 70-95 CE.*

5 I could no longer see that red bull. But that black bull grew and that heifer went with him, and

*The comet/Venus enlarged her girth as she stole some of the mass of Mars through the collision. It has long been a question why the Moon rings hollow as a bell, and why Mars has no topsoil (How do you terraform a planet with no topsoil?).*

6 I saw that many oxen proceeded from him which resembled and followed him. And that cow, that first one, went from the presence of that first bull in order to seek that red one, but found him

*The many oxen that resembled the comet/Venus were meteors within its tail that went in orbit with it. The Moons orbit was disturbed by the collisions.*

7 not, and lamented with a great lamentation over him and sought him. And I looked till that first

8 bull came to her and quieted her, and from that time onward she cried no more. And after that she bore another white bull, and after him she bore many bulls and black cows.

*The comet/Venus approaches near the Moon and has a collision or near miss bringing about the birth of meteors (Bulls & Black cows).*

9 And I saw in my sleep that white bull likewise grow and become a great white bull, and from Him proceeded many white bulls, and they resembled him. And they began to beget many white bulls, which resembled them, one following the other, (even) many.

*The comet/Venus again grows in mass from a collision.*

## Chapter 86

1 And again I saw with mine eyes as I slept, and I saw the heaven above, and behold a star fell

*A massive meteor falls to Earth.*

2 from heaven, and it arose and eat and pastured amongst those oxen. And after that I saw the large and the black oxen, and behold they all changed their stalls and pastures and their cattle, and began

*The position of the stars in the sky changed their stalls/pastures in which they were normally viewed.*

3 to live with each other. And again I saw in the vision, and looked towards the heaven, and behold I saw many stars descend and cast themselves down from heaven to that first star, and they became

*The planetary debris rains down and follows the comet/Venus.*

4 bulls amongst those cattle and pastured with them [amongst them]. And I looked at them and saw, and behold they all let out their privy members, like horses, and began to cover the cows of the oxen,

5 and they all became pregnant and bare elephants, camels, and asses. And all the oxen feared them and were affrighted at them, and began to bite with their teeth and to devour, and to gore with their

*Enoch 86:4 and 86:5 The asteroid/meteor shower multiplies in intensity with another collision.*

6 horns. And they began, moreover, to devour those oxen; and behold all the children of the earth began to tremble and quake before them and to flee from them.

*The people of Earth scramble for safety as tragedy plays itself out in the skies.*

## Chapter 87

1 And again I saw how they began to gore each other and to devour each other, and the earth

2 began to cry aloud. And I raised mine eyes again to heaven, and I saw in the vision, and behold there came forth from heaven beings who were like white men: and four went forth from that place

*Enoch 87:1 and 87:2 Four white-hot massive comet fragments strike the Earth as she cries from the toll being taken.*

3 and three with them. And those three that had last come forth grasped me by my hand and took me up, away from the generations of the earth, and raised me up to a lofty place, and showed me

*Enoch/Enkime is taken (raptured) away to heaven. I feel Enoch/Enkime to be an anthropomorphized figure versus an actual human being. Enoch leaves a 364 day calendar, he also lived 365 years (365 days), and at this point the Earth's year may have been lengthened due to the collisions or pole shift.*

4 a tower raised high above the earth, and all the hills were lower. And one said unto me: ' Remain here till thou seest everything that befalls those elephants, camels, and asses, and the stars and the oxen, and all of them.'

*I believe the tower raised high above the Earth to be the comet/proto-planet Venus as she begins to change and become more stable. The "Wheel in the Sky" with the extended pillar has been represented many times in coinage, art, glyphs, obelisks, steeples, minarets, and Jacob's Ladder! I will show my "Pillar of Fire" theory later in this book.*

Chapter 88

1 And I saw one of those four who had come forth first, and he seized that first star which had fallen from the heaven, and bound it hand and foot and cast it into an abyss: now that abyss was

2 narrow and deep, and horrible and dark. And one of them drew a sword, and gave it to those elephants and camels and asses: then they began to smite each other, and the whole earth quaked

*Enoch 88:1 and 88:2 Binding is a common term for star grouping, as a meteor falls the comet/Venus descends below the horizon into the abyss/hell (out of sight below the ecliptic). The sword the comet/Venus carried is the most potent in the known universe, that of a plasma discharge.*

3 because of them. And as I was beholding in the **vision**, lo, one of those **four** who had come forth **stoned** (them) from **heaven**, and gathered and took all the great **stars** whose **privy members** were like those of **horses**, and **bound** them all hand and foot, and **cast** them in an **abyss** of the **earth**.

*Vision, four, stoned, heaven, stars, privy members, horses, bound, cast, abyss, and Earth!*

Chapter 89

1 And one of those four went to that white bull and instructed him in a secret, without his being terrified: he was born a bull and became a man, and built for himself a great vessel and dwelt thereon;

*This is a clear and direct reference to Noah! He was born a bull (Age of Taurus) and became a man and built for himself a great vessel (Ark) to dwell on. Enoch/Enkime tosses the baton to Noah as Enoch/Enkime was an emblem of the Age of Taurus, and Noah will be the lead for the Age of Aries. The Great Flood occurred on the cusp of these two ages around 2344 BCE. As one reads this portion of the parable it will become totally clear that this is Noah and his sons with animals used versus people. The whole authenticity of Noah has long been debated. Ziusudra is from the Sumerian epics, and is the character that Noah was modeled from. This epic predates the story of Noah by almost a millennia. It will become clearer why the Book of Enoch/Enkime was left from the Torah and King James Bible, as three of his stories change three seminally important stories used in those texts.*

2 and three bulls dwelt with him in that vessel and they were covered in. And again I raised mine eyes towards heaven and saw a lofty roof, with seven water torrents thereon, and those torrents

3 flowed with much water into an enclosure. And I saw again, and behold fountains were opened on the surface of that great enclosure, and that water began to swell and rise upon the surface,

4 and I saw that enclosure till all its surface was covered with water. And the water, the darkness, and mist increased upon it; and as I looked at the height of that water, that water had risen above the height of that enclosure, and was streaming over that enclosure, and it stood upon the earth.

***Enoch 89:2 to 89:4** The pole shift has caused torrential rains to begin its deluge of the Earth as the vaults of heaven open over the planet.*

5 And all the cattle of that enclosure were gathered together until I saw how they sank and were

***The people of the Earth were engulfed by the tsunamis and the land sank and disappeared.***

6 swallowed up and perished in that water. But that vessel floated on the water, while all the oxen and elephants and camels and asses sank to the bottom with all the animals, so that I could no longer see them, and they were not able to escape, (but) perished and sank into the depths. And again I saw in the vision till those water torrents were removed from that high roof, and the chasms

***All life perishes as Noah's (White Bull) vessel weathers the storm until the water abated.***

8 of the earth were leveled up and other abysses were opened. Then the water began to run down into these, till the earth became visible; but that vessel settled on the earth, and the darkness

***The Earth's poles stabilize as the water drains from the face of the planet as darkness is still her cloak.***

9 retired and light appeared. But that white bull which had become a man came out of that vessel, and the three bulls with him, and one of those three was white like that bull, and one of them was red as blood, and one black: and that white bull departed from them.

***The White Bull (Noah) and his three sons Japheth, Shem, and Ham (3 Bulls) depart the vessel. I wonder if the three colors Red, White, and Black of the Bulls are representative of the three basic ethnicities of African, Asian, and Caucasian groups?***

10 And they began to bring forth beasts of the field and birds, so that there arose different genera: lions, tigers, wolves, dogs, hyenas, wild boars, foxes, squirrels, swine, falcons, vultures, kites, eagles, and ravens; and among them was born a white bull. And they began to bite one another; but that white bull which was born amongst them begat a wild ass and a white bull with it, and the

***In this version they generate species on their own, but, in the biblical version the animals are rescued of a kind by Noah using the Ark. Most of the animals that Enoch lists are animals from the constellations.***

12 wild asses multiplied. But that bull which was born from him begat a black wild boar and a white

***They found the 12 Tribes of Israel (12 main zodiac constellations).***

13 sheep; and the former begat many boars, but that sheep begat twelve sheep. And when those twelve sheep had grown, they gave up one of them to the asses, and those asses again gave up that sheep to the wolves, and that sheep grew up among the wolves. And the Lord brought the eleven sheep to live with it and to pasture with it among the wolves: and they multiplied and became many flocks of sheep. And the wolves began to fear them, and they oppressed them until they destroyed their little ones, and they cast their young into a river of much water: but those sheep began to

***The twelve sheep (12 Tribes) give/sell one of the sheep (Joseph) to the asses (Midianites) and they in turn sell him to the Ishmaelites, and they in turn sell him in Egypt to Potiphar. Joseph (sheep) lived/ruled Egypt, but when he passed, so did the peace among the two people. The wolves (Egyptians) felt the sheep (Israel) were too numerous and ordered their young (boys) to be cast in the river.***

16 cry aloud on account of their little ones, and to complain unto their Lord. And a sheep which had been saved from the wolves fled and escaped to the wild asses; and I saw the sheep how they lamented and cried, and besought their Lord with all their might, till that Lord of the sheep descended at the voice of the sheep from a lofty abode, and came to them and pastured them. And He called that sheep which had escaped the wolves, and spake with it concerning the wolves that it should

18 admonish them not to touch the sheep. And the sheep went to the wolves according to the word of the Lord, and another sheep met it and went with it, and the two went and entered together into the assembly of those wolves, and spake with them and admonished them not to touch the

**Enoch 89:16 to 89:18 The sheep cried to the Lord of the Sheep (Yahweh) for relief and he descended (Pillar in the Sky), pastured (orbited) among them, and ordered that sheep (Moses) to go with another sheep (Aaron) to the wolves (Pharaoh) and tell them to leave the sheep (Israel) alone.**

19 sheep from henceforth. And thereupon I saw the wolves, and how they oppressed the sheep

20 exceedingly with all their power; and the sheep cried aloud. And the Lord came to the sheep and they began to smite those wolves: and the wolves began to make lamentation; but the sheep became

**Enoch 89:19 and 89:20 The wolves (Egyptians) were slain by the sheep (Israel) and they began to cry out.**

21 quiet and forthwith ceased to cry out. And I saw the sheep till they departed from amongst the wolves; but the eyes of the wolves were blinded, and those wolves departed in pursuit of the sheep

22 with all their power. And the Lord of the sheep went with them, as their leader, and all His sheep

23 followed Him: and his face was dazzling and glorious and terrible to behold. But the wolves

**Enoch 89:21 to 89:23 As the sheep make their Exodus from the wolves (Egypt) the Lord of the sheep (Yahweh) blinds the wolves (Egyptians), leads their way, and his face was dazzling, glorious, and terrible to behold.**

24 began to pursue those sheep till they reached a sea of water. And that sea was divided, and the water stood on this side and on that before their face, and their Lord led them and placed Himself between

*The sheep (Israel) arrive at a sea of water (Red Sea/Gulf of Aqaba) and find it divided (parted) and their Lord (Wheel in the Sky) stood between them. The sea is already parted, and Moses does not do so in this version.*

25 them and the wolves. And as those wolves did not yet see the sheep, they proceeded into the midst of that sea, and the wolves followed the sheep, and [those wolves] ran after them into that sea.

*The wolves (Egyptians) blindly follow the sheep (Israel) into the parted waters.*

26 And when they saw the Lord of the sheep, they turned to flee before His face, but that sea gathered itself together, and became as it had been created, and the water swelled and rose till it covered

27 those wolves. And I saw till all the wolves who pursued those sheep perished and were drowned.

**Enoch 89:26 to 89:27 The waters close as the wolves (Egyptians) are destroyed in the deluge.**

28 But the sheep escaped from that water and went forth into a wilderness, where there was no water and no grass; and they began to open their eyes and to see; and I saw the Lord of the sheep

29 pasturing them and giving them water and grass, and that sheep going and leading them. And that

**Enoch 89:28 and 89:29 The sheep (Israel) begin to grumble for lack of food and water.**

30 sheep ascended to the summit of that lofty rock, and the Lord of the sheep sent it to them. And after that I saw the Lord of the sheep who stood before them, and His appearance was great and

*The sheep (Moses) ascend the mountain to the Lord of the sheep (Yahweh).*

31 terrible and majestic, and all those sheep saw Him and were afraid before His face. And they all feared and trembled because of Him, and they cried to that sheep with them [which was amongst

32 them]: ' We are not able to stand before our Lord or to behold Him.' And that sheep which led them again ascended to the summit of that rock, but the sheep began to be blinded and to wander

**Enoch 89:31 and 89:32 The sheep (Israel) were afraid of His (Wheel in the Sky) face and became blinded. One would be blinded when staring at a blazing star/planet/comet.**

33 from the way which he had showed them, but that sheep wot not thereof. And the Lord of the sheep was wrathful exceedingly against them, and that sheep discovered it, and went down from the summit of the rock, and came to the sheep, and found the greatest part of them blinded and fallen

34 away. And when they saw it they feared and trembled at its presence, and desired to return to their

**Enoch 89:33 and 89:34 The sheep (Israel) incurred their Lord's (Yahweh) wrath and feared His vengeance.**

35 folds. And that sheep took other sheep with it, and came to those sheep which had fallen away, and began to slay them; and the sheep feared its presence, and thus that sheep brought back those

36 sheep that had fallen away, and they returned to their folds. And I saw in this vision till that sheep became a man and built a house for the Lord of the sheep, and placed all the sheep in that house.

**Enoch 89:35 and 89:36 The head sheep (Moses) has the sheep (Israel) that were blinded (golden calf) murdered. Moses (head sheep) builds the Tabernacle to the Lord of the sheep (Yahweh), to house the Ark of the Covenant.**

37 And I saw till this sheep which had met that sheep which led them fell asleep: and I saw till all the great sheep perished and little ones arose in their place, and they came to a pasture, and

*The head sheep (Moses) dies.*

38 approached a stream of water. Then that sheep, their leader which had become a man, withdrew

*The next leader Joshua dies.*

39 from them and fell asleep, and all the sheep sought it and cried over it with a great crying. And I saw till they left off crying for that sheep and crossed that stream of water, and there arose the two sheep as leaders in the place of those which had led them and fallen asleep (lit. ' had fallen asleep and led

40 them '). **And I saw till the sheep came to a goodly place, and a pleasant and glorious land, and I saw till those sheep were satisfied; and that house stood amongst them in the pleasant land.**

41 And sometimes their eyes were opened, and sometimes blinded, till another sheep arose and led them and brought them all back, and their eyes were opened.

*The sheep (Israel) sometimes stray from the path as they make it to their Pleasant (Promised Land) Land, Babylon! Is the new sheep Saul or David?*

*Tower of Babel*

50 And that house became great and broad, and it was built for those sheep: (and) a tower lofty and great was built on the house for the Lord of the sheep, and that house was low, but the tower was elevated and lofty, and the Lord of the sheep stood on that tower and they offered a full table before Him.

*The sheep (Israel) build a lofty and great, elevated tower (Babel) to the Lord of the sheep (Yahweh)! The Lord of the sheep (Yahweh) stood on the tower (Babel). This telling passage speaks of the sheep (Israel), as the builders of the Tower of Babel (Lofty tower). That statement by Enoch seems to fly in the face of conventional teaching. Enoch/Enkime lived (maybe?) some fifteen-hundred years before the Exodus, and over seven-hundred years before the Great Flood of Noah/Ziusudra. It has become obvious that Enoch contradicts three major stories in the scriptures;*

1st – Noah          "Bull Born as a Man"

2nd – Exodus        "Already Divided Sea"

3rd – Tower of Babel     "Tower to the Lord of the Sheep"  Built in the Pleasant Land of Babylon – Plain of Shinar

51 And again I saw those **sheep** that they again **erred** and went many ways, and **forsook** that their **house**, and the **Lord** of the sheep **called** some from amongst the sheep and sent them to the sheep,

52 but the sheep began to **slay** them. And one of them was **saved** and was **not** slain, and it sped away and cried aloud over the sheep; and they **sought** to slay it, but the **Lord** of the sheep saved it from

53 the sheep, and brought it up to me, and caused it to dwell there. And many other sheep He sent to those sheep to **testify** unto them and lament over them. And after that I saw that when they forsook the **house** of the Lord and **His tower** they fell away entirely, and their eyes were blinded; and I saw the Lord of the sheep how He wrought much slaughter amongst them in their herds until

55 those sheep invited that slaughter and **betrayed** His place. And He gave them over into the hands of the **lions** and **tigers**, and **wolves** and **hyenas**, and into the hand of the **foxes**, and to all the wild

56 **beasts**, and those wild beasts began to **tear** in pieces those sheep. And I saw that He forsook that their house and their tower and gave them all into the hand of the lions, to tear and **devour** them,

*Enoch 89:51 to 89:56 Enoch claims direct ownership of the tower (Babel) by the sheep (Israel), to the Lord of the sheep (Yahweh), and not to the Babylonians, whose land the Israelites rested in. He shows that a lot of the sheep (Israel) fell into the practices of the Babylonians. "The tower (Babel) fell away entirely and their eyes were blinded!" I believe the tower (Babel) was built to touch the Pillar (cloud, wheel, bull, comet, Venus, etc.) in the Sky. The comet/proto-planet Venus passed over the area on a regular orbit (49yrs – 1 Jubilee yr) and this time it discharged plasma to the worshippers of this deity. The ones that looked directly at the discharge would be blinded, as their retinas would instantly be fried. The effect is like looking directly into the Sun at close proximity. A plasma discharge has the nuclear power of the Sun. Plasma is still a field that is being explored, but it may actually be the most powerful form of any matter.*

NOTE: El/Bel = God       Babel= Tower of God or Bel

73 house; but the wild boars tried to hinder them, but they were not able. And they began again to build as before, and they reared up that tower, and it was named the high tower; and they began again to place a table before the tower, but all the bread on it was polluted and not pure.

*The sheep (Israel) try to rebuild the tower (Babel).*

Chapter 90

1 And I saw till that in this manner **thirty-five shepherds** undertook the pasturing (of the sheep), and they severally completed their **periods** as did the **first**; and others received them into their

*Thirty-five constellations shepherd and pasture during their period (50% of El's constellations/children).*

2 hands, to pasture them for their period, each shepherd in his own period. And after that I saw in my vision all the **birds** of **heaven** coming, the **eagles**, the **vultures**, the **kites**, the **ravens**; but the eagles led all the birds; and they began to **devour** those **sheep**, and to pick out their eyes and to

*Birds, heaven, eagles, vultures, kites, and ravens are all references to the constellations*

3 devour their flesh. And the sheep cried out because their flesh was being devoured by the birds,

4 and as for me I looked and lamented in my sleep over that shepherd who pastured the sheep. And I saw until those sheep were devoured by the dogs and eagles and kites, and they left neither flesh nor skin nor sinew remaining on them till only their bones stood there: and their bones too fell

5 to the earth and the sheep became few. And I saw until that **twenty-three** had undertaken the **pasturing** and completed in their several **periods fifty-eight times**.

6 But behold lambs were borne by those white sheep, and they began to open their eyes and to see,

7 and to cry to the sheep. Yea, they cried to them, but they did not hearken to what they said to

8 them, but were exceedingly deaf, and their eyes were very exceedingly blinded. And I saw in the vision how the ravens flew upon those lambs and took one of those lambs, and dashed the sheep

9 in pieces and devoured them. And I saw till horns grew upon those lambs, and the ravens cast down their horns; and I saw till there sprouted a great horn of one of those sheep, and their eyes

10 were opened. And it looked at them [and their eyes opened], and it cried to the sheep, and the

11 **rams** saw it and all ran to it. And not withstanding all this those eagles and vultures and ravens and kites still kept tearing the sheep and swooping down upon them and devouring them: still the sheep remained silent, but the rams lamented and cried out. And those ravens fought and battled with it and sought to lay low its horn, but they had no power over it. All the eagles and vultures and ravens and kites were gathered together, and there came with them all the sheep of the field, yea, they all came together, and helped each other to break that horn of the ram.

*Enoch 90:1 to 90:11 These passages are complete astrotheology in the truest sense. Enoch/Enkime is speaking of the turmoil that will be seen in the stars as their positions (celestial position) will change, and he speaks of them fighting and biting, when it is cosmic upheaval at work, but the theology of the time has become intermingled.*

19 And I saw till a great sword was given to the sheep, and the sheep proceeded against all the beasts of the field to slay them, and all the beasts and the birds of the heaven fled before their face. And I saw that man, who wrote the book according to the command of the Lord, till he opened that book concerning the destruction which those twelve last shepherds had wrought, and showed that they had destroyed much more than their predecessors, before the Lord of the sheep. And I saw till the Lord of the sheep came unto them and took in His hand the staff of His wrath, and smote the earth, and the earth clave asunder, and all the beasts and all the birds of the heaven fell from among those sheep, and were swallowed up in the earth and it covered them.

*The sword/plasma discharge given to the comet/proto-planet Venus tears up the cosmos, as she hurts the Earth, Mars, Mercury, the Moon and others. The last Twelve Shepherds are the zodiac signs of that sky, and the Age of Aries (Exodus Disasters) had taken more lives versus the Age of Taurus (Great Flood)! The visible sky would change after any pole shift or planetary realignment. The Earth yet again falls to destruction.*

20 And I saw till a **throne** was **erected** in the **pleasant land**, and the **Lord of the sheep sat Himself thereon**, and the other took the **sealed books** and opened those books before the Lord of the sheep.

21 And the Lord called those men the **seven first white ones**, and commanded that they should bring before Him, beginning with the first star which led the way, all the stars whose **privy members**

*Thrones, pleasant land (Promised Land), seven first white ones, first lead star, and stars whose privy members (penis) were like horses! Simply about the stars!*

*NOTE: Privy member = penis = rod = obelisk = Baal's shaft*

> *Atharva Veda XI 5-12 Shouting forth, thundering red, white he carries a great penis along the Earth. The Brahmakarin sprinkles seed upon the back of the Earth, through it the four directions live.*

22 were like those of horses, and they brought them all before Him. And He said to that man who wrote before Him, being one of those seven white ones, and said unto him: ' Take those seventy shepherds to whom I delivered the sheep, and who taking them on their own authority slew more

23 than I commanded them.' And behold they were all bound, I saw, and they all stood before Him.

24 And the judgment was held first over the stars, and they were judged and found guilty, and went to the place of condemnation, and they were cast into an abyss, full of fire and flaming, and full

25 of pillars of fire. And those seventy shepherds were judged and found guilty, and they were cast

26 into that fiery abyss. And I saw at that time how a like abyss was opened in the midst of the earth, full of fire, and they brought those blinded sheep, and they were all judged and found guilty and

27 cast into this fiery abyss, and they burned; now this abyss was to the right of that house. And I saw those sheep burning and their bones burning.

28 And I stood up to see till they folded up that old house; and carried off all the pillars, and all the beams and ornaments of the house were at the same time folded up with it, and they carried

*Enoch 90:22 to 90:28 Seven white ones (planets/Pleiades), seventy shepherds (El had 70 children/constellations), bound (star grouping), stars judged, thrown in abyss (black hole), pillars of fire, right of that house, are all astronomy terms mingled with theology.*

29 it off and laid it in a place in the south of the land. And I saw till the Lord of the sheep brought a new house greater and loftier than that first, and set it up in the place of the first which had beer folded up: all its pillars were new, and its ornaments were new and larger than those of the first, the old one which He had taken away, and all the sheep were within it.

30 And I saw all the sheep which had been left, and all the beasts on the earth, and all the birds of the heaven, falling down and doing homage to those sheep and making petition to and obeying

*A new house refers to the new heavens above after the catastrophe. The Earth acquired additional days to its year, and the heavens above changed their order for a new house. In any astrological chart the 12 compartments or "houses," are imaginary divisions of the zodiac. A full 360° rotatation of the zodiac in the sky is divided into 12 equal parts of 30° each called Signs. The Hebrew calendar is 12 months of 30 days each with intercalary days inserted as needed.*

Section V. XCI-CIV (i.e. XCII, XCI. 1-1O, 18-19, XCIII. 1-1O, XCI. 12-17, XCIV-CIV.).
A Book of Exhortation and Promised Blessing for the Righteous and of Malediction and Woe for the Sinners.

**Chapter 92**

**2 Let not your spirit be troubled on account of the times;  For the Holy and Great One has appointed days for all things.**

*Remember this well! This is such an appropriate and beautiful verse!*

**Chapter 102**

2 And all the luminaries shall be affrighted with great fear, - **The stars will be in chaos**
And all the earth shall be affrighted and tremble and be alarmed. – **World quake**

3 And all the angels shall execute their commandst  - **Stars**
And shall seek to hide themselves from the presence of the Great Glory, - **Venus**
And the children of earth shall tremble and quake;  **World quake**
And ye sinners shall be cursed for ever, - *guilt placement*
**And ye shall have no peace.**

# Exodus Decoded – written @ 300 BCE

**CHAPTER 1**

1 NOW these are the names of the children of Israel, which came into Egypt; every man and his **house**hold came with Jacob.

2 Reuben *(Aquarius)*, Simeon *(Capricorn)*, Levi *(Pisces)*, and Judah *(LEO!)*,

3 Issachar *(Cancer)*, Zebulun *(Aries)*, and Benjamin *(Gemini)*,

4 Dan *(Scorpio)*, and Naphtali *(Virgo) Naptha*, Gad *(Sagittarius) Dagon?*, and Asher *(Libra) Ashera?*

5 And all the souls that came out of the loins of Jacob were **seventy souls:** for Joseph was in Egypt already.

6 And Joseph *(TAURUS!)* died, and all his brethren, and all that generation.

7 And the children of Israel were fruitful, and increased abundantly, and multiplied, and waxed exceeding mighty; and the land was filled with them.

8 Now there arose up a new king over Egypt, which knew not Joseph.

9 And he said unto his people, Behold, the people of the children of Israel are more and mightier than we:

**Exodus 1:1 to 1:9 Is the same recounting as Enoch about the Twelve Tribes of Israel. This is a purely astrological parallel to the twelve zodiac constellations. Jacob had seventy children, just as El had seventy constellations (children). Dinah is removed!**

10 Come on, let us deal wisely with them; lest they multiply, and it come to pass, that, when there falleth out any war, they join also unto our enemies, and fight against us, and so get them up out of the land.

**This statement echoes what Enoch stated in his parable of the sheep. I believe the Children of Israel dealt craftily with the Egyptians later.**

**CHAPTER 2**

10 And the child grew, and she brought him unto Pharaoh's daughter, and he became her son. And she called his name Moses: and she said, Because I drew him out of the water.

*The naming of Moses has been of speculation as it means, "One drawn from the waters."*

16 Now the priest of Midian had seven daughters: and they came and drew water, and filled the troughs to water their father's flock.

*The 7 stars of the Pleiades AKA "The Seven Sisters." Moses interestingly bumps into a priest with seven daughters.*

**CHAPTER 3**

1 NOW Moses kept the flock of Jethro his father in law, the priest of Midian: and he led the flock to the backside of the desert, and came to the mountain of God, even to Horeb.

2 And the angel of the LORD appeared unto him in a flame of fire out of the midst of a bush: and he looked, and, behold, the bush burned with fire, and the bush was not consumed.

*I wonder if this could be the result of some form of ball lightning or St. Elmo's Fire emitted from the comet.*

6 Moreover he said, I am the God of thy father, the God of Abraham, the God of Isaac, and the God of Jacob. And Moses hid his face; for he was afraid to look upon God.

*He does not once call Himself by the names man has given Him (YHWH - YWH in the land of Shasu - Yahou - Edom).*

8 And I am come down to deliver them out of the hand of the Egyptians, and to bring them up out of that land unto a good land and a large, unto a land flowing with milk and honey; unto the place of the Canaanites, and the Hittites, and the Amorites, and the Perizzites, and the Hivites, and the Jebusites.

*The passage of the comet/proto-planet Venus was depositing its carbogenous content across the globe, which helped mankind survive for decades through the famine and drought. I have wondered if the content of the manna was a good thing to enter our bodies, as it may have caused genetic aberrations over the generations.*

14 And God said unto Moses, I AM THAT I AM: and he said, Thus shalt thou say unto the children of Israel, I AM hath sent me unto you.

*This angry retort has puzzled scholars and theologians. It has been translated as, "I am that I am," as well as "The Being," which is an even odder response from a deity.*

21 And I will give this people favour in the sight of the Egyptians: and it shall come to pass, that, when ye go, ye shall not go empty:

22 But every woman shall borrow of her neighbour, and of her that sojourneth in her house, jewels of silver, and jewels of gold, and raiment: and ye shall put them upon your sons, and upon your daughters; and ye shall spoil the Egyptians.

*Exodus 3:21 and 3:22 I found the statement to ask/borrow may have meant to steal, but the Children of Israel were dealing craftily with the Egyptians, as they had done to them.*

**CHAPTER 4**

2 And the LORD said unto him, What is that in thine hand? And he said, A rod.

*The rod (penis) was a typical measuring tool in antiquity. This puzzled me as God would have known what he held in his hand.*

9 And it shall come to pass, if they will not believe also these **two signs**, neither hearken unto thy voice, that thou shalt take of the **water** of the river, and pour it upon the dry land: and the water which thou takest out of the river shall become **blood** upon the **dry land**.

30 And Aaron spake all the words which the LORD had spoken unto Moses, and **did** the **signs** in the sight of the people.

**CHAPTER 7**

11 Then Pharaoh also called the wise men and the sorcerers: now the magicians of Egypt, they also did in like manner with their enchantments.

12 For they cast down every man his rod, and they became serpents: but Aaron's rod swallowed up their rods.

*Exodus 7:11 and 7:12 The competing theologies were based on what was transpiring in the heavens above. The serpents warring in the heavens caused people to take sides in the celestial battle.*

*Onset 1st Plague – BLOOD – Iron Sulfide (Meteor) – Airborne & Direct Contact*

17 Thus saith the LORD, In this thou shalt know that I am the LORD: behold, I will smite with the rod that is in mine hand upon the waters which are in the river, and they shall be turned to blood.

18 And the fish that is in the river shall die, and the river shall stink; and the Egyptians shall lothe to drink of the water of the river.

19 And the LORD spake unto Moses, Say unto Aaron, Take thy rod, and stretch out thine hand upon the waters of Egypt, upon their streams, upon their rivers, and upon their ponds, and upon all their pools of water, that they may become blood; and that there may be blood throughout all the land of Egypt, both in vessels of wood, and in vessels of stone.

20 And Moses and Aaron did so, as the LORD commanded; and he lifted up the rod, and smote the waters that were in the river, in the sight of Pharaoh, and in the sight of his servants; and all the waters that were in the river were turned to blood.

21 And the fish that was in the river died; and the river stank, and the Egyptians could not drink of the water of the river; and there was blood throughout all the land of Egypt.

22 And the magicians of Egypt did so with their enchantments: and Pharaoh's heart was hardened, neither did he hearken unto them; as the LORD had said.

23 And Pharaoh turned and went into his house, neither did he set his heart to this also.

24 And all the Egyptians digged round about the river for water to drink; for they could not drink of the water of the river.

25 And seven days were fulfilled, after that the LORD had smitten the river.

*Exodus 7:17 to 7:25 begins the onset of the Ten Plagues of Egypt. The red (JeDOM) color of the water resulted from the iron sulfide content deposited across the globe. The bodies of water noted through records as being affected were the Nile, canals, streams, lakes, uncovered wells, and ground water. The wood troughs that fed the animals would have been left uncovered, and the stone wells also were uncovered. Covered vessels of water remained unaffected, which meant that the contaminant had to settle upon or mix with water to render it bloody and unfit for consumption. This would definitely indicate that this was an airborne toxin based on modes of transmission such as; airborne, direct, indirect, and vector. Open bodies of water that became infected would begin to smell of rotten eggs from the sulfur. The iron sulfide content in the water has been seen to color the corals of the Red Sea (Erythrean Sea) and many lakes and rivers in places like Florida. Flamingos have long been known to achieve their beautiful pink coloration from drinking of the various waters rich in iron minerals or seismic activity. The dusting that the planet Earth would receive each orbit (49-50yrs) would take about a week for the bodies of water to wash clean of the contaminants on her own accord. I believe some of the practices that the Hebrews undertook simply helped to keep their food and water sources safe, as well as residing in the land of Goshen and not Egypt, kept the settlement out of a direct debris path of the comet.*

END 1$^{st}$ Plague Blood (7 days)

**CHAPTER 8**

Onset 2$^{nd}$ Plague – FROGS – Vector-Direct/Indirect Contact

2 And if thou refuse to let them go, behold, I will smite all thy borders with frogs:

3 And the river shall bring forth frogs abundantly, which shall go up and come into thine house, and into thy bedchamber, and upon thy bed, and into the house of thy servants, and upon thy people, and into thine ovens, and into thy kneadingtroughs:

4 And the frogs shall come up both on thee, and upon thy people, and upon all thy servants.

5 And the LORD spake unto Moses, Say unto Aaron, Stretch forth thine hand with thy rod over the streams, over the rivers, and over the ponds, and cause frogs to come up upon the land of Egypt.

6 And Aaron stretched out his hand over the waters of Egypt; and the frogs came up, and covered the land of Egypt.

7 And the magicians did so with their enchantments, and brought up frogs upon the land of Egypt.

*Exodus 8:2 to 8:7 If the Egyptians practiced sorcery, is this not what Moses and Aaron are practicing?*

8 Then Pharaoh called for Moses and Aaron, and said, Intreat the LORD, that he may take away the frogs from me, and from my people; and I will let the people go, that they may do sacrifice unto the LORD.

9 And Moses said unto Pharaoh, Glory over me: when shall I intreat for thee, and for thy servants, and for thy people, to destroy the frogs from thee and thy houses, that they may remain in the river only?

10 And he said, To morrow. And he said, Be it according to thy word: that thou mayest know that there is none like unto the LORD our God.

11 And the frogs shall depart from thee, and from thy houses, and from thy servants, and from thy people; they shall remain in the river only.

12 And Moses and Aaron went out from Pharaoh: and Moses cried unto the LORD because of the frogs which he had brought against Pharaoh.

13 And the LORD did according to the word of Moses; and the frogs died out of the houses, out of the villages, and out of the fields.

***Exodus 8:2 to 8:13 begins to show how the iron sulfide kills the fish in the water with gills leaving only those in the egg. Thereby, the frogs having few predators begin to proliferate in record numbers. The frogs would begin to leave the banks of the Nile in search of food coming into the homes of the Egyptians, while the land of Goshen remained free of the pestilence because of the distance.***

14 And they gathered them together upon heaps: and the land stank.

***The frogs begin to die in piles as they find no food source to sustain their population.***

15 But when Pharaoh saw that there was respite, he hardened his heart, and hearkened not unto them; as the LORD had said.

## END2$^{nd}$ Plague – FROGS
***The poisoned river fed the frogs rapid growth***

16 And the LORD said unto Moses, Say unto Aaron, Stretch out thy rod, and smite the dust of the land, that it may become lice throughout all the land of Egypt.

17 And they did so; for Aaron stretched out his hand with his rod, and smote the dust of the earth, and it became lice in man, and in beast; all the dust of the land became lice throughout all the land of Egypt.

18 And the magicians did so with their enchantments to bring forth lice, but they could not: so there were lice upon man, and upon beast.

19 Then the magicians said unto Pharaoh, This is the finger of God: and Pharaoh's heart was hardened, and he hearkened not unto them; as the LORD had said.

20 And the LORD said unto Moses, Rise up early in the morning, and stand before Pharaoh; lo, he cometh forth to the water; and say unto him, Thus saith the LORD, Let my people go, that they may serve me.

21 Else, if thou wilt not let my people go, behold, I will send swarms of flies upon thee, and upon thy servants, and upon thy people, and into thy houses: and the houses of the Egyptians shall be full of swarms of flies, and also the ground whereon they are.

22 And I will sever in that day the land of Goshen, in which my people dwell, that no swarms of flies shall be there; to the end thou mayest know that I am the LORD in the midst of the earth.

23 And I will put a division between my people and thy people: to morrow shall this sign be.

*ONSET 3rd Plague – FLIES (Vector contact)*

24 And the LORD did so; and there came a grievous swarm of flies into the house of Pharaoh, and into his servants' houses, and into all the land of Egypt: the land was corrupted by reason of the swarm of flies.

**Exodus 8:16 to 8:24 Shows how the chain of infection continues onto the flies and lice that proliferate from the death of the frogs. The flies and lice grow in epic numbers and begin to afflict man and animal alike.**

25 And Pharaoh called for Moses and for Aaron, and said, Go ye, sacrifice to your God in the land.

26 And Moses said, It is not meet so to do; for we shall sacrifice the abomination of the Egyptians to the LORD our God: lo, shall we sacrifice the abomination of the Egyptians before their eyes, and will they not stone us?

27 We will go three days' journey into the wilderness, and sacrifice to the LORD our God, as he shall command us.

28 And Pharaoh said, I will let you go, that ye may sacrifice to the LORD your God in the wilderness; only ye shall not go very far away: intreat for me.

29 And Moses said, Behold, I go out from thee, and I will intreat the LORD that the swarms of flies may depart from Pharaoh, from his servants, and from his people, to morrow: but let not Pharaoh deal deceitfully any more in not letting the people go to sacrifice to the LORD.

30 And Moses went out from Pharaoh, and intreated the LORD.

31 And the LORD did according to the word of Moses; and he removed the swarms of flies from Pharaoh, from his servants, and from his people; there remained not one.

32 And Pharaoh hardened his heart at this time also, neither would he let the people go.

*END 3rd Plague – FLIES*
**The poisoned river fed the frogs rapid growth, whose decaying bodies fed the flies rapid growth.**

**CHAPTER 9**

*Onset 4th Plague – Beasts – Direct/Indirect Contact*
*Onset 5th Plague – Murrain (Cattle Disease) – Direct/Indirect Contact*

3 Behold, the hand of the LORD is upon thy cattle which is in the field, upon the horses, upon the asses, upon the camels, upon the oxen, and upon the sheep: there shall be a very grievous murrain.

4 And the LORD shall sever between the cattle of Israel and the cattle of Egypt: and there shall nothing die of all that is the children's of Israel.

5 And the LORD appointed a set time, saying, To morrow the LORD shall do this thing in the land.

6 And the LORD did that thing on the morrow, and all the cattle of Egypt died: but of the cattle of the children of Israel died not one.

7 And Pharaoh sent, and, behold, there was not one of the cattle of the Israelites dead. And the heart of Pharaoh was hardened, and he did not let the people go.

8 And the LORD said unto Moses and unto Aaron, Take to you handfuls of ashes of the furnace, and let Moses sprinkle it toward the heaven in the sight of Pharaoh.

9 And it shall become small dust in all the land of Egypt, and shall be a boil breaking forth with blains upon man, and upon beast, throughout all the land of Egypt.

10 And they took ashes of the furnace, and stood before Pharaoh; and Moses sprinkled it up toward heaven; and it became a boil breaking forth with blains upon man, and upon beast.

11 And the magicians could not stand before Moses because of the boils; for the boil was upon the magicians, and upon all the Egyptians.

***Exodus 9:3 to 9:11** The sorcerers have obviously become infected with boils and sores resulting from exposure to airborne particles. Volcanic ash is known to cause respiratory and skin conditions.*

18 Behold, to morrow about this time I will cause it to rain a very grievous hail, such as hath not been in Egypt since the foundation thereof even until now.

19 Send therefore now, and gather thy cattle, and all that thou hast in the field; for upon every man and beast which shall be found in the field, and shall not be brought home, the hail shall come down upon them, and they shall die.

20 He that feared the word of the LORD among the servants of Pharaoh made his servants and his cattle flee into the houses:

21 And he that regarded not the word of the LORD left his servants and his cattle in the field.

*The Hebrews had smart practices in regard to the safekeeping of their livestock. Having been a people that always cared for flocks as herdsman, they understood the need to sometimes shelter their animals as they were precious cargo. By sheltering their animals during the dustings, this would prevent any boils from afflicting their animals. I believe the genesis of Kosher and Halal practices began during these times. The animals also sensed the disasters long before their human counterparts.*

*END 4$^{th}$ Plague – Beasts – Direct Contact*
*End 5$^{th}$ Plague – Murrain (Cattle Disease) – Direct Contact*
*The poisoned rivers fed the frogs rapid growth, whose decaying bodies fed the flies rapid growth. The beasts of the field that were left unattended become infected.*

*ONSET 6$^{th}$ and 7$^{th}$ Plagues – Volcanic Ash & Meteorites – Airborne/Direct/Indirect Contacts*

22 And the LORD said unto Moses, Stretch forth thine hand toward heaven, that there may be hail in all the land of Egypt, upon man, and upon beast, and upon every herb of the field, throughout the land of Egypt.

23 And Moses stretched forth his rod toward heaven: and the LORD sent thunder and hail, and the fire ran along upon the ground; and the LORD rained hail upon the land of Egypt.

24 So there was hail, and fire mingled with the hail, very grievous, such as there was none like it in all the land of Egypt since it became a nation.

25 And the hail smote throughout all the land of Egypt all that was in the field, both man and beast; and the hail smote every herb of the field, and brake every tree of the field.

26 Only in the land of Goshen, where the children of Israel were, was there no hail.

***Exodus 9:22 to 9:25** The tail of the comet has passed, and the larger more volatile portions begin to affect the Earth. As the gravitational, piezoelectric, and tidal force of the planet are disturbed with the close flyby of the comet/proto-planet Venus. Meteorites and naphtha rain (liquid hydrocarbons) down upon the Earth as all unsheltered animals die or become affected from the fallout of debris. Not being in the direct orbital path again helps the Children of Goshen.*

31 And the flax and the barley was smitten: for the barley was in the ear, and the flax was bolled.

32 But the wheat and the rice were not smitten: for they were not grown up.

*Some crops were stunted in the bud, while others like barley's growth cycle was sped up.*

33 And Moses went out of the city from Pharaoh, and spread abroad his hands unto the LORD: and the thunders and hail ceased, and the rain was not poured upon the earth.

34 And when Pharaoh saw that the rain and the hail and the thunders were ceased, he sinned yet more, and hardened his heart, he and his servants.

35 And the heart of Pharaoh was hardened, neither would he let the children of Israel go; as the LORD had spoken by Moses.

*END 6$^{th}$ and 7$^{th}$ Plagues – Volcanic Ash & Meteorites*
*The poisoned river fed the frogs rapid growth, whose decaying bodies fed the flies rapid growth. The beasts of the field that were left unattended became infected. The close pass by of the comet/proto-planet Venus causes meteorites & naphtha to rain down, as volcanoes become active with the gravitational disturbance.*

**CHAPTER 10**

*ONSET 8$^{th}$ Plague – Locusts – Vector/Direct/Indirect Contacts*

4 Else, if thou refuse to let my people go, behold, to morrow will I bring the locusts into thy coast:

5 And they shall cover the face of the earth, that one cannot be able to see the earth: and they shall eat the residue of that which is escaped, which remaineth unto you from the hail, and shall eat every tree which groweth for you out of the field:

6 And they shall fill thy houses, and the houses of all thy servants, and the houses of all the Egyptians; which neither thy fathers, nor thy fathers' fathers have seen, since the day that they were upon the earth unto this day. And he turned himself, and went out from Pharaoh.

12 And the LORD said unto Moses, Stretch out thine hand over the land of Egypt for the locusts, that they may come up upon the land of Egypt, and eat every herb of the land, even all that the hail hath left.

13 And Moses stretched forth his rod over the land of Egypt, and the LORD brought an east wind upon the land all that day, and all that night; and when it was morning, the east wind brought the locusts.

14 And the locusts went up over all the land of Egypt, and rested in all the coasts of Egypt: very grievous were they; before them there were no such locusts as they, neither after them shall be such.

15 For they covered the face of the whole earth, so that the land was darkened; and they did eat every herb of the land, and all the fruit of the trees which the hail had left: and there remained not any green thing in the trees, or in the herbs of the field, through all the land of Egypt.

*The passage of the comet/proto-planet may have sped up the life cycle of the locusts with few predators available. A strong east wind brought the locusts, and a strong west wind removed them, as a possible disturbance in the thermal atmospheric tide brought and removed the locusts.*

*END 8$^{th}$ Plague – Locusts*
*The poisoned river fed the frogs rapid growth, whose decaying bodies fed the flies rapid growth. The beasts of the field that were left unattended became infected. The life cycle of locusts are disturbed by the thermal atmospheric tide, and are brought by an east wind, and removed by a west wind.*

*ONSET 9$^{th}$ Plague - DARKNESS*

21 And the LORD said unto Moses, Stretch out thine hand toward heaven, that there may be darkness over the land of Egypt, even darkness which may be felt.

22 And Moses stretched forth his hand toward heaven; and there was a thick darkness in all the land of Egypt three days:

23 They saw not one another, neither rose any from his place for three days: but all the children of Israel had light

in their dwellings.

*The effects of a Venusian eclipse causes darkness in the land of Egypt, as the orbital path leaves the land of Goshen still in light. This 3 days of darkness has been reported by many cultures around the globe, as well as 3 days of light (antipodal) which would stand to reason. This is the traditional period of Passover that is observed in the Jewish and Christian faiths. The populace was saved as the "Passover" of the comet/Venus seemingly spared those in Goshen who had the Blood of the Lamb on the lintels of their door posts.*

END 9$^{th}$ Plague – DARKNESS

**CHAPTER 11**

2 Speak now in the ears of the people, and let every man borrow of his neighbour, and every woman of her neighbour, jewels of silver, and jewels of gold.

*Why speak in secrecy? Why borrow of your neighbor when you know that you won't be returning? What was the need for jewels, gold, silver, and raiments in the desert? They may have deserved these because of any captivity, but it seems that the text intones that they may have been stolen? The Israelites may have been dealing "craftily" with the Egyptians, as they had dealt with the Israelites. I will continue to delve into this deeper, as this may have been a motivating factor as to why the Pharaoh decided to pursue them after freeing Israelites. Pharao in all probability thought that they were going on a three day retreat to worship their God in the wilderness.*

*ONSET 10$^{th}$ Plague – SLAYING of 1$^{st}$ BORN (Earth shock)*

3 And the LORD gave the people favour in the sight of the Egyptians. Moreover the man Moses was very great in the land of Egypt, in the sight of Pharaoh's servants, and in the sight of the people.

4 And Moses said, Thus saith the LORD, About midnight will I go out into the midst of Egypt:

5 And all the firstborn in the land of Egypt shall die, from the firstborn of Pharaoh that sitteth upon his throne, even unto the firstborn of the maidservant that is behind the mill; and all the firstborn of beasts.

6 And there shall be a great cry throughout all the land of Egypt, such as there was none like it, nor shall be like it anymore.

7 But against any of the children of Israel shall not a dog move his tongue, against man or beast: that ye may know how that the LORD doth put a difference between the Egyptians and Israel.

*The text in this chapter speaks to the death of all Egyptian firstborn, man and beasts alike. The Great Cry, heard in Egypt was from the harmonic resonance of the earthquake (shaog) as the globe vibrated in quakes around the world. The Egyptians living in stone structures were the victims of their comfortable lifestyle, while the Hebrews dwelt in homes of wood and stucco with covered roofs. If the quaking brought down any of the Hebrew (Goshen) structures or settlements, there would be minimal impact on the people and animals inside.*

**CHAPTER 12**

2 This month shall be unto you the beginning of months: it shall be the first month of the year to you.

5 Your lamb shall be without blemish, a male of the first year: ye shall take it out from the sheep, or from the goats:

6 And ye shall keep it up until the fourteenth day of the same month: and the whole assembly of the congregation of Israel shall kill it in the evening.

9 Eat not of it raw, nor sodden at all with water, but roast with fire; his head with his legs, and with the purtenance thereof.

10 And ye shall let nothing of it remain until the morning; and that which remaineth of it until the morning ye shall

burn with fire.

*The people are being taught how to handle their food to prevent contamination from the environment. If one uses water in an area that is contaminated, the food that is cooked within will spread the contaminants to the person that ingests it. The roasting of the lamb with fire destroys bacteria and microorganisms with the high temperature. If one breaks the bone, marrow comes out and may have been a source of uncooked contamination? A pig would be unsuitable for this practice, as they butt against another in their pens breaking their bones. If one transported the food outdoors to a neighbors it could get contaminated. There are many people today of Caribbean descent that wisely only cook their food with bottled water. The bottled water is highly filtered spring or tap water with more contaminants removed.*

11 And thus shall ye eat it; with your loins girded, your shoes on your feet, and your staff in your hand; and ye shall eat it in haste: it is the LORD's passover.

12 For I will pass through the land of Egypt this night, and will smite all the firstborn in the land of Egypt, both man and beast; and against all the gods of Egypt I will execute judgment: I am the LORD.

13 And the blood shall be to you for a token upon the houses where ye are: and when I see the blood, I will pass over you, and the plague shall not be upon you to destroy you, when I smite the land of Egypt.

14 And this day shall be unto you for a memorial; and ye shall keep it a feast to the LORD throughout your generations; ye shall keep it a feast by an ordinance forever.

15 Seven days shall ye eat unleavened bread; even the first day ye shall put away leaven out of your houses: for whosoever eateth leavened bread from the first day until the seventh day, that soul shall be cut off from Israel.

*I wondered why unleavened bread was so important until it hit me! A leavening agent causes bread to rise. What is a leavening agent but yeast! Yeast has long been known to cause infections (vaginal, etc.), and if one were to eat bread with yeast during this period, the probability of getting infections or diseases would be magnified exponentially. The command that all males be circumcised came into law during this period. This cross contamination between lovers would cause other ailments, therefore, removing the foreskin removes the source of contamination. An excellent decision! This new practice of circumcision came from the older Egyptian ritual process of circumcision.*

16 And in the first day there shall be an holy convocation, and in the seventh day there shall be an holy convocation to you; no manner of work shall be done in them, save that which every man must eat, that only may be done of you.

17 And ye shall observe the feast of unleavened bread; for in this selfsame day have I brought your armies out of the land of Egypt: therefore shall ye observe this day in your generations by an ordinance for ever.

18 In the first month, on the fourteenth day of the month at even, ye shall eat unleavened bread, until the one and twentieth day of the month at even.

*The 21$^{st}$ of the month being the eve of the zodiacal transition to the next month's sign.*

19 Seven days shall there be no leaven found in your houses: for whosoever eateth that which is leavened, even that soul shall be cut off from the congregation of Israel, whether he be a stranger, or born in the land.

20 Ye shall eat nothing leavened; in all your habitations shall ye eat unleavened bread.

21 Then Moses called for all the elders of Israel, and said unto them, Draw out and take you a lamb according to your families, and kill the passover.

22 And ye shall take a bunch of hyssop, and dip it in the blood that is in the bason, and strike the lintel and the two side posts with the blood that is in the bason; and none of you shall go out at the door of his house until the morning.

*Older blood and sacrifice rituals come in to play with the spreading of the blood on the door lintels and door posts.*

23 For the LORD will pass through to smite the Egyptians; and when he seeth the blood upon the lintel, and on the two side posts, the LORD will pass over the door, and will not **suffer the destroyer (comet/Venus)** to come in unto your houses to smite you.

*Here we have the onset of the Passover tradition, as the "destroyer," (Venus) will Passover the homes of the faithful.*

28 And the children of Israel went away, and did as the LORD had commanded Moses and Aaron, so did they.

29 And it came to pass, that at midnight the LORD smote all the firstborn in the land of Egypt, from the firstborn of Pharaoh that sat on his throne unto the firstborn of the captive that was in the dungeon; and all the firstborn of cattle.

30 And Pharaoh rose up in the night, he, and all his servants, and all the Egyptians; and there was a great cry in Egypt; for there was not a house where there was not one dead.

31 And he called for Moses and Aaron by night, and said, Rise up, and get you forth from among my people, both ye and the children of Israel; and go, serve the LORD, as ye have said.

32 Also take your flocks and your herds, as ye have said, and be gone; and bless me also.

*END 10$^{th}$ Plague – Slaughter of the 1$^{st}$ BORN (Earth shock)*

*Egyptian princes slept in beds similar to this as the first born. These beds were typically built lower to the floor and would be closer to any low-lying $CO_2$ type cloud or mist. The younger children slept in higher rooms and lofts, which may be a reason that the first born were afflicted by the selectivity of this killer.*

33 And the Egyptians were urgent upon the people, that they might send them out of the land in haste; for they said, We be all dead men.

34 And the people took their dough before it was leavened, their kneadingtroughs being bound up in their clothes upon their shoulders.

35 And the children of Israel did according to the word of Moses; and they borrowed of the Egyptians jewels of silver, and jewels of gold, and raiment:

*Silver, gold, and raiments.*

36 And the LORD gave the people favour in the sight of the Egyptians, so that they lent unto them such things as they required. And they spoiled the Egyptians.

37 And the children of Israel journeyed from Rameses to Succoth, about six hundred thousand on foot that were men, beside children.

38 And a mixed multitude went up also with them; and flocks, and herds, even very much cattle.

39 And they baked unleavened cakes of the dough which they brought forth out of Egypt, for it was not leavened; because they were thrust out of Egypt, and could not tarry, neither had they prepared for themselves any victual.

40 Now the sojourning of the children of Israel, who dwelt in Egypt, was four hundred and thirty years.

41 And it came to pass at the end of the four hundred and thirty years, even the selfsame day it came to pass, that all the hosts of the LORD went out from the land of Egypt.

44 But every man's servant that is bought for money, when thou hast circumcised him, then shall he eat thereof.

*Slaves? Servants? I would have thought that after "sojourning" in a land for 430 years, and having been slaves, that a religion and a people would never have slave ownership laws at the core foundations of their society. There are hundreds of occurrences of the word slave in the King James Version of the Bible. Slavery in the Bible pops up right around the time of Cain mysteriously.*

### EXODUS DISASTERS
Onset $1^{st}$ Plague – BLOOD – Iron Sulfide (Meteor) – Airborne & Direct Contact
END $1^{st}$ Plague - BLOOD (7 days)
Onset $2^{nd}$ Plague – FROGS – Vector-Direct/Indirect Contact
END $2^{nd}$ Plague – FROGS - The poisoned river fed the frogs rapid growth
Onset $3^{rd}$ Plague – FLIES (Vector contact)
END $3^{rd}$ Plague – FLIES - The poisoned river fed the frogs rapid growth, whose decaying bodies fed the flies rapid growth.
Onset $4^{th}$ Plague – BEASTS – Direct/Indirect Contact
Onset $5^{th}$ Plague – MURRAIN (Cattle Disease) – Direct/Indirect Contact
END $4^{th}$ Plague – BEASTS – Direct Contact
END $5^{th}$ Plague – MURRAIN (Cattle Disease) – Direct Contact - The poisoned rivers fed the frogs rapid growth, whose decaying bodies fed the flies rapid growth. The beasts of the field that were left unattended become infected.
Onset $6^{th}$ and $7^{th}$ Plagues – VOLCANIC ASH & METEORITES – Airborne/Direct/Indirect Contacts
END $6^{th}$ and $7^{th}$ Plagues – VOLCANIC ASH & METEORITES - The poisoned river fed the frogs rapid growth, whose decaying bodies fed the flies rapid growth. The beasts of the field that were left unattended became infected. The close pass by of the comet/proto-planet Venus causes meteorites & naphtha to rain down, as volcanoes become active with the gravitational disturbance.
Onset $8^{th}$ Plague – LOCUSTS – Vector/Direct/Indirect Contacts
END $8^{th}$ Plague – LOCUSTS - The poisoned river fed the frogs rapid growth, whose decaying bodies fed the flies rapid growth. The beasts of the field that were left unattended became infected. The life cycle of locusts are disturbed by the thermal atmospheric tide, and are brought by an east wind, and removed by a west wind.
Onset $9^{th}$ Plague - DARKNESS
END $9^{th}$ Plague – DARKNESS
ONSET $10^{th}$ Plague – SLAYING of the $1^{st}$ BORN (Earth shock)
END $10^{th}$ Plague – SLAYING of the $1^{st}$ BORN (Earth shock)

## CHAPTER 13

4 This day came ye out in the month Abib.

5 And it shall be when the LORD shall bring thee into the land of the **Canaanites**, and the **Hittites**, and the **Amorites**, and the **Hivites**, and the **Jebusites**, which he sware unto thy fathers to give thee, a land flowing with milk and honey, that thou shalt keep this service in this month.

19 And Moses took the bones of Joseph with him: for he had straitly sworn the children of Israel, saying, God will surely visit you; and ye shall carry up my bones away hence with you.

**The taking of Joseph's mummified bones with the departing Israelites gives them a source of veneration for the budding theology and society.**

21 And the LORD went before them by day in a pillar of a cloud, to lead them the way; and by night in a pillar of fire, to give them light; to go by day and night:

22 He took not away the pillar of the cloud by day, nor the pillar of fire by night, from before the people.

**The dates of the Passover of the Exodus takes course over a two month period in the early spring. The comet/Venus takes a geosynchronous orbit during this period as it seems to follow the Children of Israel in the sky.**

## CHAPTER 14

1 AND the LORD spake unto Moses, saying,

2 Speak unto the children of Israel, that they turn and encamp before Pi-hahiroth, between Migdol and the sea, over against Baal-zephon: before it shall ye encamp by the sea.

*The camp has been noted as being at Pi-hahiroth (Phi-Kharot) near the Gulf of Aqaba (Jordan-Gihon Rift).*

5 And it was told the king of Egypt that the people fled: and the heart of Pharaoh and of his servants was turned against the people, and they said, Why have we done this, that we have let Israel go from serving us?

*Could Pharoah and the Egyptians have discovered that they were missing (borrowed) their wealth?*

6 And he made ready his chariot, and took his people with him:

7 And he took six hundred chosen chariots, and all the chariots of Egypt, and captains over every one of them.

9 But the Egyptians pursued after them, all the horses and chariots of Pharaoh, and his horsemen, and his army, and overtook them encamping by the sea, beside Pi-hahiroth, before Baal-zephon.

19 And the angel of God, which went before the camp of Israel, removed and went behind them; and the pillar of the cloud went from before their face, and stood behind them:

20 And it came between the camp of the Egyptians and the camp of Israel; and it was a cloud and darkness to them, but it gave light by night to these: so that the one came not near the other all the night.

21 And Moses stretched out his hand over the sea; and the LORD caused the sea to go back by a strong east wind all that night, and made the sea dry land, and the waters were divided.

22 And the children of Israel went into the midst of the sea upon the dry ground: and the waters were a wall unto them on their right hand, and on their left.

23 And the Egyptians pursued, and went in after them to the midst of the sea, even all Pharaoh's horses, his chariots, and his horsemen.

24 And it came to pass, that in the morning watch the LORD looked unto the host of the Egyptians through the pillar of fire and of the cloud, and troubled the host of the Egyptians,

25 And took off their chariot wheels, that they drave them heavily: so that the Egyptians said, Let us flee from the face of Israel; for the LORD fighteth for them against the Egyptians.

26 And the LORD said unto Moses, Stretch out thine hand over the sea, that the waters may come again upon the Egyptians, upon their chariots, and upon their horsemen.

27 And Moses stretched forth his hand over the sea, and the sea returned to his strength when the morning appeared; and the Egyptians fled against it; and the LORD overthrew the Egyptians in the midst of the sea.

28 And the waters returned, and covered the chariots, and the horsemen, and all the host of Pharaoh that came into the sea after them; there remained not so much as one of them.

29 But the children of Israel walked upon dry land in the midst of the sea; and the waters were a wall unto them on their right hand, and on their left.

30 Thus the LORD saved Israel that day out of the hand of the Egyptians; and Israel saw the Egyptians dead upon the sea shore.

31 And Israel saw that great work which the LORD did upon the Egyptians: and the people feared the LORD, and believed the LORD, and his servant Moses.

**Pharaoh's END**

*Venus takes a station (circumpolar orbit) in the sky of the Northern hemisphere and appears there (two suns?) twenty-four hours a day. In the day she pierced pierced through the blue sky as an immense Pillar of Cloud, during the night as an immense Pillar of Fire, and always with the privy member extended towards the Earth. The close proximity of the comet/Venus causes gravitational disturbances to part the seas at a low crossing point. The Hebrews seeing their opportunity began to cross the sea. The pursuing Egyptians wait too long and are engulfed as the comet's orbit takes it away and the gravitational disturbance relents, causing the parted waters to crash down on the Pharaoh and his forces. It seems that sheer luck and timing have allowed the Children of Israel to continue their quest.*

## CHAPTER 15

14 The people shall hear, and be afraid: sorrow shall take hold on the inhabitants of Palestina.

*The Israelites begin a war with the Philistines (Palestinians) that still echoes today with problems from the past plaguing us.*

20 And Miriam the **prophetess**, the sister of Aaron, took a **timbrel** in her hand; and all the women went out after her with **timbrels** and with dances.

*Prophetess, Seer, Witch, Divinator, Sorcerer, and Magi? I thought that these things were not allowed, and were punishable by death.*

*Divination: the attempt to gain insight into a question or situation by way of an occultic process or ritual.*

*Seer: refers to the ability to gain information about an object, person, location or physical event through means other than the known human senses.*

*Prophet/Prophetess: is an individual who is claimed to have been contacted by the supernatural or the divine and to speak for them, serving as an intermediary with humanity, delivering this newfound knowledge from the supernatural entity to other people.*

*Oracle: an oracle was a person or agency considered to be a source of wise counsel or prophetic predictions or precognition of the future. As such it is a form of divination.*

## CHAPTER 16

1 AND they took their journey from Elim, and all the congregation of the children of Israel came unto the
wilderness of Sin, which is between Elim and Sinai, on the fifteenth day of the second month after their departing out of the land of Egypt.

5 And it shall come to pass, that on the sixth day they shall prepare that which they bring in; and it shall be twice as
much as they gather daily.

*The passage of the comet on a regular basis leaves what has become known as manna on a daily basis, as it settles on to rocks and streams giving the waters a milky appearance.*

8 And Moses said, This shall be, when the LORD shall give you in the evening flesh to eat, and in the morning bread to the full; for that the LORD heareth your murmurings which ye murmur against him: and what are we? your
murmurings are not against us, but against the LORD.

13 And it came to pass, that at even the quails came up, and covered the camp: and in the morning the dew lay round about the host.

*An abundance of livestock like quails proliferated without predators and became an easy food source.*

14 And when the dew that lay was gone up, behold, upon the face of the wilderness there lay a small round thing, as small as the hoar frost on the ground.

20 Notwithstanding they hearkened not unto Moses; but some of them left of it until the morning, and it bred worms, and stank: and Moses was wroth with them.

21 And they gathered it every morning, every man according to his eating: and when the sun waxed hot, it melted.

26 Six days ye shall gather it; but on the seventh day, which is the sabbath, in it there shall be none.

*The manna that was deposited spoiled in the Sun as it was being cooked by the rays, and if one collected it too late in the day it would make them sick or kill them. The manna could not be kept for long outdoors since there was no refrigeration, but could be stored in covered vessels.*

31 And the house of Israel called the name thereof Manna: and it was like coriander seed, white; and the taste of it was like wafers made with honey.

*Cakes and wafers are offered to the Queen of Heaven in the Catholic faith, as did the Egyptians in return of her bounty that she offered us during this time.*

33 And Moses said unto Aaron, Take a pot, and put an omer full of manna therein, and lay it up before the LORD, to be kept for your generations.

*This is the pot of manna that John makes reference to as the "hidden pot of manna," in Revelations 2:17*

35 And the children of Israel did eat manna forty years, until they came to a land inhabited; they did eat manna, until they came unto the borders of the land of Canaan.

*Phoenicia – Canaan*

## CHAPTER 17

1 AND all the congregation of the children of Israel journeyed from the wilderness of Sin, after their journeys, according to the commandment of the LORD, and pitched in Rephidim: and there was no water for the people to drink.

*Known water sources had changed locations in the region, and the lack of drinking water plagued the Israelites during their Exodus as drinking water became a source of wars and battles.*

## CHAPTER 18

11 Now I know that the LORD is greater than all gods: for in the thing wherein they dealt proudly he was above them.

14 And when Moses' father in law saw all that he did to the people, he said, What is this thing that thou doest to the people? why sittest thou thyself alone, and all the people stand by thee from morning unto even?

20 And thou shalt teach them ordinances and laws, and shalt shew them the way wherein they must walk, and the work that they must do.

*Jothor shows Moses how to divide the tasks of judgment by creating a ruling class with power to magistrate over the people.*

## CHAPTER 19

1 In the third month, when the children of Israel were gone forth out of the land of Egypt, the same day came they into the wilderness of Sinai.

9 And the LORD said unto Moses, Lo, I come unto thee in a thick cloud, that the people may hear when I speak with thee, and believe thee for ever. And Moses told the words of the people unto the LORD.

***The passing comet – Pillar of Cloud.***

10 And the LORD said unto Moses, Go unto the people, and sanctify them to day and to morrow, and let them wash their clothes,

11 And be ready against the third day: for the third day the LORD will come down in the sight of all the people upon mount Sinai.

12 And thou shalt set bounds unto the people round about, saying, Take heed to yourselves, that ye go not up into the mount, or touch the border of it: whosoever toucheth the mount shall be surely put to death:

13 There shall not an hand touch it, but he shall surely be stoned, or shot through; whether it be beast or man, it shall not live: when the trumpet soundeth long, they shall come up to the mount.

***People have long wondered why Moses was instructed to build a gate around the mountain to protect the people. The people seeing their God rest atop the mountain wanted to ascend to Him in their adoration. If the people had come in close proximity to the comet/Venus, they would have been exposed to radiation and plasma discharges. The voices and trumpets were the sounds of lightning, thunder, and electricity generated by the orbiting body. The practice of washing their clothes was a new one that helped to reduce the dust and cometary debris from their clothing. I believe the washing of ones feet before entering a house began during this epoch in time, as the dust would cause illness within the home.***

14 And Moses went down from the mount unto the people, and sanctified the people; and they washed their clothes.

15 And he said unto the people, Be ready against the third day: come not at your wives.

***I believe this statement to be more about cleanliness versus morality.***

16 And it came to pass on the third day in the morning, that there were thunders and lightnings, and a thick cloud upon the mount, and the voice of the trumpet exceeding loud; so that all the people that was in the camp trembled.

17 And Moses brought forth the people out of the camp to meet with God; and they stood at the nether part of the mount.

18 And mount Sinai was altogether on a smoke, because the LORD descended upon it in fire: and the smoke thereof ascended as the smoke of a furnace, and the whole mount quaked greatly.

19 And when the voice of the trumpet sounded long, and waxed louder and louder, Moses spake, and God answered him by a voice.

***The display of lightning and thunder emitted by the cloud must have been spectacular in nature and alternately horrific beyond belief.***

20 And the LORD came down upon mount Sinai, on the top of the mount: and the LORD called Moses up to the top of the mount; and Moses went up.

21 And the LORD said unto Moses, Go down, charge the people, lest they break through unto the LORD to gaze, and many of them perish.

***The people are warned not to gaze at God lest they fall. This would stand to reason that looking directly into a nuclear reaction would blind one.***

**CHAPTER 20**

5 Thou shalt not bow down thyself to them, nor serve them: for I the LORD thy God am a jealous God, visiting the iniquity of the fathers upon the children unto the third and fourth generation of them that hate me;

*The mortal aspect of God being jealous of other deities has long been debated.*

10 But the seventh day is the sabbath of the LORD thy God: in it thou shalt not do any work, thou, nor thy son, nor thy daughter, thy manservant, nor thy maidservant, nor thy cattle, nor thy stranger that is within thy gates:

11 For in six days the LORD made heaven and earth, the sea, and all that in them is, and rested the seventh day: wherefore the LORD blessed the sabbath day, and hallowed it.

12 Honour thy father and thy mother: that thy days may be long upon the land which the LORD thy God giveth thee.

13 Thou shalt not kill.

14 Thou shalt not commit adultery.

15 Thou shalt not steal.

16 Thou shalt not bear false witness against thy neighbour.

17 Thou shalt not covet thy neighbour's house, thou shalt not covet thy neighbour's wife, nor his manservant, nor his maidservant, nor his ox, nor his ass, nor any thing that is thy neighbour's.

18 And all the people saw the thunderings, and the lightnings, and the noise of the trumpet, and the mountain smoking: and when the people saw it, they removed, and stood afar off.

19 And they said unto Moses, Speak thou with us, and we will hear: but let not God speak with us, lest we die.

20 And Moses said unto the people, Fear not: for God is come to prove you, and that his fear may be before your faces, that ye sin not.

21 And the people stood afar off, and Moses drew near unto the thick darkness where God was.

22 And the LORD said unto Moses, Thus thou shalt say unto the children of Israel, Ye have seen that I have talked with you from heaven.

23 Ye shall not make with me gods of silver, neither shall ye make unto you gods of gold.

24 An altar of earth thou shalt make unto me, and shalt sacrifice thereon thy burnt offerings, and thy peace offerings, thy sheep, and thine oxen: in all places where I record my name I will come unto thee, and I will bless thee.

25 And if thou wilt make me an altar of stone, thou shalt not build it of hewn stone: for if thou lift up thy tool upon it, thou hast polluted it.

26 Neither shalt thou go up by steps unto mine altar, that thy nakedness be not discovered thereon.

*The Ten Commandments are handed down to Moses. It has been long debated that the "Law Code of Hammurabi 1800 BCE," came first as it predates the laws of Moses (@ 700 BCE) by over a millennia. I personally question the dating of the Commandments, as the earliest known Hebrew writing system is @ 1000 BCE. The Laws of Moses were handed down from 1487-1447 BCE, meaning that they would have been written in a language other than Hebrew (Egyptian or Canaanite?).*

*Curious: Hammu/rabi – Rabbi?*

## CHAPTER 21

1 Now these are the judgments which thou shalt set before them.

2 If thou buy an Hebrew servant, six years he shall serve: and in the seventh he shall go out free for nothing.

*A jubilee month is seven years!*

3 If he came in by himself, he shall go out by himself: if he were married, then his wife shall go out with him.

4 If his master have given him a wife, and she have born him sons or daughters; the wife and her children shall be her master's, and he shall go out by himself.

5 And if the servant shall plainly say, I love my master, my wife, and my children; I will not go out free:

6 Then his master shall bring him unto the judges; he shall also bring him to the door, or unto the door post; and his master shall bore his ear through with an aul; and he shall serve him for ever.

7 And if a man sell his daughter to be a maidservant, she shall not go out as the menservants do.

8 If she please not her master, who hath betrothed her to himself, then shall he let her be redeemed: to sell her unto a strange nation he shall have no power, seeing he hath dealt deceitfully with her.

*More slave and concubine laws!*

## CHAPTER 22

18 Thou shalt not suffer a witch to live.

*Both sides had sorcerers!*

20 He that sacrificeth unto any god, save unto the LORD only, he shall be utterly destroyed.

28 Thou shalt not revile the gods, nor curse the ruler of thy people.

*The Gods? The plurality of this statement leaves speculation once again to the singularity of deity, or a plurality? For a religion to make their people subservient to a rulership that may not be the best for the people or the faith is strange. There is clearly no separation of church and state.*

## CHAPTER 23

24 Thou shalt not bow down to their gods, nor serve them, nor do after their works: but thou shalt utterly overthrow them, and quite break down their images.

*The divine right to destroy other belief systems.*

## CHAPTER 24

1 AND he said unto Moses, Come up unto the LORD, thou, and Aaron, Nadab, and Abihu, and seventy of the elders of Israel; and worship ye afar off.

*The seventy elders of Israel are representative of the seventy children of the Canaanite God El, which are the seventy constellations that He gave birth to.*

13 And Moses rose up, and his minister Joshua: and Moses
went up into the mount of God.

*It seems that Moses needed a bodyguard, as Joshua is his attendant. This shows why after the death of Moses, the Children of Israel became more military minded, waging battles across the region.*

15 And Moses went up into the mount, and a cloud covered the mount.

16 And the glory of the LORD abode upon mount Sinai, and the cloud covered it six days: and the seventh day he called unto Moses out of the midst of the cloud.

*A seven day orbit of close proximity.*

17 And the sight of the glory of the LORD was like devouring fire on the top of the mount in the eyes of the children of Israel.

18 And **Moses** went into the **midst** of the **cloud**, and gat him up into the **mount**: and Moses was in the mount **forty days** and **forty nights.**

*Adam tilled the Garden of Eden for 40 days, Moses was on the mountain 40 days and 40 nights, Jesus fasted in the desert 40 days and 40 nights, the Great Flood was 40 days and 40 nights, Abraham was mourned for 40 days and 40 nights upon his death, the Children of Israel wandered 40 years, the Children of Israel ate manna for 40 years, the scribe Endusbar ate and drank once before fasting for 40 days & nights, while taking down the Book of Enki from his lord, and curiously 40 is the sacred number of the Sumerian Lord Ea (Enki).*

## CHAPTER 32

1 AND when the people saw that Moses delayed to come down out of the mount, the people gathered themselves together unto Aaron, and said unto him, Up, make us gods, which shall go before us; for as for this Moses, the man that brought us up out of the land of Egypt, we wot not what is become of him.

2 And Aaron said unto them, Break off the golden earrings, which are in the ears of your wives, of your sons, and of your daughters, and bring them unto me.

3 And all the people brake off the golden earrings which were in their ears, and brought them unto Aaron.

4 And he received them at their hand, and fashioned it with a graving tool, after he had made it a molten calf: and they said, These be thy gods, O Israel, which brought thee up out of the land of Egypt.

5 And when Aaron saw it, he built an altar before it; and Aaron made proclamation, and said, To morrow is a feast to the LORD.

6 And they rose up early on the morrow, and offered burnt offerings, and brought peace offerings; and the people sat down to eat and to drink, and rose up to play.

*Aaron takes the gold and silver from the people to make a molten calf (this is why they borrowed gold and silver). The calf worship belonged to the former Age of Taurus, and Moses represented the new Age of Aries the ram.*

*Age od Taurus: 4468 BCE to 2308 BCE     Age of Aries: 2308 BCE to 148 BCE*

7 And the LORD said unto Moses, Go, get thee down; for thy people, which thou broughtest out of the land of Egypt, have corrupted themselves:

8 They have turned aside quickly out of the way which I commanded them: they have made them a molten calf, and have worshipped it, and have sacrificed thereunto, and said, These be thy gods, O Israel, which have brought thee up out of the land of Egypt.

9 And the LORD said unto Moses, I have seen this people, and, behold, it is a stiffnecked people:

10 Now therefore let me alone, that my wrath may wax hot against them, and that I may consume them: and I will make of thee a great nation.

*God is ANGRY!*

13 Remember Abraham, Isaac, and Israel, thy servants, to whom thou swarest by thine own self, and saidst unto them, I will multiply your seed as the stars of heaven, and all this land that I have spoken of will I give unto your seed, and they shall inherit it for ever.

**The Cosmic Covenant! This is a direct celestial reference of multiplying his seed as the stars of heaven.**

*Abraham: Abram – Brama / Brahmaa – Abraham  More on this clue later!*

18 And he said, It is not the voice of them that shout for mastery, neither is it the voice of them that cry for being overcome: but the noise of them that sing do I hear.

*Let the festivities begin!*

19 And it came to pass, as soon as he came nigh unto the camp, that he saw the calf, and the dancing: and Moses' anger waxed hot, and he cast the tables out of his hands, and brake them beneath the mount.

20 And he took the calf which they had made, and burnt it in the fire, and ground it to powder, and strawed it upon the water, and made the children of Israel drink of it.

21 And Moses said unto Aaron, What did this people unto thee, that thou hast brought so great a sin upon them?

22 And Aaron said, Let not the anger of my lord wax hot: thou knowest the people, that they are set on mischief.

23 For they said unto me, Make us gods, which shall go before us: for as for this Moses, the man that brought us up out of the land of Egypt, we wot not what is become of him.

24 And I said unto them, Whosoever hath any gold, let them break it off. So they gave it me: then I cast it into the fire, and there came out this calf.

25 And when Moses saw that the people were naked; (for Aaron had made them naked unto their shame among their enemies:)

*This has been an act that has puzzled researchers to Aaron's culpability in leading them further down the road in idolatry against God's dictates.*

34 Therefore now go, lead the people unto the place of which I have spoken unto thee: behold, mine Angel shall go before thee: nevertheless in the day when I visit I will visit their sin upon them.

35 And the LORD plagued the people, because they made
the calf, which Aaron made.

*Aaron is forgiven and the people are killed. The comet/Venus leaves the area and the Israelites begin to follow it out of the valley. I wondered if Aaron feared the people attacking him while the warrior Joshua was on the mount.*

## CHAPTER 33

1 AND the LORD said unto Moses, Depart, and go up hence, thou and the people which thou hast brought up out of the land of Egypt, unto the land which I sware unto Abraham, to Isaac, and to Jacob, saying, Unto thy seed will I give it:

2 And I will send an angel before thee; and I will drive out the Canaanite, the Amorite, and the Hittite, and the Perizzite, the Hivite, and the Jebusite:

3 Unto a land flowing with milk and honey: for I will not go up in the midst of thee; for thou art a stiffnecked people: lest I consume thee in the way.

4 And when the people heard these evil tidings, they mourned: and no man did put on him his ornaments.

5 For the LORD had said unto Moses, Say unto the children of Israel, Ye are a stiffnecked people: I will come up into the midst of thee in a moment, and consume thee: therefore now put off thy ornaments from thee, that I may know what to do unto thee.

*Lest I bring on you another plague?*

6 And the children of Israel stripped themselves of their ornaments by the mount Horeb.

7 And Moses took the tabernacle, and pitched it without the camp, afar off from the camp, and called it the Tabernacle of the congregation. And it came to pass, that every one which sought the LORD went out unto the tabernacle of the congregation, which was without the camp.

*The new converts come to the tabernacle for conversion.*

8 And it came to pass, when Moses went out unto the tabernacle, that all the people rose up, and stood every man at his tent door, and looked after Moses, until he was gone into the tabernacle.

9 And it came to pass, as Moses entered into the tabernacle, the cloudy pillar descended, and stood at the door of the tabernacle, and the LORD talked with Moses.

10 And all the people saw the cloudy pillar stand at the tabernacle door: and all the people rose up and worshipped, ,every man in his tent door.

*Moses wisely pitches his tent of the tabernacles underneath the orbiting cloud.*

11 And the LORD spake unto Moses face to face, as a man speaketh unto his friend. And he turned again into the camp: but his servant Joshua, the son of Nun, a young man, departed not out of the tabernacle.

*Joshua leaves.*

19 And he said, I will make all my goodness pass before thee, and I will proclaim the name of the LORD before thee; and will be gracious to whom I will be gracious, and will shew mercy on whom I will shew mercy.

20 And he said, Thou canst not see my face: for there shall no man see me, and live.

*The Israelites again receive another stern warning not to look upon the face of God, lest they be destroyed by His brilliance!*

21 And the LORD said, Behold, there is a place by me, and thou shalt stand upon a rock:

22 And it shall come to pass, while my glory passeth by, that I will put thee in a clift of the rock, and will cover thee with my hand while I pass by:

23 And I will take away mine hand, and thou shalt see my back parts: but my face shall not be seen.

*The Israelites cower in the narrow passage way ("Valley of the Shadow of Death") as the comet/Venus passes overhead. Their fear was derived from this horrifying passage as they were only able to look down. The brilliance alone would have blinded one. The ROD and STAFF are astrological references.*

> **Psalms 23:4** Yea, though I walk through the valley of the shadow of death, I will fear no evil: for thou *art* with me; thy rod and thy staff they comfort me.

## CHAPTER 34

5 And the LORD descended in the cloud, and stood with him there, and proclaimed the name of the LORD.

*The Pillar of Cloud orbits above the Mount.*

11 Observe thou that which I command thee this day: behold, I drive out before thee the Amorite, and the Canaanite, and the Hittite, and the Perizzite, and the Hivite, and the Jebusite.

12 Take heed to thyself, lest thou make a covenant with the inhabitants of the land whither thou goest, lest it be for a snare in the midst of thee:

*This covenant now grants them the lands of Canaan, Syria, Israel, Palestine, Syria, Anatolia, and more. This covenant is at the heart of the world's issues in the Middle East today.*

*Cove: narrow waterway*     *Coven: 13 Witches*     *Covenant: Witches agreement or pact*

13 But ye shall destroy their altars, break their images, and cut down their groves:

*We still have altars, images, and groves in our places of worship!*

28 And he was there with the LORD forty days and forty nights; he did neither eat bread, nor drink water. And he wrote upon the tables the words of the covenant, the ten commandments.

*Moses again spends 40 days and 40 nights with God on the mountain and did not partake of bread or water. This statement is a metaphor as Moses is the symbol of that present age (Aries).*

29 And it came to pass, when Moses came down from mount Sinai with the two tables of testimony in Moses' hand, when he came down from the mount, that Moses wist not that the skin of his face shone while he talked with him.

30 And when Aaron and all the children of Israel saw Moses, behold, the skin of his face shone; and they were afraid to come nigh him.

*The glow of his skin may have been a sun tan from radiation exposure. The effects of radiation poisoning has not been noted however. Moses (Tuthmoses III) has always been depicted with stubby little goat horns, as it is his symbolism for the Age of Aries.*

## CHAPTER 40

37 But if the cloud were not taken up, then they journeyed not till the day that it was taken up.

38 For the cloud of the LORD was upon the tabernacle by day, and fire was on it by night, in the sight of all the house of Israel, throughout all their journeys.

*Forty years! For forty years the Children of Israel followed the orbit and dictates of this cloud. Their extended Exodus seems to have been caused by the following of this heavenly body. The lands that they wandered into were ones along the orbit of the comet/Venus.*

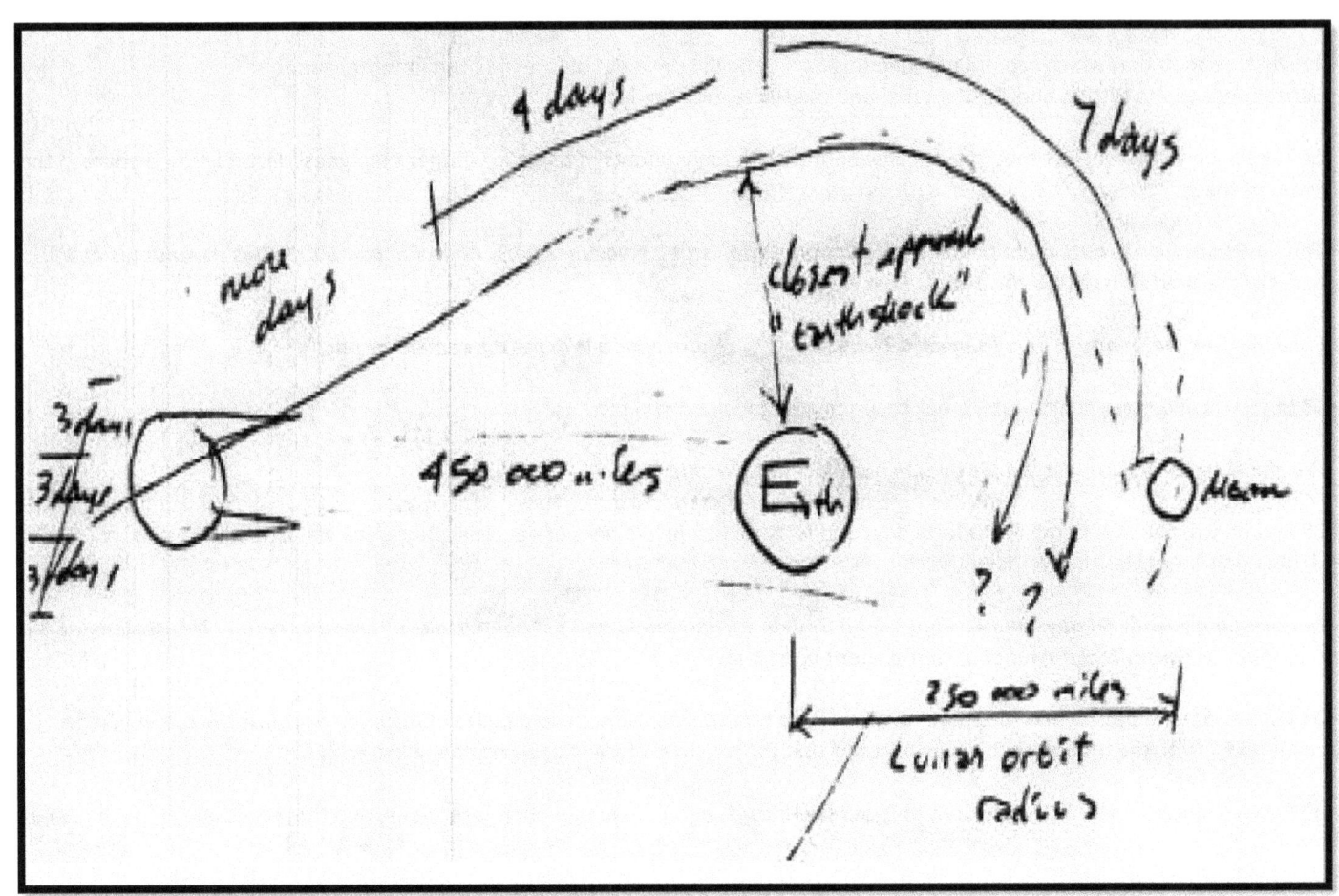

*Mr. Velikofsky's Planetary Passover theory*

# *"Sacrificial Scapegoat of the Hebrews"*

*The word scapegoat has two meanings. The most common one is "one that bears the blame for others." That person may or may not be guilty. The original meaning was, "a goat upon whose head are symbolically placed the sins of the people after which he is sent into the wilderness in the Biblical ceremony for Yom Kippur" (Day of Atonement). "Ez azael" the "goat" (ez) which "escapes" (azel) is what Azazel means.*

*Two nearly identical he-goats would be chosen from among the congregation and presented to the high priest. The high priest would cast lots to determine which was for Jehovah/Yahweh and which for Azazel. Each goat stood by one side of the priest, and the fate of each was determined by the lot chosen by the hand on that side.*

*The goat selected for Jehovah was sacrificed for a sin offering to atone for the sins of the people. Afterward, the high priest laid both hands on the head of the goat chosen for Azazel, and placed on him all the sins of the Children of Israel. Then, an appointed man would lead the goat into the wilderness, to a land not inhabited, and there release the goat.*

*The goat was taken to a certain place in the wilderness to the projecting edge of a steep cliff below which had many jagged rocks. It was steep enough to insure the death of the goat from the fall. So technically, it was released in the wilderness, but over the edge of a cliff! In actual practice it was not released to freedom, but to die a horrible death. This prevented the goat from returning to the encampment as once happened and this return was seen as a bad omen.*

# *Ipuwer Papyrus - @ 1300 BCE*

*"Lament of an Egyptian Scribe"*

**IPUWER PAPYRUS – LEIDEN 344 TORAH-EXODUS**

The sole surviving manuscript dates to the latter **13th** century BCE. The dating of the original composition of the poem is disputed, but several scholars have suggested a date between the late 12th dynasty and the Second Intermediate Period (**ca. 1850 BCE – 1600 BCE**).

## Chapter 1

The brewers/[. . .] sad. A man regards his son as his enemy. Confusion [. . .] another. Come and conquer; judge [. . .] what was ordained for you in the time of Horus, in the age [of the Ennead . . .]. The virtuous man goes in mourning because of what has happened in the land [. . .] goes [. . .] the tribes of the desert have become Egyptians everywhere.

*Ipuwer laments the state of the land and how nomadic tribes from the desert have now become Egyptians (Hebrews/Hyksos?).*

Indeed, the face is pale;/[. . .] what the ancestors foretold has arrived at [fruition . . .] the land is full of confederates, and a man goes to plough with his shield.

*Those with more of a Caucasian complexion are beginning to supplant the true Egyptian populace. Things have degraded to a warrior of the wastelands society. A man has to defend himself with the sword just to sow his fields.*

Indeed, the **women** are **barren** and **none conceive**. Khnum fashions (men) no more because of the **condition** of the **land**.

*The post-apocalypse effects brought by the comet/Venus caused women to be barren. This could be caused by a myriad of issues like the iron sulfide to drought and desertification. There are numerous examples of women in religious texts during this period being barren until late in their lives. Science does not know what the effects of an exchange between Earth and another heavenly body will result in. The life cycles of plants and animals may be severely affected.*

## Chapter 2

Indeed, poor men have become owners of wealth, and he who could not make sandals for himself is now a possessor of riches.

*Due to the upheaval in their caste system, the poor and former slaves now own the wealth of the dead and dispossessed.*

> **Exodus 3:21 And I will give this people favour in the sight of the Egyptians, and whenever ye shall escape, ye shall not depart empty.**
>
> **Exodus 3:22 But (every) woman shall ask of her neighbor and fellow lodger, articles of gold and silver, and apparel; and ye shall put them upon your sons and upon your daughters, and ye the Egyptians.**

Indeed, men's slaves, their hearts are sad, and magistrates do not fraternize with their people when they shout.
Indeed, [hearts] are violent, pestilence is throughout the land, blood is everywhere, death is not lacking, and the mummy-cloth speaks even before one comes near it.
Indeed, many dead are buried in the river; the stream is a sepulcher and the place of embalmment has become a stream.
Indeed, noblemen are in distress, while the poor man is full of joy. Every town says: "Let us suppress the powerful among us."

*Society has broken down, violence is in the hearts of man, bodies once buried float in the river, and the once lower class are taking revenge against the former ruling elite.*

Indeed, men are like ibises. Squalor is throughout the land, and there are none indeed whose clothes are white in these times.

Indeed, the land turns around as does a potter's wheel; the robber is a possessor of riches and [the rich man is become] a plunderer.
Indeed, trusty servants are [. . .]; the poor man [complains]: "How terrible! What am I to do?"

*All men wear clothes that are dirty, and the reversal in the caste system has left the rich to rob.*

Indeed, the river is blood, yet men drink of it. Men shrink from human beings and thirst after water.

*We see that the river has turned the color of blood according to Ipuwer, but, no theological significance is noted as the cause. The iron sulfide has destroyed life in the waters rendering it unfit for human or animal consumption. This event in all probability occurred during the period of the Exodus of the Children of Israel from Egypt.*

> **Exodus 7:17** These things saith the Lord: Hereby shalt thou know that I am the Lord: behold, I strike with the rod that is in my hand on the water which is in the river, and it shall change into blood.

> **Exodus 7:18** And the fish that are in the river shall die, and the river shall stink thereupon, and the Egyptians shall not be able to drink water from the river.

Indeed, gates, columns and walls are burnt up, while the hall of the palace stands firm and endures.

*The effects of the cometary Passover damaged the exterior portions of the palace, but the excellent construction kept the structure intact.*

> **Exodus 9:24** So there was hail and flaming fire mingled with hail; and the hail was very great, such as was not in Egypt, from the time there was a nation upon it.

> **Exodus 9:25** And the hail smote in all the land of Egypt both man and beast, and the hail smote all the grass in the field, and the hail broke in pieces all the trees in the field.

Indeed, the ship of [the southerners] has broken up; towns are destroyed and Upper Egypt has become an empty waste.

*Ipuwer shows that Lower Egypt suffered the same fate as Upper Egypt.*

## Chapter 3

/Indeed, the desert is throughout the land, the homes are laid waste, and barbarians from abroad have come to Egypt.
Indeed, men arrive [. . .] and indeed, there are no Egyptians anywhere.

*Nomads have traveled in a massive influx to supplant the Egyptian populace.*

## Chapter 4

Indeed, every dead person is as a well-born man. Those who were / Egyptians [have become] foreigners and are thrust aside.

*Egyptian royalty and ruling class are killed in the destruction, as new people begin to enforce a new rule.*

Indeed, hair [has fallen out] for everybody, and the man of rank can no longer be distinguished from him who is nobody.

*This loss of hair sounds like the effects of iron sulfide or leprosy?*

Indeed, [. . .] because of noise; noise is not [. . .] in years of noise, and there is no end [of] noise.

*The massive and continual quaking of the planet makes noises that keep the people in fear.*

Indeed, great and small {say}: "I wish I might die." Little children say: "He should not have caused {me} to live."
Indeed, the children of princes are dashed against walls, and the children of the neck are laid out on the high ground.

*The situation is one so dire that children wish never to have been born. The princes (First born) have been crushed by falling walls or thrown and killed against those walls in an earthquake in all probability.*

> **Exodus 11:5 And all the firstborn in the land of Egypt shall die, from the firstborn of Pharaoh that sitteth upon his throne, even unto the firstborn of the maidservant that is behind the mill; and all the firstborn of beasts.**

Indeed, the Delta in its entirety will not be hidden, and Lower Egypt puts trust in trodden roads. What can one do? No [. . .] exist anywhere, and men say: **"Perdition to the secret place!"** Behold, it is in the hands of those who do not know it like those who know it.

*The roads are not safe to travel. The secret place (pyramids?) has been overrun by those that know not how to interpret what they have found.*

The desert dwellers are skilled in the crafts of the Delta.

*The same lower class craftsmen that toiled in helping to make the marvelous buildings have now become leaders in the Egyptian society. Ipuwer laments the inability to stop the Asiatic influence.*

### Chapter 6

Indeed, everywhere barley has perished and men are stripped of clothes, spice, and oil; everyone says: "There is none." The storehouse is empty and its keeper is stretched on the ground; a happy state of affairs! . . ./
Would that I had raised my voice at that moment, that it might have saved me from the pain in which I am.

*There is no barley to be found in the lands, as Ipuwer wishes that he had perished to avoid the pain that he feels. Joseph had previously profited from the storage of grain and barley from a period of drought.*

> **Exodus 9:31 And the flax and the barley was smitten: for the barley was in the ear, and the flax was bolled.**

> **Exodus 9:32 But the wheat and the rice were not smitten: for they were not grown up.**

Indeed, the private council-chamber, its writings are taken away and the mysteries which were {in it} are laid bare.

*This could mean a prison or hall of records, where great mysteries were housed now have fallen into the hands of those less enlightened.*

Indeed, **magic spells** are **divulged**; smw- and shnw-spells are **frustrated** because they are **remembered** by **men**.

*The magic spells and documents that were taken from the private judgment-hall are being used by those that do not know their use.*

Indeed, **public offices** are **opened** and their **inventories** are **taken** away; the **serf** has become an **owner** of serfs.
Indeed, [scribes] are **killed** and their **writings** are **taken** away. **Woe** is me because of the misery of this time!
Indeed, the **writings** of the **scribes** of the **cadaster** are **destroyed**, and the **corn** of **Egypt** is **common property**.

*It's always curious to me when a serf or slave becomes the owner of serfs or slaves! You would think that through the bondage one suffered it would cause them to never make another suffer as they had in bondage.*

## Chapter 7

Behold, the fire has gone up on high, and its burning goes forth against the enemies of the land.

*This is yet another supporting report to the "pillar in the sky." The fire that has gone on up high is the comet/Venus as she takes a different orbit. This is the same object that appeared before the Israelites as their protecto,r and Ipuwer states that it goes against the enemies of Egypt!*

> **Exodus 19:18 The mount of Sina was altogether on a smoke, because God had descended upon it in fire; and the smoke went up as the smoke of a furnace, and the people were exceedingly amazed.**

Behold, he who was buried as a falcon {is devoid} of biers, and what the pyramid concealed has become empt

*The falcon of Horus.*

# *The Lament for Sumer and Urim – written @ 2000 BCE*

"The Lament for Sumer and Urim," is an ancient epic Sumerian poem that speaks to the blight upon the land that echoes the disasters of the Exodus and the Ipuwer Papyrus. I have only highlighted common words from these epics to show the same theme of disasters that runs through these sacred texts.

**31**  To **overturn** the appointed times,
to **obliterate** the divine plans,
the **storms** gather to **strike** like a **flood**.

**32**  to overturn the divine powers of **Sumer**,
to lock up the favorable reign in its home,
to **destroy** the **city**, to destroy the **house**,
to destroy the **cattle-pen**, to level the **sheepfold**;
that the cattle should not stand in the pen,
that the sheep should **not multiply** in the fold,
that **watercourses** should carry **brackish** water,
that weeds should grow in the fertile fields,
that mourning plants should grow in the open country,
that the mother should not seek out her child,
that the father should not say "O my dear wife!",
that the **junior wife** should take no joy in his embrace,
that the young child should not grow vigorous on his knee,
that the wet-nurse should not sing lullabies;

**33**  that on the two banks of the **Tigris** and of the **Euphrates**
bad weeds should grow,
that no one should set out on the **road**,
that no one should seek out the **highway**,
that the city and its settled surroundings
should be **razed** to ruin-mounds;
that its numerous **black-headed** people should be **slaughtered**;
that the hoe should not attack the fertile fields,
that seed should not be planted in the ground,
that the melody of the cowherds' songs
should not resound in the open country,
that butter and cheese should not be made in the cattle-pen,
that dung should not be stacked on the ground,
that the shepherd should not enclose
the **sacred sheepfold** with a fence,
that the song of the churning should not resound in the sheepfold;

**34**  to decimate the animals of the open country,
to finish off all living things,
that the four-legged creatures of Cakkan
should lay no more dung on the ground,
that the marshes should be so dry
as to be full of cracks and have no new seed,
that sickly-headed reeds should grow in the reed-beds,
that they should be covered by a **stinking morass,**
that there should be no new growth in the orchards,
that it should all collapse by itself—
so as quickly to subdue Urim like a roped ox,

to bow its neck to the ground: the great charging wild bull,
confident in its own strength,
the primeval city of lordship and kingship,
built on sacred ground.

**35**  The people, in their **fear, breathed** only with difficulty.
The **storm** immobilized them,
the storm did not let them return.
There was **no return** for them,

**36**  The extensive countryside was destroyed,
no one moved about there.
The **dark time** was **roasted** by **hailstones** and **flames**.
The **bright time** was **wiped out** by a **shadow**.
On that **bloody day,**
**mouths** were crushed, **heads** were **crashed**.
The **storm** was a harrow coming from **above**,
the city was **struck** by a hoe.

**37**  Large **trees** were **uprooted**, the forest growth was ripped out.
The orchards were stripped of their fruit,
they were cleaned of their offshoots.
The crop **drowned** while it was still on the **stalk**,
the yield of the **grain** diminished.

**38**  There were **corpses floating** in the Euphrates,
**brigands** roamed the roads.
The father turned away from his wife
without saying "O my wife!"
The mother turned away from her child
without saying "O my child!"
He who had a **productive** estate **neglected** his estate
without saying "O my estate!"
The **rich man** took an unfamiliar path away from his possessions.
In those days the kingship of the Land was **defiled**.
The **tiara** and **crown** that had been on the king's head
were both spoiled.
The lands that had followed the same path were split into disunity.

**39**  As the day grew dark, the eye of the sun was eclipsing,
the people experienced **hunger**.
There was no **beer** in the beer-hall,
there was no more **malt** for it.
There was no food for him in his palace,
it was **unsuitable** to live in.
**Grain** did not fill his lofty storehouse,
he could not save his life.
The grain-piles and granaries of **Nanna** held no grain.

**40**  Wine and syrup ceased to flow in the great dining hall.
The butcher's knife that used to slay oxen and sheep
lay hungry in the grass.
Its mighty oven no longer cooked oxen and sheep,
it no longer emitted the aroma of roasting meat.

**41**  The mortar, pestle and grinding stone lay idle;

no one bent down over them.

**42** The ***Shining Quay*** of Nanna was silted up.
the sound of water against the boat's prow ceased,
there was no rejoicing.

**43** The rushes grew, the rushes grew,
the mourning reeds grew.
Boats and barges ceased docking at the Shining Quay.
Nothing moved on your watercourse which was fit for barges.

**44** Its watercourse was empty, barges could not travel.

**45** There were no paths on either of its banks,
long grass grew there.

**46** The reed huts were overrun, their walls were breached.
The cows and their young were captured
and carried off to enemy territory.
The munzer-fed cows took an unfamiliar path
in an open country that they did not know.
*Gayau*, who loves cows, dropped his weapon in the dung.
*Cuni-dug*, who stores butter and cheese,
did not store butter and cheese.
***Those*** who are ***unfamiliar*** with butter were ***churning*** the ***butter***.
***Those*** who are ***unfamiliar*** with milk were ***curdling*** the ***milk***.
The sound of the churning vat did not resound in the cattle-pen.

**47** The ***trees*** of **Urim** were ***sick***, its reeds were sick.
**Laments** sounded all along its city wall.
Daily there was ***slaughter*** before it.
Large ***axes*** were sharpened in front of Urim.
The ***spears***, the arms of ***battle***, were prepared.
The large ***bows, javelin*** and ***shield*** gathered together to ***strike***.
The ***barbed arrows*** covered its outer side like a raining cloud.
***Large stones***, one after another, fell with ***great thuds***.

**48** ***Urim***, confident in its own strength,
stood ready for the ***murderers***.
Its people, oppressed by the enemy,
could not withstand their ***weapons***.

**49** In the city, those who had not been felled by weapons
succumbed to hunger.
***Hunger*** filled the city like water, it would not cease.
This hunger contorted people's faces, ***twisted*** their muscles.
Its people were as if drowning in a pond,
they gasped for breath.
Its king breathed heavily in his palace, all alone.
Its people ***dropped*** their ***weapons***,
their weapons hit the ground.
They ***struck*** their ***necks*** with their ***hands*** and cried.
They sought counsel with each other,
they searched for clarification:
"Alas, what can we say about it?
What more can we add to it?

How long until we are *finished* off by this *catastrophe*?
Inside Urim there is *death*, outside it there is death.
Inside it we are to be finished off by *famine*.
Outside it we are to be finished off by *Elamite* weapons.
In Urim the *enemy* oppresses us, oh, we are *finished*."

**50**   The *people* took *refuge* behind the city walls.
They were *united* in *fear*.
The *palace* that was *destroyed* by *onrushing water* was defiled,
its doorbolts were torn out.
Elam, like a swelling flood wave, left only the *ghosts*.
In Urim *people* were *smashed* as if they were clay pots.
Its *refugees* were *unable* to flee,
they were *trapped* inside the walls.
Like fish living in a pond, they tried to escape.

**51**   Its mighty cows with shining horns were captured,
their horns were cut off.
Its *unblemished oxen* and grass-fed *sheep* were slaughtered.
The palm-trees, strong as mighty copper, the heroic strength,
were *torn* out like rushes, were plucked like rushes,
their trunks were turned sideways.
Their tops lay in the dust, there was no one to *raise* them.
The midriffs of their palm fronds were cut off
and their tops were burnt off.
Their date *spadices* that used to fall on the well were torn out.

**52**   The great *tribute* that they had *collected* was hauled off to the *mountains*.

# JUBILEES DECODED – written @ 100 BCE

## JUBILEES 1

3 And He called to Mosheh on the seventh day out of the midst of the cloud, and the appearance of the splendor of YAHWEH was like a flaming fire on the top of the mount.

4 And Mosheh was on the Mount forty days and forty nights, and YAHWEH taught him the earlier and the later history of the division of all the days of the Torah and of the testimony.

*Moses spends forty days (40) and forty nights (40) on the mountain.*

7 And do you write for yourself all these words which I declare unto, you this day, for I know their rebellion and their stiff neck, before I bring them into the land of which I swore to their fathers, to Abraham and to Yitschaq and to Yacob, saying: ' Unto your seed will I give a land flowing with milk and honey.

11 And they will make to themselves high places and groves and graven images, and they will worship, each his own (graven image), so as to go astray, and they will sacrifice their children to demons, and to all the works of the error of their hearts.

*Milk and honey prophecy.*

20 Let your mercy, O YAHWEH, be lifted up upon Your people, and create in them an upright spirit, and let not the spirit of Belial rule over them to accuse them before You, and to ensnare them from all the paths of righteousness, so that they may perish from before Your face.

*Belial is a name for the devil, Mastema AKA Venus.*

29 And the **malak** of the presence who went before the camp of Yisrael took the tables of the divisions of the years -from the time of the creation- of the Torah and of the testimony of the weeks of the jubilees, according to the individual years, according to all the number of the jubilees [according, to the individual years], from the day of the [new] creation when the heavens and the earth shall be renewed and all their creation according to the powers of the heaven, and according to all the creation of the earth, until the sanctuary of YAHWEH shall be made in Yerusalem on Mount Zion, and all the luminaries be renewed for healing and for shalom and for blessing for all the elect of Yisrael, and that thus it may be from that day and unto all the days of the earth.

*In the King James version of the story, God leads the way in a Pillar of fire/smoke, but in the Hebrew version, it is an angel (malak) AKA comet/Venus. The camp of Israel took the Tables of the division of Years (calendar), as opposed to the Ten Commandments of the Christian version. There was a call for a renewal in healing for the luminaries (stars/planets/zodiac). This would suggest that the cosmos had suffered a trauma in a recent time period. In Arabic, Malak al-Maut is the Angel of Death in the Islamic faith, and is comparable to the Archangel Michael in the Judeo-Christian faiths.*

## JUBILEES 3

4 And YAHWEH said to us: 'It is not good that the man should be alone: let us make a helpmeet for him.

5 'And YAHWEH our Sovereign Ruler caused a deep sleep to fall upon him, and he slept, and He took for the woman one rib from amongst his ribs, and this rib was the origin of the woman from amongst his ribs, and He built up the flesh in its stead, and built the woman.

*Yahweh creates woman for Adam out of one of his ribs. The use of a rib for extracting DNA from the red blood cells in the bone marrow would make it a perfect choice.*

9 And after Adam had completed forty days in the land where he had been created, we brought him into the garden of Eden to till and keep it, but his wife they brought in on the eightieth day, and after this she entered into the garden of Eden.

*Adam begins a long continuation of the forty days and forty nights concept (Enki's sacred number is 40).*

15 And in the first week of the first jubilee, [1-7 A.M.] Adam and his wife were in the garden of Eden for seven years tilling and keeping it, and we gave him work and we instructed him to do everything that is suitable for tillage.

*Adam begins the seven years concept.*

34 And they had no son till the first jubilee, [8 A.M.] and after this he knew her.

*Adam finally gets the woman pregnant after forty-nine years (7 X 7 years).*

## JUBILEES 4

1 And in the third week in the second jubilee she gave birth to Cain, and in the fourth she gave birth to Abel, and in the fifth she gave birth to her daughter Awan.

*The naming of Abel is very curious. The name Abel (Herdsman or Breath of El) denotes that he is a follower of the Canaanite God El, or is he a followe of Bel? The naming of the second son born to Adam and Eve as a follower of El shows a clear and early synthesis of local deities.*

*Awan=Aswan?*

9 And Cain took Awan his sister to be his wife and she bare him Enoch at the close of the fourth jubilee. [190-196 A.M.] And in the first year of the first week of the fifth jubilee, [197 A.M.] houses were built on the earth, and Cain built a city, and called its name after the name of his son Enoch.

*Enoch the prophet is born.*

15 And in the second week of the tenth jubilee [449-55 A.M.] Mahalalel took unto him to wife DinaH, the daughter of Barakiel the daughter of his father's brother, and she bare him a son in the third week in the sixth year, [461 A.M.] and he called his name Jared, for in his days the malakim of YAHWEH descended on the earth, those who are named the Watchers, that they should instruct the children of men, and that they should do judgment and uprightness on the earth.

*The Watchers (meteorites) descend to teach mankind. They are called Warners in the Qur'an.*

17 And he was the first among men that are born on earth who learnt writing and knowledge and wisdom and who wrote down the signs of heaven according to the order of their months in a book, that men might know the seasons of the years according to the order of their separate months.

*The first lessons imparted to mankind was how to chart the heavens and to track the seasons. There is a curious lack of any theology in the initial instructions.*

20 And in the twelfth jubilee, [582-88] in the seventh week thereof, he took to himself a wife, and her name was Edna, the daughter of Danel, the daughter of his father's brother, and in the sixth year in this week [587 A.M.] she bare him a son and he called his name Methuselah.

21 And he was moreover with the malakim of YAHWEH these six jubilees of years, and they showed him everything which is on earth and in the heavens, the rule of the sun, and he wrote down everything.

*In the Hebrew version Methuselah learns about the heavens three-hundred years from the angels. In the Apocryphal Texts, Enoch, Methuselah's father learns the heavens from the angel Uriel, and walks with God three-hundred years. It is noted that Enoch lived sixty-five years and walked with God three-hundred years, and then was no more. Methuselah was the person that Enoch dictated his books to. There is only a one line mention of Methuselah in the Christian Bible, but he is the longest lived person in the Bible at nine-hundred and sixty-nine years. Establishing an understanding of the celestial placement and function was always of primary importance to this era.*

## JUBILEES 5

6 And against the angels whom He had sent upon the earth, He was exceedingly wroth, and He gave commandment to root them out of all their dominion, and He bade us to bind them in the depths of the earth, and behold they are bound in the midst of them, and are (kept) separate.

*Rooting out of their dominion would be the stars transgressing their appointed order. The binding is the grouping of those stars into the zodiac constellation characters.*

7 And against their sons went forth a command from before His face that they should be smitten with the sword, and be removed from under heaven.

8 And He said 'My spirit shall not always abide on man; for they also are flesh and their days shall be one hundred and twenty years'.

*The comet/Venus was portrayed as wielding a cosmic sword to judge mankind for its sins. The lifespan of humans were cut to one-hundred and twenty years by decree after the comet/Venus destroyed the delicate ecosystem of the Earth.*

24 And YAHWEH opened seven flood-gates of heaven,
And the mouths of the fountains of the great deep, seven mouths in number.

25 And the flood-gates began to pour down water from the heaven forty days and forty nights, And the fountains of the deep also sent up waters, until the whole world was full of water.

*The seven flood-gates (firmament concept) of heaven open and it rains forty days and forty nights.*

26 And the waters increased upon the earth: Fifteen cubits did the waters rise above all the high mountains, And the ark was lift up above the earth, And it moved upon the face of the waters.

*The waters crested 22' 1/2' feet higher than the surrounding mountains.*

## JUBILEES 6

1 And on the new month of the third month he went forth from the ark, and built an altar on that mountain.

2 And he made atonement for the earth, and took a kid and made atonement by its blood for all the guilt of the earth; for everything that had been on it had been destroyed, save those that were in the ark with Noah.

3 And he placed the fat thereof on the altar, and he took an ox, and a goat, and a sheep and kids, and salt, and a turtle-dove, and the young of a dove, and placed a burnt sacrifice on the altar, and poured thereon an offering mingled with oil, and sprinkled wine and strewed frankincense over everything, and caused a goodly savior to arise, acceptable before YAHWEH.

*These animals just made the arduous journey for the survival of their species, and then they're sacrificed right away?*

4 And YAHWEH smelt the goodly savior, and He made a covenant with him that there should not be any more a flood to destroy the earth; that all the days of the earth seed-time and harvest should never cease; cold and heat, and summer and winter, and day and night should not change their order, nor cease forever.

*This is the covenant that Yahweh makes with Noah to never destroy the Earth by flood again. He does not agree to never destroy it by fire, earthquake, or other means though!*

17 For this reason it is ordained and written on the heavenly tablets, that they should celebrate the "Feast of Weeks" in this month once a year, to renew the covenant every year.

18 And this whole festival was celebrated in heaven from the day of creation till the days of Noah -twenty six jubilees and five weeks of years [1309-1659 A.M.]: and Noah and his sons observed it for seven jubilees and one week of years (350 years), till the day of Noah's death, and from the day of Noah's death his sons did away with it until the days of Abraham, and they eat blood.

21 For it is the "Feast of Weeks" and the "Feast of First Fruits:" this feast is twofold and of a double nature: according to what is written and engraved concerning it, celebrate it.

23 And on the new month of the first month, and on the new month of the fourth month, and on the new month of the seventh month, and on the new month of the tenth month are the days of remembrance, and the days of the seasons in the four divisions of the year. These are written and ordained as a testimony forever.

*The Feast of Weeks and the Feast of First Fruits are harvest festivals that trace their origins back to Sumeria.*

*Sumeria/Sumer = Summer*

29 And they placed them on the heavenly tablets, each had thirteen weeks; from one to another (passed) their memorial, from the first to the second, and from the second to the third, and from the third to the fourth.

30 And all the days of the commandment will be fifty two weeks of days, and (these will make) the entire year complete. Thus it is engraved and ordained on the heavenly tablets.

*A calendar year of 4 seasons of 13 weeks (52) for a calendar year of 364 days. There is a notable day missing from the Hebrew and Enoch Fixed Calendars to that of the present day calendar of 365 days which seems to suggest a lengthening of the year, due a slowing of the Earth's rotation and axial shifting. A Jubilee Year is every 52 years in the Mayan Calendar.*

33 But if they do neglect and do not observe them according to His commandment, then they will disturb all their seasons and the years will be dislodged from this (order), [and they will disturb the seasons and the years will be dislodged] and they will neglect their ordinances.

34 And all the children of Yisrael will forget and will not find the path of the years, and will forget the new months, and seasons, and Shabbats and they will go wrong as to all the order of the years.

35 For I know and from henceforth will I declare it unto you, and it is not of my own devising; for the book is written before me, and on the heavenly tablets the division of days is ordained, lest they forget the feasts of the covenant and walk according to the feasts of the Gentiles after their error and after their ignorance.

36 For there will be those who will assuredly make observations of the moon -how it disturbs the seasons and comes in from year to year ten days too soon.

37 For this reason the years will come upon them when they will disturb (the order), and make an abominable (day) the day of testimony, and an unclean day a feast day, and they will confound all the days, the kodesh with the unclean, and the unclean day with the kodesh; for they will go wrong as to the months and Shabbats and feasts and jubilees.

38 For this reason I command and testify to you that you may testify to them; for after your death your children will disturb them, so that they will not make the year three hundred and sixty-four days only, and for this reason they will go wrong as to the new months and seasons and Shabbats and festivals, and they will eat all kinds of blood with all kinds of flesh.

*Order, seasons, years, paths, months, covenants, feasts, heavenly tablets, and the moon!*

## JUBILEES 7

19 The sons of Japheth: Gomer and Magog and Madai and Javan, Tubal and Meshech and Tiras: these are the sons of Noah.

*Magog only bears mention in the Book of Revelations.*

## JUBILEES 8

3 And he found a writing which former (generations) had carved on the rock, and he read what was thereon, and he transcribed it and sinned owing to it; for it contained the teaching of the Watchers in accordance with which they used to observe the omens of the sun and moon and stars in all the signs of heaven.

*Did Kainam find a star map or zodiac charts?*

19 And he knew that the Garden of Eden is the kodesh of kodeshim, and the dwelling of YAHWEH, and Mount Sinai the centre of the desert, and Mount Zion -the centre of the navel of the earth: these three were created as kodesh places facing each other.

20 And he blessed the ALMIGHTY of gods, who had put the Word of YAHWEH into his mouth, and YAHWEH forevermore.

21 And he knew that a blessed portion and a blessing had come to Shem and his sons unto the generations forever -the whole land of Eden and the whole land of the Red Sea, and the whole land of the east and India, and on the Red Sea and the mountains thereof, and all the land of Bashan, and all the land of Lebanon and the islands of Kaftur, and all the mountains of Sanir and 'Amana, and the mountains of Asshur in the north, and all the land of Elam, Asshur, and Babel, and Susan and Ma'edai, and all the mountains of Ararat, and all the region beyond the sea, which is beyond the mountains of Asshur towards the north, a blessed and spacious land, and all that is in it is very good.

22 And for Ham came forth the second portion, beyond the Gihon towards the south to the right of the Garden, and it extends towards the south and it extends to all the mountains of fire, and it extends towards the west to the sea of 'Atel and it extends towards the west till it reaches the sea of Ma'uk -that (sea) into which everything which is not destroyed descends.

*Ma'uk = Marduk?*

25 And for Japheth came forth the third portion beyond the river Tina to the north of the outflow of its waters, and it extends north-easterly to the whole region of Gog, and to all the country east thereof.

*The region of Gog bears large mention in the book of Revelations.*

**JUBILEES 10**

7 And YAHWEH our Sovereign Ruler bade us to bind all.

*The binding would be the formation of zodiac groupings.*

8 And the chief of the spirits, **Mastema**, came and said: 'YAHWEH, Creator, let some of them remain before me, and let them listen to my voice, and do all that I shall say unto them; for if some of them are not left to me, I shall not be able to execute the power of my will on the sons of men; for these are for corruption and leading astray before my judgment, for great is the wickedness of the sons of men.'

*Mastema is yet another name for Satan, Belial, Baalzebub, Venus, etc., and is allowed to tempt mankind yet again.*

12 And we explained to Noah all the medicines of their diseases, together with their seductions, how he might heal them with herbs of the earth.

13 And Noah wrote down all things in a book as we instructed him concerning every kind of medicine. Thus the evil spirits were precluded from (hurting) the sons of Noah.

*Noah was trained as a physician and healer, as the evil spirits (planets/stars/comets/meteors) were toxins and diseases introduced to the Earth by the comet/Venus.*

18 And in the three and thirtieth jubilee, in the first year in the second week, Peleg took to himself a wife, whose name was Lomna the daughter of Sina'ar, and she bare him a son in the fourth year of this week, and he called his name Reu; for he said: 'Behold the **children of men** have become evil through the wicked purpose of building for themselves a city and a tower in the land of **Shinar**.'

19 For they departed from the land of **Ararat** eastward to Shinar; for in his days **they built** the **city** and the **tower**, saying, **'Go to, let us ascend thereby into heaven.'**

20 And **they** began to build, and in the fourth week **they** made **brick with fire**, and the bricks served **them** for stone, and the clay with which **they** cemented them together was **asphalt** which comes out of the **sea**, and out of the **fountains** of **water** in the land of **Shinar**.

*The tower later called Bavel (Babel), because there God confused their languages, was under construction to reach God in the heavens. The land of Shinar had received large deposits of asphalt (oil) which added natural resources to the building effort.*

21 And they built it: forty and three years [1645-1688 A.M.] were they building it; its breadth was 203 bricks, and the height (of a brick) was the third of one; its height amounted to 5433 cubits and 2 palms, and (the extent of one wall was) thirteen stades (and of the other thirty stades).

Building time: 43 years
Brick = 8" x 4"    Stade = 600'    Cubit = 18"
Breadth/Width: 203 bricks = 202.5'          Height: 5433 cubits = 8149.5' or 1.54 miles
One Wall: 13 stades (7,800 feet) or 1.4 miles     Second wall: 30 stades = 18,600' or 3.4 miles

*This tower would surely pass into the upper atmosphere. The size is almost unfathomable to imagine in scale, yet we have no remains or satellite imaging of the remains of any tower of that possible length in the region. The Great Wall of China can be seen from space as well as other enormous remaining ancient structures. The builders would run out of oxygen before they were able to build the tower too high. The tower took 43 years to build, and would have been ready to be struck down on the next Jubilee Passover year (49yrs.).*

22 And YAHWEH our Sovereign Ruler said to us: Behold, they are one people, and (this) they begin to do, and now nothing will be withheld from them. Go to, let us go down and confound their language, that they may not understand one another's speech, and they may be dispersed into cities and nations, and one purpose will no longer abide with them till the Day of Judgment.'

*This is a curious act by God? This act has been the subject of much debate, but may become clearer through the book.*

23 And YAHWEH descended, and we descended with him to see the city and the tower which the children of men had built.

24 And he confounded their language, and they no longer understood one another's speech, and they ceased then to build the city and the tower.

25 For this reason the whole land of Shinar is called Babel, because YAHWEH did there confound all the language of the children of men, and from thence they were dispersed into their cities, each according to his language and his nation.

26 And YAHWEH sent a mighty wind against the tower and overthrew it upon the earth, and behold it was between Asshur and Babylon in the land of Shinar, and they called its name 'Overthrow'.

*Yahweh descends to destroy the tower that was dedicated to Him, as He Overthrows it by a mighty wind in this tradition. The "Evil Wind," is spoken of in Sumerian tradition, and the Hurricane (Hurakan) Wind in Mesoamerican tradition.*

33 But he did not listen to them, and dwelt in the land of Lebanon from Hamath to the entering of Egypt, he and his sons until this day.

34 And for this reason that land is named Canaan.

35 And Japheth and his sons went towards the sea and dwelt in the land of their portion, and Madai saw the land of the sea and it did not please him, and he begged a (portion) from Ham and Asshur and Arpachshad, his wife's brother, and he dwelt in the land of Media, near to his wife's brother until this day.

36 And he called his dwelling-place, and the dwelling-place of his sons, Media, after the name of their father Madai.

*This is one of the roots of our modern day issues.*

## JUBILEES 11

7 And he grew up, and dwelt in Ur of the Chaldees, near to the father of his wife's mother, and he worshipped idols, and he took to himself a wife in the thirty-sixth jubilee, in the fifth week, in the first year thereof, [1744 A.M.] and her name was Melka, the daughter of Kaber, the daughter of his father's brother.

8 And she bare him Nahor, in the first year of this week, and he grew and dwelt in Ur of the Chaldees, and his father taught him the researches of the Chaldees to divine and augur, according to the signs of heaven.

**The Chaldees or Chaldeans have long been known to be a society of astronomers, astrologers, and magis that hailed from southern Mesopotamia (Iraq) and ruled Babylon for a period.**

11 And the prince Mastema sent ravens and birds to devour the seed which was sown in the land, in order to destroy the land, and rob the children of men of their labours. Before they could plough in the seed, the ravens picked it from the surface of the ground.

**Mastema AKA Satan, Lucifer, Ishtar, Venus, etc. God gives the devil yet another chance to bother mankind. The comet/Venus destroyed the crops and vegetation with her continual Passovers.**

16 And the child began to understand the errors of the earth that all went astray after graven images and after uncleanness, and his father taught him writing, and he was two weeks of years old, and he separated himself from his father, that he might not worship idols with him.

17 And he began to pray to the Creator of all things that He might save him from the errors of the children of men, and that his portion should not fall into error after uncleanness and vileness.

**At fourteen, Abraham leaves home because of his father's religious practices.**

20 And he caused the clouds of ravens to turn back that day seventy times, and of all the ravens throughout all the land where Abram was there settled there not so much as one.

**Seventy (70) is a known repeated zodiac number, and the number of children (constellations) of the Canaanite God El.**

## JUBILEES 12

16 And in the sixth week, in the fifth year thereof, [1951 A.M.] Abram sat up throughout the night on the new month of the seventh month to observe the stars from the evening to the morning, in order to see what would be the character of the year with regard to the rains, and he was alone as he sat and observed.

17 And a word came into his heart and he said: All the signs of the stars, and the signs of the moon and of the sun are all in the hand of YAHWEH. Why do I search them out?

**Abram spends the whole day and night of the new moon tracking its path. Abram was very cognizant of the signs in the stars.**

26 And I opened his mouth, and his ears and his lips, and I began to speak with him in Hebrew in the tongue of the creation.

27 And he took the books of his fathers, and these were written in Hebrew, and he transcribed them, and he began from henceforth to study them, and I made known to him that which he could not (understand), and he studied them during the six rainy months.

**Abram takes credit for Hebrew being the tongue of creation, as he studies the books of his fathers. The rain that he sought to understand from signs in the skies for six months finally came.**

## JUBILEES 13

13 And it came to pass when Pharaoh seized Sarai, the wife of Abram that YAHWEH plagued Pharaoh and his house with great plagues because of Sarai, Abram's wife.

**This also unnamed Pharaoh gets plagued as well as well for kidnapping Sarah.**

22 And in this year came Chedorlaomer, king of Elam, and Amraphel, king of Shinar, and Arioch king of Sellasar, and Tergal, king of nations, and slew the king of Gomorrah, and the king of Sodom fled, and many fell through wounds in the vale of Siddim, by the Salt Sea.

**The Vale of Siddim (DMP - Disaster Miracle Path) is an area near the southern end of the Dead Sea that has been found to contain recent bitumen deposits along with tar pits. It has been theorized to be the result of the Jordan-Gihon rift area sinking due to tectonic shifting. The army was destroyed by a meteor shower along with active faults in the area. It has been theorized that fire and brimstone (Venus – atmosphere comprised mainly of sulfur) caused Siddim to become the Dead Sea.**

## JUBILEES 15

13 He that is born in your house shall surely be circumcised, and those whom you have bought with money shall be circumcised, and My covenant shall be in your flesh for an eternal ordinance.

**Slave laws are always the first enacted. The process of Circumcision began in the Egyptian culture.**

## JUBILEES 16

30 And to this there is no limit of days; for it is ordained forever regarding Yisrael that they should celebrate it and dwell in booths, and set wreaths upon their heads, and take leafy boughs, and willows from the brook.

**The wreaths upon the heads and leafy boughs of willow are harvest festival apparel.**

31 And Abraham took branches of palm trees, and the fruit of goodly trees, and every day going round the altar with the branches seven times [a day] in the morning, he praised and gave thanks to YAHWEH his Sovereign Ruler for all things in joy.

**The familiar occurrence of seven times in Biblical texts.**

## JUBILEES 17

16 And the prince Mastema came and said before YAHWEH, 'Behold, Abraham loves Yitschaq his son, and he delights in him above all things else; bid him offer him as a burnt-offering on the altar, and You will see if he will do

**Mastema (comet/Venus) pushes Abraham to the point of murdering his son. The fearful people often sacrificed their children to Gods like Moloch.**

## JUBILEES 18

7 And he said, ' YAHWEH will provide for himself a sheep for a burnt-offering, my son.' And he drew near to the place of the mount of YAHWEH.

**Yitshaq senses that something is amiss, as he asks his father where the sacrificial sheep is? Abraham replies that Yahweh will provide the sheep, knowing that Yitshaq was the sacrificial sheep.**

12 And the prince Mastema was put to shame; and Abraham lifted up his eyes and looked, and, behold a ram caught by his horns, and Abraham went and took the ram and offered it for a burnt-offering in the stead of his son.

**Comet/Venus (Mastema) loses this time! We have yet another reference to the Age of Aries.**

## JUBILEES 19

25 And these shall serve To lay the foundations of the heaven, And to strengthen the earth, And to renew all the luminaries which are in the firmament.

*Foundations, heaven, luminaries, and firmaments (snow globe) are all astronomy and astrology terms.*

## JUBILEES 21

7 And if you do slay a victim as an acceptable shalom offering, slay you it, pour out its blood upon the altar, and all the fat of the offering offer on the altar with fine flour and the meat offering mingled with oil, with its drink offering -offer them all together on the altar of burnt offering; it is a sweet savor before YAHWEH.

8 And you will offer the fat of the sacrifice of thank offerings on the fire which is upon the altar, and the fat which is on the belly, and all the fat on the inwards and the two kidneys, and all the fat that is upon them, and upon the loins and liver you shall remove, together with the kidneys.

9 And offer all these for a sweet savor acceptable before YAHWEH, with its meat-offering and with its drink-offering, for a sweet savor, the bread of the offering unto YAHWEH.

10 And eat its meat on that day and on the second day, and let not the sun on the second day go down upon it till it is eaten, and let nothing be left over for the third day; for it is not acceptable [for it is not approved] and let it no longer be eaten, and all who eat thereof will bring sin upon themselves; for thus I have found it written in the books of my forefathers, and in the words of Enoch, and in the words of Noah.

*Slay, victims, offering, pour, blood, fat, flour, meat, oil, drink, savor, fire, belly, kidneys, loins, liver, and bread! After blood, everything sounds yummy, until one remembers that it's not a chef's recipe, but a ritual sacrifice! There are a lot of rules in the sacrificial tradition that began in the time of Enoch/Enkime, that coincides with the entrance of the comet/Venus. Men begin to call upon God/Gods (time of Jared) because of the danger that appeared in the heavens and began to rain down upon the Earth.*

## JUBILEES 22

8 The sword of the adversary has not overcome me in all that You have given me and my children all the days of my life until this day.

*The fiery Pillar in the Sky (Sword of the Adversary) did not destroy Abraham and his people during his lifetime.*

## JUBILEES 23

7 And his sons Yitschaq and Ishmael buried him in the double cave, near Sarah his wife, and they wept for him forty days, all the men of his house, and Yitschaq and Ishmael, and all their sons, and all the sons of Keturah in their places; and the days of weeping for Abraham were ended.

*The forty days and forty nights practice.*

## JUBILEES 27

10 'Do not take you a wife of any of the daughters of **Canaan**; arise and go to **Mesopotamia** to the house of Bethuel, your mother's father, and take you a wife from thence of the daughters of Laban, your mother's brother.

*He goes to the Fertile Crescent, land of Babylon, the Chaldees, and Ur!*

21 And he dreamt that night, and behold a ladder set up on the earth, and the top of it reached to heaven, and behold, the malakim of YAHWEH ascended and descended on it: and behold, YAHWEH stood upon it.

*The puzzling imagery is easily discerned once we understand the language of scriptural authors. Yacob's vision is of the fiery Pillar in the Sky, whose privy member reached toward the Earth. It must have appeared in the sky that a ladder (tower, obelisk, minaret, steeple, etc.) could reach it. The malakim (angels) that went up and down are the flames that circulated about.*

25 And Yacob awoke from his sleep, and said, 'Truly this place is the house of YAHWEH, and I knew it not.' And he was afraid and said: 'Dreadful is this place which is none other than the house of YAHWEH, and this is the gate of heaven.'

*We have the comet/Venus being associated with the house of Yahweh and the Gate of Heaven!*

26 And Yacob arose early in the morning, and took the stone which he had put under his head and set it up as a pillar for a sign, and he poured oil upon the top of it. And he called the name of that place Bethel; but the name of the place was Luz at the first.
*The act of Yacob setting up a pillar (privy member, penis, Baal's shaft) speaks of the object that he saw. Naming the spot as Bethel (House of God-El) gives another link to the Canaanite God El.*

## JUBILEES 29

9 But before they used to call the land of Gilead the land of the Rephaim; for it was the land of the Rephaim, and the Rephaim were born (there), giants whose height was ten, nine, eight down to seven cubits.

*1 cubit-12" to 18" – the giants ranged from seven feet tall to fifteen feet tall.*

## JUBILEES 40

7 And he clothed him with **byssus garments (mollusks)**, and he put a **gold chain** upon his neck, and (a herald) proclaimed before him ' **'El 'El wa 'Abirer (Mighty One of God aka Magician),'** and placed a ring on his hand and made him **ruler** over all his **house (cosmic heavens)**, and **magnified (sun/star/etc.)** him, and said to him. 'Only on the **throne (orbit)** shall I be **greater** than you.'

10 And the king called **Yoseph's** name **Sephantiphans**, and gave Yoseph to wife the daughter of **Potiphar**, the daughter of the **priest of Heliopolis (Egypt!)**, the chief cook.

## JUBILEES 48

5 And **YAHWEH** executed a great **vengeance** on them for **Yisrael's** sake, and **smote** them through (the plagues of) **blood** and **frogs, lice** and **dog-flies**, and malignant **boils** breaking forth in **blains**; and their **cattle** by death; and by **hail-stones**, thereby He destroyed everything that **grew** for them; and by **locusts** which devoured the **residue** which had been left by the **hail**, and by **darkness**; and (by the death) of the **first-born** of **men** and **animals**, and on all their **idols** YAHWEH took vengeance and **burned** them with **fire**.

*The plagues of Egypt! What edible residue does hail stones (METEORS or MANNA) leave for locusts to eat?*

15 And on the fourteenth day and on the fifteenth and on the sixteenth and on the seventeenth and on the eighteenth the prince Mastema was bound and imprisoned behind the children of Yisrael that he might not accuse them.

*Comet/Venus (prince Mastema) is finally bound (star binding) so that she (he) no longer persecutes (accuses) the Children of Yisrael (Mankind).*

18 And on the fourteenth we bound him that he might not accuse the children of Yisrael on the day when they asked the Egyptians for vessels and garments, vessels of silver, and vessels of gold, and vessels of bronze, in order to despoil the Egyptians in return for the bondage in which they had forced them to serve.

19 And we did not lead forth the children of Yisrael from Egypt empty handed.

*They borrowed/asked gold, silver, and raiment from the Egyptians.*

## JUBILEES 49

2 For on this night -the beginning of the festival and the beginning of the joy- you were eating the Passover in Egypt, when all the powers of Mastema had been let loose to slay all the first-born in the land of Egypt, from the first-born of Pharaoh to the first-born of the captive maid-servant in the mill, and to the cattle.

**The Angel of Death in the Passover narrative is typically portrayed as an agent of Yahweh. Mastema (comet/Venus) is directly attributed as the angel of death on this night.**

## JUBILEES 50

13 The man who does any of these things on the Shabbat shall die, so that the children of Yisrael shall observe the Shabbats according to the commandments regarding the Shabbats of the land, as it is written in the tablets, which He gave into my hands that I should write out for you the laws of the seasons, and the seasons according to the division of their days.

**Laws to live by, and a calendar to chart the days and seasons.**


***NOTE: This is the Toltecs of Mesoamerica Jubilee tradition***

*Prophecy of the Return of Quetzalcoatl **(Venus)** in the 13th Toltec Era – Thirteenth 52 year cycle*

| | |
|---|---|
| 0 Toltec Era | 1168 ACE |
| 1st Toltec Era | 1220 ACE |
| 2nd Toltec Era | 1272 ACE |
| 3rd Toltec Era | 1324 ACE |
| 4th Toltec Era | 1376 ACE |
| 5th Toltec Era | 1428 ACE |
| 6th Toltec Era | 1480 ACE |
| 7th Toltec Era | 1532 ACE |
| 8th Toltec Era | 1584 ACE |
| 9th Toltec Era | 1636 ACE |
| 10th Toltec Era | 1688 ACE |
| 11th Toltec Era | 1740 ACE |
| 12th Toltec Era | 1792 ACE |
| 13th Toltec Era | 1844 to 1896 |

**1948 And then 2000? 2052? Etc.**

# *Job Decoded - written @ 400 – 600 BCE*

**CHAPTER 1**

1 There was a man in the land of *Uz*, whose name was Job; and that man was perfect and upright, and one that feared God, and eschewed evil.

*The Apocalypse of Abraham has Job as a chief officer to Pharaoh in Egypt trying to kill the newborn infant Abram!*

13 And there was a day when his sons and his daughters were eating and drinking wine in their eldest brother's house:

14 And there came a messenger unto Job, and said, The oxen were plowing, and the asses feeding beside them:

15 And the Sabeans fell upon them, and took them away; yea, they have slain the servants with the edge of the sword; and I only am escaped alone to tell thee.

*Tragedy #1 – Sabeans (Yemen) kill all servants working in the fields – 1 survivor*

16 While he was yet speaking, there came also another, and said, The fire of God is fallen from heaven, and hath burned up the sheep, and the servants, and consumed them; and I only am escaped alone to tell thee.

*Tragedy #2 – Naptha falls from the sky killing the sheep and servants – 1 survivor*

17 While he was yet speaking, there came also another, and said, The Chaldeans made out three bands, and fell upon the camels, and have carried them away, yea, and slain the servants with the edge of the sword; and I only am escaped alone to tell thee.

*Tragedy #3 – Three bands of Chaldeans (Iraq) kill his servants and steal the camels – 1 survivor*

18 While he was yet speaking, there came also another, and said, Thy sons and thy daughters were eating and drinking wine in their eldest brother's house:

19 And, behold, there came a great wind from the wilderness, and smote the four corners of the house, and it fell upon the young men, and they are dead; and I only am escaped alone to tell thee.

*Tragedy #4 – All of Jobs children were killed by a great wind that destroyed the home of his son – 1 survivor*

20 Then Job arose, and rent his mantle, and shaved his head, and fell down upon the ground, and worshipped,

*Job rent his mantle. I believe that Job shaved his head due to the onset of leprosy! This will become clearer as one reads the later text. Persons afflicted with leprosy often have bad scalp ailments. Leprosy seems to have become a major problem in the world after the Great Flood. It was customary in sacred texts to rent ones mantle and to place ashes on ones head in mourning (Enki, Marduk), but I believe that Job's actions served a dual purpose.*

21 And said, Naked came I out of my mother's womb, and naked shall I return thither: the LORD gave, and the LORD hath taken away; blessed be the name of the LORD.

*The Book of Job is one of my favorite texts of any religious or philosophical nature, as the author was highly intellectual with excellent philosophical discussions during the story. The to and fro, up and down, that Satan (comet/Venus) refers to is the dusting of the planet that this heavenly body did on a regular basis.*

**CHAPTER 2**

3 And the LORD said unto Satan, Hast thou considered my servant Job, that there is none like him in the earth, a perfect and an upright man, one that feareth God, and escheweth evil? and still he holdeth fast his integrity,

although thou movedst me against him, to destroy him without cause.

*This testing of Job that God allows Satan to attempt has elicited various viewpoints. I think this has to be more allegorical to the suffering that Job will encounter, and how he stood up to the trials that he had to endure. I take from Job the context that we must all endure some hardship in this life, and the test of our soul is how we endure these trials.*

7 So went Satan forth from the presence of the LORD, and smote Job with sore boils from the sole of his foot unto his crown.

8 And he took him a potsherd to scrape himself withal; and he sat down among the ashes.

*The text tells us that Venus (Satan) smote Job with boils. The cometary dust/debris that Venus continually deposited on the Earth helped diseases like leprosy proliferate. Boils on the soles of the feet are common in sufferers of leprosy with itching scaling skin, so that he had to scrape himself with a sharp object and roll in ash for some measure of relief.*

9 Then said his wife unto him, Dost thou still retain thine integrity? curse God, and die.

10 But he said unto her, Thou speakest as one of the foolish women speaketh. What? shall we receive good at the hand of God, and shall we not receive evil? In all this did not Job sin with his lips.

11 Now when Job's three friends heard of all this evil that was come upon him, they came every one from his own place; Eliphaz the Temanite, and Bildad the Shuhite, and Zophar the Naamathite: for they had made an appointment together to come to mourn with him and to comfort him.

*Let the philosophy flow!*

## CHAPTER 3

3 Let the day perish wherein I was born, and the night in which it was said, There is a man child conceived.

4 Let that day be darkness; let not God regard it from above, neither let the light shine upon it.

5 Let darkness and the shadow of death stain it; let a cloud dwell upon it; let the blackness of the day terrify it.

6 As for that night, let darkness seize upon it; let it not be joined unto the days of the year, let it not come into the number of the months.

*This is a dark metaphor to the birth of the comet/Venus, as there were extended periods of darkness and seasons were off schedule.*

## CHAPTER 7

5 My flesh is clothed with worms and clods of dust; my skin is broken, and become loathsome.

*The leprosy has continued to advance as Jobs' body deteriorates.*

6 My days are swifter than a weaver's shuttle, and are spent without hope.

7 O remember that my life is wind: mine eye shall no more see good.

*Job laments his condition.*

## CHAPTER 8

8 For inquire, I pray thee, of the former age, and prepare thyself to the search of their fathers:

9 (For we are but of yesterday, and know nothing, because our days upon earth are a shadow:)

**Bildad speaks about not knowing who they were yesterday, as knowledge of the prior times was lost with each successive catastrophe.**

## CHAPTER 9

5 Which removeth the mountains, and they know not: which overturneth them in his anger.

6 Which shaketh the earth out of her place, and the pillars thereof tremble.

7 Which commandeth the sun, and it riseth not; and sealeth up the stars.

8 Which alone spreadeth out the heavens, and treadeth upon the waves of the sea.

**Verses 9:5 to 9:8 speak to the mountains falling, mega earthquakes, and extended darkness. These are all classic signs of the effects from the passage of a heavenly body in close proximity to the Earth.**

9 Which maketh Arcturus, Orion, and Pleiades, and the chambers of the south.

**The references to the chambers of the south and the constellation of Arcturus, Orion, and the Pleiades, shows Jobs strong knowledge of astronomy. Arcturus is the brightest star in the constellation Bootes (The Good Shepherd). The constellation of Orion is portrayed as the Mighty Hunter, and the Pleiades constellation holds the Seven Sisters.**

## CHAPTER 12

6 The tabernacles of robbers prosper, and they that provoke God are secure; into whose hand God bringeth abundantly.

**Job speaks about the church at that time being a tabernacle of robbers! The church prospers even though they are not following their own dictates.**

## CHAPTER 13

27 Thou puttest my feet also in the stocks, and lookest narrowly unto all my paths; thou settest a print upon the heels of my feet.

28 And he, as a rotten thing, consumeth, as a garment that is moth eaten.

**Job laments as his leprosy continues to advance.**

## CHAPTER 15

8 Hast thou heard the secret of God? and dost thou restrain wisdom to thyself?

**Eliphaz the Temanite (Edom) asks this of Job, as Job shows that he was of the priest class or magi, with his extensive knowledge of astronomy.**

15 Behold, he putteth no trust in his **saints**; yea, the **heavens** are **not clean** in his sight.

**This is a clear astrotheology statement. The saints are the heavenly bodies, and the uncleanliness is the chaos that was reigning in the skies.**

21 A dreadful sound is in his ears: in prosperity the destroyer shall come upon him.

**The dreadful sound is the comet as it approaches, and Venus has long been known as The Destroyer (Typhon, Phaeton, Nibiru, Blue Star, etc)!**

22 He believeth not that he shall return out of darkness, and he is waited for of the sword.

23 He wandereth abroad for bread, saying, Where is it? He knoweth that the day of darkness is ready at his hand.

*The comet/Venus was portrayed as carrying a sword (plasma sword). The bread is a reference to the manna that it once deposited, and extended darkness was to come with its appearance.*

## CHAPTER 16

2 I have heard many such things: miserable comforters are ye all.

*Job lets his three visitors know of his displeasure with their thoughts.*

15 I have sewed sackcloth upon my skin, and defiled my horn in the dust.

16 My face is foul with weeping, and on my eyelids is the shadow of death;

*Verses 16:15 and 16:16 The sackcloth was made of coarse animal hair. Sackcloth was sometimes worn in penitence, but I believe that Job wore it to help scratch his scaling skin. Job was so distraught that he scraped his penis (horn) in the dust in a vain attempt at relief.*

## CHAPTER 19

13 He hath put my **brethren** far **from** me, and mine **acquaintance** are verily **estranged** from me.

14 My **kinsfolk** have **failed**, and my familiar **friends** have **forgotten** me.

15 They that **dwell** in **mine house**, and my **maids**, count me for a **stranger**: I am an **alien** in their **sight**.

16 I **called** my **servant**, and he gave me **no answe**r; I **intreated** him with my mouth.

17 My **breath** is **strange** to **my wife**, though I **intreated** for the **children's** sake of **mine** own **body**.

*Verses 19:13 to 19:17 clearly shows that although it has always been related that Jobs' wife stood firmly by his side through his travails, but his breath is strange to her, meaning that she had not been around in quite some time.*

18 Yea, young children despised me; I arose, and they spake against me.

19 All my inward friends abhorred me: and they whom I loved are turned against me.

*Job laments his situation as he shows how friends and family have distanced themselves from him, and how his own servants treat him as a stranger, and that his own wife has not been around to see him. No one wants to be near Job for fear of catching his leprosy, except for the three wise (Wise Men/Magi?) visitors.*

20 My bone cleaveth to my skin and to my flesh, and I am escaped with the **skin of my teeth.**

21 Have pity upon me, have pity upon me, O ye my friends; for the hand of God hath touched me.

*Verses 19:20 and 19:21 shows how Job begs God to relent and have pity upon him, as his disease is almost to the point of killing him.*

26 And though after my skin worms destroy this body, yet in my flesh shall I see God:

*The skin worms clearly show the effects of leprosy.*

## CHAPTER 20

17 He shall not see the rivers, the floods, the brooks of honey and butter.

*We have the reference to lands of honey and butter AKA milk and honey.*

## CHAPTER 22

12 Is not God in the **height** of **heaven**? and behold the **height** of the **stars**, how high they are!

13 And thou sayest, How doth God know? can he **judge** through the **dark cloud**?

14 Thick clouds are a covering to him, that he seeth not; and he walketh in the circuit of heaven.

*The God in the clouds cannot see through the dark cloud that encompassed it to judge man, as he resided in the heavens and traversed its circuit. This is pure astrotheology as this is the belief system for Eliphaz.*

## CHAPTER 26

1 BUT Job answered and said,

2 How hast thou helped him that is without power? How savest thou the arm that hath no strength?

3 How hast thou counselled him that hath no wisdom? And how hast thou plentifully declared the thing as it is?

4 To whom hast thou uttered words? and whose spirit came from thee?

5 Dead things are formed from under the waters, and the inhabitants thereof.

6 Hell is naked before him, and destruction hath no covering.

7 He stretcheth out the north over the empty place, and hangeth the earth upon nothing.

8 He bindeth up the waters in his thick clouds; and the cloud is not rent under them.

9 He holdeth back the face of his throne, and spreadeth his cloud upon it.

10 He hath compassed the waters with bounds, until the day and night come to an end.

11 The pillars of heaven tremble and are astonished at his reproof.

12 He divideth the sea with his power, and by his understanding he smiteth through the proud.

13 By his spirit he hath garnished the heavens; his hand hath formed the crooked serpent.

14 Lo, these are parts of his ways: but how little a portion is heard of him? but the thunder of his power who can understand?

*I thoroughly enjoy this portion as Job speaks about how God hung the firmaments with no firm foundation (dark matter). Job speaks of the crooked serpent, which so many cultures around the globe have depicted in the skies.*

## CHAPTER 28

1 SURELY there is a vein for the silver, and a place for gold where they fine it.

2 Iron is taken out of the earth, and brass is molten out of the stone.

*Job lives in the Copper Age, as iron is now being mined by mankind.*

3 He setteth an end to darkness, and searcheth out all perfection: the stones of darkness, and the shadow of death.

*Meteorites would be the stones of darkness (barads), as the comet/Venus is the shadow of death.*

4 The flood breaketh out from the inhabitant; even the waters forgotten of the foot: they are dried up, they are gone away from men.

5 As for the earth, out of it cometh bread: and under it is turned up as it were fire.

*Verses 28:4 and 28:5 Job speaks of the floods and drought, the manna that he sees coming from the Earth, and the volcanoes that were initiated by the comet/Venus.*

## CHAPTER 30

29 I am a brother to dragons, and a companion to owls.

*Is this a reference to a cult of Venus? The comet/Venus was noted as a dragon by many civilizations. The companion to the owls may be a reference to Moloch, or quite simply that he has to dwell in the wilderness?*

30 My skin is black upon me, and my bones are burned with heat.

*The necrosis of Job's skin continues to progress, as he suffers in the intense desert heat.*

## CHAPTER 31

10 Then let my wife grind unto another, and let others bow down upon her.

*This graphic statement by Job set me back for a moment. Job declares that if he has ever slept with another man's wife then let his wife be with another man.*

## CHAPTER 32

2 Then was kindled the wrath of Elihu the son of Barachel the Buzite, of the kindred of Ram: against Job was his wrath kindled, because he justified himself rather than God.

*Could the kindred of the Ram be a reference to the Age of Aries, or quite simply because he was a shepherd?*

## CHAPTER 34

25 Therefore he knoweth their works, and he overturneth them in the night, so that they are destroyed.

26 He striketh them as wicked men in the open sight of others;

*Elihu speaks of how the comet/Venus comes in the night to destroy the wicked.*

29 When he giveth quietness, who then can make trouble? and when he hideth his face, who then can behold him? whether it be done against a nation, or against a man only:

*The heavens spread like a scroll as the comet/Venus crosses the sky. The tabernacle that Elihu speaks of is within the cloud of the comet/Venus!*

## CHAPTER 37

15 Dost thou know when God **disposed** them, and caused the **light** of his **cloud** to **shine**?

16 Dost thou know the **balancings** of the **clouds**, the wondrous **works** of him which is **perfect** in **knowledge**?

17 How thy garments are warm, when he **quieteth** the **earth** by the **south wind**?

18 Hast thou with him **spread** out the **sky**, which is **strong**, and as a **molten looking glass**?

19 Teach us what we shall say unto him; for we cannot **order** our **speech** by reason of **darkness**.

20 Shall it be told him that I speak? if a man speak, surely he shall be swallowed up.

21 And now men see not the **bright light** which is in the **clouds**: but the **wind** passeth, and **cleanseth** them.

22 **Fair** weather cometh out of the **north**: with **God** is **terrible majesty**.

*Verses 37:15 to 37:22 Another eloquently stated testimony to the knowledge of the Earth, astronomy, and the comet/Venus.*

**CHAPTER 38**

1 THEN the LORD answered Job out of the whirlwind, and said,

2 Who is this that darkeneth counsel by words without knowledge?

3 Gird up now thy loins like a man; for I will demand of thee, and answer thou me.

*God told Job to man up!*

7 When the **morning stars (Venus)** sang together, and all the **sons** of **God** shouted for joy?

8 Or who **shut** up the **sea** with **doors**, when it **brake** forth, as if it had **issued** out of the **womb**?

9 When I made the **cloud** the **garment** thereof, and thick **darkness** a **swaddlingband** for it,

13 That it might take **hold** of the **ends** of the **earth**, that the **wicked** might be **shaken** out of it?

14 It is turned as **clay** to the **seal**; and they **stand** as a garment.

19 Where is the way where **light** dwelleth? and as for darkness, where is the place thereof,

20 That thou shouldest take it to the **bound** thereof, and that thou shouldest know the **paths** to the **house** thereof?

22 Hast thou **entered** into the **treasures** of the snow? or hast thou seen the treasures of the hail,

23 Which I have reserved against the time of trouble, against the **day** of **battle** and **war**?

24 By what way is the **light** parted, which scattereth the **east wind** upon the earth?

*The previous ten verses were all astronomy, geology, and cosmic events mingled with theology.*

25 Who hath divided a watercourse for the overflowing of waters, or a way for the lightning of thunder;

*God reminds Job that it was He who did all of these wonderful and frightful things.*

31 Canst thou bind the sweet influences of Pleiades, or loose the bands of Orion?

*The binding or loosening of the stars of the Pleiades and Orion is a clear astronomy term, as stars that are grouped in the zodiac are known to be banded.*

32 Canst thou bring forth Mazzaroth in his season? or canst thou guide Arcturus with his sons?

*Mazzaroth is a reference to the zodiac constellations. In Kabalistic astrology, mazalot was a general term for astrology. In Assyrian the term manzaltu means station (360 stations - 1° each – 72 years per station (celestial portion/man's life portion) = 25,920 years or 1 complete Zodiac Cylce), which is a position that the stars take in the heavens. The constellation of Arcturus is located in the zodiac binding of the Bootes constellation (Good Shepherd).*

**CHAPTER 40**

15  Behold now behemoth, which I made with thee; he eateth grass as an ox.

16 Lo now, his strength is in his loins, and his force is in the navel of his belly.

17 He moveth his tail like a cedar: the sinews of his stones are wrapped together.

18 His bones are as strong pieces of brass; his bones are like bars of iron.

19 He is the chief of the ways of God: he that made him can make his sword to approach unto him.

20 Surely the mountains bring him forth food, where all the beasts of the field play.

21 He lieth under the shady trees, in the covert of the reed, and fens.

22 The shady trees cover him with their shadow; the willows of the brook compass him about.

23 Behold, he drinketh up a river, and hasteth not: he trusteth that he can draw up Jordan into his mouth.

24 He taketh it with his eyes: his nose pierceth through snares.

*Job 40:15 to 40:4 is a metaphorical reference of the hippopotamus as behemoth.*

**CHAPTER 41**

1 CANST thou draw out leviathan with an hook? or his tongue with a cord which thou lettest down?

2 Canst thou put an hook into his nose? or bore his jaw through with a thorn?

3 Will he make many supplications unto thee? will he speak soft words unto thee?

4 Will he make a covenant with thee? wilt thou take him for a servant for ever?

5 Wilt thou play with him as with a bird? or wilt thou bind him for thy maidens?

6 Shall the companions make a banquet of him? shall they part him among the merchants?

7 Canst thou fill his skin with barbed irons? or his head with fish spears?

8 Lay thine hand upon him, remember the battle, do no more.

9 Behold, the hope of him is in vain: shall not one be cast down even at the sight of him?

10 None is so fierce that dare stir him up: who then is able to stand before me?

11 Who hath prevented me, that I should repay him? whatsoever is under the whole heaven is mine.

12 I will not conceal his parts, nor his power, nor his comely proportion.

13 Who can discover the face of his garment? or who can come to him with his double bridle?

14 Who can open the doors of his face? his teeth are terrible round about.

15 His scales are his pride, shut up together as with a close seal.

16 One is so near to another, that no air can come between them.

17 They are joined one to another, they stick together, that they cannot be sundered.

18 By his neesings a light doth shine, and his eyes are like the eyelids of the morning.

19 Out of his mouth go burning lamps, and sparks of fire leap out.

20 Out of his nostrils goeth smoke, as out of a seething pot or caldron.

21 His breath kindleth coals, and a flame goeth out of his mouth.

22 In his neck remaineth strength, and sorrow is turned into joy before him.

23 The flakes of his flesh are joined together: they are firm in themselves; they cannot be moved.

24 His heart is as firm as a stone; yea, as hard as a piece of the nether millstone.

25 When he raiseth up himself, the mighty are afraid: by reason of breakings they purify themselves.

26 The sword of him that layeth at him cannot hold: the spear, the dart, nor the habergeon.

27 He esteemeth iron as straw, and brass as rotten wood.

28 The arrow cannot make him flee: slingstones are turned with him into stubble.

29 Darts are counted as stubble: he laugheth at the shaking of a spear.

30 Sharp stones are under him: he spreadeth sharp pointed things upon the mire.

31 He maketh the deep to boil like a pot: he maketh the sea like a pot of ointment.

32 He maketh a path to shine after him; one would think the deep to be hoary.

33 Upon earth there is not his like, who is made without fear.

34 He beholdeth all high things: he is a king over all the children of pride.

**Verses 41:1 to 41:34** Job speaks of the crocodile as leviathan in metaphorical terms. When crocodiles/alligators are mating, the males attract females by bellowing, snapping their snouts, or blowing water out of their noses, which causes the water to foam and boil like a pot!

> **Verse 10:10 & 11: I am appointed to hold the Leviathans, because through me is subjugated the attack and menace of every reptile!**
> ***Apocalypse of Abraham***

## CHAPTER 42

1 THEN Job answered the LORD, and said,

2 I know that thou canst do every thing, and that no thought can be withholden from thee.

3 Who is he that hideth counsel without knowledge? therefore have I uttered that I understood not; things too wonderful for me, which I knew not.

4 Hear, I beseech thee, and I will speak: I will demand of thee, and declare thou unto me.

5 I have heard of thee by the hearing of the ear: but now mine eye seeth thee.

6 Wherefore I abhor myself, and repent in dust and ashes.

7 And it was so, that after the LORD had spoken these words unto Job, the LORD said to Eliphaz the Temanite, My wrath is kindled against thee, and against thy two friends: for ye have not spoken of me the thing that is right, as my servant Job hath.

8 Therefore take unto you now seven bullocks and seven rams, and go to my servant Job, and offer up for yourselves a burnt offering; and my servant Job shall pray for you: for him will I accept: lest I deal with you after your folly, in that ye have not spoken of me the thing which is right, like my servant Job.

9 So Eliphaz the Temanite and Bildad the Shuhite and Zophar the Naamathite went, and did according as the LORD commanded them: the LORD also accepted Job.

10 And the LORD turned the captivity of Job, when he prayed for his friends: also the LORD gave Job twice as much as he had before.

11 Then came there unto him all his brethren, and all his sisters, and all they that had been of his acquaintance before, and did eat bread with him in his house: and they bemoaned him, and comforted him over all the evil that the LORD had brought upon him: every man also gave him a piece of money, and every one an earring of gold.

12 So the LORD blessed the latter end of Job more than his beginning: for he had fourteen thousand sheep, and six thousand camels, and a thousand yoke of oxen, and a thousand she asses.

13 He had also seven sons and three daughters.

14 And he called the name of the first, Jemima; and the name of the second, Kezia; and the name of the third, Keren-happuch.

15 And in all the land were no women found so fair as the daughters of Job: and their father gave them inheritance among their brethren.

16 After this lived Job an hundred and forty years, and saw his sons, and his sons' sons, even four generations.

17 So Job died, being old and full of days.

**Job's wealth is restored to make him richer than even previously, but it states nothing about Job being healed. It says that Job's captivity was turned, or he was restored, and speaks of wealth but not health!**

**Addendum:**

**Leprosy or Hansen's disease is a chronic disease caused by Mycobacterium leprae, and by Mycobacterium lepramatosis. Leprosy is primarily a granulomatous disease of the peripheral nerves and mucosa of the upper respiratory tract, with skin lesions being**

*the primary external sign.* Leprosy when left untreated can be progressive, causing permanent damage to the skin, nerves, limbs, and eyes. Investigators believe that M. leprae is spread through droplets (airborne, direct, indirect contacts). Approximately 95% of people are naturally immune. Sufferers are no longer infectious after two weeks typically. There are eight different classifications of leprosy, with the Multibacillary or Borderline being the category that I believe Job suffered with. This form is of immediate severity with the skin lesions resembling tuberculoid leprosy. This type is unstable and may become like lepromatous leprosy or may undergo a reversal reaction becoming more like the tuberculoid form. The nine-banded armadillo has been found to be naturally infected with leprosy. The disease was known in ancient Greece as elephantiasis, and at various times blood was considered to be the prescribed treatment either as a beverage or as a bath. Virgins or children were considered to be especially potent for this use. The iron sulfide deposited in mass quantities began to foul the water supply during the time of Jared, and the first Biblical reference to leprosy is with Noah. Job lived in the post-flood era when the land was still decimated and contaminating the populace.

*The story of Job was crafted from a Babylonian poem about a pious man named Tabu-utul-bel, and an Egyptian poem Lament for Ipuwer, that predates Job by several hundred years.

# Tabu-utul-bel – written @ 1500 BCE

*"Tabu-utul-bel," is an ancient epic Sumerian poem that speaks to the suffering of a pious man, and the blight upon the land. This poem echoes the suffering of Job, and the disasters of the Exodus and the Ipuwer Papyrus. I have only highlighted common words from these epics to show the same theme of disasters that runs through these sacred texts.*

*Tabu-utul-bel*

I will **praise** the **lord** of **wisdom**,
protection
[The **staff** of thy **divinity**?] I seize hold of.
[**Mine eyes** he closed, bolting them as with] a **lock**,
[**Mine ears** he stopped] like those of a **deaf** person ;
A **king**—I have been **changed** into a **slave**. (xxx. 26)
A **madman**—my **companions** became **estranged** from me.
In the midst (?) of the assembly, they **spurned me**. . . . (xix. 19)
At the mention (?) of my **piety**. . . .terror.
By **day**—deep sighs, at **night**—weeping ;
The month—cries, the year—**distress**.
I **experience**, O my mistress, **mournful** days, **distressful** months,
years of **misery**. (vii. 3)
I had reached and **passed** the **allotted** time of life;
Whithersoever I **turned**—evil **upon** evil. (xxx. 27 ff)
Misery had increased, **happiness** had **disappeared**,
I cried to **my god**, but he **granted** me not his **countenance** ;
I prayed to my **goddess**, but **she** did **not** raise her head, (xxiii. 8, 9)
The **seer-priest** could not **determine** the **future** by an **inspection**.
The **sacrificial-priest** did **not** by an **offering** justify my suit.
The **oracle-priest** I appealed to, but he revealed **nothing**,
**TABI-UTUL-BEL, THE PIOUS SUFFERER. 507**
The **exorciser-priest** did not by his **rites** release me from the **ban**.
(xiii. 4; xvi. 2)
The **like** of this had **never** been **seen**
;
**Whithersoever** I turned, **trouble** was in pursuit. (iii. 26)
As though I **had not** always set **aside** the **portion** for **my god**,
(xxix. 2-5)
And had not **invoked** my **goddess** at my **meals**,
Had not **bowed** down my **face**, and brought my **tribute**
;
As **one** in whose mouth **supplication** and **prayer** were not **constant**,
Who had **passed over** the **day** of **his god**, had forgotten the **newmoon festival**,
Had **spurned** them, neglected their **images**,
Not **taught** his **people fear** and **reverence**, (iv. 3)
Not **invoked** his **god**, but eaten of **his food,**
Neglected his **goddess**, not **offering** her **drink**,
As though one who had always honored **his lord** could forget him
!
Like unto one who has **lightly** uttered the **sacred name** of **his god**
—
thus I appeared.
Whereas I was always **steadfast** in **supplication** and **prayer**
;
**Prayer** was my **practice**, sacrifice my law, (i. 5, last clause)
The **day** of worship of **the gods** was the **joy** of my heart,

The *day* of *devotion* to the *goddess* more to me than *riches* ;

The *prayer* of a *king*,—that was my joy ;
And *hymns* of *praise*—in them was my *delight*.
I *taught* my *country* to *commemorate* the *name* of *God*, (iv. 3)
To *honor* the *name* of the *goddess* I *accustomed* my *people*.
The *fear* of the *king* I made *like* unto that of *God*,
And in *reverence* for the *palace* I instructed the people.
For, indeed, I thought that such things were pleasing to God.
What, however, *seems* good in itself, to God is *displeasing*,
What in itself is held in *contempt* finds *favor* with God ;

Who is there that can *grasp* the will of the *gods* in *heaven* ?
The *mysterious plan of God*—who can *fathom* it? (xviii. 20)
How can *mere mortals* learn the way of God?
He who is *alive* at *evening* is *dead* the next *morning*; (iv. 20)
Suddenly he is cast into *grief*, in haste he is *stricken* down ;
In one *moment* he is singing and playing.
In a twinking he wails like a *mourner*.
As day and night the *spirit* [of mankind] changes;
Now they are *hungry* and are like a *corpse*.
Again they are filled, and feel *equal* to God ;

If things go well, they *prate* of *mounting* to heaven. *(Prate = Tower) – babel = Mount heaven = Tower of Babel?)*
If they are in *distress*, they speak of *descending* into Irkalla *(hell-like).*
An *evil demon* has taken hold of me (?) ; (i. 12)
From *yellowish*, the *sickness* became *white*, (xxx. 30) *(LEPROSY)*
It threw me to the *ground* and *stretched* me on my back,
It *bent* my high *stature* like a *poplar*;
Like a *strong tree* I was *uprooted*, like a lofty tree *thrown* down. (xviii. 16)
As one whose food is *putrid* I grew *old*. (xxx. 27)
The *malady* dragged on its *course*.
Though *without* food, *hunger* diminished ( ?) ;
my *blood* [became sluggish ( ?) ]
With *nourishment* cut off (?).
Though my *armor* was *burnished*, the *bow* [strung], (xxix. 29)
*Tied* to the *couch* with the outlet closed, I was stretched out. (xii.146)
My *dwelling* had become a *prison* ;

In the bonds of my flesh my *members* were *powerless*,
In *fetters* of my own, my feet were *entangled*,
My discomfiture was *painful*, the downfall severe.
A *strap* of many twists held me fast,
A sharply-pointed *spear* pierced me, (vi. 4a)
My *persecutor tracked* me all the day,
Nor in the night time did my *pursuer* let me draw a *breath*, (vii. 4)
Through *wrenching* my joints were torn *asunder* (xvi. 9)
My limbs were *shattered* and rendered helpless;
In my *stall* I passed the night like an *ox*,
I was *saturated* like a *sheep* in my *excrements* ;

My *diseased* joints the *exorciser* tore apart (?) – *an exorcism = one who casts out with spells? Exorcisor= disentangler or doctor?*
And my *omens* the *seer-priest* set aside,
The *prophet-priest* could not *interpret* the *character* of my disease.

And the limit of my malady the **seer-priest** could not determine.
(xiii. 4)
**No god** came to my **aid**, taking me by the hand,
**No goddess** had **compassion** for me, walking by my side.
The **grave** was **open**, my burial **prepared**; (xvii. 1)
Though I was not yet **dead**, the **lamentation** for me was over
;
The **people** of my land had already said *"alas"* over me.
(vii. 6 ; ix. 25-26)
My **adversary** heard it and **his** face **shone** ; (xxx. 1-10) *(comet/Venus, Satan, Mastema, etc.)*
As the joyful tidings were announced to him, his heart rejoiced,
**Supposing** that it was the day for my whole family,
When among the **shades**, their **deity** would be honored ( ?)
TABI-UTUL-BEL, THE PIOUS SUFFERER. 509
The **weight** of his hand I was no longer able to **endure** ....
(Tabi-utul-Bel dwelling in **Nippur**,
He spake, "How long yet!" deeply sighing,
The strong ruler, **decked** with the **turban**.)
My **sins** he caused the **wind** to carry away,
[Mine **eyes** which had been **bolted** he **opened**;]
Mine **ears** had been closed and **bolted** as a **deaf** person's
—
He took away their deafness, he **restored** my hearing
;
The net( ?) which had shut (me) in, he released from round about me,
He **healed**, and my **breast** resounded like a flute,
The **fetters** which enclosed (me) like a lock he **unlocked**.
The one weakened by hunger he made strong like a powerful, wellknitted sprout.
He brought me **food**, he provided **drink**.
The neck that had been bent **downwards** and worn
He **raised** erect like a cedar;
He made my form like one **perfect** in strength.
Like one **rescued** from an evil spirit, my lips ( ?) cry out,
He poured out their **wealth**, he embellished their **property**.
My **knees** that were caught like a mountain bird,
**My entire body he restored**
;
(xlii. 10)
He wiped out the **anger**, he freed from his wrath (?),
The **depressed** form he cheered up.
(To the shores of Naru, the place of the judgment of humanity they crossed over,
The **forehead brand** was removed, the slave mark taken away.) – **forehead seal!**
He who sins against **E-sagila**, through me let him see.
In the **jaw** of the **lion** about to conquer me **Marduk** placed a bit
;
**Marduk** seized the one ready to **overwhelm** me, and completely encircled me with his bulwark. (xi. 13-17)

# *The Apocalypse of Peter Decoded (1 CE – 76 CE)*

**THE AKHMIM FRAGMENT**

6 And as we prayed, suddenly there appeared **two men** standing **before** the **Lord** (perhaps add, to the **east**) upon whom we were **not able to look.**

7 For there issued from their countenance a **ray** as of the **sun**, and their **raiment** was **shining** so as the eye of man never saw the like: for no mouth is able to declare nor heart to conceive the glory wherewith they were clad and the beauty of their countenance.

8 Whom when we saw we were astonied, for their bodies were **whiter** than any **snow** and **redder** than any **rose**.

*Verses 6,7, and 8 – Two heavenly bodies that shine like a sun is what Peter speaks of. Again, we are unable to look directly into the sun, eclipse, nuclear explosion, or a plasma discharge. A welder has to wear a protective visor when welding (plasma, arc, etc.), if this were not done, there would be a myriad of eye ailments to deal with. The white and red appearance is descriptive of Noah at his birth. The color white speaks to the comet/Venus, and the red stands for Mars.*

9 And the redness of them was mingled with the whiteness, and, in a word, I am not able to declare their beauty.

10 For their hair was **curling** and **flourishing** (flowery), and **fell comely** about their **countenance** and their shoulders like a garland woven of nard and various flowers, or like a **rainbow in the air:** such was their comeliness.

*Verses 9 and 10 – The appearance of the two heavenly bodies in the sky would seem to have curling flowery hair streaming from it (Cockatrice - Rooster with a Dragon's body).*

12 And I drew near to the Lord and said: Who are these?

13 He saith to me: These are your (our) righteous brethren whose appearance ye did desire to see.

*Verses 12 and 13 – Peter desired to see what appeared in the skies.*

21 And I saw also another place over against that one, very squalid; and it was a place of punishment, and they that were punished and the angels that punished them had their raiment dark, according to the air of the place.

22 And some there were there hanging by their tongues; and these were they that blasphemed the way of righteousness, and under them was laid fire flaming and tormenting them.

**THE ETHIOPIC TEXT**

And we besought and entreated him severally and prayed him, saying unto him: Declare unto us what are the signs of thy coming and of the end of the world, that we may perceive and mark the time of thy coming and instruct them that come after us, unto whom we preach the word of thy gospel, and whom we set over (in) thy church, that they when they hear it may take heed to themselves and mark the time of thy coming.

*We once again have a reestablishment of when the next catastrophe is to take place. The common mindset of these prior times (our time) was always preoccupied with the next disaster, and the signs that will be seen in the skies in order to prepare themselves.*

And our Lord answered us, saying: Take heed that no man deceive you, and that ye be not doubters and serve other gods. Many shall come in my name, saying: I am the Christ. Believe them not, neither draw near unto them. For the coming of the Son of God shall not be plain (i.e. foreseen); but as the **lightning** that shineth from the **east** unto the **west**, so will I come upon the **clouds** of heaven with a **great host** in my majesty; with my **cross** going before my face will I come in my majesty, shining **sevenfold** more than the **sun** will I come in my majesty with all my **saints**, mine **angels** (mine holy angels). And my Father shall set a **crown** upon mine head, that I may judge the **quick** and the **dead** and recompense every man according to his works.

*This statement is astrotheology wholly and completely. The cults that arose serving the other Gods in the region had a similar pantheon of deities. The sun rises in the east and sets in the west, as Peter gives us the path. The host of the comet/Venus will be meteorites.*

even the **first Christ** whom they crucified and therein sinned a great sin. And when they reject him he shall slay with the sword, and there shall be many martyrs.

*This statement has followed us over time. Peter speaking of the second Christ has been interpreted to be many historical men over time. The 2nd Christ is a forecast of another destructive event to come from the comet/Venus.*

**Enoch** and Elias shall be sent to **teach** them that this is the deceiver which must come into the **world** and do **signs** and **wonders** to deceive.

*The book of Enoch was not accepted into the modern Bible, but was commonly cleaved to by the early Church as having been divinely inspired. Enoch as noted earlier in the book was an astronomer/magi, who was the first noted man (?) taught to write. Again Enoch will teach the world of the true signs!*

And this shall come at the **day of judgement** upon them that have fallen away from faith in **God** and that have committed sin: **Floods** (cataracts) of **fire** shall be let loose; and **darkness** and **obscurity** shall come up and **clothe** and **veil** the whole **world** and the **waters** shall be **changed** and turned into **coals** of **fire** and all that is in them shall **burn**, and the **sea** shall become **fire**. Under the **heaven** shall be a **sharp fire** that **cannot** be **quenched** and floweth to fulfil the **judgement** of wrath. And the **stars shall fly in pieces** by **flames** of fire, as if they had not been created and the **powers (firmaments)** of the heaven shall pass away for lack of water and shall be as though they had not been. And the **lightnings of heaven** shall be no more, and by their **enchantment** they shall **affright** the world (probably: The heaven shall turn to lightning and the lightnings thereof shall affright the world. The spirits also of the dead bodies shall be like unto them (the **lightnings?**) and shall become **fire** at the **commandment** of God.

*Floods of fire, darkness, waters shall be changed, coals of fire, burn, stars shall fly, the heavens shall pass away, lightnings of heaven, and dead bodies. This all too common a theme at this point again exhibits all of the same noted catastrophes of the Great Flood and the Exodus.*

And so soon as the whole creation dissolveth, the men that are in the east shall flee unto the west, unto the east; they that are in the south shall flee to the north, and they that are in the south. And in all places shall the wrath of a fearful fire overtake them and an unquenchable flame driving them shall bring them unto the judgement of wrath, unto the stream of unquenchable fire that floweth, flaming with fire, and when the waves thereof part themselves one from another, burning, there shall be a great gnashing of teeth among the children of men.

*When the sky and stars above (creation dissolveth) are changed in order of their appearance the fire from heaven will destroy mankind.*

Then shall they all behold me coming upon an **eternal cloud of brightness**: and the **angels** of **God** that are with me shall sit (prob. And I shall sit) upon the **throne** of my glory at the right hand of my **Heavenly Father**; and he shall set a **crown** upon mine head. And when the nations behold it, they shall weep, every nation apart.

And there are **wheels of fire** and **men** and **women hung** thereon by the strength of the whirling thereof.

*This is an example of sadomasochistic torture.*

And the angel Tatirokos shall come and chastise them with yet greater torment, and say unto them:

*Tatirokos is Greek for the keeper of hell, but I feel it is the constellation of Tarturus (Taurus).*

And my Lord Jesus Christ our King said unto me: Let us go unto the holy mountain. And his disciples went with him, praying. And behold there were two men there, and we could not look upon their faces, for a light came from them, shining more than the sun, and their rairment also was shining, and cannot be described, and nothing is sufficient to be compared unto them in this world. And the sweetness of them . . . that no mouth is able to utter the beauty of their appearance (or, the mouth hath not sweetness to express, &c.), for their aspect was astonishing and wonderful. And the other, great, I say, shineth in his aspect above crystal. Like the flower of roses is the appearance of the colour of his aspect and of his body . . . his head (al. their head was a marvel). And upon his (their) shoulders (evidently something about their hair has dropped out) and on their foreheads was a crown of nard woven of fair flowers. As the rainbow in the water, so was their hair.

**Again the white and red appearance is descriptive of Noah at his birth. The color white speaks to the comet/Venus, and the red stands for Mars.**

Satan maketh war against thee, and hath veiled thine understanding; and the good things of this world prevail against thee. Thine eyes therefore must be opened and thine ears unstopped that a tabernacle, not made with men's hands, which my heavenly Father hath made for me and for the elect.

**Satan (Venus) has caused mankind to have their understanding, of their place in the cosmos veiled from sight. The word revelation has been mistranslated from the Greek, meaning a lifting of the veils. Here Peter clearly speaks of the veils that have been placed over our understanding.**

And great fear and commotion was there in heaven and the angels pressed one upon another that the word of the scripture might be fulfilled which saith: Open the gates, ye princes.

**There is war in heaven as the angels (planets/stars) battle, and the gates are finally closed as Venus is defeated (fizzles) as a comet.**

## SECOND BOOK OF THE SIBYLLINE ORACLES

190 Woe unto all them that are found great with child in that day, and to them that give suck to infant children, and to them that dwell by the sea (the waves). Woe to them that shall behold that day. For a dark mist shall cover the boundless world, of the east and west, the south and north. And then shall a great river of flaming fire flow from heaven and consume all places, the earth and the great ocean and the grey sea, lakes and rivers and fountains, and merciless

**190 – The droughts caused women to be unable to breast feed their babies. The coastal populations are always at the mercy of tsunamis, and ninety percent of the worlds' population lives by the coastline. A fire from heaven shall engulf the planet. We see that this same sentiment is echoed by two other authors;**

> **Luke 21:23 But woe unto them that are with child, and to them that give suck in those days! For there shall be great distress in the land, and wrath upon this people.**

> **Matthew 24:19 And woe unto them that are with child, and to them that give suck in those days!**

200 Hades and the pole of heaven: but the lights of heaven shall melt together in one and into a void (desolate) shape (?). For the stars shall all fall from heaven into the sea (?), and all souls of men shall gnash their teeth as they burn in the river of brimstone and the rush of the fire in the blazing plain, and ashes shall cover all things. And then shall all the elements of the world be laid waste, air, earth, sea, light poles, days and nights, and no more shall the multitudes of birds fly in the air nor swimming creatures any more swim the sea no ship shall sail with its cargo over the waves;

**200 – The constellation Hyades (Hades), along with the pole of heaven and the lights (stars) will lose their recognizable form on that day. The meteors will rain fire and brimstone upon mankind. We have the four zodiac elements; earth, air, fire, and water.**

214 Now when the immortal angels of the undying God **Barakiel, Ramiel, Uriel, Samiel, and Azael**, [These names are from Enoch.] knowing all the evil deeds that any hath wrought aforetime -then out of the misty darkness they shall bring all the souls of men to judgement, unto the seat of God the immortal, the great.

*214 – Peter qoutes from Enoch/Enkime to show the fondness held for his books in antiquity. We have shown that Enoch was totally based on astrotheology, and if the early church clung to his canons, this shows that their theology was based in the stars. It's curious that Azazel will be one of the angels that judges the souls of men, as Venus is Azazel! All of the planets are noted as angels represent heavenly bodies.*

220 For he only is incorruptible, himself the Almighty, who shall be the judge of mortal men. And then unto them of the underworld shall the heavenly one give their souls and spirit and speech, and their bones joined together, with all the joints, and the flesh and sinews and veins, and skin also over the flesh, and hair as before, and the bodies of the dwellers upon earth shall be moved and arise in one day, joined together in immortal fashion and breathing.

Then shall the great angel Uriel break the monstrous bars framed of unyielding and unbroken adamant, of the brazen

230 gates of Hades, and cast them down straightway, and bring forth to judgement all the sorrowful forms, yea, of the ghosts of the ancient Titans, and of the giants, and all whom the flood overtook. And all whom the wave of the sea hath destroyed in the waters, and all whom beasts and creeping things and fowls have feasted on: all these shall he bring to the judgement seat; and again those whom flesh-devouring fire hath consumed in the flames, them also shall he gather and set before God's seat.

And when he shall overcome Fate and raise the dead, then shall Adonai Sabaoth the high thunderer sit on his heavenly

*230 – Hades (Hyades), Titans (Greeks), Giants (Nephilim), Floods (Noah & Ducalion), these are all familiar things at this point. We have another name for God as Adonai Sabaoth.*

240 throne, and set up the great pillar, and Christ himself, the undying unto the undying, shall come in the clouds in glory with the pure angels, and shall sit on the seat on the right of the Great One, judging the life of the godly and the walk of ungodly men.

And Moses also the great, the friend of the Most High shall come, clad in flesh, and the great Abraham himself shall come, and Isaac and Jacob, Jesus, Daniel, Elias, Ambacum (Habakkuk), and Jonas, and they whom the Hebrews slew: and all the Hebrews that were with (after ?) Jeremias shall be judged at the judgement seat, and he shall destroy them, that they may receive a due reward and expiate all that they did in their mortal life.

*240 – A great pillar with Christ, Moses (friends?), Abraham, Isaac, Jacob, Jesus, Daniel, Elias, Ambacum, and Jonas! This seems to be an indictment of the Hebrews for all of the people murdered during their wars and campaigns. The Sibylline speaks of Christ and Jesus, as two seemingly separate people altogether!*

# THE PROPHET EZEKIEL DECODED - @ 600 BCE

*"Wheels, wheels, & more wheels"*

**CHAPTER 1**

1 NOW it came to pass in the thirtieth year, in the fourth month, in the fifth day of the month, as I was among the captives by the river of Chebar, that the heavens were opened, and I saw visions of God.

2 In the fifth day of the month, which was the fifth year of king Jehoiachin's captivity,

> *"In the seventh year after the Great Calamity, in the second month, on the seventeenth day, I was summoned by my master the Lord Enki, great god, benevolent fashioner of Mankind, omnipotent and merciful. I was among the remnants of Eridu who had escaped to the arid steppe just as the Evil Wind was nearing the city."*
> **Endusbar – Book of Enki - A retelling of a Babylonian narrative!**

3 The word of the LORD came expressly unto Ezekiel the priest, the son of Buzi, in the land of the Chaldeans by the river Chebar; and the hand of the LORD was there upon him.

**Chaldean is a word known to be associated with a people and their culture as astronomers in Sumeria/Babylon.**

4 And I looked, and, behold, a whirlwind came out of the north, a great cloud, and a fire infolding itself, and a brightness was about it, and out of the midst thereof as the colour of amber, out of the midst of the fire.

> *"And I looked up and to and behold, a Whirlwind came out of the south."*
> **Endusbar – Book of Enki**

5 Also out of the midst thereof came the likeness of four living creatures. And this was their appearance; they had the likeness of a man.

6 And every one had four faces, and every one had four wings.

**Verses 1:5 and 1:6 are clear zodiacal references that were echoed by Ezekiel and Enoch, and later most notably by John of Patmos, in the Book of Revelations. The four faces are yet again the four elements of the zodiac:**

> *"And as it reached the ground, four straight feet spread out from its belly and the brilliance disappeared."*
> *"And when I lifted my eyes, there were two divine emissaries standing near me. And they had the faces of men, and their garments were sparkling like burnished brass."*
> **Endusbar – Book of Enki**

7 And their feet were straight feet; and the sole of their feet was like the sole of a calf's foot: and they sparkled like the colour of burnished brass.

**I feel this to be a reference to the Bull (Taurus), and their custom of creating statues of the Bull God out of metals such as gold, silver, bronze, and brass.**

8 And they had the hands of a man under their wings on their four sides; and they four had their faces and their wings.

9 Their wings were joined one to another; they turned not when they went; they went every one straight forward.

**Verses 1:8 and 1:9 echo the same quote as Enoch and John. When the 12 zodiac constellations are viewed in the round the members of the zodiac overlap two months, and their wings touch another.**

10 As for the likeness of their faces, they four had the face of a man, and the face of a lion, on the right side: and they four had the face of an ox on the left side; they four also had the face of an eagle.

*If one starts the zodiac with Leo at twelve o'clock, Scorpio at three o'clock, Aquarius at six o'clock, and Taurus at the nine o'clock positions on a wheel chart, they sit at four cardinal points opposite another, and form a cosmic/equinox cross. Three noted times these four elements are mentioned in the Bible and Sacred texts; Revelations, Enoch, Apocalypse of Abraham, and Ezekiel.*

| Zodiac Sign | Representation | Element |
|---|---|---|
| Leo | Lion | Fire |
| Aquarius | Man | Air |
| Scorpio* | Eagle | Water |
| Taurus | Bull | Earth |

*\* Scorpio is often represented by an Eagle on some zodiac charts*

*This fresco rests in Westminster Cathedral in England. Christ is depicted sitting upon a rainbow with his feet resting upon the Earth, as his Sun rays covers the four corners of the heavens. Christ holds a chalice in his left hand, signs a mudra with his right hand, and has a Coptic wheel cross behind his head. The zodiac imagery is unmistakable and the reference is clear! The creator of the painting knew the correct position of the icons in relation to each other. We go from Aquarius (Man) to Scorpio (Eagle/Scorpion), down to the Calf (Taurus), and finally over to the Lion (Leo). These are the fearful images that have kept us afraid of the End Time, since the beginning of remembered time!*

11 Thus were their faces: and their wings were stretched upward; two wings of every one were joined one to another, and two covered their bodies.

*The Hindu God Brahma has 4 heads, 4 faces, 4 arms, and 4 hands! This is a common theme that represents the 4 cardinal directions of north, south, east, and west, as Brahma is one of the three Creator Gods. This common synthesis of deities and beliefs into different religious systems is clearly evident with many theologies.*

*NOTE:*

*Brahma - Abraham - Brama - Abram - Rama - Ramadan*

*Sumeria/Babylon gave us our conception of winged creatures, Gods, Angels, and Cherubim, as we see Gilgamesh has two (4) sets of wings, and the Chaos beast has two wings and a tail.*

12 And they went every one straight forward: whither the spirit was to go, they went; and they turned not when they went.

*When the twelve constellations are viewed in the round the members of the zodiac overlap from month to month. The signs appear to be connected and traveling as one through the heavens.*

15 Now as I beheld the living creatures, behold one wheel upon the earth by the living creatures, with his four faces.

*Taurus has his wheel upon the Earth as he represents that element.*

16 The appearance of the wheels and their work was like unto the colour of a beryl: and they four had one likeness: and their appearance and their work was as it were a wheel in the middle of a wheel.

*Stones like Beryl, Jasper, and Carnelian, were used as ornamentation or as gemstones in the Jewish High Priest's breastplate, as well as ornamentation for ornate zodiac wheels and formed the basis for gemstones being associated with the zodiac sign.*

17 When they went, they went upon their four sides: and they turned not when they went.

*This is another reference to the inner connectivity of the zodiac wheel and elements.*

18 As for their rings, they were so high that they were dreadful; and their rings were full of eyes round about them four.

19 And when the living creatures went, the wheels went by them: and when the living creatures were lifted up from the earth, the wheels were lifted up.

20 Whithersoever the spirit was to go, they went, thither was their spirit to go; and the wheels were lifted up over against them: for the spirit of the living creature was in the wheels.

21 When those went, these went; and when those stood, these stood; and when those were lifted up from the earth, the wheels were lifted up over against them: for the spirit of the living creature was in the wheels.

**Verses 1:18 to 1:21 are basically rehashing the wheel inner connectivity. Did Ezekiel have knowledge of the Mesoamerican calendar half a world away?**

*Mayan Sacred Round Calendar (20 x 13 = 260 Venus cycle) – "Wheel within a Wheel!"*

22 And the likeness of the firmament upon the heads of the living creature was as the colour of the terrible crystal, stretched forth over their heads above.

**The heavens above the zodiac wheel was the color of the terrible crystal. I believe the terrible crystal to represent the comet/Venus.**

25 And there was a voice from the firmament that was over their heads, when they stood, and had let down their wings. was the likeness of a throne, as the appearance of a sapphire stone: and upon the likeness of the throne was the likeness as the appearance of a man above upon it.

27 And I saw as the colour of amber, as the appearance of fire round about within it, from the appearance of his loins even upward, and from the appearance of his loins even downward, I saw as it were the appearance of fire, and it had brightness round about.

**I believe these verses to be a reference to Aquarius the Age to come.**

*I have tried to take great care in my analysis of **chapters 3, 4, and 5**, as these acts show the fearful, superstitious, and schizophrenic state of mind that Ezekiel (Saint John as well) was in. The true fact is that when our friends and loved ones behave in an irrational manner, such as Ezekiel's eating dung (feces) bread, eating a scroll, laying on one side while sleeping **390 nights** and **40 nights (430 years in Egypt!) outside the city walls.** We would go to court to have them deemed mentally unfit. I have much* *respect for Ezekiel as a highly intelligent person that was driven to their breaking point by circumstances unfolding of cosmic proportions.*

**CHAPTER 3**

1 Moreover he said unto me, Son of man, eat that thou findest; eat this roll, and go speak unto the house of Israel.

2 So I opened my mouth, and he caused me to eat that roll.

***Ezekiel ate a scroll!!! The theologian says that by Ezekiel eating the scroll, his words would flow forth directly as the words of the Almighty.***

**CHAPTER 4**

15 Then he said unto me, Lo, I have given thee cow's dung for man's dung, and thou shalt prepare thy bread therewith.

***This act by Ezekiel has spawned many questions from religious and scholarly figures alike. The theologian sees this order by God as a testing of Ezekiel's faith, but I feel this to be clearly the act of a manic person.***

**CHAPTER 5**

1 And thou, son of man, take thee a barber's razor, and cause it to pass upon thine head and upon thy beard: then take the balances to weigh, and divide the hair.

2 Thou shall **burn** with **fire** a **third** part in the **midst** of the city, when the **days** of the **siege** are **fulfilled**: and thou shalt take a third part, and **smite** about it with a **knife**: and a third part thou shalt **scatter** in the **wind**; and I will **draw** out a **sword** after them

***This is ritual not unlike those practiced by so-called Pagan beliefs!***

**CHAPTER 7**

2 Also, thou son of man, thus saith the Lord GOD unto the land of Israel; An end, the end is come upon the four corners of the land.

3 Now is the end come upon thee, and I will send mine anger upon thee, and will judge thee according to thy ways, and will recompense upon thee all thine abominations.

6 An end is come, the end is come: it watcheth for thee; behold, it is come.

7 The morning is come unto thee, O thou that dwellest in the land: the time is come, the day of trouble is near, and not the sounding again of the mountains.

***As Earthquakes trembled the land and mountains, Ezekiel, expects another extinction level event, and Divine judgment as the "day of trouble nears."***

14 They have blown the trumpet, even to make all ready; but none goeth to the battle: for my wrath is upon all the multitude thereof.

***The sounds of the Earth moaning signals the trumpet of battle, but no stars in the sky appear ready for war. Ezekiel is pulling from older texts about the destruction of Noah and Moses.***

15 The **sword** is without, and the **pestilence** and the **famine** within: he that is in the **field** shall **die** with the **sword**; and he that is in the city, **famine** and **pestilence** shall devour him.

16 But they that escape of them shall escape, and shall be on the **mountains** like doves of the valleys, all of them **mourning**, every one for his **iniquity**.

17 All **hands** shall be **feeble**, and all knees shall be **weak** as water.

18 They shall also **gird** themselves with **sackcloth**, and horror shall **cover** them; and **shame** shall be **upon** all **faces**, and **baldness** upon all their **heads**.

*This statement is reminiscent of the trials of Job. Ezekiel is speaking about leprosy that was prevalent in the land after the time of the Great Flood. The horror that covered them was from the lesions and the pathology of the disease. The shame sprang from the infected person being ostracized by the people of the land. Job shaved his head immediately after putting on sackcloth. The scalp is often affected with the onset and duration of leprosy.*

**CHATER 8**

9 And he said unto me, Go in, and behold the wicked abominations that they do here.

10 So I went in and saw; and behold every form of creeping things, and abominable beasts, and all the idols of the house of Israel, portrayed upon the walls round about.

11 And there stood before them **seventy men** of the ancient house of Israel, and in the midst of them stood Ja-azanran the son of Shapnan with every man his censer in hand; and a thick cloud of incense rose up.

*We see that the children of Israel revert back to their Canaanite roots in the worship of El and the 70 children of his constellations. Abraham (Brahma) previously destroyed his father's 70 idols and chased back the ravens 70 times in a day. Incense and branches (olive branch) are still used in religious rituals up to the present time.*

**This passage by Ezekiel shows how Judaism and Islam sprang from shared practices and beliefs.**

*Chapter 9:4 and said to him, "Go throughout the city of Jerusalem and put a mark on the foreheads of those who grieve and lament over all the detestable things that are done in it." 5 As I listened, he said to the others, "Follow him through the city and kill, without showing pity or compassion. 6 Slaughter old men, young men and maidens, women and children, but do not touch anyone who has the mark. Begin at my sanctuary." So they began with the elders who were in front of the temple.*

*The use of the "forehead seal," will allow the destruction to Passover the protected, but Ezekiel states that all were killed with him being the exception. We have a destruction from a passing body that destroys all life in the city, but espoused in his theology.*

# THE REVELATION OF JOHN DECODED – written @ 70-95 CE

*Introduction to John of Patmos*

*"Early star clues"*

**CHAPTER 1**

1 THE Revelation of Jesus Christ, which God gave unto him, to shew unto his servants things which must shortly come to pass; and he sent and signified it by his angel unto his servant John:

*This brief statement speaks to John's fearful state of mind. When John says; "Even the things which must come to pass." John expects tremendous upheaval of the Earth in the near future. John is reliving the trauma of the Flood of Noah and the disasters of the Exodus.*

4 JOHN to the **seven churches** which are in Asia: Grace be unto you, and peace, from him which is, and which was, and which is to come; and from the **seven Spirits** which are before his **throne**;

*Ancient star charts from around the globe from a diversity of cultures lead us back to the Pleiades constellation. The references to the seven stars (Seven Sisters) of the Pleiades that form the Leg of the Sacred Bull sit before what has been called; Star of David, Star of Bethlehem, Star of Ra, Star of Solomon, Blazing Star, and the Star of Judas. The star known as Atlas forms a trinity of stars with Alcyone and Pleione to form the end of the Key of Solomon. This is yet another astrotheological reference based on anthropomorphism. Many cultures that are isolated from each other share a link to the stars in this system, so I will not discount the importance the system has played in man's development and place in creation.*

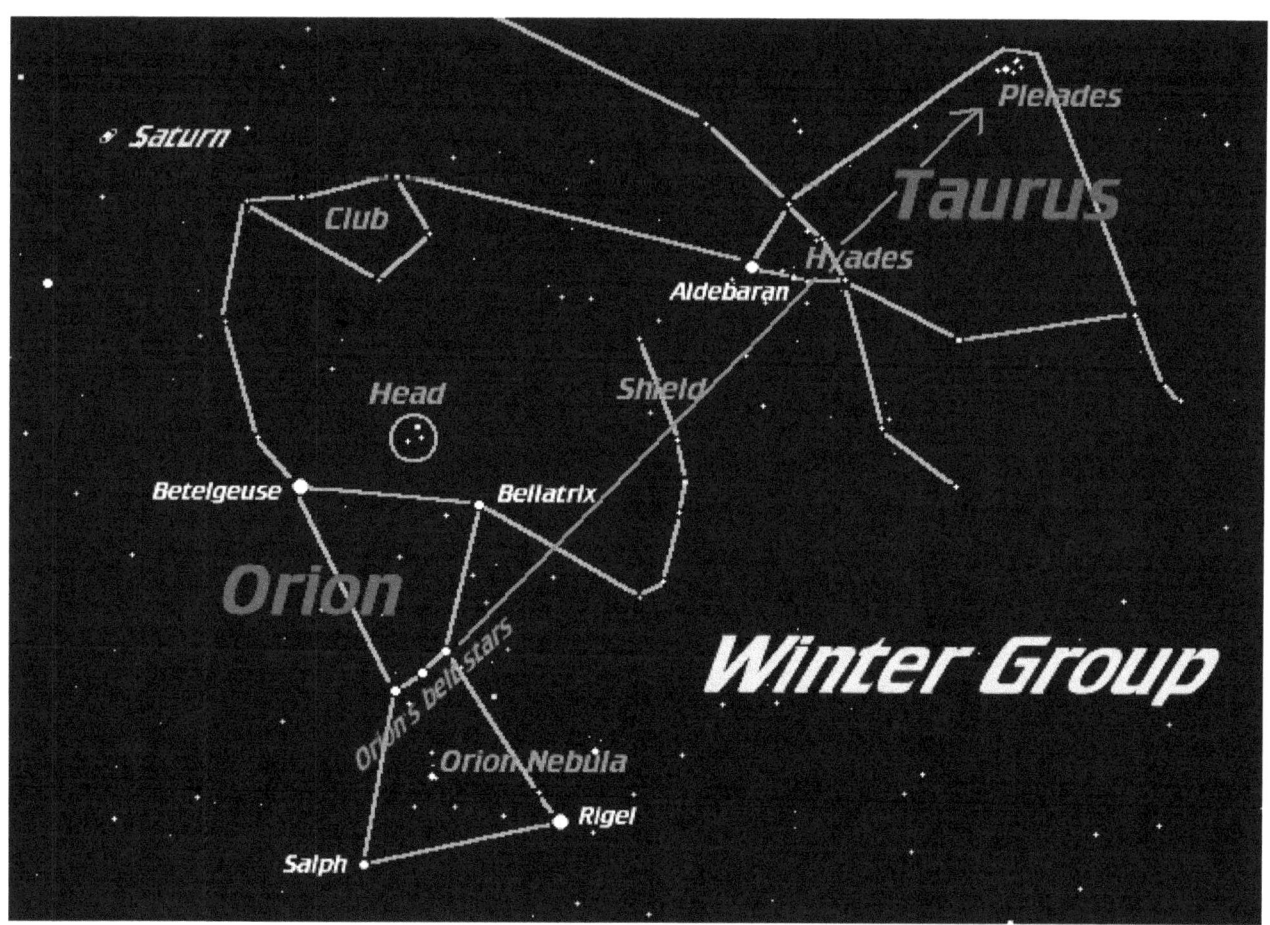

8 I am Alpha and Omega, the beginning and the ending, saith the Lord, which is, and which was, and which is to come, the Almighty.

*I find this passage interesting as it is shared by the Qur'an.*

> *Surah 53:25 But it is to Allah that the End and the Beginning belong.*

12 And I turned to see the voice that spake with me. And being turned, I saw seven golden candlesticks;

**The seven golden candlesticks represent the seven stars of the Pleiades in John's menorah (minarah).**

13 And in the midst of the seven candlesticks one like unto the Son of man, clothed with a garment down to the foot, and girt about the paps with a golden girdle.

14 His head and his hairs were white like wool, as white as snow; and his eyes were as a flame of fire;

15 And his feet like unto fine brass, as if they burned in a furnace; and his voice as the sound of many waters.

**Verses 1:13 to 1:15 are clear references to the next Age of Aquarius. White hair (Galzu) is seen as representing the wisdom of years. Priests wore breastplates studded with precious jewels such as Jasper and Carnelion, and set in gold. Aquarius is the Water Bearer, so his would be the voice of many waters.**

16 And he had in his right hand seven stars: and out of his mouth went a **sharp two edged sword**: and his countenance was as the sun shineth in his strength.

*The seven stars are yet another reference to the Pleiades constellation (Leg of the Sacred Bull). The appearance (countenance) of the comets body was that of a sharp two-edged sword streaming from its mouth, and its brightness rivaled the Sun.*

18 I am he that liveth, and was dead; and, behold, I am alive for evermore, **Amen**; and have the keys of hell and of death.

*This is a reference to the Hyades (Hades-Hell) constellation in the constellation of Taurus. These systems are also a part of the Key of Solomon. Amen aka Amun = Hidden One*

20 The mystery of the **seven stars** which thou sawest in my right hand, and **the seven golden candlesticks**. The **seven stars** are the **angels** of the **seven churches**: and the **seven candlesticks** which thou sawest are the **seven churches**.

*This is a clear astrotheological statement. John all but lets the reader know the context of his premonition. John has an obvious understanding of the stars and religious training. The seven stars in the Pleiades are; Merope, Electra, Celeano, Maia, Taygeta, Asterope, and Arope. The seven (angels) churches represent one of the seven stars that sit before the throne.*

**Addressing the Churches**

*"Morning Star"*

**CHAPTER 2**

9 I know thy works, and tribulation, and poverty, (but thou art rich) and I know the blasphemy of them which say they are Jews, and are not, but are the synagogue of Satan.

*John speaks to the sociopolitical and false worshippers within his church that are worshipping deities other than those of the recognized faith.*

*Synagogue – syn/a/gog/ue = At one/ Together with Gog?*

13 I know thy works, and where thou dwellest, even where Satan's seat is: and thou holdest fast my name, and hast not denied my faith, even in those days wherein Antipas was my faithful martyr, who was slain among you, where Satan dwelleth.

**This is a reference to the martyrdom of Antipas who was burned alive in a brazen bull for not denouncing his faith.**

17 He that hath an ear, let him hear what the Spirit saith unto the churches; To him that overcometh will I give to eat of the hidden manna, and will give him a white stone, and in the stone a new name written, which no man knoweth saving he that receiveth it.

*John is speaking of the manna that Moses in Exodus 16:33 placed in a vessel as the hidden manna. The noted researcher and theorist Immanuel Velikofsky, postulated that manna was created from the carbogenous content from the tail of the comet/Venus. This manna fed the people of the Exodus for forty years, as well as dozens of cultures around the globe that describe manna, ambrosia, and madhu. A common practice in the past was to place the names of people (rulers in particular) with complaints written upon them on a stone. It is also a common practice for a deity to have multiple names to encompass their various personifications: man has also been described as having multiple names.*

20 Notwithstanding I have a few things against thee, because thou sufferest that woman Jezebel, which calleth herself a prophetess, to teach and to seduce my servants to commit fornication, and to eat things sacrificed unto idols.

*I feel Jezebel to be one of the most unfairly maligned people down through the ages. Her marriage to King Ahab brought her into a region that was already beset with religious and political turmoil. Jezebel was the Phoenician daughter of King Ethbaal, and the worship of Baal was allowed by the royal couple. The "el" in Jezebel (El/Bel) denotes her to be a follower of the Canaanite God El or Bel. The fact that power and wealth now lay in the city caused the landowners who were losing wealth because of the sea trade to become restless. The prophet Elisha caused the overthrow of the House of Ahab, and the eventual defenestration of Jezebel. This was an unfitting end in my view, as there have been more suitable candidates for such treatment in Biblical history.*

28 And I will give him the **morning star.**

*This is a clear reference that should be read as; "and I will give him Venus." Many cultures, civilizations, and religions worshipped Venus at various points. Venus is known to be called by more names than any other planet such as; Morning Star, Evening Star, Blazing Star, Smoking Star, Satan, Beelzebub, Azazel, Azzael, Azza, Quetzalcohuatl, Kukulkan, Gukumatz, Gula, al-Uzza, Uzza, Phaeton, Aphrodite, Astarte, Astarte Isadore, Ishtar, Ishetar, Isis, Minerva, Athene, Chaska, Shiva, Vishnu (pervade), Visnu, (Visnu-Venus), Pallas Athene, and most notably Lucifer. Venus is central in our understanding of past events as it has caused tremendous carnage in our solar system. I will show later how Mr. Velikofsky's theories on past Earth upheavals may be borne out in the Revelation to Saint John.*

Curious?

*Azazel & Azael – The el in their names denote that they were of the Canaanite God El, thus, how could they be the Devil and Satan of the God Yahweh/Jehovah? In this tradition Azazel was basically the number two to Yahweh.*

## CHAPTER 3

7 And to the angel of the church in Philadelphia write; These things saith he that is holy, he that is true, he that hath the key of David, he that openeth, and no man shutteth; and shutteth, and no man openeth;

*When John speaks of the Key of David, he again references the stars in this grouping that has come to be understood as the seat of the progenitors of humanity. When one's mind has been opened and the veils have dropped, then no one can close that door, and no one may enter unwillingly. True knowledge and understanding will free your soul to find the truth in all things. The seven churches are representative of the Seven Sisters of the Pleiades.*

Astrotheology

"Wheels, Stars, and Zodiac Creatures"

## CHAPTER 4

4 And round about the throne were four and twenty seats: and upon the seats I saw four and twenty elders sitting, clothed in white raiment; and they had on their heads crowns of gold.

*The four and twenty thrones that held the four and twenty seated elders represent the twenty-four hours of the day quite simply.*

5 And out of the throne proceeded lightnings and thunderings and voices: and there were seven lamps of fire burning before the throne, which are the seven Spirits of God.

*The seven stars of the Pleiades and the Star of David (Atlas) are referenced as the seven lamps of fire burning before the throne, which are the seven spirits of God.*

> *Seven Sisters of the Pleiades: Maia, Electra, Taygeta, Aerope, Celeano, Asterope, Merope.*

6 And before the throne there was a sea of glass like unto crystal: and in the midst of the throne, and round about the throne, were four beasts full of eyes before and behind.

*The surface of the structure had a crystalline (water/clear) appearance. The four creatures sit at opposite points to one another, north, south, east, and west. This can also be seen as the opposite points on a clock at the twelve, three, six, and nine o'clock positions.*

And the first beast was like a lion, and the second beast like a calf, and the third beast had a face as a man, and the fourth beast was like a flying eagle.

*This statement has puzzled researchers and theologians alike since its acceptance into the Bible. I believe this to be another telling statement from John based on his knowledge of astronomy and his deep religious fervor. When one looks at this statement without emotional attachment, it becomes clear that this is a reference to four of the twelve zodiac manifestations. The first creature that was like a lion represents Leo. The second creature that was like a calf represents Taurus. The third creature had a face as a man represents Aquarius. The fourth creature was like a flying Eagle represents Scorpio. The Ages of Leo, Taurus, Aquarius, and Scorpio are opposite the other as zodiac signs and form a cross on the zodiac wheel. John has borrowed the symbolism and imagery evoked by Enoch and Ezekiel in the earlier prophecies.*

> *Ezekiel 1:10 As for the likeness of their faces, they four had the face of a man, and the face of a lion, on the right side: and they four had the face of an ox on the left side; they four also had the face of an eagle.*

> *Apocalypse of Abraham 18:3 - 5. and it did not cease from the plentitude of the fire. And as the fire rose up, soaring to the highest point, I saw under the fire a throne of fire and the many-eyed ones round about, reciting the song, under the throne four fiery living creatures, singing.*

> *4. ,5And the appearance of each of them was the same, each having four faces, And this (was) the aspect of their faces: of a lion, of a man, of an ox, and of an eagle.*

8 And the four beasts had each of them six wings about him; and they were full of eyes within: and they rest not day and night, saying, Holy, holy, holy, Lord God Almighty, which was, and is, and is to come.

*When the twelve constellations of the zodiac are viewed in the round, the eyes of all of the manifestations are looking without rest day and night. John adds two more wings to his creatures than those of Ezekiel. The "Holy, Holy, Holy," is a common trinity statement.*

> *Ezekiel 1:9 Their wings were joined one to another; they turned not when they went; they went every one straight forward.*

> *Ezekiel 1:19 And when the living creatures went, the wheels went by them: and when the living creatures were lifted up from the earth, the wheels were lifted up.*

*The zodiac signs touch one another in the sky and on the calendar. There is an overlap of zodiac signs from month to month, (ex: November 23rd to December 22nd – Sagittarius) and this can be viewed on a zodiac chart with the four elements as wheels around the chart. In astrological charts there is a synthesis of time and elements.*

*And John Wept*

*"No Noble Plea"*

**CHAPTER 5**

4 And I wept much, because no man was found worthy to open and to read the book, neither to look thereon.

5 And one of the elders saith unto me, Weep not: behold, the Lion of the tribe of Juda, the Root of David, hath prevailed to open the book, and to loose the seven seals thereof.

*These two verses open a window into the mind of John. The fact that John cried because he thought that there would be no one worthy of destroying mankind is telling. John wished to see mankind destroyed because he feels that everyone should perish because of their sins. Many men in the Bible and other sacred texts have all made eloquent pleas to the powers to be for the salvation of mankind without destruction. John makes no such attempt to save his brethren, but yearns for the onset of that terrible day. Those seeking the end of the world as fulfillment of prophecy still thrive today. We have an inbred fear of living and an intense desire for destruction. It is time that we move from ignorance to knowledge, and not to allow our primal fears to be stoked for gain.*

*Seven Seals*

*"Birth of a Comet/Planet"*

**CHAPTER 6**

*The symbolism enclosed in the Seven Seals has been interpreted in many different ways, and I will relay it as it has come to my understanding. There is typically a literal understanding for the masses, a secret understanding for the priest class, and an even higher level of understanding for the elite or illuminated.*
*\* From "The Clavicula Solemnis" –" The Key of Solomon"*

| Day | Saturday | Thursday | Tuesday | Sunday | Friday | Wednesday | Monday |
|---|---|---|---|---|---|---|---|
| Archangel | Tzaphqiel | Tzadiqel | Khaniel | Raphael | Haniel | Michael | Gabriel |
| Angel | Cassiel | Sachiel | Zamael | Michael | Anael | Raphael | Gabriel |
| Planet | Saturn | Jupiter | Mars | Sun | Venus | Mercury | Moon |
| Metal | Lead | Tin | Iron | Gold | Copper | Mercury | Silver |
| Colour | *Black | Blue | *Red | Yellow | Green | *Purple/Mix Colors | *White |

*\*Solomon's Four Horses - Black Horse: Saturn    Red Horse: Mars   White Horse: Moon    Pale Horse: Mercury  @ 1600CE*
*\*Pyramids in Egypt - White, Black, and Red 10,500BCE - 2,500BCE*
*\*Atharva Veda - Brahmakarin Red & White 1,000BCE*
*\*Enoch - White, Black, and Red Bulls 400BCE*
*\*Apocalypse of Peter - Red & White 1-76BCE*
*\*John - White, Black, Red, and Pale Horses 40-96CE*

1 AND I saw when the Lamb opened one of the seals, and I heard, as it were the noise of thunder, one of the four beasts saying, Come and see.

*The Lamb is inextricably tied with the constellation of Virgo, and is symbolic for the absolution of mans sins. The use of the scapegoat by the post-deluvial Hebrew people evolved into the use of the sheep (Aries) to represent the faith. Sheep were venerated long before the Hebrew culture by the ancient Sumerian people, as they believed that they were not of the Earth. As the comet/Venus enters the neighborhood the "voice of thunder," is the sound that this massive body made across the heavens. As the meteors exploded in the atmosphere, the sound that they made was interpreted as YA or Yahu (NetanYAHU)! The Hebrews said that the name of their God was Yahweh based on this sound. The Chinese document this same sound in the skies as the name of their God, Yahou. The sound of the passing comet with meteor storm beyond comparison would have made* ancient or modern man cringe in fear of the end. The YWH or Land of the Shasu People document YWH as the name of their God, where Moses dwelt in their land of Midian for forty years.

* Disaster - Miracle Path * DMP
This is an update to a forthcoming book that will show the correlation between all Biblical Miracles and Disasters that fall in almost a straight line. The relationship between John, those events, and the Four Horsemen that he speaks of will be outlined below with the corresponding body of water.

2 And I saw, and behold a white horse: and he that sat on him had a bow; and a crown was given unto him: and he went forth conquering, and to conquer.

The White Horse that John envisions is Venus when she was born as a comet and entered our planetary orbit from the direction of the constellation of Sagittarius. Ancient texts relate Venus as wearing a crown/diadem and carrying a bow. Mr. Velikofsky has postulated that the bow Venus carried was an electrical/plasma discharge in her early life. I believe that John is pulling from archival documents for his source knowledge in regard to the entrance of the White Horse.

WHITE HORSE: Sea of Galilee (DMP) is the Lowest Fresh Water body on Earth, and sits between the Black Sea (Black Horse) and the Dead Sea (Pale Horse) on the Biblical DMP with the Arabian plate running the middle length. The Sea of Galilee region is associated with 25 Miracles of Jesus Christ and this is a body of pure water!

4 And there went out another horse that was red: and power was given to him that sat thereon to take peace from the earth, and that they should kill one another: and there was given unto him a great sword.

The Red Horse is a reference to Mars, and the role that it played in these cosmic collisions/wars in the heavens. Mars has been described as carrying a sword, which to me is representative of its ability during the past to cause wars on Earth.

RED HORSE: Red Sea / Gulf of Aqqaba (DMP) sits at the southern end of the DMP below the Dead Sea (White Horse), and is the site of the Biblical Red Sea Crossing of Moses, and is also bisected by the Jordan-Gihon Fault Line (Arabian Plate). The Red Sea is the saltiest ocean on the planet and sits near the Dead Sea (Salt Sea).

5 And when he had opened the third seal, I heard the third beast say, Come and see. And I beheld, and lo a black horse; and he that sat on him had a pair of balances in his hand.

I believe the Black Horse bears a correlation to Saturn, and the balance refers to the constellation of Libra who carries the balance to judge mankind. Saturn is also known as the planet of judgement, time, and restriction.

BLACK HORSE: The Black Sea sits at the top of the Disaster - Miracle Path above the Sea of Galilee ( White Horse) and is the supposed sea that overflowed in the Biblical narrative of Noah. The Black Sea is a part of the Eurasian plate, and this area of Turkey contains many otherly worldly terrains.

6 And I heard a voice in the midst of the four beasts say, A measure of wheat for a penny, and three measures of barley for a penny; and see thou hurt not the oil and the wine.

The constellation of Virgo is the focal point of this portion of the Revelation, as she is always depicted holding a stalk of wheat and barley in her hand. John knows that several crops survived destruction in the past.

8 And I looked, and behold a pale horse: and his name that sat on him was Death, and Hell followed with him. And power was given unto them over the fourth part of the earth, to kill with sword, and with hunger, and with death, and with the beasts of the earth.

This is yet another reference to Mars as death, and its companion moons Phobos and Deimos. Phobos and Deimos have been described as driving the chariot of Mars across the sky. Mr. Velikofsky relates that the passing of Mars during this chaotic period brought wars, pestilence, death, the fall of civilizations, and the birth of others.

PALE HORSE: The Dead Sea (Salt Sea) is the lowest and saltiest body of water on Earth, and sits between the Sea of Galilee (White Horse) and the Red Sea (Red Horse). The Dead Sea is the body of water and held the cities that were destroyed by the *periodic Passovers from Venus and other planetary bodies. The five destroyed Biblical cities of Sodom, Gomorrah, Bela, Zoar, and Admah, were obliterated from a Passover @ 1900 BCE during the time of the Biblical patriarch Abraham. The Red Sea and Gulf of Aqaba rests along the Arabian plate that leads to the Jordan-Gihon fault line. The Pale Horse is considered death as that Passover brought a massive destruction in its wake. The Dead Sea was destroyed as well as the 5 cities and vales were opened in the Earth.*

WHITE HORSE - Sea of Galilee - fresh water - Miracles of Jesus Christ - 0 BCE
RED HORSE - Red Sea/Gulf of Aqaba - salt water - Exodus Disasters - 1487 - 1447 BCE
BLACK HORSE - Black Sea - fresh water - Great Flood - 2344 BCE
PALE HORSE - Dead Sea - salt water - 5 Destroyed Cities of the Valley - @ 1900 BCE

<u>Disaster - Miracle Path North to South</u>

BLACK HORSE - Turkey   WHITE HORSE - Jordan / Israel   PALE HORSE - Israel / Jordan   RED HORSE - Saudia Arabia / Egypt

9 And when he had opened the fifth seal, I saw under the altar the souls of them that were slain for the word of God, and for the testimony which they held:

10 And they cried with a loud voice, saying, How long, O Lord, holy and true, dost thou not judge and avenge our blood on them that dwell on the earth?

11 And white robes were given unto every one of them; and it was said unto them, that they should rest yet for a little season, until their fellowservants also and their brethren, that should be killed as they were, should be fulfilled.

**Verses 6:6 to 6:11 I feel are more theological in statement as John speaks of the Altar (Ara Constellation), this is a reference to the star Ara, but espouses the theology of his religion.**

12 And I beheld when he had opened the sixth seal, and, lo, there was a great earthquake; and the sun became black as sackcloth of hair, and the moon became as blood;

**As the planetary body passes in an orbit that disturbs the Earth's rotation, this causes a great or worldwide earthquake. The passage of a planetary body across the face of the sun and moon would cover their faces with its cometary tail. Sackcloth is clothing made from animal hair and is quite uncomfortable. The connotation would be that it took on a fuzzy appearance.**

13 And the stars of heaven fell unto the earth, even as a fig tree casteth her untimely figs, when she is shaken of a mighty wind.

One can imagine the meteor storm that barraged the sky with flaming rocks blanketing the heavens, as though a great wind were shaking a tree.

14 And the heaven departed as a scroll when it is rolled together; and every mountain and island were moved out of their places.

**As this body passes overhead the atmosphere of the Earth was peeled away like a scroll as it rolled up. This was yet another in a series of close encounters that our planet has had in the past with large planetary bodies. The repeated stripping of the Earth's atmosphere through depositing of iron meteors and other elements took place.**

15 And the kings of the earth, and the great men, and the rich men, and the chief captains, and the mighty men, and every bondman, and every free man, hid themselves in the dens and in the rocks of the mountains;

**This verse shows that there was time for people to attempt an evacuation, but there was no safe place to hide. The caves that they occupied became their tombs as some mountains sank and new ones rose in their stead. The destruction was not limited to the wealthy or the poor.**

16 And said to the mountains and rocks, Fall on us, and hide us from the face of him that sitteth on the throne, and from the wrath of the Lamb:

*John relates the folly that they exhibited by trying to use the caves in the mountains for safety.*

*Tribes of the Zodiac*

*"1 Baktun"*

**CHAPTER 7**

4 And I heard the number of them which were sealed: and there were sealed an hundred and forty and four thousand of all the tribes of the children of Israel.

5 Of the tribe of Juda were sealed twelve thousand. Of the tribe of Reuben were sealed twelve thousand. Of the tribe of Gad were sealed twelve thousand.

6 Of the tribe of Aser were sealed twelve thousand. Of the tribe of Nepthalim were sealed twelve thousand. Of the tribe of Manasses were sealed twelve thousand.

7 Of the tribe of Simeon were sealed twelve thousand. Of the tribe of Levi were sealed twelve thousand. Of the tribe of Issachar were sealed twelve thousand.

8 Of the tribe of Zabulon were sealed twelve thousand. Of the tribe of Joseph were sealed twelve thousand. Of the tribe of Benjamin were sealed twelve thousand.

**Verses 7:4 to 7:8 Of the Tribe of Judah were sealed (forehead) twelve thousand, of the tribe of Reuben, Gad, Asher, Nepthali, Dan, Manasseh, Simeon, Levi, Issachar, Zebulun, Joseph, and Benjamin, were sealed twelve thousand.**

This is a charting of the zodiac using the twelve tribes of Israel to represent each zodiac sign. The Bible relates that in the book of the Exodus 600,000 of the Tribe of Israel went out of Egypt. The 144,000 is 1 Baktun! A baktun is 20 katun cycles of the ancient Maya and Olmec (many Mesoamerican cultures) Long Count Calendar. It contains 144,000 days, equal to 394.26 tropical years. The current (13th) baktun will end, or be completed, on 13.0.0.0.0 (December 21, 2012). The Maya had two calendar systems. The Tzolkin or "Sacred Round" is a 260 day calendar based on the planet Venus, and the Haab is a 365 day calendar. The Maya share the Jubilee tradition with the Hebrews, but their Jubilee Year comes every 52 years, versus, every 49 years. I believe this is a direct connection to as why the Maya recognized the elements of Christianity when it was brought to them by Spanish explorers and missionaries. These correlations shows a common basis for these calendar systems from Mesoamerica to the Middle East. The question then becomes, how did John have an understanding of a calendrical system half a world away? Did the monks in the 16th century synchronize Revelations timing with that of the Mayan Calendar? Was the original basis for these joint calendars based on the circuits of Venus? Each Tribe of Israel has 12,000 days sealed in their zodiac constellation for a total of 144,000! Just as in Ezekiel chapter 9, the forehead seal will protect the chosen ones from death.

12,000 X 12 = 144,000 - Is the recently rediscovered 13th zodiac constellation Ophiuchus the Lost Tribe of Israel?

| | | | |
|---|---|---|---|
| Reuben – Aquarius | Gad – Sagittarius | Asher – Libra | Napthali – Virgo |
| Dan – Scorpio | Judah – Leo | Simeon – Capricorn | Levi – Pisces |
| Isaachar – Cancer | Zebulun – Aries | Joseph – Taurus | Benjamin – Gemini |

Table of Mayan Long Count Units

| Days | Long Count Periods | Long Count Units | Approximate Solar Years |
|---|---|---|---|
| 1 | | 1 Kin | |
| 20 | 20 Kin | 1 Unial | |
| 360 | 18 Unial | 1 Tun | ~1 |

| 7,200 | 20 Tun | 1 Ka'tun | 19.7 |
| --- | --- | --- | --- |
| 144,000 | 20 Ka'tun | 1 Bak'tun | 394.3 |
| 2,880,000 | 20 Bak'tun | 1 Pictun | 7885 |
| 57,600,000 | 20 Pictun | 1 Kalabtun | 157,808 |
| 1,152,000,000 | 20 Kalabtun | 1 K'inchiltun | 3,156,164 |
| 23,040,000,000 | 20 K'inchiltun | 1 Alautun | 63,123,288 |

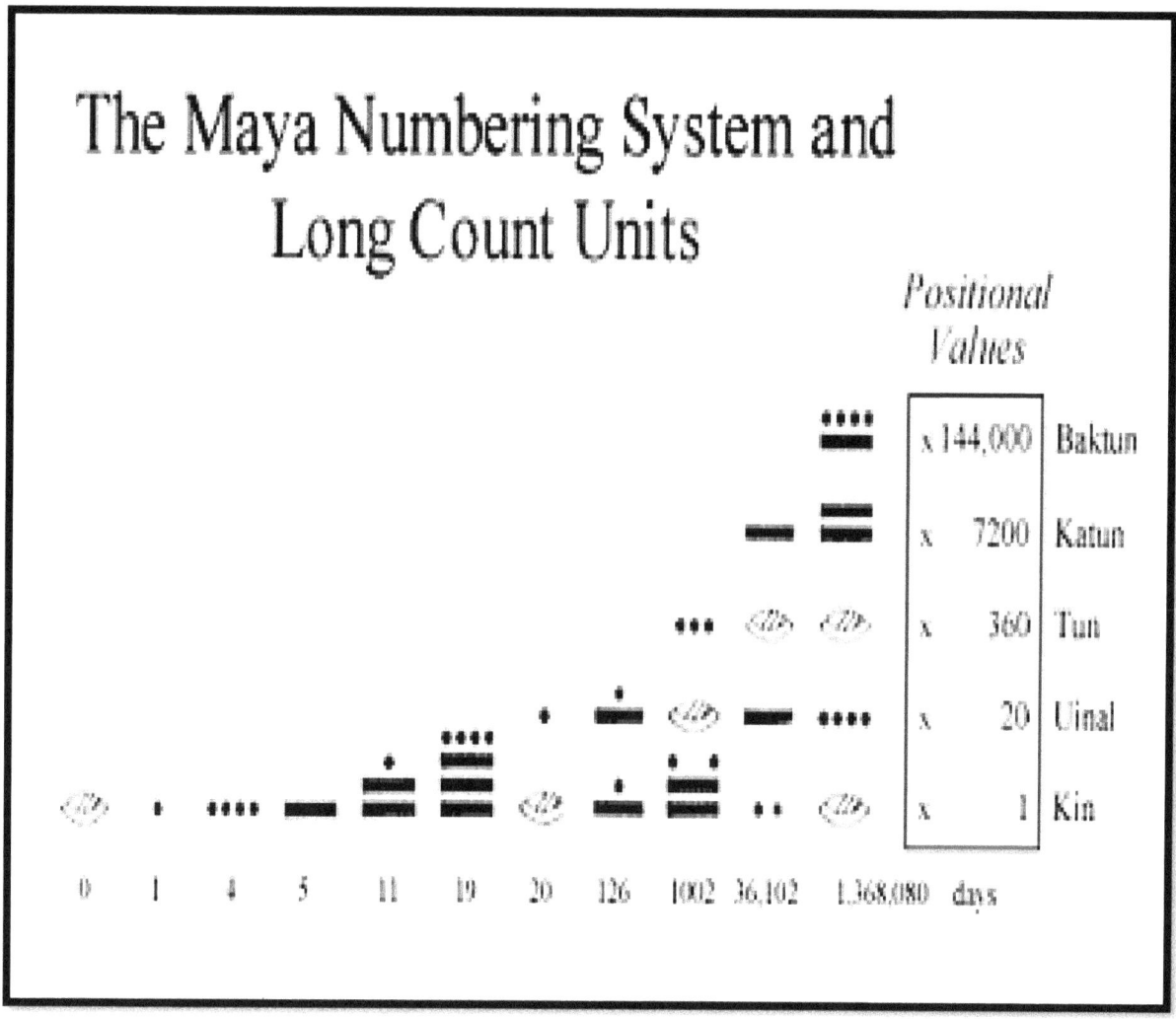

*"Baktun"*

*One Baktun on the Mayan Long Count calendar is equal 394.26 tropical years, or 144,000 days. The Mayan belief is that we are currently in the 13th Baktun which marks the end of a Great Age. The Mayans believed in World Suns versus Zodiac Ages, and that each Sun ended in destruction. Based on the end date of the 13th Baktun on December 21, 2012 (13.0.0.0.0) the understanding is that doom lurks behind the Sun or a devastating celestial alignment will occur. There have been several worldwide catastrophes that coincide with these Baktuns as listed below. I have attempted to line up the logical World Sun with the right period based on known events during those World Suns.*

| Sun/Baktun | Date - Age | Notable Events |
|---|---|---|
| End 5th? - 13th Baktun | 2011.9 - 1617.6 / Aquarius 2012-4172 CE | * rounded 394.3yrs |
| 12th Baktun | 1617.6 – 1223.3 | End Dark Ages 1500 CE - Columbus discovers America 1492 BCE |
| 11th Baktun | 1223.3 – 829 | |
| 10th Baktun | 829 – 434.7 | Start of Dark Ages |
| 9th Baktun | 434.7 – 40.4 CE | Book of Revelations@ 81-96 CE, New Testament @ 30-96 CE, Zohar 100 CE, Popul Vuh 100 CE |
| 5th - 8th Baktun | 40.4 CE – 353.9 BCE / Pisces 149 BCE – 2012 | Book of Enoch @ 160-300 BCE, Septuagint 300 BCE |
| 7th Baktun | 353.9 – 748.2 | Rome Founded @ 730 BCE |
| 4th – 6th Baktun | 748.2 – 1142.5 | Maya Rise @ 1100 BCE |
| 3rd – 5th Baktun | 1142.5 – 1536.8 | Fall of Troy 1194 BCE, Exodus Disasters @ 1487 – 1447 BCE, Thera in Greece destroyed 1500 BCE, Krishna's City of Dwarka sinks in the sea 1500 BCE, Bharata battle fought 1424 BCE |
| 4th Baktun | 1536.8 – 1931.1 | Enuma Elish (Flood story) 1800 BCE, Code of Hammurabi 1792 BCE, Epic of Gilgamesh 1760 BCE, Downfall of Indus Valley Civilization 1750 BCE |
| 2nd – 3rd Baktun | 1931.1 – 2325.4 / Aries 2308-148 CE | Great Flood @ 2344 BCE – 5 Cities of the Valley destroyed @ 2200 BCE |
| 2nd Baktun | 2325.4 – 2719.7 | |
| 1st – 1st Baktun | 2719.7 – 3114/ Taurus 4468-2309 CE | Start of Maya time 3114 BCE, Kali Yuga start 3102 |

Red – MAJOR GLOBAL DISASTERS

1st Sun – Ends during the disaster of the Great Flood and the 2nd Sun begins

2nd Sun – Ends during the turbulent period of the Exodus disasters, eruption of Thera (Santorini) in Greece, and the sinking of the city of Dwarka in India. The 3rd Sun begins

3rd Sun – Falls during the next Baktun as disasters continue and lead to the rise of the Maya and 400 hundred years later the Romans rise as the 4th Sun begins

4th Sun – Ends in the early part of the Age of Pisces (Christian era) – ongoing disaster from the sky brings the 4th Sun to a close and the 5th Sun begins

9th Baktun – John writing @ 81-96 CE Apocalyptic visions based on his knowledge of the Mayan calendar expected disaster soon to come. We see Jewish, Christian, and Mayan Sacred books created within twenty years of each other.

5th Sun – This is our current sun, and hopefully stable for an infinite number of Baktuns

16 They shall hunger no more, neither thirst any more; neither shall the sun light on them, nor any heat.

*The Children of Israel hungered and thirsted with little reprieve from the excessive dessert heat for forty years. This statement was in recognition and appeasement for those hardships.*

17 For the Lamb which is in the midst of the throne shall feed them, and shall lead them unto living fountains of waters: and God shall wipe away all tears from their eyes.

*This refers to Jesus (Pisces) leading the way to the man that carries the water Aquarius. Pisces precedes Aquarius in the Zodiac Ages.*

> Matthew 28:20 Teaching them to observe all things whatsoever I have commanded you: and, lo, I am with you alway, even unto the end of the (Age/Aeon) world.

*Luke 22:10 And he said unto them, Behold, when ye are entered into the city, there shall a man meet you, bearing a pitcher of water (Aquarius); follow him into the house where he entereth in.*

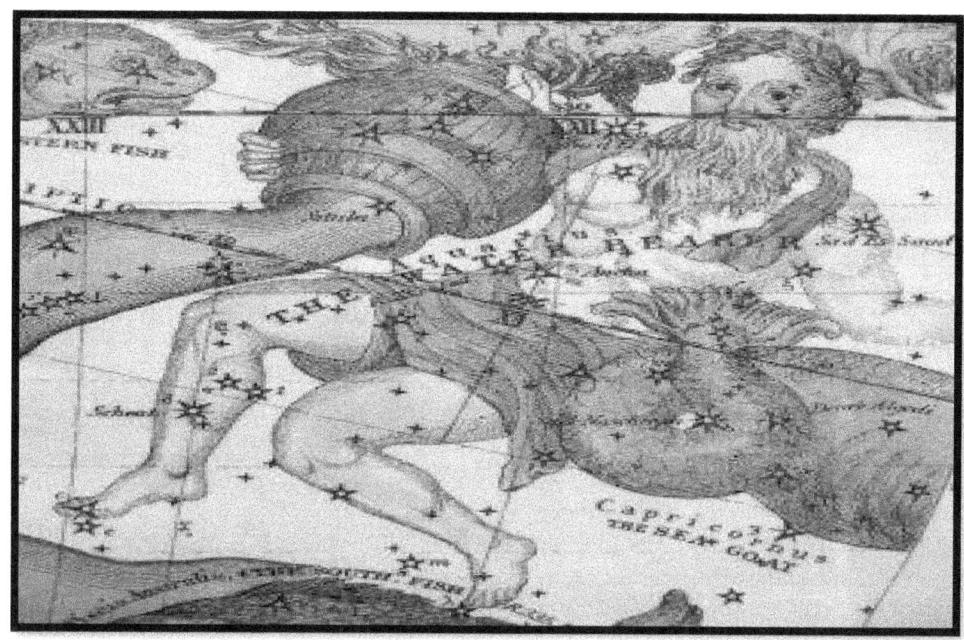

*Aquarius – The Waterman*

*The Last Seal & Seven Woes*

*"Wormwood"*

## CHAPTER 8

1 AND when he had opened the seventh seal, there was silence in heaven about the space of half an hour.

*This is the proverbial calm before the storm, as the comet/Venus enters close to the Earth's orbit.*

5 And the angel took the censer, and filled it with fire of the altar, and cast it into the earth: and there were voices, and thunderings, and lightnings, and an earthquake.

*The censer that the angel carries is the Cup (Crater - enmity) that rests on the back of the Serpent (Hydra). The Altar (Ara) is the cosmic place of sacrifice. The event related through astrotheology was one that the Earth suffered in association with the passing of a large body in close orbit to our planet.*

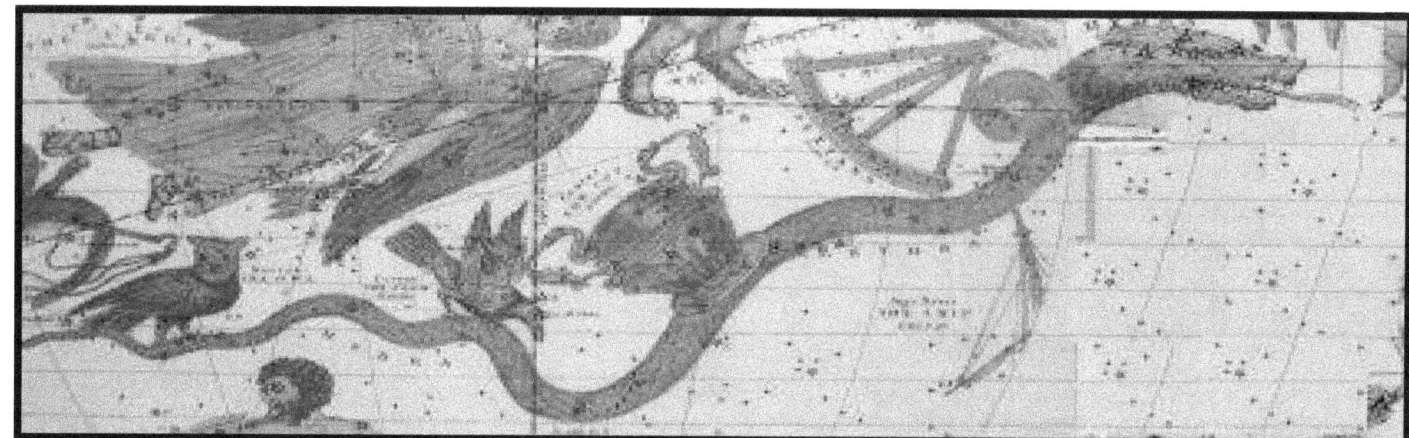

*The constellation of Hydra (Serpent) wraps 1/3 of the heavens & sits near the Virgin (Virgo) as the Cup of Wrath (Crater) rests on its' back, and some of the birds that fly in midheaven.*

7 The first angel sounded, and there followed hail and fire mingled with blood, and they were cast upon the earth: and the third part of trees was burnt up, and all green grass was burnt up.

*A meteor shower bombards the planet with meteors (barads) and fire from above. The metallic content of the meteors turns the land and waters red. The firestorm that the meteors brought scorched 1/3 of the vegetation.*

8 And the second angel sounded, and as it were a great mountain burning with fire was cast into the sea: and the third part of the sea became blood;

*A massive meteor fell into the sea with the metallic content leaching into the water bringing death to anything in the water that came in contact with it.*

9 And the third part of the creatures which were in the sea, and had life, died; and the third part of the ships were destroyed.

*The loss of sea life-fish kill was due to the massive meteor.*

10 And the third angel sounded, and there fell a great star from heaven, burning as it were a lamp, and it fell upon the third part of the rivers, and upon the fountains of waters;

*Another encounter with these heavenly bodies deposited a large meteor/comet fragment that turned a third of the potable water acrid and not fit for use.*

11 And the name of the star is called Wormwood: and the third part of the waters became wormwood; and many men died of the waters, because they were made bitter.

*The wormwood root was in common use in the region and its bitter qualities would be an easy analogy for them to use in the description. The term Longwood was used in the Book of Enki (Sumerian cylinder seals) to describe a similar event, but it described a celestial bow and arrow. Those that drank of the waters died because it was unfit for anyone to use.*

12 And the fourth angel sounded, and the third part of the sun was smitten, and the third part of the moon, and the third part of the stars; so as the third part of them was darkened, and the day shone not for a third part of it, and the night likewise.

*The tail of the comet/Venus would blot out 1/3 of the heavens as it passed near the sun. The coverage of the sky would cause the side of the Earth facing the sun to go into darkness. This would relate to an extended period of light on the other side of the globe that has been documented by other civilizations.*

13 And I beheld, and heard an angel flying through the midst of heaven, saying with a loud voice, Woe, woe, woe, to the inhabiters of the earth by reason of the other voices of the trumpet of the three angels, which are yet to sound!

*The Angel (Eagle) that flies in mid heaven is none other than Aquila. The Eagle (Angel) that is the Aquila constellation signals the common trinity of woes to come from the three angels yet to sound.*

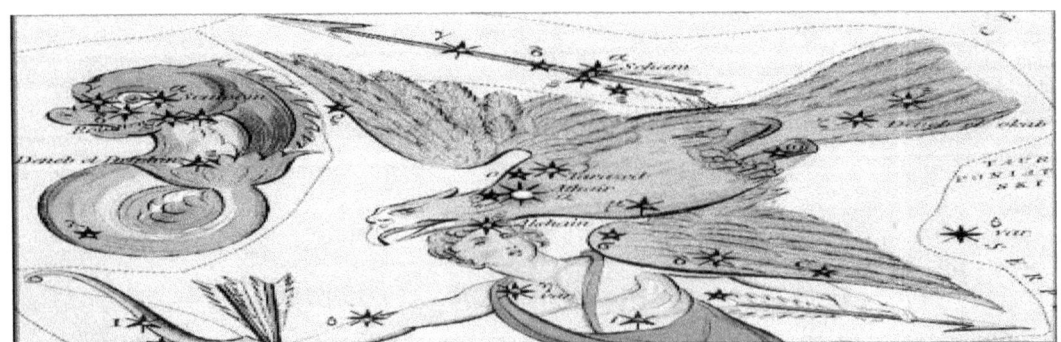

*Angels, Apollyon, and Demons*

*"Forehead Seals"*

**CHAPTER 9**

1 AND the fifth angel sounded, and I saw a star fall from heaven unto the earth: and to him was given the key of the bottomless pit.

2 And he opened the bottomless pit; and there arose a smoke out of the pit, as the smoke of a great furnace; and the sun and the air were darkened by reason of the smoke of the pit.

**Verses 9:1 and 9:2 A meteor falls into the sea as the comet/Venus descends below the ecliptic plane into hell. The resulting steam and heat blocked out the visible sun in the region, as the meteor gouges a deep pit in the Earth.**

3 And there came out of the smoke locusts upon the earth: and unto them was given power, as the scorpions of the earth have power.

4 And it was commanded them that they should not hurt the grass of the earth, neither any green thing, neither any tree; but only those men which have not the seal of God in their foreheads.

**The meteor plague begins to affect the region as the meteors shower the region in numbers. The selective statement of forehead seals again brings us back to this practice used by many religions and cultures.**

5 And to them it was given that they should not kill them, but that they should be tormented five months: and their torment was as the torment of a scorpion, when he striketh a man.

**The meteor showers tormented the populace for five months as the Earth was caught in an orbit with the umbra/penumbra of the comet/Venus.**

6 And in those days shall men seek death, and shall not find it; and shall desire to die, and death shall flee from them.

**The constant Earth changes, plagues, and standard of life made mankind long for an end to their suffering. This nervous breakdown still inhabits the souls of man today, as we long to be raptured away from this world of sorrow.**

7 And the shapes of the locusts were like unto horses prepared unto battle; and on their heads were as it were crowns like gold, and their faces were as the faces of men.

8 And they had hair as the hair of women, and their teeth were as the teeth of lions.

9 And they had breastplates, as it were breastplates of iron; and the sound of their wings was as the sound of chariots of many horses running to battle.

| Tribe | Tribe | Tribe |
|---|---|---|
| Zebulon | Issachar | Judah |
| Gad | Naphtali | Dan |
| Levi | Simeon | Reuben |
| Benjamin | Joseph | Asher |

10 And they had tails like unto scorpions, and there were stings in their tails: and their power was to hurt men five months.

*Verses 9:7 to 9:10 Speaks to the appearance of the meteor showers as they streak across the sky like war horses. The breastplates of iron is a reference to the metallic content of the meteorites, as high priests wore breastplates adorned with precious jewels. Their deafening sound as they shattered in the atmosphere must have made the ancients long for death, so as not to endure any more hardship.*

11 They have over them as king the angel of the abyss: his name in Hebrew is Abaddon, and in the Greek tongue he hath the name Apollyon.

*This references the king of the angels of the abyss as Satan. The Greek name Apollyon, has been referenced to Apollo the Sun God. This is more a statement to the deification of Apollo during that time.*

14 one saying to the **sixth angel** that had one trumpet, Loose the **four angels** that are **bound** at the great river **Euphrates**.

15 And the four angels were **loosed**, that had been prepared for the **hour** and **day** and **month** and **year**, that they should **kill** the **third part** of men.

16 And the **number** of the **armies** of the **horsemen** was twice **ten thousand times ten thousand**: I heard the number of them.

17 And thus I saw the horses in the **vision**, and them that sat on them, having **breastplates** as of **fire** and of **hyacinth** and of **brimstone**: and the **heads** of **lions**; and out of their **mouths** proceedeth **fire** and **smoke** and **brimstone**.

18 By these **three plagues** was the **third part** of men **killed**, by the fire and the smoke and the brimstone, which proceeded out of their mouths.

19 For the **power** of the **horses** is in their **mouth**, and in their **tails**: for their tails are **like** unto **serpents**, and have **heads; and with them they hurt.**

*Revelations 9:14 to 9:19 speaks to a catastrophic series of events from a flood, to a protracted meteor storm, and then a plague of insects. The distortion of a massive body in the gravitational field of the earth would cause a massive flood. As the tail of the comet passes over the earth, it will stream projectiles into the atmosphere. The resulting meteors and dust would have an immediate effect on our ecosystem and inhabitants. The river Euphrates has changed course in the past as proven by satellite imaging, as millions of meteorites (barads/horsemen) kill 1/3 of life on the planet.*

20 And the rest of mankind, who were not killed with these plagues, repented not of the works of their hands, that they should not worship demons, and the idols of gold, and of silver, and of brass, and of stone, and of wood; which can neither see, nor hear, nor walk:

*The populace after suffering these tragedies probably clung closer to their old Gods and Idols more than ever.*

*Pillar of Fire*

*"Pillar of cloud-Pillar of fire"*

**CHAPTER 10**

1 And I saw another strong angel coming down out of heaven, arrayed with a cloud; and the rainbow was upon his head, and his face was as the sun, and his feet as pillars of fire;

*Exodus 13:21 And the Lord went before them by day in a pillar of a cloud, to lead them the way; and by night in a pillar of fire, to give them light; to go by day and night.*

*I awed in the marvelous beauty and terror of this photograph. The volcanic activity caused a pillar of fire and ash, with electricity crackling about with the heavens laid above. This is exactly the type of feature that the Hebrews of the Exodus, and many other civilizations around the globe saw at that time in the sky. The comet / proto-planet Venus appeared as a circular cloud with a giant horn (pillar) extended pointing toward the earth. This celestial event has been documented on ancient Roman coins and artwork from around the world. The ancients are relating to us actual events, we just have to decipher what was meant.*

*By day He led them in a pillar of cloud*

*Atharva Veda XI 5-12 Shouting forth, thundering red, white he carries a great penis along the Earth. The Brahmakarin sprinkles seed upon the back of the Earth, through it the four directions live.*

*The "Wheel in the Sky," with extended pillar (Privy Member/penis) radiating Earthward. This Roman coin captures the sight that has been recorded by countless civilizations around the globe. This is the pillar of fire/cloud that the Children of the Exodus witnessed. This is the ladder that Jacob saw in his vision with flaming angels ascending and descending. The comet/Venus came around the neighborhood every forty-nine years (Jubilee Year) and brought destruction with her, as attested by the Mayans, Aztecs, Toltecs, Hebrews, Sumerians, Hindu, Chinese, and Japanese. On this regular path that the comet/Venus took carried her over the Arabian Peninsula toward the Indus Valley to points further East. The object that became worshipped and feared began to settle down over millennia from its cosmic wars and lose its cometary aspects. The wheel also appeared as the Flower of Life that is often depicted in church windows and architectural features. The ancients believed that it was the source of life, it did leave life giving elements in her wake, but robbed us of our former lifespan. I think that a portion of the Children of Israel's journey in the desert was spent in alignment with the path of the item of their worship for forty years.*

*"Opportunus Adest" – It is here at an opportune time!*

*"Opportunus Adest" – It Is Here at an Opportune Time!*

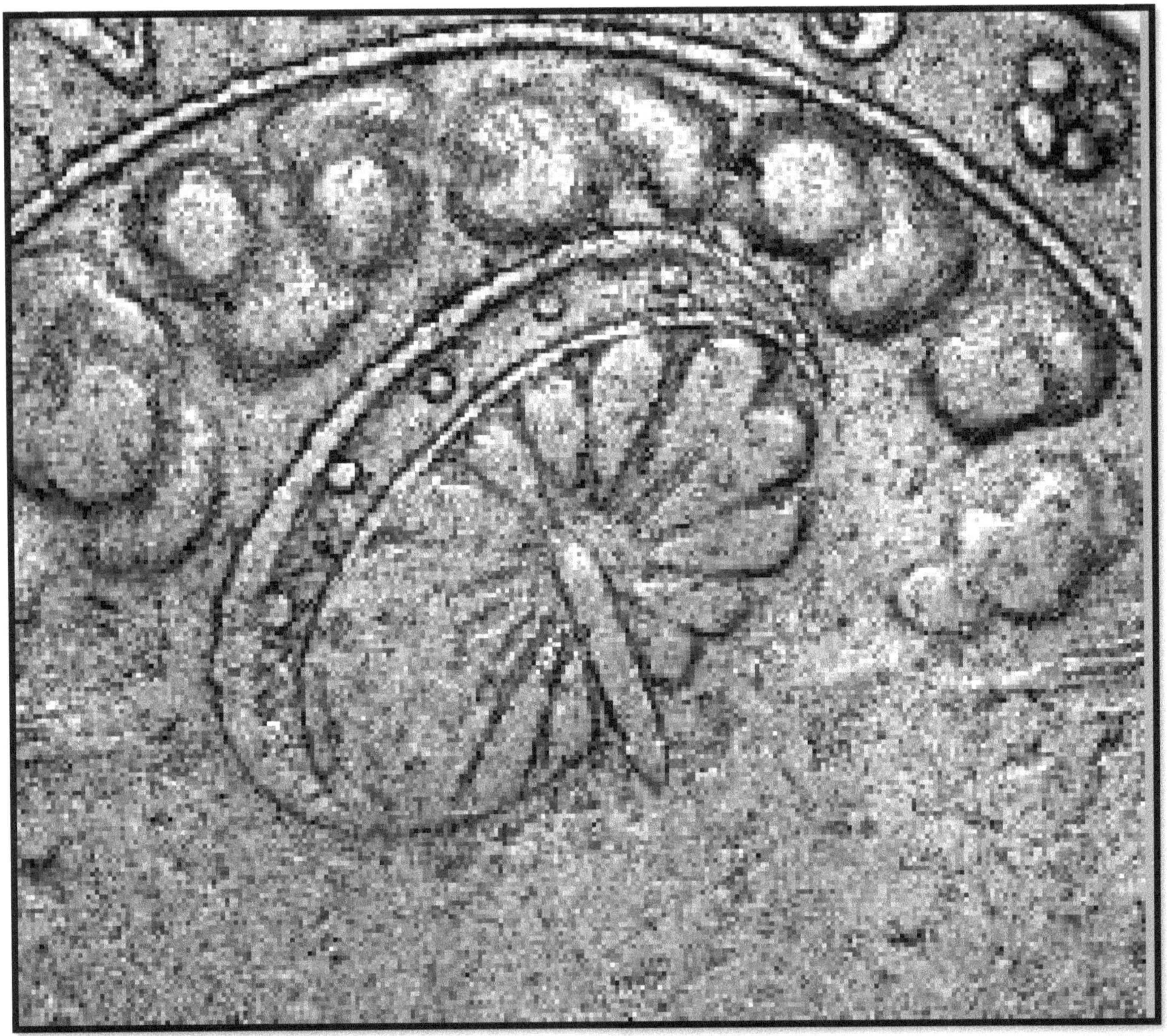

*Roman coin with wheel with flaming privy member*  *Sanskrit coin with Flower of Life – Wheel in the Sky*

*Norway Spiral/Lights 2011 – Failed Russian missile launch?*  *French medal showing the Flower of Life as a shield for Earth*

*Shield in the sky with privy member*

*This cropping of a medieval painting of a Saint sheds a new perspective on the halo. This halo is clearly a wheel with extended privy member!*

Resurrection

*"The Walls Fall Down"*

**CHAPTER 11**

3 And I will give unto my two witnesses, and they shall prophesy a thousand two hundred and threescore days, clothed in sackcloth.

**The period of 3 1/3 years (40 mo.), is again echoed, as they will wear the sackcloth in penitence with the approach of the hairy comet.**

6 These have the power to shut the heaven, that it rain not during the days of their prophecy: and they have power over the waters to turn them into blood, and to smite the earth with every plague, as often as they shall desire.

7 And when they shall have finished their testimony, the beast that cometh up out of the abyss shall make war with them, and overcome them, and kill them.

**The passage of the comet brought drought, disease, pestilence, and the iron sulfide turned the waters and land to blood.**

8 And their dead bodies lie in the street of the great city, which spiritually is called Sodom and Egypt, where also their Lord was crucified.

*The catastrophe caused the dead not to be removed due to the level of the event. The Egyptian God Horus (Mercury) was crucified before the time of Jesus according to Egyptian lore. A short list of deities that were crucified as well include; Prometheus, Adonis, Apollo, Arys, Bacchus, Buddha, Christna, Indra, Mithras, Osiris, Pythagorus, Quetzalcoatl, Semiramis, and Jupiter. There is a list of over thirty deities that were crucified on the cross and the larger amount predate the Christian era. When we look at the astrological references in all of these deities, one must conclude that they are all Gods of the celestial heavens, as religious lessons were taught through the skies to a populace largely incapable of reading or writing.*

*9 And from among the peoples and tribes and tongues and nations do men look upon their dead bodies three days and a half, and suffer not their dead bodies to be laid in a tomb.*

*10 And they that dwell on the earth rejoice over them, and make merry; and they shall send gifts one to another; because these two prophets tormented them that dwell on the earth.*

*11 And after the three days and a half the breath of life from God entered into them, and they stood upon their feet; and great fear fell upon them that beheld them.*

*Here we have the tradition of 3 days dead before resurrection from hell (Hyades) in several traditions. This typically occurs on December 22$^{nd}$, when the sun is at its lowest point on the horizon it sits near the Southern Crux (Cross) constellation (why is the cross located near the Centaur's penis?) and is said to die on the cross. On December 25$^{th}$, the sun begins to rise 1-degree higher on the horizon, as it signals the onset of warmer weather to come. This 3-day period is venerated in Egyptian, Persian, and Christian texts.*

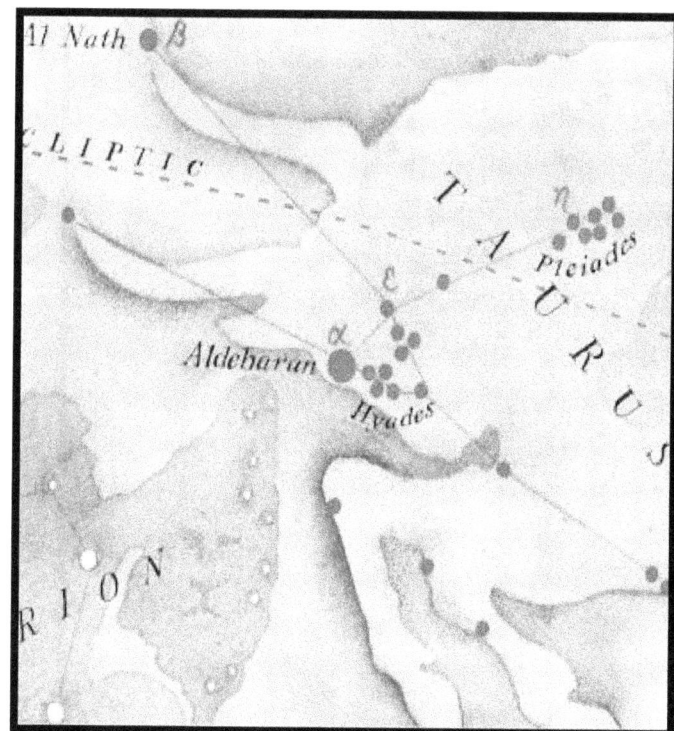
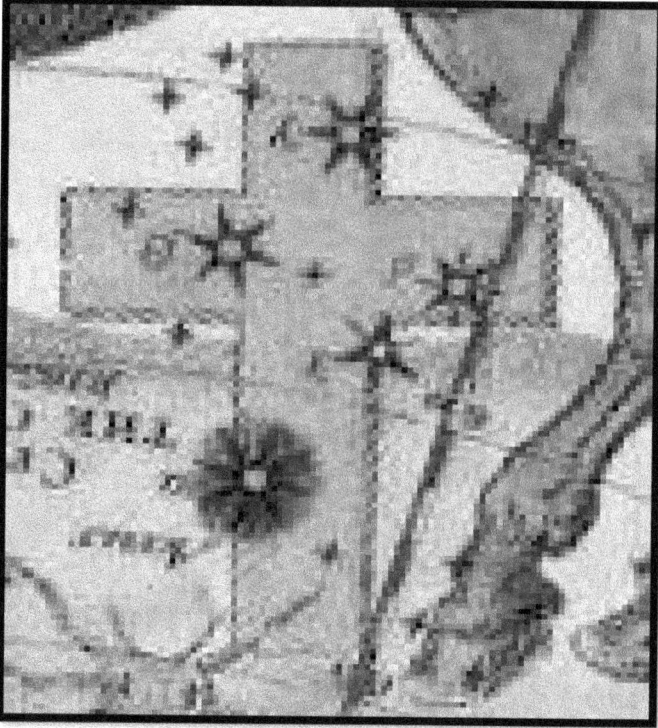

*Hyades (HELL– HADES) constellation*    *Southern Crux (Cross) constellation*

13 And in that hour there was a great earthquake, and the tenth part of the city fell; and there were killed in the **earthquake seven thousand persons**: and the rest were **affrighted**, and gave **glory** to the **God** of **heaven**.

*A devastating earthquake strikes the 2 cities and brings utter devastation. John directly attributes the seven thousand deaths in Sodom and Egypt to an earthquake. The theology states that it was a judgment because of their wickedness, versus a global event as can be attested to by many cultures. These disasters continued to create a power and leadership vacuum, as the once great cities were prime for plunder being weakened through catastrophe.*

"War In Heaven"

# CHAPTER 12

## "Venus versus Mars"

Rev.12:1 And a great sign was seen in heaven; a woman arrayed with the sun, and the moon under her feet, and upon her head a crown of twelve stars;

*This verse that is completely an astrologic reference jumped off the pages at me. On the next page is a reproduction of the Virgin of Guadalupe constellation. A woman arrayed with the sun, refers to the constellation of Virgo that represents the Virgin Mary in Christian faith. And the moon under her feet, and upon her head a crown of twelve stars; the crown is a direct reference to the Corona Borealis constellation that forms a crown on the head of the Virgin. The astrologic conjunction of the constellation Virgo, sun, and the moon signaled the entrance of the comet Venus as a threat to mans survival. The Virgin Mary is often depicted as standing on a crescent moon, and is also referred to as the Queen of Heaven! The way in which John presents this verse shows clear and definitive astrotheology as his fundamental way of relaying cosmic events.*

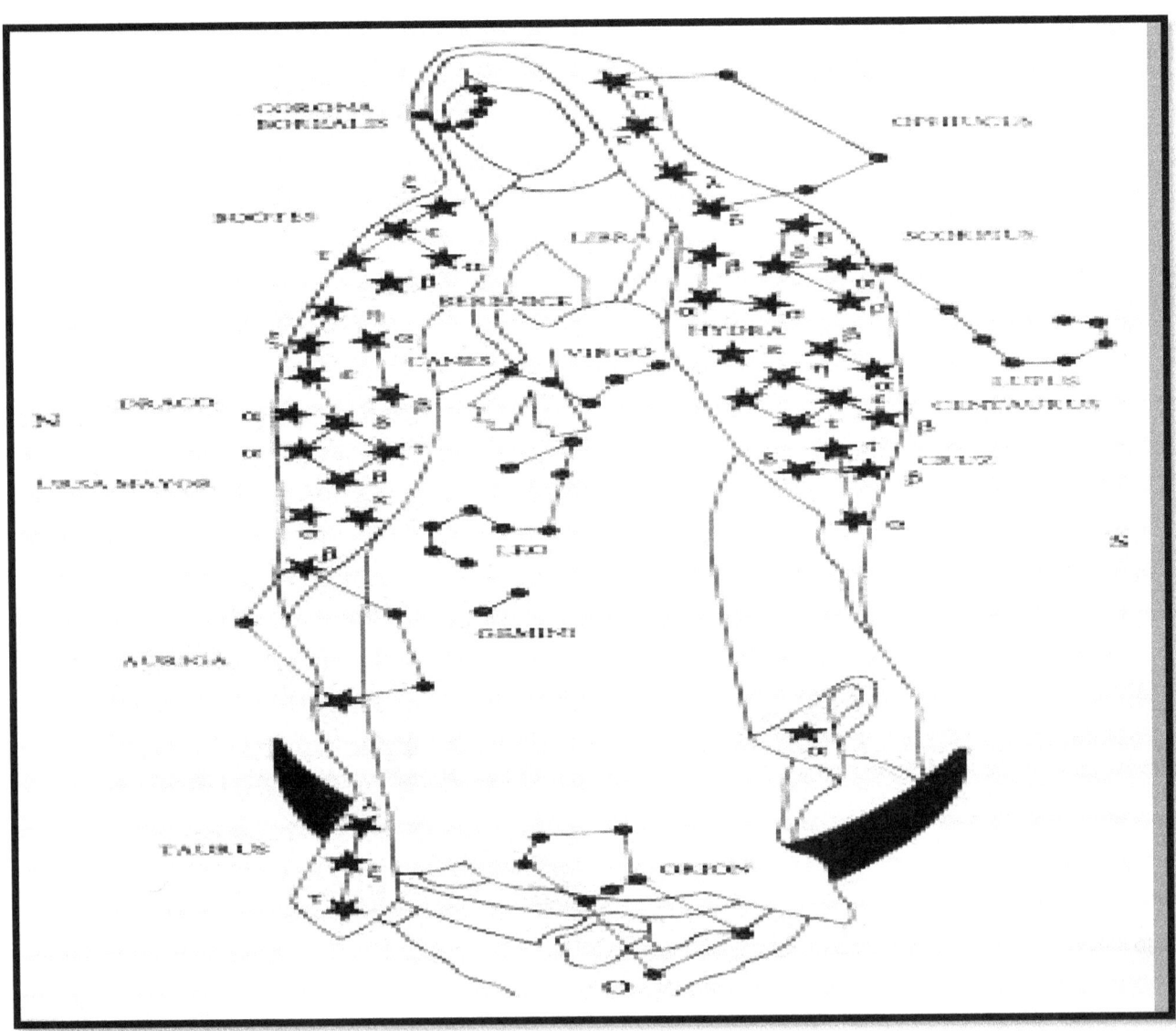

2 and she was the child; and she crieth out, travailing in birth, and in pain to be delivered.

*This symbolizes the Virgin birth of Mary using the cosmic chalkboard.*

3 And there was seen another sign in heaven: and behold, a great red dragon, having seven heads and ten horns, and upon his heads seven diadems.

*The great red dragon, having seven heads (Ages) and ten horns, and upon his head seven diadems (crowns) is a symbolic description of the appearance of Venus as a comet. Cultures around the globe speak of the dragon in the sky or the smoking star. Ancients describe Venus as bringing disaster with her, and being brighter than the sun. The appearance of Venus as a comet streaking across the sky would have resembled a badminton shuttlecock in the sky.*

4 And his tail draweth the third part of the stars of heaven, and did cast them to the earth: and the dragon standeth before the woman that is about to be delivered, that when she is delivered he may devour her child.

*We have another cosmic event that has been related in astrotheology, as the passing tail of the comet would have encompassed the larger part of the heavens. The Water Serpent (Hydra) covers 1/3 of the sky and stands near the constellation of the Virgin that he may devour her newborn. This is prophesied by John, as it is a recollection of the Serpent in the sky bringing disaster from that region.*

5 And she was delivered of a son, a man child, who is to rule all the nations with a rod of iron: and her child was caught up unto God, and unto his throne.

*I believe that the comet entered from the direction of the Virgo constellation, but, she was ascribed as giving birth to it. The age that John wrote during was the Iron Age, and the rod (penis, privy member) was a common tool for measurements.*

6 And the woman fled into the wilderness, where she hath a place prepared of God, that there they may nourish her a thousand two hundred and threescore days.

*The constellation of Virgo retreated from the visible sky with the approach of the comet. The third part of the sentence implies that for 1,230 or 3 1/3 years (41mos.) she was not seen in the visible sky.*

7 And there was war in heaven: Michael and his angels going forth to war with the dragon; and the dragon warred with his angels;

*A collision or near collision between Mars/Sun (Michael) and Venus (Dragon/Satan) played out in the skies above the earth in the distant past. The angels that accompanied Michael (Mars/Sun) were Phobos and Deimos, the moons of Mars.*

8 And they prevailed not, neither was their place found any more in heaven.

*They fought to a standstill with all combatants suffering in the battle, as Mars/Sun and its satellites were displaced from their old order in the cosmos, and Venus lost its cometary tail.*

9 And the great dragon was cast down, the old serpent, he that is called the Devil and Satan, the deceiver of the whole world; he was cast down to the earth, and his angels were cast down with him.

*After this last interstellar battle between the heavenly bodies Venus loses its coma and tail taking a position in orbit within our solar system. I believe that it was this final battle that robbed Mars of its habitability, usurping its atmosphere of water and oxygen, along with a large portion of its iron content. Mars and Venus have both shared the role of demon and savior alike. It was dependent upon the culture, religion, military gains, plagues, pestilence, agricultural plenty or lack, due to these cosmic disturbances. Venus is known by many names in many cultures as the dragon (Dagon = Gonad?), Satan, Azazel, Baalzebub, Quetzocoatl, and more. The deception that John speaks of is in regard to the worship and cults to Venus that arose during these fearful times. Mankind and religions were led astray by the worship of this body as a savior of light aka the devil. When Venus was cast into the sea below the visible horizon it appeared to the ancients that is where she went. This phenomenon is caused by the precession of the planets orbit taking it out of sight for thirteen days before it is resurrected as the Morning Star.*

10 And I heard a great voice in heaven saying, Now is come the salvation, and the power, and the kingdom of our God, and the authority of his Christ: for the accuser of our brethren is cast down, who accuseth them before our God day and night.

*The salvation of the earth was now complete, as the accuser (Venus-Satan) was sent to Hell (Hyades constellation). Venus is represented on the zodiac chart by the constellation of Libra, whose symbol is the Scales of balance. Scales have always been seen as a check and balance for sins, good & evil, pain & pleasure, and Venus stood as the balancer and accuser of mankind.*

11 And they overcame him because of the blood of the Lamb, and because of the word of their testimony; and they loved not their life even unto death.

*John makes this statement to enforce that it was because of their faith they were overcome.*

12 Therefore rejoice, O heavens, and ye that dwell in them. Woe for the earth and for the sea: because the devil is gone down unto you, having great wrath, knowing that he hath but a short time.

*This verse tells all that salvation has come as Venus is no longer the threat that it was. Woe for the sea, as many meteors fell to the bottom causing issues for the planet. John expects another flare-up from Satan/Venus based on known timeframes.*

13 And when the dragon saw that he was cast down to the earth, he persecuted the woman that brought forth the man child.

*This could be a reference to Venus taking an orbit in line with the constellation of Virgo. This can also refer to the Coma Berenice constellation that sits above Virgo. Berenice is depicted as a mop-haired comet named after the famous Queen.*

14 And there was given unto the woman the two wings of the great eagle, that she might fly into the wilderness unto her place where she is nourished for a time, and times, and half a time, from the face of the serpent.

*The constellation of the Virgin typically shows a woman with angel's wings, and the great Eagle is the constellation of Cancer. The wilderness and time reference may apply to the disaster or zodiac movements.*

15 And he cast out of his mouth after the woman water as a river, that he might cause her to be carried away by the stream.

*The water as a river is a reference to the Cetus (Sea Monster) constellation.*

16 And the earth helped the woman, and the earth opened her mouth and swallowed up the river which the dragon cast out of his mouth.

*This refers to the vaults of heaven opening up. The water that the earth was deluged with by the passing comet inundated the earth with a catastrophic amount of water that the Dragon (Venus) cast from his mouth.*

## "The War in Heaven in Art"

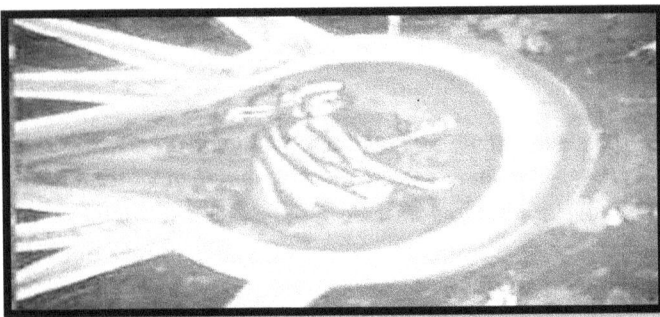

Venus                                                                                           Mars

**This painting titled, "The Crucifixion," sits above the altar at the Visoki Decani Monastery in Kosovo, Yugoslavia. This painting dates back to 1350 AD, and depicts the Cricifixion of Christ. The painting has come under scrutiny in recent years as it seems to depict a UFO pursuit through the skies in the background. The two streaking craftlike objects do seem to be some sort of flying vehicle with a female pilot chasing a male pilot that is checking behind to see how close she is to catching him. This is our**

proverbial "War in Heaven!" Venus (female) chases Mars (male) through the heavens in a cosmic battle that left both planets utter wastes. I have shown throughout the book how Jesus Christ has been linked to Venus and the zodiac in symbolism and statements several times. The ancients often synthesized two events into one, as actual contacts or events become joined.

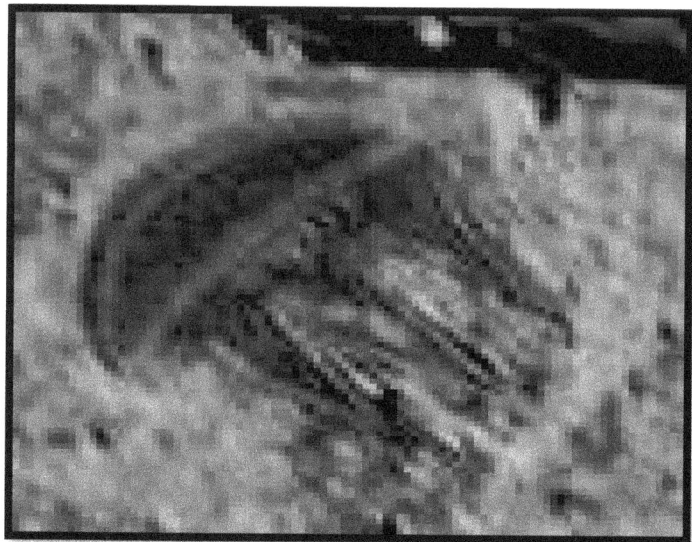
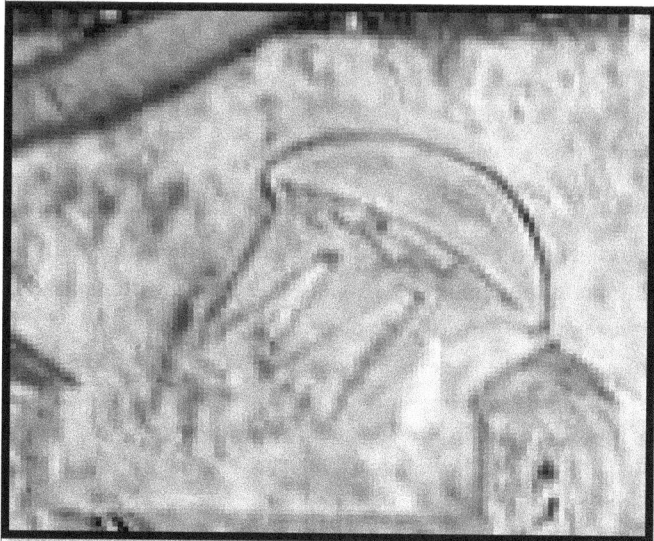

This painting of the Crucifixion stored in Svetishoveli Cathedral in Mtskheta, Georgia appear to be some sort of UFO, but once again represent Venus (female face) and Mars (male face).

 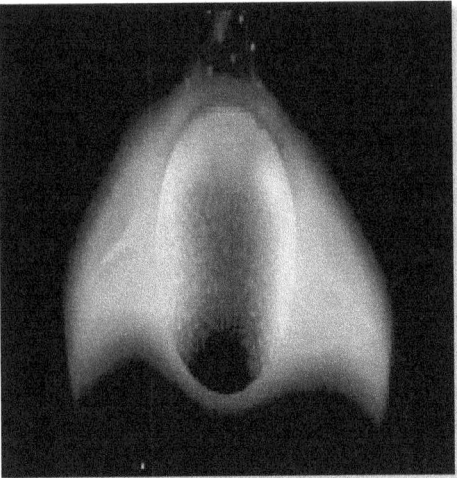 

Nuns Habit  |  Artist conception of planet Nibiru  |  Flying Nun show from 1967-1970

The Nun's habit (Cornette) with exaggerated wings have long been a point of puzzlement, from the television show "The Flying Nun," to Nuns that we have seen our whole lives long. As the artist conception of the planet Nibiru shows, we have been mimicking the comet/Venus as she appeared streaking through the skies in ancient periods. The imagery has been before us all along, we need but link these images together as they are shown.

## The Beast

"666?" - Purposely placed in unlucky chapter 13

## CHAPTER 13

1 and he stood upon the sand of the sea. And I saw a beast coming up out of the sea, having ten horns, and seven heads, and on his horns ten diadems, and upon his heads names of blasphemy.

*After another in a series of disasters between Venus and Mars, Mars rises above the horizon with Phobos & Deimos driving his war chariot and meteors accompanying them. The names of blasphemy pertain to the cults, cultures, and many names given to Mars.*

2 And the beast which I saw was like unto a leopard, and his feet were as the feet of a bear, and his mouth as the mouth of a lion; and the dragon gave him his power, and his throne, and great authority.

*I could not decipher the Leopard (Leopardalis constellaton?) symbolism, but, the bear is a reference to Ursa Major or Ursa Minor, and the Lion is Leo. I believe this to be a statement that backs up one of Mr. Velikofsky's primary theories. The dragon (Venus) gave him (Mars) his power, and his throne (order), and great authority (destroyer). Mr. Velilovsky posited the theory that a collision between Mars and Venus in the not too distant past caused a switch between the two planets in their position (throne) in the heavens.*

3 And I saw one of his heads as though it had been smitten unto death; and his death-stroke was healed: and the whole earth wandered after the beast;

*Mr. Velikovsky also theorized that a plasma discharge between Venus and Mars resulted in a massive trauma to Mars. The death-stroke that was healed is the large scar on the planet (Valles Marinaris). With Mars bringing destruction to Earth on a periodic basis, cults and worshippers sprang up around the globe.*

4 and they worshipped the dragon, because he gave his authority unto the beast; and they worshipped the beast, saying, Who is like unto the beast? And who is able to war with him?

*The worship of Venus had long been a fixture in antiquity since her emergence with cults in the Middle East, Africa, The Mediterranean, The Indus Valley, Europe, South America, and the Far East. Venus began to settle in as a normal resident, as Mars became the destroyer of note. Venus probably lost her cometary aspects gradually over the course of hundreds of years and exchanges with bodies in our area of the solar system. The other cults and religions in the region gave their worship and praise to Mars, and not to the God of John.*

5 and there was given to him a mouth speaking great things and blasphemies; and there was given unto him authority to continue forty and two months.

*This statement echoes the 3 1/3 yrs. period that the Virgin (Virgo) spends in the wilderness being nourished after giving birth to the Lamb (Southern Crux).*

11 And I saw another beast coming up out of the earth; and he had two horns like unto lamb, and he spake as a dragon.

*As Mars rises from below the ecliptic plane after the collision with Venus, it now bears horns similar to Venus from transference of cometary and planetary debris.*

12 And he exerciseth all the authority of the first beast in his sight. And he maketh the earth and them dwell therein to worship the first beast, whose death-stroke was healed.

*With its' newfound look, Mars, has become the heavy hand that will affect the earth for some time to come. The denizens of earth now fearing destruction at the hands of Mars begin to worship Venus as their savior.*

13 And he doeth great **signs**, that he should even make fire to come down out of heaven upon the earth in the sight of men.

*The passage of the planet periodically during this period brought impending terror, as flaming meteors rained down on the Earth with its' passage.*

14 And he deceiveth them that dwell on the earth by reason of the **signs** which it was given him to do in the sight of the beast; saying to them that dwell on earth, that they should make an image to the beast who hath the stroke of the sword and lived.

*The populace of the planet fearing near total destruction, begin to make graven images once again to Mars as a deity.*

16 that there be given them a mark on their right hand, or even upon their **forehead**;

*Forehead marking and branding was a common practice of some of these cults in antiquity, as we still follow along those lines by having a cross placed on our foreheads on Ash Wednesday, as we are marked Children of God!*

18 **Here is wisdom**. He that **hath understanding**, let him **count** the **number** of the **beast**; for it is the **number** of a **man**: and **his number is Six hundred and sixty and six.**

*This statement has been interpreted to be many people, most notably a parallel to Caesar Nero. The numerical equivalent to his name in the Greek alphabet is 666, thus, most historians and theologians believe it to be a reference to Nero, since it is believed that John lived during this epoch. I have found another possible clue! The bible has related that King Solomon received 666 talents of gold a year. A talent in the Middle-East during that time was about 57 pounds. That would be an annual gold intake of 37,962 pounds. If this amount were multiplied over 40 years of rulership, the total would be 1,518,480 pounds of gold! This is an astronomical amount of gold, and maybe John felt that this type of wealth acquisition went against the doctrines of the faith. Maybe this is the wisdom that John speaks of? The use of "score" or a "20" count (finger/toes) is another link to the Maya and Mesoamerica.*

> *1st Kings 10:14 Now the weight of gold that came to Solomon in one year was six hundred threescore and six talents of gold, (666)*

**2ND Chronicles 9:13** *Now the weight of gold that came to Solomon in one year was six hundred and threescore and six talents of gold;* (666)

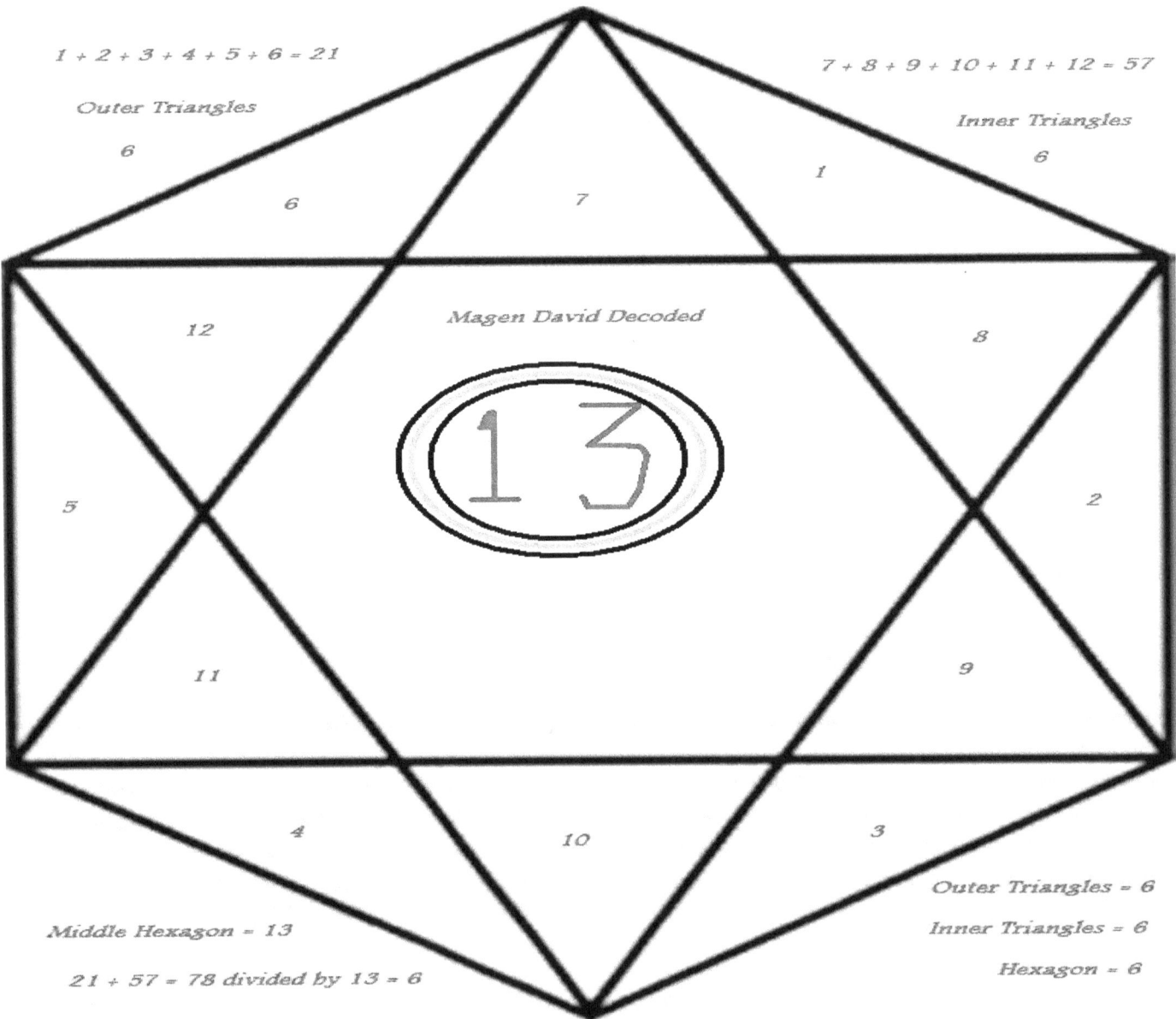

2/19/2012 – Gold = $1,722.93 ounce

666 Talents = 37, 962lbs

$ 27,566.88lb x 57lbs = @ 10.7 Billion Annual

10.7 Billion x 40 years = @ 428 Billion

This only accounts for the possible annual gold intake

$1 + 2 + 3 + 4 + 5 + 6 = 21$
Outer Triangles

$7 + 8 + 9 + 10 + 11 + 12 = 57$
Inner Triangles

Magen David Decoded

Middle Hexagon = 13
$21 + 57 = 78$ divided by $13 = 6$

Outer Triangles = 6
Inner Triangles = 6
Hexagon = 6

**Outer Triangles:** 6   **Inner Triangles:** 6   **Hexagon:** 6   **TOTAL:** 666

The symbol known as the Star of David, Magen David, Star of Remphan, Star of Molech, and more, has on a symbolic level been decoded. The Shield of David was adopted in the 17th century CE as a symbol to represent the Jewish faithful, and in the 18th century came to represent the Zionist Movement and has been adopted as the symbol of the state of Israel. The Kabbalist began use of the Star of David as early as the 3rd century CE. The star is also known from the Seals of Solomon, such as the Seal of Saturn!

The Star of David is a symbol that has stretched way back into antiquity, and whose use was predated by many other cultures. The symbol has been used by the Egyptians in the "As Above – So Below," of philosophy, alchemy, Hinduism, Buddhism, Shinto, and many other cultures and religions. I believe this decoding to be just one level of a complex much studied and worshipped symbol throughout remembered history.

*13 Unlucky      13 Witches = Coven      13 Original Colonies      13th Amendment - Freed Slaves*
*13 Wooden sticks in a Fasces      Chapter 13 - Bankrupcy      Venus Synod Cycle - 13 days in hell*
*Revelations Chapter 13 = 666      13 years to build Solomon's Temple      13 Baktuns-Mayan Calendar (2012)*
*13th Zodiac sign - Ophiuchus constellation aka Lost Tribe of Israel*

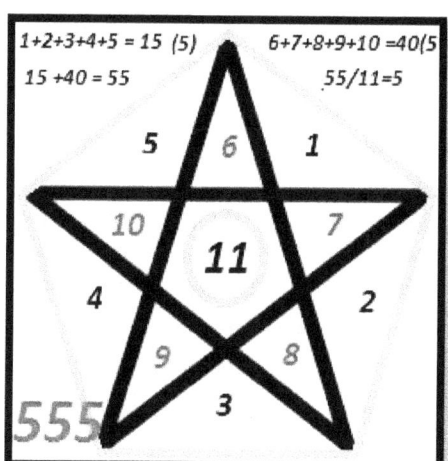 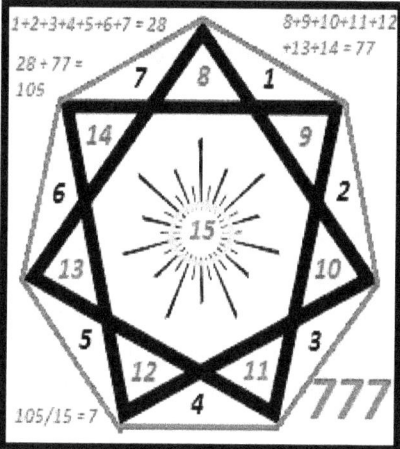 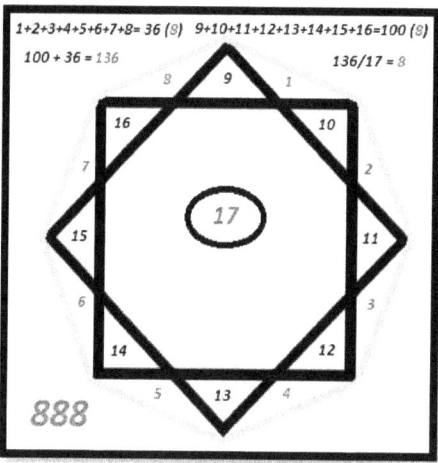

555 - (11)          777 (15)          888 (17)

*The mathematical aproach to solving the 5, 6, 7, and 8 pointed stars holds acurate for those shapes*

Chapter 14

**Fallen is Babylon**

"Grapes of Wrath"

1 And I saw, and behold, the Lamb standing on the mount Zion, and with him a hundred and forty and four thousand, having his name, and the name of his Father, written on their **foreheads**.

**John references the 144,000 from the Tribe of Judah that will carry a mark with the name of God and the Lamb written on their foreheads. This is yet again a reference to the Mayan Baktun tradition of 144,000 days (394.26 years) per Baktun.**

8 And another, a second angel, followed saying, Fallen, fallen is Babylon the great, that hath made all the nations to drink of the wine of the wrath of her fornication.

*This is a reference to prior times when Babylon was the Las Vegas, New York, and Paris, of the Middle East. Babylon was a seat of knowledge, teaching, religion, arts, architecture, and carnal delights. Babylon was looked upon by other cultures as the ultimate cosmopolitan center of the day.*

14 And I saw, and behold, a white cloud; and on the cloud I saw one sitting like unto a son of man, having on his head a golden crown, and in his hand a sharp sickle.

*This is Mars yet again bringing disaster to the Earth. The constellation Bootes is often pictured with a sickle in hand and the Corona Borealis (crown) constellation sits across from Bootes in the heavens.*

19 And the angel cast his sickle into the earth, and gathered the vintage of the earth, and cast it into the winepress, the great winepress, of the wrath of God.

*Another passage of Mars leaves red dust with a high metallic content all over the globe. Crops failed as they were stunted and famine took hold, and this was related as caused by God's wrath.*

20 And the winepress are trodden without the city, and there came out blood from the winepress, even unto the bridles of the horses, as far as a thousand and **six hundred furlongs**.

*The soil and water became as blood, as the metallic ore poisoned the land and sea. Animals that had the dust covering them became sick, and the land was smitten for seventy-five miles.*

### Beasts & Blood

## CHAPTER 16

### "Har-Megiddo"

2 And the first went, and poured out his bowl into the earth; and it became a noisome and grievous sore upon the men that had the mark of the beast, and that worshipped his image.

*The cometary debris begins to cover the globe with its strong iron sulfide content. These poisons that have been seeded upon the earth begin to affect mankind. The subjective allocation of the sores upon men, were more based on the debris path versus theology.*

3 And the second poured out his bowl into the sea; and it became blood as of a dead man; and every living soul died, even the things that were in the sea.

*The debris begins to affect the water as the larger portion of sea-life died from the sulphur and metallic content that was deposited.*

4 And the third poured out his bowl into the rivers and the fountains of the waters; and it became blood.

*The rivers and streams that dump into the larger bodies of water begin to show the same affect as only water in covered containers would have remained potable.*

5 And I heard the angel of the waters saying, Righteous art thou, who art and who wast, thou Holy One, because thou didst thus judge:

6 for they poured out the blood of the saints and the prophets, and blood hast thou given them to drink: they are worthy.

*The theology is that the current disaster is due to the past deaths of saints, that this has befallen man. As they have spilled blood, so shall they now have blood to drink.*

7 And I heard the altar saying, Yea, O Lord God, the Almighty, true and righteous are thy judgments.

*The altar (Ara) speaks praises as this is where the Beast (Cetus) is to be sacrificed.*

8 And the fourth poured out his bowl upon the sun; and it was given unto it to scorch men with fire.

9 And men were scorched men with great heat: and they blasphemed the name of God who hath the power over these plagues; and they repented not to give him glory.

**The passage of the comet obliterates the sun as it passes before it causing a dramatic temperature increase on the planet, possibly due to the thermal atmospheric tide.**

10 And the fifth poured out his bowl upon the throne of the beast; and his kingdom was darkened; and they gnawed their tongues for pain,

11 and they blasphemed the God of heaven because of their pains and their sores; and they repented not of their works.

**The next series of events causes the Earth to fall into a protracted darkness, as a heavenly body puts (Venus/Mars) the Earth in the umbra or a penumbra of an eclipse as diseases like leprosy abound.**

12 And the sixth poured out his bowl upon the great river, the river Euphrates; and the water thereof was dried up, that the way might be made ready for the kings that come from the sunrising.

**The water of the Euphrates River changed course due to meteoric deposition, drained , or dried out due to the extreme Earth changes taking place.**

13 And I saw coming out of the mouth of the dragon, and out of the mouth of the beast, and out of the mouth of the false prophet, three unclean spirits, as it were frogs:

**The collision between the two heavenly bodies leaves them with the appearance of bladed tongues (frogs) coming from their faces.**

14 for they are spirits of **demons**, working **signs**; which go forth unto the kings of the whole world, to gather them together unto the war of the great day of God, the Almighty.

**The astrotheology relates the planets (spirits) that are behaving unpleasantly, as demons working signs in the heavens they prepare for God's great day.**

15 (Behold, I come as a thief. Blessed is he that watcheth, and keepeth his garments, lest he walked naked, and they see his shame.)

**This relates that the event will come upon mankind without warning and one must be vigilant, lest they be caught with their clothing off and must flee while naked. I guess this is the genesis for the term being, "caught with your pants down!"**

16 And they gathered them together into the place which is called in Hebrew Har-magedon.

**This has been the second most feared and misunderstood place in history. It is called Harmagedon and Har-Megiddo, among other names. This is the supposed location of the final battle between good and evil. This was an area in antiquity that sat at a vital military and trade crossroads, and was the scene of many conflagrations. The word Armageddon has become synonymous with the end times prophecies of the book of Revelations. The spiritual enslavement of the masses by those that manipulate this fearful doctrine for their own purpose has proliferated upon the planet.**

17 And the seventh poured out his bowl upon the air; and there came forth a great voice out of the temple, from the throne, saying, It is done:

18 and there were lightnings, and voices, and thunders; and there was a great earthquake, such as was not since there were men upon the earth, so great an earthquake, so mighty.

*The Earth moans from the gravitational disturbance of the passing body. The electrical discharges from a positively charged and negatively charged body caused lightning and thunderstorms on a cosmic level around the Earth. This worldwide quake was of a nature unseen by man since that event.*

19 And the great city was divided into three parts, and the cities of the nations fell: and Babylon the great was remembered in the sight of God, to give unto her the cup of the wine of the fierceness of his wrath.

*The cosmic disturbances, yet again breaks down civilization as traditionally strong nations begin to be plundered by bands and tribes of other peoples. Babylon is still fondly remembered as God destroys her for her iniquities with His Cup (Crater) of wrath.*

Rev.16:20 And every island fled away, and the mountains were not found.

*Islands and mountains that formerly stood above ground now lay below, as the topography begins to change because of these disasters.*

21 And great hail, every stone about the weight of a talent, cometh down out of heaven upon men: and men blasphemed God because of the plague of the hail; for the plague thereof is exceeding great.

*The tail of the comet distributes substantial sized meteorites upon the planet. A talent in ancient times was around fifty-seven pounds. The specter of a sky filled with flaming rocks that hit the Earth at terminal velocity was enough to cause mankind of all faiths to curse God (all Gods?) because of this barrage.*

## Mother of Harlots

## CHAPTER 17

1 And there came one of the seven angels that had the seven bowls, and spake with me, saying, Come hither, I will show thee the judgment of the great harlot that sitteth upon many waters;

2 with whom the kings of the earth committed fornication, and they that dwell in the earth were made drunken with the wine of her fornication.

*Rev. 17:1 & 17:2 are yet again more indictments against Babylon, and the sway that she held over men with her culture and life style. 7 angels, 7 bowls = 7 planets!*

3 And he carried me away in the Spirit into a wilderness: and I saw a woman sitting upon a scarlet-colored beast, full of names of blasphemy, having seven heads and ten horns.

*Venus is the woman sitting upon a scarlet-colored beast (Cetus). Cetus strides the outer portion of the zodiac wheel near Taurus, and spans the Ages of Aries and Pisces. John expects upheaval to come during the Age of Pisces (Was/Is/Yet!).*

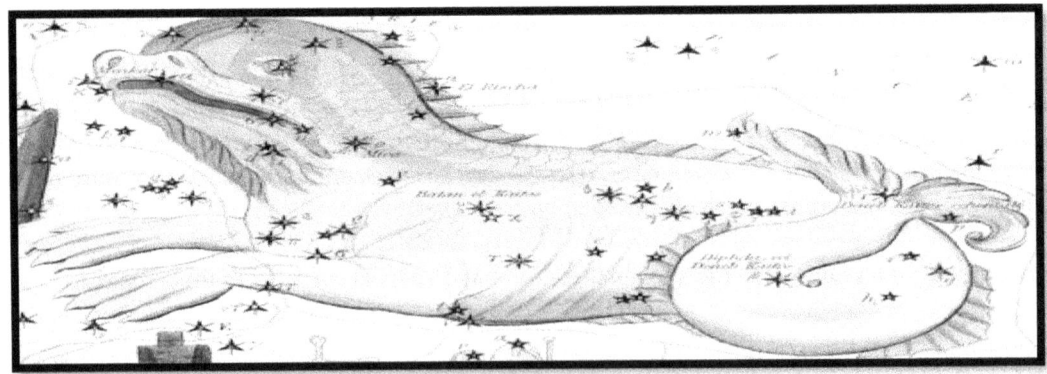

*"The Beast" – Cetus constellation*

Rev.17:4 And the woman was arrayed in purple and scarlet, and decked with gold and precious stone and pearls, having in her hand a golden cup full of abominations, even the unclean things of her fornication,

Rev.17:5 and upon her forehead a name written, **MYSTERY, BABYLON THE GREAT, THE MOTHER OF THE HARLOTS AND OF THE ABOMINATIONS OF THE EARTH.**

Rev.17:6 And I saw the woman drunken with the blood of the saints, and with the blood of the martyrs of Jesus. And when I saw her, I wondered with a great wonder.

Rev.17:7 And the angel said unto me, Wherefore didst thou wonder? I will tell thee the mystery of the **woman**, and of the **beast** that carrieth her, which hath the **seven heads** and the **ten horns**.

Rev.17:8 The beast that thou sawest **was**, and **is not**; and is **about** to come up out of the **abyss**, and to go into **perdition**. And they that dwell on the earth shall wonder, they whose name hath not been written in the book of life from the foundation of the world, when they behold the beast, how that he was, and is not, and shall come.

Rev.17:9 Here is the **mind** that hath **wisdom**. The **seven heads** are **seven mountains**, on which the woman sitteth:

Rev.17:10 and they are **seven kings**; the **five** are **fallen**, the one **is,** the other is **not yet come**; and when **he cometh**, he must **continue** a **little while**.

*The comet/Venus (Phaeton?) appeared to have crowns, horns, and tails, as she blazed through the sky. Venus descends into the abyss (horizon) and is reborn later. The seven heads, mountains, and kings, are a reference to the Zodiac Ages. Modern man is believed to have existed as far back as 10-12K years ago. This would put us at the start of the Age of Leo as cognizant beings with opposable thumbs. John was waiting and watchful of impending doom from the stars, as the Age of Aries killed more of mankind than any previous period of existence. Five ages had passed (150 BCE to 10,949 BCE; Aries, Taurus, Gemini, Cancer, and Leo) during John's time as he lived in the Age of Pisces as, "the one is." The one that is yet to come is the Age of Aquarius that begins possibly on December 21, 2012. John curiously shares the same end of Age date as the Mayan Calendar, which suggests a common genesis for these world ages, understanding (misunderstandings!), and dates. How could John have come up with the same date as the Mayan/Aztecs who based their calendar on the cycles of Venus! This statement reinforces my theory of why the Mayans recognized Christianity when it was brought to them by the Spanish missionaries. "The beast that was, and is not, and yet is," is also a reference to Cetus as that constellation sits between Aries and Pisces in the sky and spans the two Ages.* Daniel/Belteshazzar the Prophet speaks of Ten Horns in his Old Testament book.

*Was: When it spanned the sky during the Age of Aries*

*Is not: When it spanned the sky on the cusp of Aries transition to Pisces*

*Shall come: It still spans the sky during a portion of the Age of Pisces*

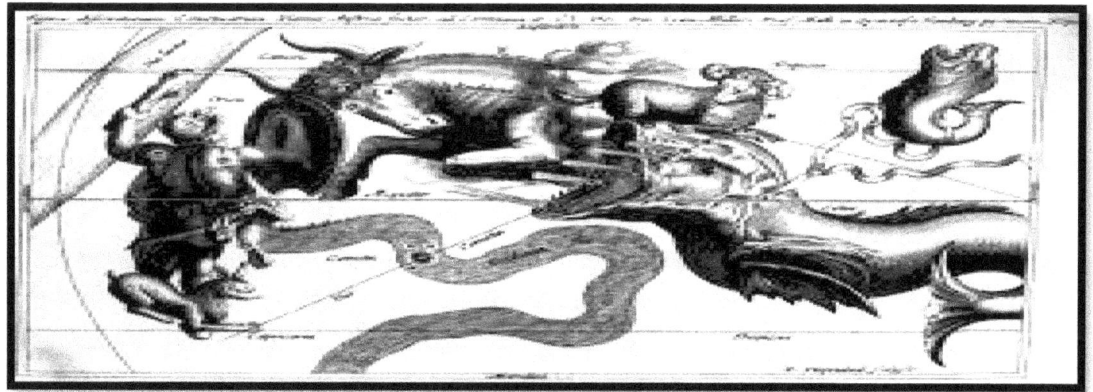

*Cetus(Beast) spans Aries, and the Pisces constellations in this zodiac arrangement*

*The apocalyptic mindset that ran rampant worldwide is quite understandable given my viewpoint 4-5K years later. One can only imagine the horrors at that time, as we have become desensitized from the tragedies and minor disasters that we see nightly on the news. These events do not hit home, until they hit home!*

*Zodiac Age = 2,160 years (i.e. – Kings, Mountains, Diadems/Crowns)*

| Zodiac Age (Kings) | Start Date | End Date |
|---|---|---|
| 1st Leo | 10,949 BCE | 8790 BCE |
| 2nd Cancer | 8789 BCE | 6630 BCE |
| 3rd Gemini | 6,629 BCE | 4470 BCE |
| 4th Taurus | 4469 BCE | 2309 BCE |
| 5th Aries | 2308 BCE | 151 BCE |
| 6th Pisces | 150 BCE | 2011 BCE |
| 7th Aquarius | 2012 AD | 4172 AD |

*\* John lived near the early portion of the Age of Pisces. The Ages are based on common timelines*

11 And the beast that was, and is not, is himself also an eighth, and is of the seven; and he goeth into perdition.

*The beast that was the comet/Venus began to lose her coma and massive tail as she goes beneath the horizon into perdition. John believes that in the 8th Age of Capricorn is when the beast (Cetus/Venus) will go into perdition.*

12 And the ten horns that thou sawest are ten kings, who have received no kingdom as yet; but they receive authority as kings, with the beast, for one hour.

*The ten kings have been noted to be various nations during the past and present history.*

Woe, Woe

## CHAPTER 18

*"Dust on their heads"*

2 And he cried with a mighty voice, saying, Fallen, fallen is Babylon the great, and is become a habitation of demons, and a hold of every unclean spirit, and a hold of every unclean and hateful bird.

3 For by the wine of the wrath of her fornication all the nations are fallen; and the kings of the earth committed fornication with her, and the merchants of the earth waxed rich by the power of her wantonness.

10 standing afar off for the fear of her torment, saying, Woe, woe, the great city, Babylon, the strong city! For in one hour is thy judgment come.

*John is making reference to Babylon's prior destruction. There is a continual demonization of the practices of Babylon's citizens.*

19 And they cast dust on their heads, and cried, weeping and mourning, saying, Woe, woe, the great city, wherein all that had their ships in the sea were made rich by reason of her costliness! For in one hour is she made desolate.

*Casting dust on one's head is seen as an act of penitence for sins committed. The ships that were not in the harbors and ports when the devastation occurred were spared their vessels. I believe the fact that Babylonian vessels at sea were spared, shows us this particular event was location based, versus sin based against Babylon.*

Sword in Mouth

CHAPTER 19

"Diadems"

7 Let us rejoice and be exceeding glad, and let us give the glory unto him: for the **marriage** of the Lamb is come, and his wife hath made herself ready.

*This curious statement about the marriage of the lamb and his wife hath made herself ready? The concept of a deity having a mate or consort holds in Egyptian, Canaanite, Mesopotamian, and many other cultures. The Hebrew/Christian sect the Essenes, Book of Revelations states; the seven stars are the Angels of the Heavenly Father, And the seven stars are the Angels of the Earthly Mother. The traditional Judeo-Christian theology does not have a male-female union at the God level.*

11 and I saw the heaven opened; and behold, a white horse, and he that sat thereon called Faithful and True; and in righteous he doth judge and make war.

12 And his eyes are a flame of fire, and upon his head are many diadems; and he hath a name written which no one knoweth but he himself.

13 And he is arrayed in a garment sprinkled with blood: and his name is called The Word of God.

**Rev. 19:11 to 13 This is yet another reference to Venus, as the comet streaked across the sky with her tail and many meteor fragments following. The toll that this comet/proto-planet took on the earth has been extremely profound.**

*Above is a Mycanae royal crown having seven diadems (years) and seven circles (planets) each (7 x 7 = 49 = A Jubilee Year). This cropped and rotated view shows what looks like a comet streaking across the sky. This crown dates to circa 1600 BCE, which dovetails into an excellent timeline of disasters based on the Bible and sacred texts.*

14 And the armies which are in heaven followed him upon white horses, clothed in fine linen, white and pure.

*The comet's tail trailed meteoric debris with it.*

15 And out of his mouth proceedeth a sharp sword, that with it he should smite the nations: and he shall rule them with a rod of iron: and he treadeth the winepress of the fierceness of the wrath of God, the Almighty.

*The comet appears to have a sharp tongue protruding from its mouth that will smite the nations. The rod is the common measuring tool, and iron is the age that they were in. The resulting catastrophe brought drought, plague, pestilence, and failed crops.*

    *Mayan Calendar Wheel*              *Kali Ma – India*              *Jesus Christ*

16 And he hath on his garment and on his thigh a name written, KINGS OF KINGS, AND LORD OF LORDS.

17 And I saw an angel standing in the sun; and he cried with a loud voice, saying to all the birds that fly in mid heaven, Come and be gathered together unto the great supper of God;

*The angel standing in the Sun may be the constellation of Scorpio as it is also represented by an eagle on the zodiac chart. The birds that fly in mid-heaven and are invited to the feast are the Raven (Corvus), the Swan (Cygnus), and the Eagle (Aquila).*

  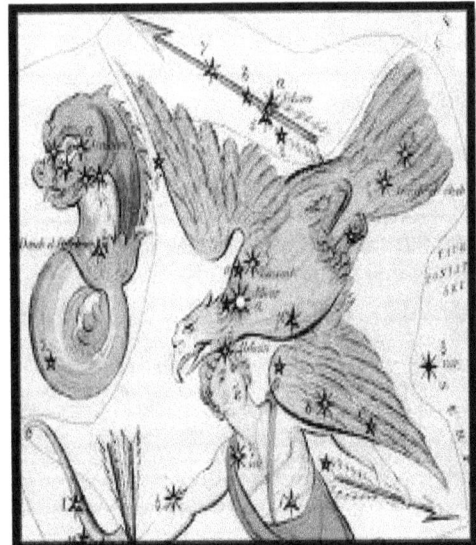

    *Raven (Corvus)*              *Cygnus (Swan)*             *Eagle (Aquila)*

18 that ye may eat the flesh of kings, and the flesh of captains, and the flesh of mighty men, and the flesh of horses and of them that sit thereon, and the flesh of all men, both free and bond, and small and great.

**The comet/Venus was an equal opportunity destroyer of men, as station, rank, and theology bore no witness in who would be saved.**

19 And I saw the beast, and the kings of the earth, and their armies, gathered together to make war against him that sat upon the horse, and against his army.

20 And the beast was taken, and with him the **false prophet** that wrought the signs in his sight, wherewith he deceived them that had received the mark of the beast and them that worshipped his image: they two were cast alive into the lake of fire that burneth with brimstone:

21 and the rest were killed with the sword of him that sat upon the horse, even the sword which came forth out of his mouth: and all the birds were filled with their flesh.

**The cults to Venus and Mars that arose in the region were decimated from the passage of the thing that they bore worship to, and their corpses were eaten by the scavengers.**

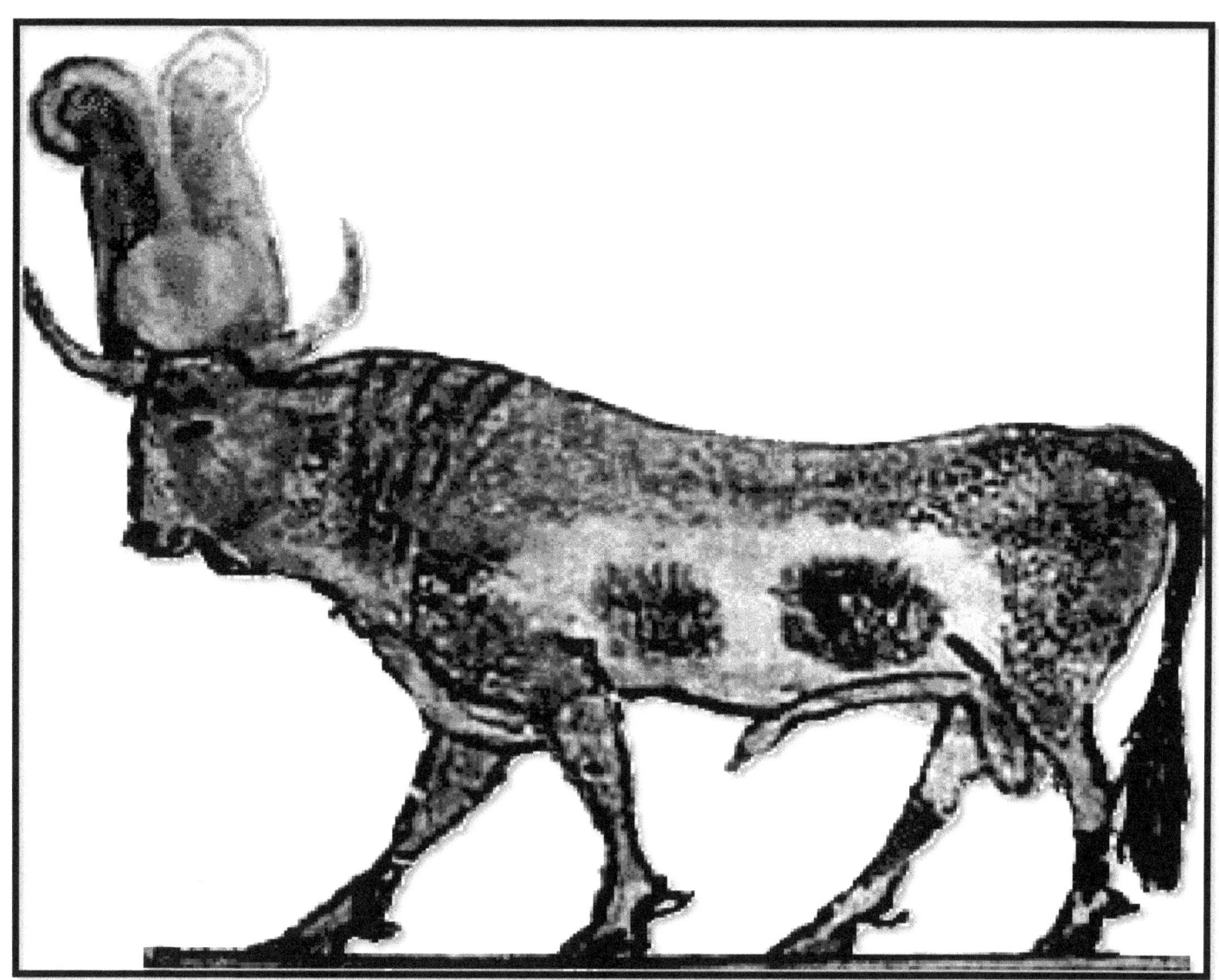

*Apis Bull – Egypt – Venus*

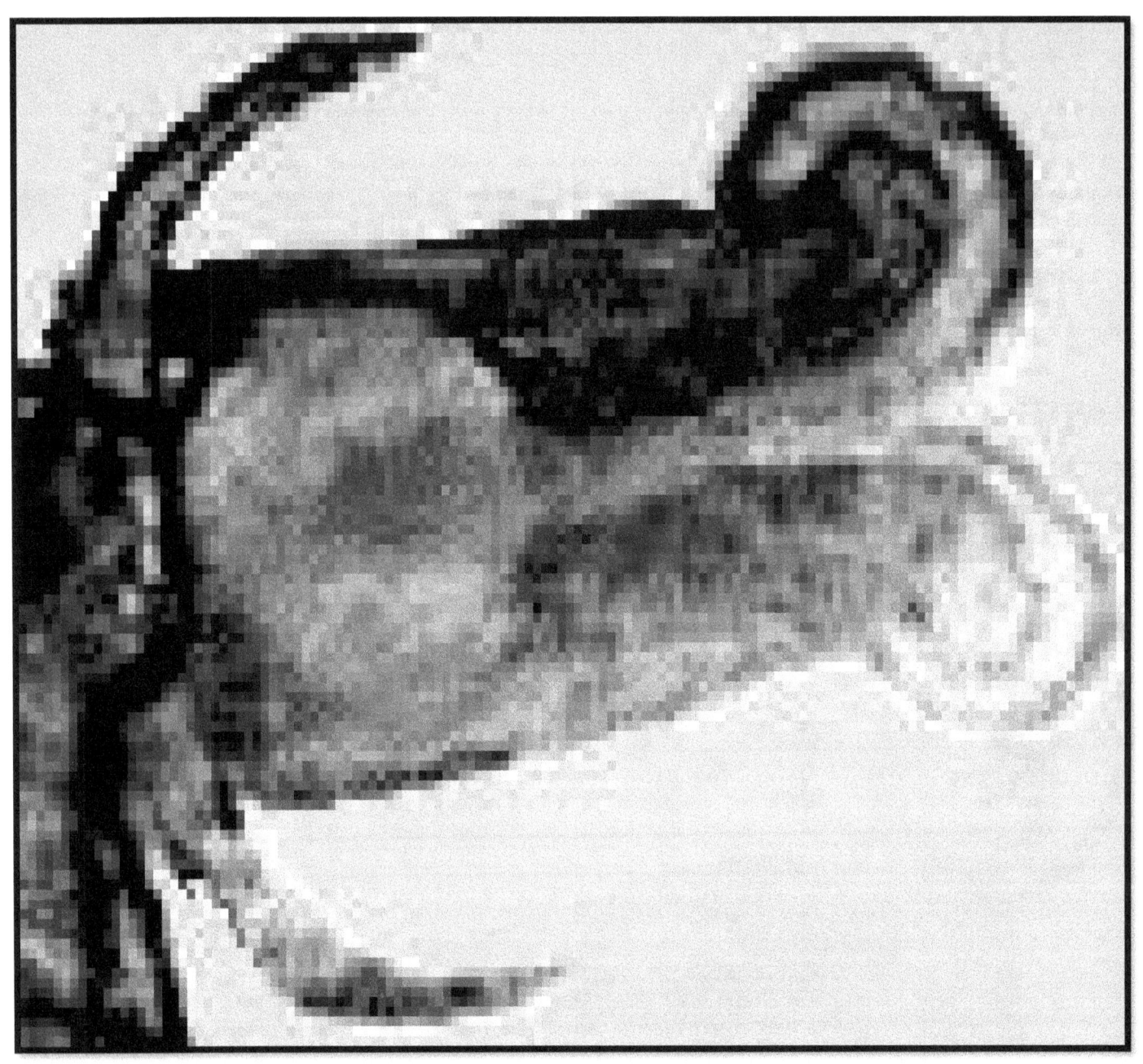

## Apis Bull horn's side-view

*I believe the horns of the Apis Bull and red ball with curled tail to be deciphered! The bull has been long known to represent different deities and the Age of Taurus. The Apis bull has been likened to the "Bull of Heaven," and the "Sacred Bull." The common belief is that the fireball is a rendering of our sun. When the fireball and horns of the bull are cropped and rotated, the fireball takes on a whole new understanding. The fireball is none other than the comet/proto-planet Venus! Venus entered the picture during the Age of Taurus, and became the Great Bull that tore through the heavens. The Pervader, The Destroyer, and the Judge of Man. We have overlooked the thing that sat before us all along. The artist represented the fireball and hot tail as it tore through the heavens wreaking havoc in its wake. What appears, at first glance to be support-pillars are actually streaks of fire above and below the comet. The curling of the tail forms a twin crescent effect. The tail of the fireball may also represent rams horns in dual symbolism. The Age of Taurus (bull horns) is being brought to a catastrophic end by the comet/proto-planet Venus, thereby ushering in the Age of Aries (ram's horns). The Apis Bull has not been accurately dated, but I believe it to be from the pre-Exodus period during the Age of Taurus. While the Egyptians did venerate the Sun, the exact culprit in each celestial encounter is not always clear.*

*Notice the change in the Feathers of Shu from the Apis Bull to a later dynasty. This bust of Thutmose III is dated from 1479 – 1425 BCE during his possible fifty-four years of rule. The two pillars are designed less as pillars of fire, as the Feathers of Shu now rest upon the Ram's horns! This shows a clear transition in practice from the Age of Taurus with the Apis Bull being representative of that time, and the horns being representative of the current Age of Aries the Ram. The pharaoh now supplanted the Bull as being conjoined with the heavens. Notice the gold ( once red) disk, the Uraeus, and the wiggly horns extending left and right from the headdress reaffirms Thutmoses III link to the Age of Aries. Thutmoses III died aournd 1450 BCE, about 3 years before the children of Israel made it to the Promised Land!*

*Uraeus – Ur/ae/us – Ur/Anu/s – Uranus – Ur of Anu? Could Uranus have been a destroyer of note as well? The Viper?*

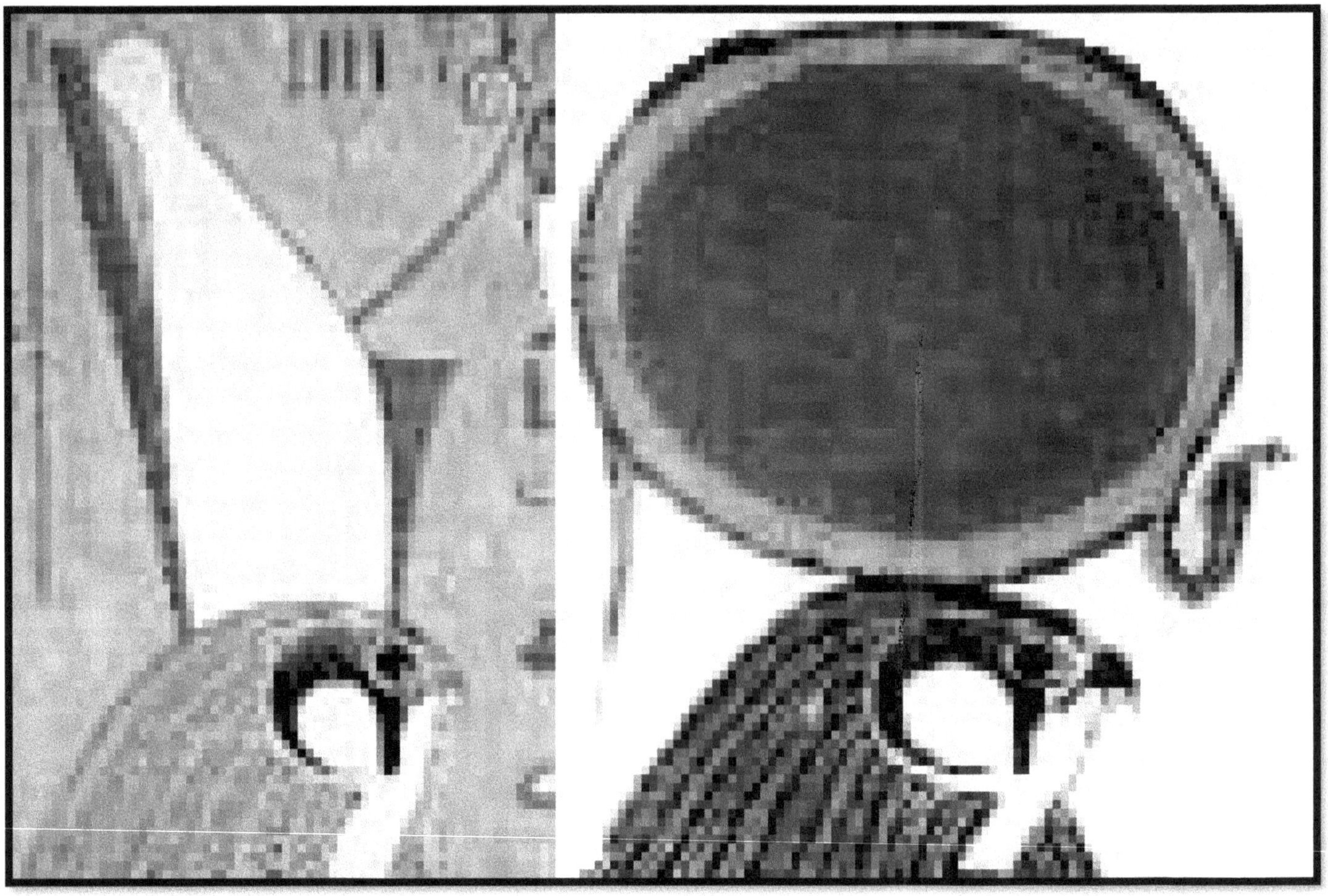

*The Pschent and another headresses of Horus (Mercury)*

<u>Left Picture:</u>

The headdress of Horus on the left has the comet/Venus with head 600' (1 league) in length, and the tail spreading out across the heavens of 30,000' (50 leagues) in length.

<u>Right Picture</u>

The headdress of Horus on the right bears what has traditionally been seen as the Sun with viper on the front. The red globe actually represents the Uranus (Uraeus) during a period of solar destructiveness. The head of the viper (Uranus) spits (pours) its venom (poison) over the Earth, as it does in other traditions. The tail dangles from the back of the dragon (Hydra/Serpentus) as it wrapped a third of the way around the heavens.

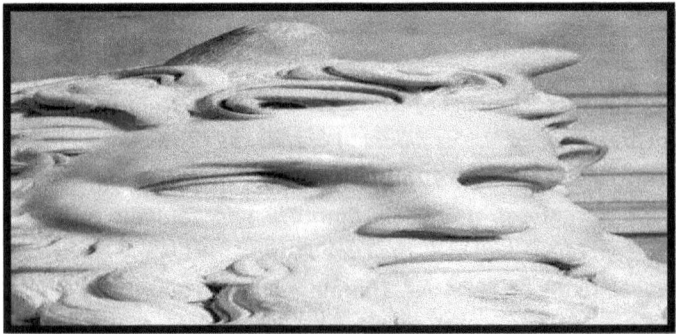

*Statue of Moses by Michaelangelo with goat horns - Age of Aries*   *Tuthmosis III with goat horns - Age of Aries*

*When the Double Crown Hedjet of Horus above is cropped and rotated, we can see the telltale comet shape. The ball is the coma, and the tail is the bottle-shaped portion. It is 1 league (3miles) long, and the tail is 50 leagues (150 miles) long per the Book of Enki.*

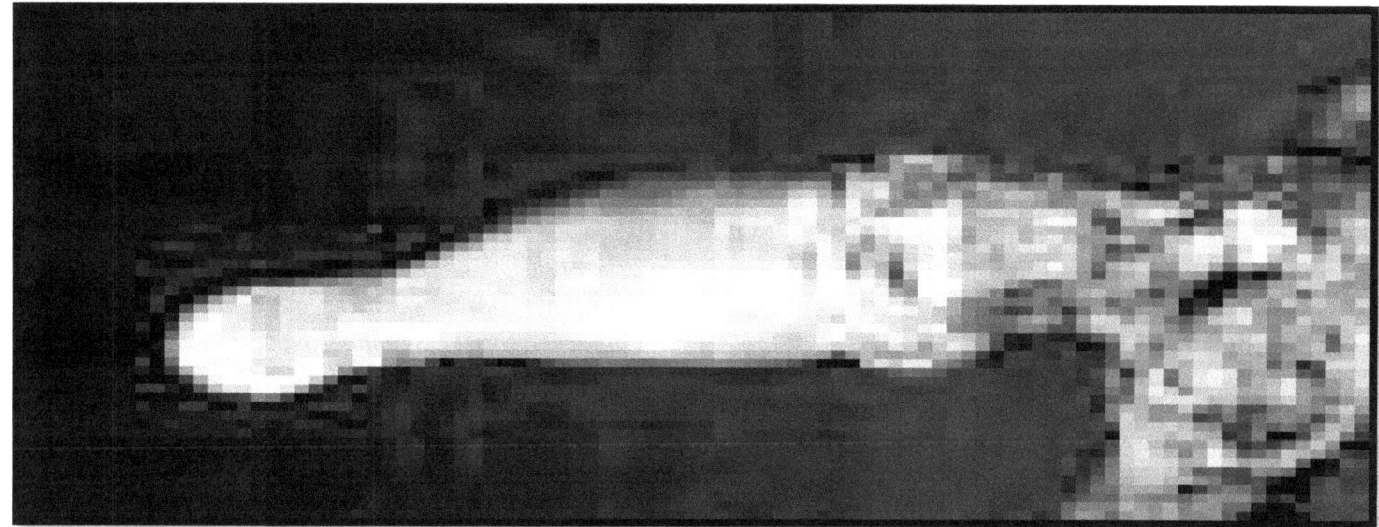

*Above we see the Upper Crown Hedjet (Venus) from the statue of Baal cropped and rotated. We have again the prototypical coma and tail feature of the comet. This is a clear link to a shared theology with Horus and Baal.*

*Starting to get the picture?*

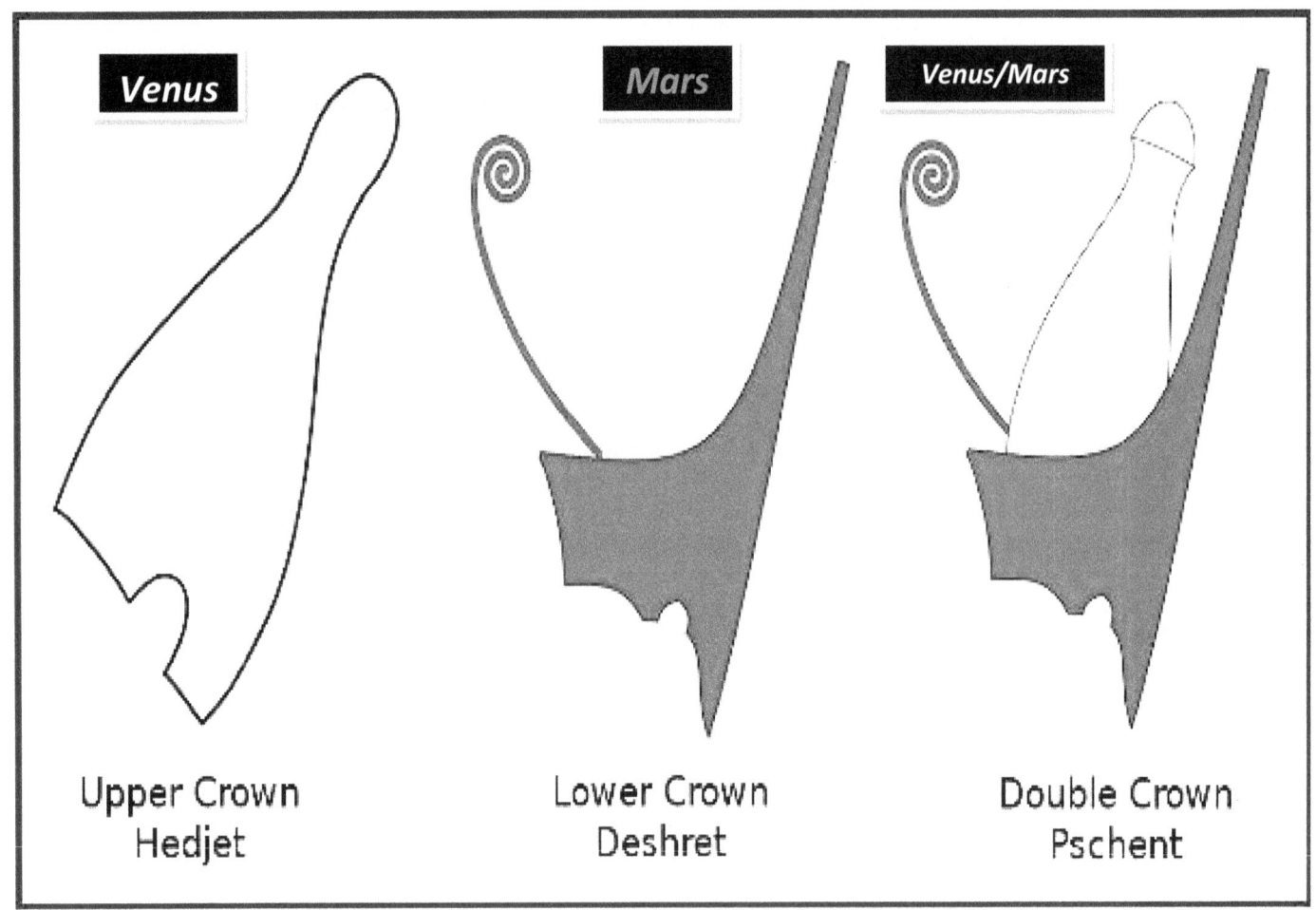

Upper Egypt Crown – Venus venerators     Lower Egypt Crown – Mars venerators     United Kingdom of Venus/Mars

Keys to the Abyss

"At One with Gog"

## CHAPTER 20

1 And I saw an angel coming down out of heaven, having the key of the abyss and a great chain in his hand.

2 And he laid hold on the dragon, the old serpent, which is the Devil and Satan, and bound him for a thousand years,

3 and cast him into the abyss, and shut it, and sealed it over him, that he should deceive the nations no more, until the thousand years should be finished: after this he must be loosed for a little time.

*Rev. 20:1 to 20:3 speaks to the final pass of Venus (Devil/Satan) as a comet as she settles into a normal orbit and loses her coma through interstellar collisions. Venus descends below the horizon as the dragon has been defeated. The binding could be a reference to the zodiac binding of the Serpent star group. Based on prior tragedies, John, expects Venus (Devil/Satan) to be back to cause tragedy within a thousand years. There was a five hundred to seven hundred and fifty year period between the Flood of Noah and the catastrophes of The Exodus. John's research brought him to the opinion that another disaster would be soon to come. Since, Venus (Devil/Satan) had lost its coma and ferocity, the cults to Venus began to fall by the wayside in favor of other Gods.*

   *The stars that form the Key of Solomon (Keys of life & death) are Orion, Hyades, Alderbarran, Taurus, and the Plieades.

4 And I saw thrones, and they sat upon them, and judgment was given unto them: and I saw the souls of them that had been beheaded for the testimony of Jesus, and for the word of God, and such as worshipped not the beast, neither his image, and received not the mark upon their forehead and upon their hand; and they lived, and reigned with Christ a thousand years.

*John speaks to the political – religious climate that produced atrocities against the clergy.*

8 and shall come forth to deceive the nations which are in the four corners of the earth, Gog and Magog, to gather them together to the war: the number of whom is as the sand of the sea.

*This has been a hotly debated statement in Revelations. The Gog (giant king?) has yet to be deciphered. The Magog, refers to the city of that name. I feel this to definitely be a statement of John's time and political – religious climate.*

*Curious? – Synagogue: syn-a-gog-ue – At one/Together with Gog?*

11 And I saw a great white throne, and him that sat upon it, from whose face the earth and the heaven fled away; and there was found no place for them.

*The terror that Venus wrought caused the skies to peel away and for men to hide in fear.*

*New Jerusalem*

## CHAPTER 21

*"The Great Promise"*

1 And I saw a new heaven and a new earth: for the first heaven and the first earth are passed away; and the sea is no more.

2 And I saw the holy city, new Jerusalem, coming down out of heaven of God, made ready as a bride adorned for her husband.

*Again we have the troubling statement of the marriage of heaven and Earth! This yet again echoes the Egyptian philosophy of "As above, So below." The Bride may be the Andromeda constellation and the husband is the Perseus constellation.*

*Rev.21:3 to Rev.21:9 "The Great Promise"*

3 And I heard a great voice out of the throne saying, Behold, the tabernacle of God is with men, and he shall dwell with them, and they shall be his peoples, and God himself shall be with them, and be their God:

4 and he shall wipe away every tear from their eyes; and death shall be no more; neither shall there be mourning, nor crying, nor pain, any more: the first things are passed away.

5 And he that sitteth on the throne said, Behold, I make all things new. And he saith, Write: for these words are faithful and true.

6 And he said unto me, They are come to pass. I am the Alpha and the Omega, the beginning and the end. I will give unto him that is athirst of the fountain of the water of life freely.

7 He that overcometh shall inherit these things; and I will be his God, and he shall be my son.

8 But for the fearful, and unbelieving, and abominable, and murderers, and fornicators, and sorcerers, and idolaters, and all liars, their part shall be in the lake that burneth with fire and brimstone; which is the second death.

9 And there came one of the seven angels who had the seven bowls, who were laden with the seven last plagues; and he spake with me, saying, Come hither, I will show thee the bride, the wife of the Lamb.

*Artist's conception of John's description of the Holy City Jerusalem!*
*Wall great & high - 12 angels at the 12 gates (12 tribes of Zodiac/Israel) - 3 East gates - 3 North gates - 3 South gates - 3 West gates - 12 foundations city wall (12 apostles of the Lamb)*
*Bride: Andromeda constellation*

10 And he carried me away in the Spirit to a **mountain** great and high, and **showed** me the **holy city Jerusalem**, coming **down** out of **heaven** from **God**,

11 having the glory of God: her **light** was like unto a **stone** most precious, as it were a **jasper** stone, clear as **crystal**:

12 having a **wall great** and **high**; having **twelve gates**, and at the **gates twelve angels**; and **names** written thereon, which are the names of the **twelve tribes** of the **children** of **Israel**:

13 on the **east** were **three gates**; and on the **north three gates**; and on the **south three gates**; and on the **west three gates**.

14 And the **wall** of the **city** had **twelve foundations**, and on them **twelve names** of the **twelve apostles** of the **Lamb**.

*Rev.21:10 to 21:14 "The Holy City Jerusalem" The description of the Holy City Jerusalem has led artist and people alike to imagine the splendor of the Holy City Jerusalem. I instantly noticed a continual pattern of similarly descriptive items in the texts. By analyzing what John says in regard to the Holy City (Cube?), we see what he was truly imagining.*

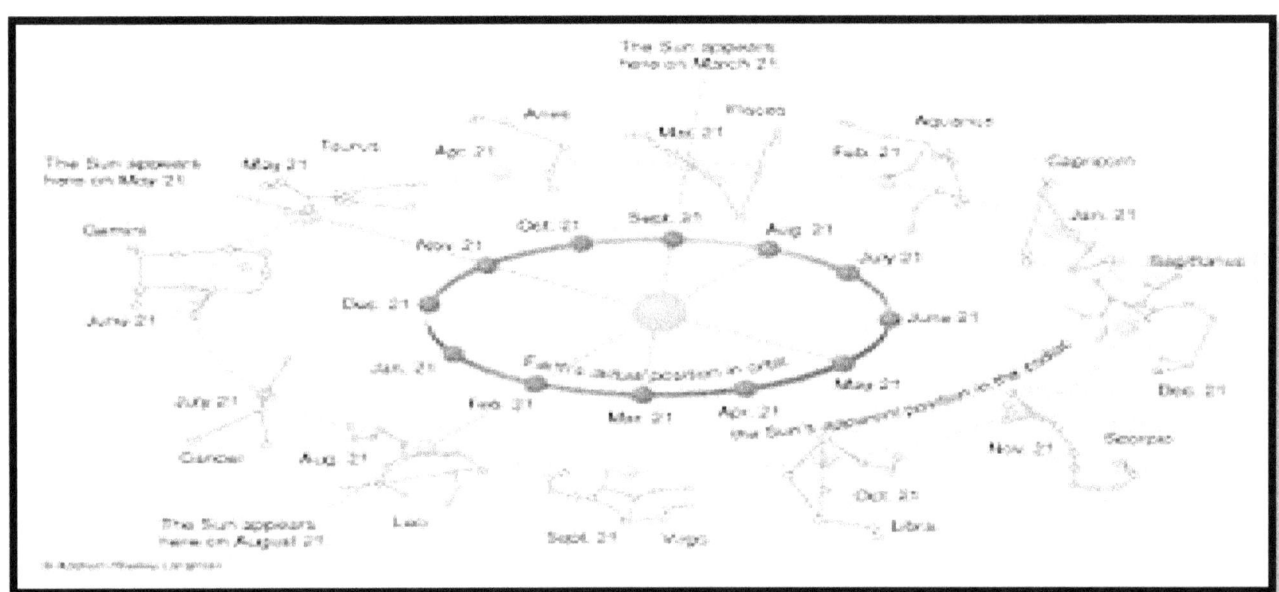

23 And the city hath no need of the **sun**, neither of the **moon**, to **shine** upon it: for the **glory** of **God** did **lighten** it, and the **lamp** thereof is the **Lamb**.

*Morning Star*

**CHAPTER 22**

*"Venus"*

16 I Jesus have sent mine angel to testify unto you these things for the churches. I am the root and the offspring of David, the bright, the morning star.

***The Bright, the Morning Star, has been long known to be the planet Venus.***

*Venus – "The bright! The Morning Star!"*    *Venus – "The bright, the Evening Star!"*

# Essene Book of Revelations – written @ 80 - 150 BCE

*"The Essene Book of Revelations," speaks to the same vision as John in his book of Revelations. The Essene's practiced a different spiritual approach with reverence for the Earth Mother and other concepts. John has clearly borrowed the Essene's visions, who borrowed other writers texts. I have only highlighted common words from these epics to show the same theme of disasters tha trun through these sacred texts. Written @ 80 - 150 CE*

The Essene Book of Revelations
Translated by E B Szekely

**Behold, the Angel of the Air shall bring him,**
And every eye shall see him,
And the **brotherhood,** *(John's brotherhood?)*
All the vast brotherhood of the Earth
Shall raise their voice as one and sing,
Because of him.
Amen *(Hidden One – Amen Ra, Amun Ra, Amenhotep)*

"I am the **Alpha** and **Omega**, the Beginning and the End;
What is, what was, and what is to come."

And the voice spoke, and I turned to see
The voice that spoke to me,
And being turned, I saw **seven golden candles**;
And in the midst of their blazing light
I saw someone **like a son of man,** *(Sun, Galzu, Aquarius)*
Clothed in white, **white** as the **snow**. *(clouds?)*
And his voice filled the air with the **sound of rushing water;** *(Aquarius)*
And in his hands were **seven stars,** *(Pleiades)*
And when he spoke, his face was streaming light,
Blazing and golden like a **thousand suns.** *(the Sun!)*
And he said, "Fear not, **I am the first and the last;** *(shared with the Bible and the Qur'an)*
**I am the beginning and the end.**
Write the things that **you have seen**,
And the things that are, and the things that will come after;
The mystery of the **seven stars** which fill my hands,
And the seven golden candles, blazing with eternal light.
**The seven stars are the Angels(planets, stars, zodiac) of the Heavenly Father, (Pleiades)**
**And the seven stars are the Angels of the Earthly Mother.** *(Earth Mother? – Gaia, Mary, Cybele, Juno, Maya, Hera, etc.)*
And the spirit of man is the flame *(Ezekiel)*
That streams between the **starlight** and the **glowing candle;** *(comet/Venus/wheel in the sky)*
A bridge of holy light between Heaven and Earth." *(Pillar of Fire in the Sky)*

These things said he who held the seven stars in his hands,
Who walked within the flames of the seven golden candles. *(John)*
He that has an ear, let him hear what the spirit said:
"To him that overcomes I will allow to eat from the tree of life,
That stands in the midst of the shining paradise of God."

And then I looked, and behold,
A door was opened in heaven:
And a voice which sounded from all sides, like a trumpet,
Spoke to me: "Come up here, *(John)*
And I will show you the things which must be hereafter."

And immediately I was there, in spirit, *(Enoch, Ezekiel, John)*
At the threshold of the open door.
And I entered through the open door
Into a sea of blazing light.
And in the midst of the blinding ocean of radiance was a throne:
And on the throne sat one whose face was hidden.
And there was a rainbow around about the throne,
Which looked like emerald.
**And round about the throne were thirteen seats: (changed from John's 4 & 20 elders)**
**And upon the seats I saw thirteen elders sitting,**
Clothed in white raiment;
And there faces were hidden by swirling clouds of light.
And seven lamps of fire burned before the throne,
**The fire of the Earthly Mother.**
And seven stars of heaven shone before the throne,
The fire of the Heavenly Father.
And before the throne
There was a **sea of glass like crystal**:
And reflected within it
Were all the mountains and valleys of the Earth,
And all the creatures abiding therein.
And the thirteen elders bowed down before the 168dmixtur of him
Who sat upon the throne, whose face was hidden,
And rivers of light streamed from their hands, one to the other,
And they cried, **"Holy, Holy, Holy,**
Lord God Almighty,
Which was, and is, and is to come.
Thou art worthy, O Lord,
To receive glory and honour and power:
For thou hast created all things."
And then I saw in the right hand
Of him that sat on the throne,
A book written within and on the back,
Sealed with seven seals.
**And I wept, because the book could not be opened, *(John wept as well)***
Nor was I able to read what there was written.
And one of the elders said to me, 'Weep not.
Reach out your hand and take the book.'
And I reached out my hand and touched the book.
And behold, the cover lifted,
And my hands touched the golden pages,
And my eyes beheld the mystery of the **seven seals.**

And I beheld, and I heard the voice of many angels
Round about the throne,
And the number of them was **ten thousand times ten thousand**,
And thousands of thousands, saying with a loud voice,
"All glory, and wisdom, and strength,
and power forever and ever,
To him who shall reveal the **Mystery of Mysteries.**"
And I saw the swirling clouds of golden light
Stretching like a ***fiery bridge*** between my hands,
And the hands of the ***thirteen*** elders,
And the feet of him who sat on the throne,
Whose face was hidden.

And I opened the ***first seal***.
And I saw, and beheld the ***Angel of the Air,***
And between her lips flowed ***the breath of life***,
And she knelt over the earth
And gave to man the winds of wisdom,
And man breathed in.
*And when he breathed out, the sky darkened,*
*And the sweet air became fetid,*
*And clouds of evil smoke hung low over all the earth. (Evil Wind?)*
And I turned my face away in shame.

And I opened the ***second seal.***
And I saw, and beheld the ***Angel of the Water.***
And between her lips flowed the ***water of life***,
And she knelt over the Earth
And gave to man an ocean of love.
*And man entered the clear and shining waters.*
*And when he touched the water, the clear streams darkened,*
*And the crystal waters became thick with slime,*
*And the fish lay gasping in the foul blackness,*
*And all the creatures died of thirst. (Exodus, Ipuwer, Enki)*
And I turned my face away in shame.

And I opened the ***third seal.***
*And I saw and beheld the Angel of the Sun.*
And between her lips flowed the ***light of life,***
And she knelt over the earth
And gave to man the Fires of Power.
*And the strength of the Sun entered the heart of man,*
*And he took the power, and made with it a false sun (Venus/comet),*
*And he spread the fires of destruction,*
*Burning the forests,*
*Laying waste the green valleys,*
*Leaving only charred bones of his brothers.*
And I turned away in shame.

And I opened the *fourth seal.*
And I saw, and beheld the Angel of Joy.
And between her lips flowed the *music of life,*
And she knelt over the Earth
And gave to man the song of peace.
And peace and joy like music
Flowed through the soul of man.
*But he heard only the harsh discord of sadness and discontent,*
*And he lifted up his sword*
*And cut off the heads of the singers.*
And I turned my face away in shame.

And I opened the *fifth seal.*
And I saw, and beheld the *Angel of Life*.
And between her lips
Flowed the holy alliance between God and Man,
And she knelt over the Earth
And gave to man the gift of Creation.
*And man created a sickle of iron in the shape of a serpent, (dragon in the sky, iron meteors, droughts, & famine)*
*And the harvest he reaped was of hunger and death.*
And I turned my face away in shame.

And I opened the *sixth seal.*
And I saw, and beheld the *Angel of the Earth*.
And between her lips flowed the river of eternal life,
And she knelt over the Earth
And gave to man the secret of eternity,
And told him to open his eyes
*And behold the mysterious Tree of Life in the Endless Sea.*
*But man lifted up his hand and put out his own eyes,*
*And said there is no eternity.*
And I turned my face away in shame.

And I opened the *seventh seal*.
*And I saw, and beheld the Angel of the Earthly Mother.*
*And she brought with her a message of blazing light*
*From the throne of the Heavenly Father.*
*And this message was for the ears of Man alone,*
He who walks between the Earth and Heaven,
And into the ear of man was whispered the message.
And he did not hear.
But I did not turn away my face in shame.
Lo, I reached out my hand to the wings of the angel,
And turned my voice to heaven saying,
"Tell me the message. For I would eat of the fruit
Of the Tree of Life that grows in the Sea of Eternity."

And the angel looked upon me with great sadness,
*And there was silence in Heaven.*

And then I heard a voice,
Which was like the voice that sounded like a trumpet,
Saying, "O Man, would you look upon the evil you have done
When you turned your face away from the throne of God?
When you did not make use of the gifts
Of the seven Angels of the Earthly Mother,
And the seven angels of the Heavenly Father?"

And a terrible pain seized me
*As I felt within me the souls of all those*
*Who had blinded themselves,*
*So as to see only their own desires of the flesh.*
And I saw the seven angels who stood before God;
And to them were given *seven trumpets*
And another angel came and stood at the *alter,*
Having a *golden censer;*
And there was given to him much *incense,*
That he should offer it with the prayers of all the angels
Upon the golden alter that was before the throne.

And the smoke of the incense ascended up before God
Out of the angels hand.
And the angel took the *censer,*
And filled it with *fire* of the *alter,*
And cast it onto the Earth,
And there were *voices*

And *lightnings*, and *earthquakes.*
And the *seven* angels that had the *seven* trumpets
Prepared themselves to sound.

The *first angel* sounded,
*And there followed hail and fire mixed with blood,*
*And they were cast upon the Earth.*
*And the green forests and trees were burnt up,*
*And all the green grass to cinders.*

The *second angel* sounded,
*And a great mountain burning with fire*
*Was cast into the sea*
*And blood rose from the earth as a vapour.*

And the *fourth angel* sounded,
*And there was a great earthquake;*
*And the sun became as black as sackcloth of hair,*
*And the moon became as blood.*

And the *fifth angel* sounded
*And the stars of heaven fell onto the earth*

*Like figs from fig tree*
*Shaken by a mighty wind.*

And the *sixth angel* sounded
*And the heaven departed as a scroll when it is rolled together.*
*And over the whole earth there was not one tree,*
*Nor one flower, nor one blade of grass.*
*And I stood on the earth,*
*And my feet sank into the soil,*
*soft and thick with blood,*
Stretching as far as the eye could see.
And all over the earth was silence.

And the *seventh angel* sounded. *(7 Angels = 7 Planets)*
And I saw *a mighty being come down from Heaven,*
*Clothed with a cloud;*
*And a rainbow on his head,*
*And his face was as is it were the Sun (WOW!),*
*And his feet were pillars of fire. (Enoch, Ezekiel, John)*
And he had in his hand a book open:
And he set his right foot upon the *sea*, and his left foot on the *earth*,
And he cried with aloud voice, which was wondrous to hear:
*'O Man, would you have this vision come to pass?'*
And I answered, *'You know I would do anything*
*So that these terrible things might not come to pass.'*

And he spoke: "Man has created these powers of destruction.
He has made them from his own mind.
He has turned his face away
From the *angels* of the *Heavenly Father* and the *Earthly Mother*,
And he has fashioned his own destruction."

And I spoke: "Then is there no hope, bright angel?"
And a blazing light streamed like a river from his hands
As he answered, *"There is always hope,*
*O thou for whom Heaven and Earth were created."*

And then the angel,
He who stood upon the sea and upon the earth,
Lifted up his hand to heaven,
And swore by him who lives for ever and ever,
Who created heaven and the things that therein are,
And the Earth, and the things that therein are,
And the sea, and the things that are therein,
*That there should be time no longer:*
But in the days of the voice of the seventh angel,
When he shall begin to sound,
The mystery of God should be revealed to those
*Who have eaten from the Tree of Life*

*Which stands forever in the Eternal Sea.*

And the voice spoke again saying:
"Go take the book that is in the hand of the angel,
who stands upon the sea and upon the earth."
And I went to the angel, and said to him,
"Give me the book,
For I would eat from the Tree of Life
Which stands in the middle of the Eternal Sea."
And the angel gave to me the book,
And I opened the book, and I read therein
What had always been, what was now, and what would come to pass.

I saw the holocaust that would engulf the Earth,
And the great destruction
**That would drown all her people in oceans of blood.**
And I saw too the eternity of man
And the endless forgiveness of the Almighty.
The souls of men were as blank pages in the book,
Always ready for a new song to be there inscribed.

And I lifted up my face
To the *seven Angels of the Earthly Mother*
And the *seven Angels of the Heavenly Father,*
And I felt my feet touching the holy brow of the Earthly Mother,
And my fingers touching the holy feet of the Heavenly Father,
And I uttered a hymn of thanksgiving:
"I thank thee, heavenly father,
Because thou hast put me at a source of running streams,
At a living spring in a land of drought,
Watering an eternal garden of wonders,
The Tree of Life, Mystery of mysteries,
Growing everlasting branches for eternal planting,
To sink their roots into the stream of life from an eternal source.
And thou, Heavenly Father,
Protect their fruits
With the angels of day and night,
And with flames of Eternal Light lighting every way.

But again the voice spoke,
And again my eyes were drawn away
From the splendours of the realm of light,
"Heed thou, O man!
You may walk on the right path
And walk in the presence of the angels,
You may sing of the Earthly Mother by day
And of the Heavenly Father by night,
And through your being course the golden stream of the Law,
**But would you leave your brothers**

*To plunge through the gaping chasm of blood,*
*As the pain-wracked Earth shudders and groans*
*Under her chains of stone?*
*Can you drink from the cup of eternal life*
*While your brothers die of thirst?"*

And my heart was heavy with compassion.
And I looked, and lo,
There appeared a great wonder in heaven:
*A woman clothed with the sun, and the moon under her feet, (John)*
*And upon her head a crown of seven stars.*
*And I knew she was the source of running streams*
*And the mother of the forests.*

And I stood upon the sand of the sea,
*And saw a beast rise up out of the sea,*
And from his nostrils wafted foul and loathsome air,
And where he rose from the sea, the clear waters turned to slime,
*And his body was covered with black and steaming stone.*

*And the woman clothed with the sun*
*Reached out her arms to the beast,*
*And the beast drew near and embraced her.*
*And lo, her skin of pearl withered beneath his foul breath,*
*And her back was broken by his arms of crushing rock,*
*And with tears of blood she sank into the pool of slime.*

*And from the mouth of this beast there poured armies of men,*
*Brandishing swords and fighting, one with the other.*
*And they fought with a terrible anger,*
And they cut off their own limbs and clawed out their own eyes,
Until they fell into the pit of slime,
Screaming in agony and pain.

And I stepped to the edge of the pool and reached down my hand,
And I could see the swirling maelstrom of blood,
And the men therein, trapped like flies in a web.
And I spoke in a loud voice, saying,
"Brothers, drop your swords and take hold of my hand.
Leave off this defiling and desecration
Of she who has given thee birth,
And he who has given thee thy inheritance.
For you the days of buying and selling are over
And over, too, the days of hunting and killing.
For he that leadeth into captivity will go into captivity,
And he who kills with the sword must be killed by the sword.
And the merchants of the earth shall weep and mourn
Because no man buys their merchandise any more.
The merchants of gold, and silver, and precious stones,

And of pearls, and fine linen, and **purple dyes**, and **silk,** and **scarlet,**
And marble, and beasts, and sheep, and horses,
And chariots, and slaves, and souls of men,
***All these things you cannot buy and sell,***
***For all is buried in a sea of blood***
***Because you have turned your back on your father and mother,***
***And worshipped the beast who would build a paradise of stone.***
Drop thy swords, my brothers, and take hold of my hand!"

And as our fingers clasped,
I saw in the distance a great city,
***White and shining on the far horizon, glowing alabaster,***
***And there were voices and thunders, and lightnings,***
***And there was a great earthquake,***
***Such as was not since men were on the Earth,***
***So mighty an earthquake, and so great.***
***And the great city was divided into three parts,***
***And the cities of the nations fell.***
***And the great city came in remembrance before God***
***To give unto her the cup of the wine***
***Of the fierceness of his wrath,***

***And every island fled away,***
***And the mountains were not found,***
***And there fell upon men a great hail out of heaven,***
***Every stone about the weight of a talent.***
***And a mighty angel took up a stone like a great millstone,***
***And threw it into the sea, saying,***
***"Thus, with violence shall the great city be thrown down,***
***And shall be found no more at all.'***

And the voice of harpists, and musicians, and of pipers,
And of singers, and trumpeters,
Shall be heard no more in thee;
And no craftsmen, of whatever craft he be,
Shall be found anymore in thee;
And the sound of the millstone shall be heard no more in thee.
And the light of the candle will shine no more in thee
And the voice of the bridegroom and of the bride
Shall be heard no more in thee
For your merchants were great men of the Earth;
By there sorceries all nations were deceived.
***And in her was found the blood of prophets and saints,***
And all those who were slain upon Earth.`

And my brothers laid hold of my hand,
And they struggled out of the pool of slime
And stood bewildered on the sea of sand,
And the skies opened and washed their naked bodies with rain.

And I heard a voice from heaven, as the voice of many waters,
And as the voice of great thunder:
And I heard the sound of harpists playing their harps,
And they sang a new song before the throne.

And I saw another angel fly in the midst of Heaven,
Having the songs of day and night
And the everlasting gospel to preach to them that dwell on the Earth,
Unto them that have climbed from the pit of slime,
And stand naked and washed by rain before the throne.
And the angel cried out, "Fear God, and give glory to him;
For the hour of his judgement has come:
And worship him that made Heaven and Earth,
And the sea, and the fountains of waters."

And I saw Heaven open, and beheld a white horse;
And he that sat upon him was called Faithful and True,
And in righteousness he does judge.
His eyes were like a flame of fire,
And on his head were many crowns,
And he was cloaked in blazing light
*And his feet were bare.*
*And his name is called the Word of God.*
*And the holy brotherhood followed him upon white horses,*
*Clothed in fine linen, white and clean.*
And they entered the eternal Infinite Garden,
In whose midst stood the Tree of Life.

And the rain washed naked throngs came before them,
Trembling to receive their judgement.
For their sins were many, and they had defiled the Earth,
Yea, they had destroyed the creatures of the land and sea,
Poisoned the ground, fouled the air,
And buried alive the mother who had given them birth.

But, I saw not what befell them, for my vision changed,
And I saw a new Heaven and a new Earth;
For the first Heaven and the first Earth had passed away;
And there was no more sea.
*And I saw the holy city of the brotherhood (John, New Jerusalem, brotherhood?)*
*Coming down from God out of Heaven,*
Prepared like a bride adorned for her husband. *(Bride: Andromeda constellation, Bridegroom: Perseus constellation!)*
And I heard a great voice out of heaven saying:
"Lo, the mountain of the Lord's house
Is established in the top of the mountains
And is exalted above the hills;
And all people shall flow to it.
Come, and let us go up to the mountain of the Lord,
To the house of God;

And he will teach us of his ways,
And we will walk in his paths:
For out of the Holy Brotherhood shall go forth the Law.
Behold, the **Tabernacle of God** is with men,
And he will dwell with them, and they shall be his people,
And God himself will be with them, and be their God.'
And God shall wipe away all **tears** from their **eyes**;
And there shall be no more death,
Neither sorrow, nor crying,
Neither shall there be any more pain:
For the former things have all passed away.
***Those who made war shall beat their swords into ploughshares,***
***And their spears into pruning hooks:***
***Nation shall not lift up sword against nation,***
***Neither shall they learn war anymore:***
***For the former things have passed away.***

And he spoke again: "Behold I make all things new.
I am Alpha and Omega, the Beginning and the End.
I will give to him that thirsts at the Fountain of the Water of Life freely.
He who overcomes shall inherit all things,
And I will be his God, and he shall be my son.
But the fearful, and the unbelieving,
And the abominable, and murderers, and all liars,
Shall dig their own pit which burns with **fire and brimstone**."

And again my vision changed,
And I heard the voices of the holy brotherhood raised in song,
Saying, "Come ye, and let us walk in the **light of the Law (Sun)**."
And I saw the Holy City,
And the brothers were **streaming** to it.
And the city had **no need of the sun**,
Neither of the **moon** to shine on it:
For the glory of God did lighten it.

And I saw the pure river of the Water of Life,
Clear as crystal, proceeding out of the throne of God.
And in the middle of the river stood the Tree of Life,
***Which bore fourteen kinds of fruits,***
And yielded her fruit to those who would eat of it,
And the leaves of the tree were for the healing of the nations.

***And there shall be no night there;***
***And they need no candle, neither light of the sun,***
For the **Lord gives them light**:
And they shall reign for ever and ever.

I have reached the inner vision
And through thy spirit in me

I have heard thy wondrous secret.
Through thy mystic insight
Thou hast caused a spring of knowledge
To well up within me,
A fountain of power pouring forth living waters;
A flood of love and all embracing wisdom
Like the 178dmixtur of eternal light.

# Book of Enki Decoded – written @ 3100 – 1000 BCE

*Transcibed from Summerian tablets by Zecharia Sitchin*

The words of **Endubsar, master scribe**, son of Eridu city, servant of the lord Enki, great god.
In the seventh year after the Great Calamity, in the second month, on the seventeenth day, I was summoned by my master the Lord Enki, great god, benevolent fashioner of Mankind, omnipotent and merciful. I was among the remnants of Eridu who had escaped to the arid steppe just as the **Evil Wind** was nearing the city. And I wandered off into the wilderness to seek withered twigs for firewood. And I looked up and to and behold, a **Whirlwind** came out of the south. There was a **reddish brilliance** about it and it made no sound. And as it reached the ground, **four straight feet** spread out from its belly and the brilliance disappeared. And I threw myself to the ground and prostrated myself, for I knew that it was a divine vision. And when I lifted my eyes, there were **two divine emissaries** standing near me. And they had the **faces** of **men**, and their garments were sparkling like **burnished brass**. And they called me by name and spoke to me, saying: You are summoned by the great god the lord Enki. Fear not, for you are blessed. And we are here to take you aloft, and carry you unto his retreat in the Land of **Magan**, on the island amidst the **River of Magan**, where the sluices are.

*We've heard this story before, but this story was written first! The prophecy of Ezekiel was preceded by the texts created for the Sumerian Lord Enki. Ezekiel leads right into his prophecy with the exact same dialogue!*

> *Ezekiel 1:1 NOW it came to pass in the thirtieth year, in the fourth month, in the fifth day of the month, as I was among the captives by the river of Chebar, that the heavens were opened, and I saw visions of God.*
>
> *Ezekiel 1:2 In the fifth day of the month, which was the fifth year of king Jehoiachin's captivity,*
>
> *Ezekiel 1:3 The word of the LORD came expressly unto Ezekiel the priest, the son of Buzi, in the land of the Chaldeans by the river Chebar; and the hand of the LORD was there upon him.*
>
> *Ezekiel 1:4 And I looked, and, behold, a whirlwind came out of the north, a great cloud, and a fire infolding itself, and a brightness was about it, and out of the midst thereof as the colour of amber, out of the midst of the fire.*
>
> *Ezekiel 1:5 Also out of the midst thereof came the likeness of four living creatures. And this was their appearance; they had the likeness of a man.*
>
> *Ezekiel 1:6 And every one had four faces, and every one had four wings.*
>
> *Ezekiel 1:7 And their feet were straight feet; and the sole of their feet was like the sole of a calf's foot: and they sparkled like the colour of burnished brass.*

And as they spoke, the **Whirlwind** lifted itself as a fiery chariot and was gone. And they took me by my hands, each one grasping me by one hand. And they lifted me and carried me swiftly between the Earth and the heavens, as the eagle soars. And I could see the land and the waters, and the plains and the mountains. And they let me down on the island at the gateway of the great god's abode. And the moment they let go of my hands, a brilliance as I had never seen before engulfed and overwhelmed me, and I collapsed on the ground as though voided of the spirit of life.
Not since the Great Deluge **(Flood of Noah)** had such a calamity befallen the Earth and the gods and the Earthlings. But the Great Deluge was destined to happen, not so the great calamity **(Exodus)**. This one, seven years ago, need not have happened.
And was it fate or was it destiny? In the future shall it be judged, for at the end of days a Day of judgment there shall be. On that day the **Earth** shall **quake (sheog)** and the **rivers shall change course,** and there shall be darkness at noon and a fire in the heavens in the night, the day of the returning celestial god will it be.

For **forty days** and **forty nights** shall I speak and you will write; **forty** shall be the count of the days and the nights of your task here, for **forty is my sacred number** among the gods. For **forty** days and **forty** nights you shall neither eat nor drink; only this once of bread and water you shall partake, and it shall sustain you for the duration of your task.

*This is the common forty days and forty nights concept, and forty is the sacred number of the Lord Enki.*

And they shall learn all that I have dictated to you; and that true account of the **Beginnings** and the **Prior Times** and the **Olden Times** and the **Great Calamity** shall henceforth be known as The Words of the **Lord Enki**. And it shall be a Book of **Witnessing** of the past, and a Book of **Foretelling** the *future*, for the future in the *past lies* and the *first things* shall also be the *last things*. And there was a pause, and I took the **tablets**, and put them one by one in their **correct order** in the **chest**. And the chest was made of **acacia wood** and it was **inlaid** with **gold** on the outside. And the **voice** of **my lord** said: Now close the chest's cover and fasten its **lock**. And I did as directed.

*Enki speaks of basically four World or Zodiac Ages; Beginnings, Prior Times, Olden Times, Great Calamity. Most civilizations relate that their have been four worlds that were previously destroyed, and that we are currently living in the fifth world on the onset of the sixth. Books of Witnessing and Foretelling, tablets, chest, and commands! These items are all too familiar in religious history.*

And the voice of the lord Enki said: The **signs** will be in the **heavens**, and the words to utter shall come to you in **dreams** and in **visions**. And after you there will be **other** chosen **prophets**. And in the end there will be a **New Earth** and a **New Heaven**, and for prophets there will be no more need.

*Signs, heavens, dreams, visions, prophets, New Earth (post-disaster), and New Heaven (sky above), are all familiar in religious history as well.*

## THE FIRST TABLET

How **smitten** is the **land**, its people delivered to the **Evil Wind**, its **stables** abandoned, its **sheepfolds** emptied.
How smitten are the cities, their people **piled** up as **dead corpses**, afflicted by the Evil Wind. How smitten are the fields, their **vegetation withered**, touched by the Evil Wind. How smitten are the **rivers**, nothing **swims** anymore, pure sparkling **waters** turned into **poison**.

*This disaster sounds eerily like the disasters of the Exodus. We have three separate sources linking same or similar issues in the same epoch of time, and in the same region; Hebrew, Egyptian, and Sumerian!*

Of its **black-headed** people, **Shumer** is emptied, **gone** is all **life**;

*The Shumerians: Sumerians-Babylonians-Akkadians-Iraqis     Sumer=Summer*

The temples whose heads to heaven arose by their gods have been abandoned. Of lordship and kingship command there is none; scepter and tiara are gone.

*Just as Ipuwer lamented loss of crown and tiara, and the loss of respect for the Uraeus (Uranus), Enki laments this tragedy.*

A death-dealing wind born in the west its way to the east has made, its course set by fate. A storm devouring as the deluge, by wind and not by water a destroyer; by poisoned air, not tidal waves, overwhelming.

*Poison gasses that have been theorized to be volcanic or nuclear, destroys the Shumerians versus a deluge, just as in the Egyptian/Hebrew plagues of the Exodus.*

Against Marduk, my firstborn, did the two sons destruction direct; vengeance was in their hearts.

*The planet Mars is antrhopromorphized as Marduk the Destroyer! The two sons are Phobos and Deimos (moons of Mars) as this cosmic war in the heavens begins to play out. The Sumerian name for Mars has been related as Nergal, and Jupiter as Marduk. I believe Enlil represented Jupiter, as Mars is the combatant in this celestial war.*

Ishkur, Enlil's youngest, punishment demanded; in my lands to whore after him the people he made! He said.

*Ishkur AKA Ishtar AKA Venus seeks vengeance against Marduk, as the people have begun to worship Mars as a deity.*

Utu, son of **Nannar**, at **Marduk's** son **Nabu** his wrath directed: The **Place** of the **Celestial Chariots** he tried to **seize**!

*The Sun (Utu) lashes out at Phobos or Deimos (Nabu) as Nabu attempts to take the Sun's position (celestial Chariots).*

**Inanna**, twin of **Utu**, was furious of all; the **punishment** of **Marduk** for the **killing** of her beloved **Dumuzi** she still demanded.]

*Venus (Inanna) twin of the Sun (Utu) demands the death of Mars (Marduk) for the death of the Bootes constellation (Dumuzi/Tammuz). Venus is implied as being as bright as the Sun at some point, as she is considered his twin in many tales.*

**Ninharsag**, mother of gods and men, her gaze diverted. Why is not Marduk here? She only said. **Gibil**, my own son, with gloom replied: Marduk has all entreaties put aside; by the **signs** of **heaven** his **supremacy** he claims!

*Utu – Utu Shamash (Akkadian) – Sun God*
*Inanna – Venus (twin of the Sun God!)*
*Nannar – Moon God*
*Marduk – Mars*
*Celestial Chariots – position in heavens (Earth is 3$^{rd}$)*
*Dumuzi/Tammuz – Son of the Sun (Bootes constellation)*
*Ninharsag – Earth*
*Gibil – Mercury*

**This is all about a war in the skies with the planets anthropomorphized as Gods.**

Husband and wife let them be, as one flesh to become.

*This speaks of binding by capturing, but relates the common belief of man in regard to marriage.*

THE SECOND TABLET

**Little Gaga**, the One Who Shows the Way, by its circuit Alalu was greeting, to him a welcome extending.

*Gaga – Pluto*

*Pluto was not (re) discovered until 1930*

With a leaning gait, before and after the celestial **Antu** it was destined to travel, To face forward, to face backward, with two facings was it endowed.

*Antu – Neptune*

**Enki understands Neptune's axis and rotation, even though we didn't (re) discover Neptune until 1846 with the use of modern telescopes. Due to the axial tilt of Neptune (28.3°) it experiences seasons similar to Earth's (23°) and seasons that last "40 YEARS!**

The giant Kishar, foremost of the Firm Planets, its size was overwhelming. Swirling storms obscured its face, colored spots they moved about; A host beyond counting, some quickly, some slowly, the celestial god encircled.
Troublesome were their ways, back and forth they were surging. Kishar itself a spell was casting, divine lightnings it was thrusting.

*Kishar – Jupiter   Anshar – Saturn*

*Enki knows that Saturn is the largest planet with a red dust storm that swirls about the equator. The hosts are the meteors and rocks that circulate near Jupiter and the ones that comprises its ring system.*

The Hammered Bracelet ahead was reigning, to demolish it was awaiting! Of rocks and boulders was it together hammered, like orphans with no mother they banded together.

***The Hammered Bracelet is what we call the asteroid belt! This area lies between Mars and Jupiter, and is considered to be the remnants of a planetary collision. The ancients possibly knew more about the cosmos than we could have guessed!***

Before it, a red-brown planet on its circuit was coursing; the sixth in the count of celestial gods it was.

*Mars!*

Then snow-hued Earth appeared, the seventh in the celestial count.

*Earth AKA Ki AKA Tiamat!*

It is an account of the **Beginning** and how the **celestial gods created** were. In the Beginning, **When** in the **Above** the **gods** in the heavens had not been **called** into being, And in the *Below Ki*, the **Firm Ground**, had not yet been named, Alone in the **void** there existed **Apsu**, their **Primordial Begetter**. In the heights of the Above, the celestial gods had **not** yet been **created**; In the **waters** of the **Below**, the celestial gods had not yet **appeared**. **Above** and **Below**, the gods had not yet been formed, **destinies** were not yet **decreed**.

*Beginning, celestial gods, called, firm ground, void, primordial beggeter, above and below! Another all too familiar theme from Biblical and sacred texts. The, "As Above – So Below," theme of philosophy is present in the Sumerian, Egyptian, and Judeo-Christian doctrines.*

Male and female were the celestials created; **Lahmu** and **Lahamu** by names they were called. In the Below did Apsu and Tiamat make them an abode.

*Lahmu – Mars*
*Lahamu – Venus*
*Apsu – Sun*
*Tiamat – Primordial Earth*

Their ways to Apsu were verily loathsome; Tiamat, getting no rest, was aggrieved and raged. A throng to march by her side she formed, A growling, raging host against the sons of Apsu she brought forth. Withal eleven of this kind she brought forth;

*The primordial Earth with her eleven hosts (11 moons/satellites) take their rage out on the sons of the Sun!*

She made the firstborn, Kingu, chief among them.

*Kingu is the Moon.*

A Tablet of Destiny to his chest she has attached, his own circuit to acquire,

*A Tablet of destiny would be an orbital path/trajectory!*

By an artful Creator was he fashioned, the son of his own Sun he was. From the Deep where he was engendered, the god from his family in a rushing departed;

*A planet from the deep who is the son of another Sun, is fashioned to accept the celestial battle with Tiamat.*

To leadership you shall be consigned, a host by your side will be your servants! Let Nibiru be your name, as Crossing forever known!

*Nibiru (Destroyer, Phaeton, etc.) with his hosts (moons/satellites) is sent to combat the Earth (Tiamat) as the Planet of the Crossing.*

And how the **Earth** lead **come** to be, and of **Nibiru's** destiny. The **lord** went forth, his **fated** course he followed, Toward the raging Tiamat he **set** his **face**, a **spell** with his **lips** he uttered. As a **cloak** for **protection** he the **Pulser** and the **Emitter** put on; With a **fearsome radiance** his **head** was **crowned**.

*Earth, Nibiru, lord, fated, Tiamat, face, spell, lips, cloak, Pulser, Emitter, fearsome radiance, head crowned! The Sumerians tell of an epic cosmic battle.*

Tiamat's band tightly her encircled, with terror they trembled. Tiamat to her roots gave a shudder, a mighty roar she emitted; On Nibiru she cast a spell, engulfed him with her charms.

The Evil Wind charged her belly, into her innards it made its way. Her innards were howling, her body was distended, her mouth was open wide. Through the opening Nibiru shot a brilliant arrow a lightning most divine.

***As Tiamat passes Nibiru, the gravitational disturbance causes the planet to shudder and an Evil Wind (depleted Uranium-235 mine in Oklo, Gabon) is discharged from within Tiamat (Earth) as Nibiru arcs a plasma discharge toward Tiamat.***

Beside their lifeless mistress, her eleven helpers trembled with terror; In Nibiru's net they were captured, unable they were to flee. Kingu, who by Tiamat was made the host's chief, was among them. The Lord put him in fetters, to his lifeless mistress he bound him. The others of Tiamat's band as captives he bound, in his circuit he them ensnared.

***Tiamat lay lifeless as her eleven satellites are now captured by Nibiru. The Moon is left bound (satellite) to the Earth (Tiamat).***

He bound them all to his circuit; to turn around he made them, backward to course.

***The eleven moons that Nibiru captured from Tiamat (Earth) now have a retrograde orbit.***

Her inner channels he cut apart, her golden veins he beheld with wonder.

***The collision exposes gold that was deep within Tiamat (Earth).***

In a brilliance was Tiamat's upper part to a region unknown carried.

***Tiamat's (Earth's) inards are carried into space.***

A Firmament to divide the waters from the waters. The Upper Waters above the Firmament from the Waters Below it he separated; Let the waters to one place be gathered, let firm land appear! By Firm Land let her be called, Ki henceforth her name to be!

***This echoes the biblical sentiment in Genesis.***

> ***Genesis 1:6 and 1:7*** *And God said , Let there be a firmament in the midst of the waters, and let it divide the waters from the waters. And God made the firmament, and divided the waters which were under the firmament from thewaters which were above the firmament: and it was so.*

Let Kingu be a creature of the night, to shine at night I shall appoint him Earth's companion, the Moon forever to be! Their circuits he destined that none shall transgress nor fall short of each other.

***The Moon is bound forever with the Earth (Ki) to be in unison.***

Most radiant of the gods he is, let him truly the Son of the Sun be!

***The Moon as Son of the Sun!***

## THE THIRD TABLET

Impatient, Ea donned his Fish's suit; within his chest his heart was like a drum beating. Into the marsh he jumped, toward its edge hurried steps he directed. High were the marshes flooding, deeper was the bottom than he expected. He changed his gait to swimming, with bold strokes forward he advanced.

***We have the Mayan concept of the White God swimming from the waters.***

A sight never seen before their eyes was unfolding: The Sun, as a red ball, on the horizon was disappearing! Fear seized the heroes, of a Great Calamity afraid they were! Alalu with laughter words of comfort was saying: A setting of the Sun it is,

*The Anunnaki have never witnessed an Earth sunset and are struck with fear!*

*NOTE: Anu/nnaki = Anu's meteorites! I feel that those who from heaven came, and were associated in the Sumerian pantheon were meteorites from the planet Uranus.*

Evil serpents in the pond were swarming! So did Engur to Ea say.

*We have our first introduction to the snake as an Evil Serpent.*

Mushdammu to lay foundations he directed, dwelling abodes to erect.

*Is the name Muhammad derived from Mushdammu?*

Ulmash, he who what in the waters swarms knows, who of fowl that fly has

*Ulmash – Shamash – Utu Shamash aka the Sun*

Let this day be a day of rest; the seventh day hereafter a day of resting always to be!

*The Sabbath day!*

His mouth was wide open, swiftly he the malehood of Anu bit off, The malehood of Anu did Alalu swallow! In pained agony did Anu a cry to the heavens shout; to the ground wounded he fell.

*Alalu bit off Anu's malehood and swallowed it!*

Of the tall trees in the cedar forest long beams were prepared, The Abode of the North Crest he named it.

*The Cedar Forests of Lebanon.*

The image of Alalu upon the great rock mountain with beams they carved. They showed him wearing an Eagle's helmet; his face they made uncovered. Let the image of Alalu forever gaze toward Nibiru that he ruled, Toward the Earth whose gold he discovered!

*Could this be the famed image on the Cydonia region of Mars?*

Those who on Earth are shall as Anunnaki be known, Those Who from Heaven to Earth Came!

*Those to Earth from heaven came. The Biblical Anakim (Anak)!*

Those who on Lahmu are, Igigi shall be named, Those Who Observe and See they shall be!

*The Watchers!*

Now this is the account of Enki and Enlil and Ninmah,

In the cages there were odd creatures, their likes in the wild no one had seen: Foreparts of one kind they had, hindparts of another creature they possessed; Creatures of two kinds by their essences combined to Ninmah Enki was showing!

*A Gene splicing laboratory.*

The two entwined strands separate and combine an offspring to fashion. Let a male Anunnaki a two-legged female impregnate, let a combination offspring be born! Thus did Ninmah say.

*Human DNA is combined with Anunnaki DNA. This statement says that the meteorites from Uranus (Anunnaki) begin to change mankind on a genetic level causing abnormalities and diseases (leprosy!).*

Shaggy with hair all over was the newborn, his foreparts like of the Earth creatures were, His hindparts to those of the Anunnaki more akin they were.

*A hairy reject is born.*

Again and again Ninmah rearranged the admixtures, of the ME formulas she took bits and pieces; One Being had paralyzed feet, another his semen was dripping,

*More unsuitable offspring occur as a result of the meteoric content.*

Shaggy like the wild ones he was not, dark black his head hair was, Smooth was his skin, smooth as the Anunnaki skin it was, Like dark red blood was its color, like the clay of the Abzu was its hue. They looked at his malehood: Odd was its shape, by a skin was its forepart surrounded, Unlike that of Anunnaki malehood it was, a skin from its forepart was hanging!

*The first man is born with the appearance of an African/Hindu/Arabic person. The human male is born with a foreskin around his penis, unlike that of the Anunnaki.*

Adamu I shall call him! Ninmah was saying. One Who Like Earth's Clay Is, that will be his name! For the newborn Adamu a crib they fashioned, in a corner of the House of Life they placed him.

*The first man is named Adamu (constellation? House of life).*

In seven vessels of the clay of the Abzu made, Ninmah ovals of the two-legged females placed, The life essence of Adamu she extracted, bit by bit in the vessels she it inserted. Then in the malepart of Adamu an incision she made, a drop of blood to let out;

*DNA is extracted from Adamu for implantation.*

Shaggy she was not, like beach sands was the hue of her head hair, Her skin smooth was, as that of the Anunnaki in smoothness and color it was.

*The first female is Caucasian in appearance with blonde hair.*

Ti-Amat let her name be, the Mother of Life! Ninki was saying.

*Ti-Amat is the first female so named.*

An abode in an enclosure for them was built, to roam therein they could.

*Our fabled Garden of Eden sounds like a large cage!*

Day and night the Earthlings he was watching, their doings to ascertain.

*Watcher!*

From the rib of Enki the life essence he extracted, Into the rib of Adamu the life essence of Enki he inserted;
From the rib of Ninmah the life essence he extracted, Into the rib of Ti-Amat the life essence he inserted.

*The rib would be a perfect choice for cell extraction as the bone marrow is rich in red blood cells.*

Then let them be where they are needed! Enlil with anger said. To the Abzu, away from the Edin, let them be expelled!

*Enlil (El, Yahweh, Elul, Toru-el, etc.) expels mankind from the Edin.*

To be with the Anunnaki they were eager, for food rations they toiled well, Of heat and dust they did not complain, of backbreaking they did not grumble; Of the hardships of work the Anunnaki of the Abzu were relieved.

*Our ancient fathers and mothers seemed to be little more than a cargo cult! At the end of World War 2 when the U.S. Air Force took down their temporary bases, villagers on Tanna Island built effigees and prayed to the Gods that left and no longer gave them rations to eat.*

Upon the Earth the warmth was rising, vegetation flourished, wild creatures overran the land;

*Global temperatures rose as plant life and wildlife teemed.*

The rains were heavier, rivers were gushing, abodes repairing needed. Upon the Earth the heat was increasing, the snow white parts to water were melting,

*The rains and temperature increased (not from industry!) as the polar regions melted.*

The bars of the seas the oceans were not containing. From the depths of the Earth volcanoes were fire and brimstones belching, The grounds were trembling, each time the Earth was shaking. In the Lower World, the snow white-hued place, the Earth was grumbling;

*The oceans were flooding, volcanoes rained fire and brimstone, worldquakes, and Antartica was shaking. Scientists have recently reported in a major nature publication, that the collapse of an ancient ice sheet in the Antarctic some 14,000 years ago caused sea level to rise 45 feet during a period of rapid climate change known as the Bolling Warming. This is one of Mr. Sitchin's transcriptions that came under heavy criticism, and may have been shown to be correct?*

In the Hammered Bracelet, turmoils are occurring! Upon the Earth, brimstones from the skies were falling.
Pitiless demons havoc causing, violently the Earth they approached, Into flaming fires in the skies they were bursting. In a clear day darkness they were causing, with storms and Evil Winds they raged around. Like stony missiles the Earth they were attacking, Kingu, Earth's Moon, and Lahmu too by these havocs were afflicted, The faces of all three with countless scars were covered!

*Hammered Bracelet (Asteroid Belt), Earth, brimstones, falling, Pitiless demons, havoc, violently, approached, flaming, skies, bursting, darkness, storms, Evil Winds, raged, stony missiles, attacking, Kingu, Lahmu, three, scars, covered!*

Bereft of the celestial bar, Lahamu with Mummu near the Sun were crouching,

*Venus (Lahamu) and Mercury (Mummu) near the Sun as they loose footing in the celestial bar.*

In the heavens Lahamu her glorious dwelling place was abandoning, Toward Nibiru the heavenly king she was attracted, a queen of heaven she wished to be!

*Lahamu (Venus) takes an orbit towards Nibiru (Phaeton, Destroyer, etc.) by gravitational pull.*

To quell her, Nibiru from the celestial deep a monstrous demon made appear. A monster once to Tiamat's host belonging, by the Celestial Battle fashioned,

*Nibiru sends a former Moon of Tiamat (Earth) to do battle with Lahamu (Venus).*

From horizon to the midst of heaven like a flaming dragon it was stretched, One league was its head, fifty leagues in length it was, awesome was its tail.

*The satellite's coma was 1 mile long with the tail 150 miles in length, as it stretched across 1/3 of the visible heavens.*

By day the skies of Earth it darkened, By night upon the face of the Moon a spell of darkness it cast.

*We have an extended period of darkness recorded.*

Lahamu its dwelling place did not abandon, The stony missiles upon the Earth and Lahmu ceased their raining.

*Venus kept her order in the celestial seating, as meteors ceased raining down on the Earth and Mars.*

The Landing Platform was intact; in the valleys of the north the Earth fiery liquids was pouring!

*Magma from volcanoes flowed in the north.*

So was Ninurta to his father Enlil telling; sulfuric mists and bitumens he was discovering.

*The Moon God, tells the Bull God, of the sulfur and bitumen that the celestial collisions have deposited on the Earth.*

On Lahmu the atmosphere was damaged, dust storms were with life and work interfering,

*The Sumerians tell us what we've spent billions to find out. That the atmosphere of Mars was damaged causing dust storms to rage across the surface of the planet.*

The handiwork of the Creator of All in this solitude we can admire!

*Enki consistently refers to the Creator of All!*

Its motions about the Earth they measured, the duration of a month they calculated. How the two were entwined, causing the luminaries to disappear, they recorded.

*The Moon is studied to establish a Lunar Calendar.*

With the Earth and the Moon, Lahmu the Sums second quarter constituted, Six were the celestials of the Lower Waters. So was Enki to Marduk explaining. Six were the celestials of the Upper Waters, beyond the bar, the Hammered Bracelet, they were: Anshar and Kishar, Anu and Nudimmud, Gaga and Nibiru; these were the six others,

*Inner Planets: Mercury (Mummu), Venus (Lahamu), Earth (Ki, Tiamat), Moon (Kingu), and Lahmu (Mars)*
*Hammered Bracelet: Asteroid Belt*
*Outer Planets: Anshar (Jupiter), Kishar (Saturn), Anu (Uranus), Nudimmud (Neptune), Gaga (Pluto), and Nibiru (Phaeton)*

Twelve were they in all, of twelve did the Sun and its family make the count.

*We have the twelve children of the family of the Sun!*

By the circuit of the heavens, from horizon to horizon, he drew images of twelve constellations.

*Enki/Enoch creates the twelve zodiac constellations.*

In the Great Band, the Way of Anu, one each with the Sun's family of twelve he paired, To each one he designated a station, by names they were to be called. Then in the heavens below the Way of Anu, whence Nibiru the Sun is approaching, A bandlike way he designed, the Way of Enki he it designated; To it twelve constellations by their shapes he also allotted. The heavens above the Way of Anu, the Upper Tier, the Way of Enlil he called, Therein too the stars into twelve constellations he assembled. Thirty-six were the stars' constellations, in the three Ways were they located.

*The zodiac constellations are broken down into twelve major figures with thirty-six decans or sub-groups of banded stars. The three decans of twelve each for a total of thirty-six are;*

*The Way of Enlil - The celestial sphere above the 30$^{th}$ parallel north – Yahweh, Jehovah, Brahma – The Lord of Heaven*
*The Way of Anu - The central band of the celestial sphere containing the zodiacal constellations; on Earth, the central band between the northern Way of Enlil and the southern Way of Enki – Anubis – Great Lord of All Heaven*
*The Way of Enki - The celestial sphere below the 30$^{th}$ parallel south – Satan, Baalzebub, etc. – The Lord of the Underworld*

When on Earth I had arrived, the station that was ending by me the Station of the Fishes was named,

*Enki/Enoch arrived during the end of the Age of Pisces which just finished possibly in 2012. This would mean that one complete Zodiac Age has elapsed or 26-28K years since his arrival on Earth. We curiously have cave drawings in France and other countries that date back to this period!*

The one that followed after my name title, He of the Water., I called!

*The Age of Aquarius (Galzu) follows the sign of Pisces.*

But on Earth and on Nibiru, knowledge and rulership are separated! So did Marduk to his
father say.

*And it stays that way up to this day!*

Sweet were her lips, firm with ripeness were her breasts. Into her womb he poured his semen, in a mating he knew her. Into her womb she took the holy semen, by the semen of the lord Enki she was impregnated. The second young one to him Enki called, berries from the field she him offered. Enki bent down, the young one he embraced, on her lips he kissed her; Sweet were her lips, firm with ripeness were her breasts. Into her womb he poured his semen, in a mating he knew her. Into her womb she took the holy semen, by the semen of the lord Enki she was impregnated.

*Lord Enki is up to his old tricks mating with Earth women.*

Among the bulrushes in reed baskets have I them found! Thus to all you will say!

*This is the story of Moses, but with twins (Romulus & Remus)!*

Ninurta teaches Ka-in crop cultivation

*Ka-in learns to farm.*

Marduk teaches Abael shepherding and toolmaking

*Abael learns shepherding.*

Fighting over water, Ka-in strikes and kills Abael Ka-in is tried for murder, sentenced to exile

*Water has been fought over since we were first taught to direct its course.*

Adapa and Titi have other offspring who intermarry On his deathbed Adapa blesses his son Sati as his heir A descendant, Enkime, is taken by Marduk to Lahmu

*Adam's son Sati (Satu, Satan), and Marduk (Mars) takes Enkime/Enoch to Mars.*

Adapa, to Nibiru, the planet whence we had come, you will be going, Before Anu our king you will come, to his majesty you will be presented; Before him you shall bow. Speak only when asked, to questions short answers give!
New clothing you will be given; the new garments put on. A bread on Earth not found they to you will give; the bread is death, do not eat! In a chalice an elixir to drink they to you will give; the elixir is death, do not drink!
With you Ningishzidda and Dumuzi my sons will journey, to their words hearken, and you shall live! So did Enki Adapa instruct.
This I shall remember! Adapa said.

*Enki tricks Adapa into giving up long life, and thus begins the legend of the deception of mankind by the Evil Serpent.*

Never before was there a ewe on Earth, a lamb has never to Earth from the heavens been dropped, A she-goat has never before to her kid given birth,

*The first lamb is born on Earth as this was seen as a gift from heaven, and is in all probability why it was of primary sacrificial importance.*

After the Celebration of Firsts was over, sullen was Ka-in's face; By the lack of Enki's blessing greatly he was aggrieved.

**The Sumerians had a Feast of Firstfruits, just as the Hebrews now observe! Enki is pleased with Abel's offering, but not that of Ka-in. This seeming favoritism further deepens the divide between brothers.**

As to their tasks the brothers returned, Abael before his brother was boasting: I am the one who abundance brings, who the Anunnaki satiates,

**Abael rubs it in that the Anunnaki (meteorites of Uranus) are fed by him.**

Into the fields of his brother Abael his flocks drove, from the Furrows and the canals to drink water. By this Ka-in was angered; to move the flocks away his brother he commanded. Farmer and shepherd, brother and brother, words of accusation uttered. They spat on each other, with their fists they fought. Greatly enraged, Ka-in a stone picked up, with it he Abael in the head struck. Again and again he hit him until Abael fell, his blood from him gushing. When Ka-in his brother's blood saw, Abael, Abael, my brother! He shouted. Motionless on the ground did Abael remain, from him his soul had departed.

**Flocks, water, trespass, accusations, spat, fists, stoned! Just like that, we have the first murder on the books.**

In the field they found Ka-in, by the dead Abael he was still seated.

**Ka-in mourns what he has done as he stays by his brother's side.**

What have you done? What have you done? To Ka-in they shouted. Silence was Ka-in's answer; to the ground he threw himself and wept. To Eridu city Adapa returned, what had happened to the lord Enki he told. With fury Enki Ka-in confronted. Accursed you shall be! To him he said. From the Edin you must depart, among Anunnaki and Civilized Earthlings you shall not stay

**Ka-in is cast out by Lord Enki and cursed for his actions.**

As the Anunnaki custom is, he in a grave, below a stone pile, shall be buried. How Abael to bury Enki to Adapa and Titi showed, for the custom to them was not known.

**Burial cairns (meteorite piles?) are the Anunnaki (meteorites of Uranus) tradition. This may help to explain this practice in the United Kingdom and many other countries.**

For **thirty days** and **thirty nights** was Abael by his parents mourned.

**The mourning period begins at thirty days.**

Eastward to a land of wandering for his evil deed Ka-in must depart,
That his life must be spared, he and his generations shall be distinguished! By Ningishzidda was the life essence of Ka-in altered: That his face a beard should not grow, Ka-ins life essence Ningishzidda changed.

**Ka-in's DNA is altered so that he and his offspring are unable to grow beards.**

With his sister Awan as a spouse Ka-in from the Edin departed, to the Land of Wandering he set his course.

**Awan – Aswan?**

In all, **thirty sons** and **thirty daughters** Adapa and Titi had,

**30/30 club.**

By, the name Enki-Me, by Enki ME Understanding, in the annals he was called.

**Enkime/Enoch is born.**

About the heavens and all matters celestial he was constantly curious. To him the lord Enki took a liking, secrets once to Adapa revealed to him he told. Of the family of the Sun and the twelve celestial gods Enki him was teaching, And how the months by the Moon were counted and the years by the Sun, And how by Nibiru the Shars were counted, and how the counts by Enki were combined, How the lord Enki the circle of the heavens to twelve parts divided, A constellation to each one how Enki assigned, twelve stations in a grand circle he arranged,

**Enki teaches Enkime/Enoch all about the stars and constellations, and one Shar is 3,600 Earth years.**

Utu in his bright abode a Prince of Earthlings him installed. The rites him he taught, the functions of priesthood to begin. In Sippar with his spouse Edinni, a half sister, Enkime resided, To them in the one hundred and fourth Shar a son was born, Matushal his mother him named, Who by the Bright Waters Raised the name meant.

**The Biblical Methusaleh (Matushal) is born to Enkime/Enoch.**

To the hands of Matushal, his firstborn son, the writings he entrusted, With his brothers Ragim and Gaidad to study and abide by. In the one hundred and fourth Shar was Matushal born, To the Igigi troubles and what Marduk had done he was a witness.

**Matushal (Methusaleh) goes into witness protection as he speaks out against the Igigi. Enoch/Enkime goes into hiding because of the Watchers in the Biblical accounting.**

By his spouse Ednat a son to Matushal was born, Lu-Mach, Mighty Man, was his name. In his days conditions on Earth became harsher; the toilers in field and meadow raised complaints. As a workmaster the Anunnaki Lu-Mach appointed, the quotas to enforce, the rations to reduce.

**Lu-Mach (Lemech) is born to be a taskmaster over his fellow Earthlings.**

And the face of Ka-in on the right was beardless, and the face of Sati on the left with beard was. And Adapa put his right hand on the head of Sati, the one on the left, And he blessed him and said: Of your seed shall the Earth be filled, And of your seed as a tree with three branches Mankind a Great Calamity shall survive. And he put his left hand on the head of Ka-in on his right, and to him said: For your sin of your birthright you are deprived, but of your seed seven nations shall come, In a realm set apart they shall thrive, distant lands they shall inhabit;

**The tradition of the Patriarch giving his blessings before closing his eyes begins.**

In the Edin Lu-Mach as a workmaster the Anunnaki served, In the days of Lu-Mach did Marduk and the Igigi with Earthlings intermarry.

**The Igigi (altered human offspring?) intermarry with Earth women during the days of Lu-Mach. The Bible has them doing this in the days of Jared.**

On the Sun they observed, in the netforces of Earth and Lahmu there were disruptions. In the Abzu, at the tip the Whiteland facing, instruments far observing they installed;

**The Sun is causing gravitational problems on Earth and Mars. In Africa instruments recording the continent of Antartica picks up the anomalies.**

In our image and in our likeness Civilized Earthling is, except for the long life, he is we!

**In OUR image man was created!**

Now this is the account of how the Igigi the daughters of the Earthlings abducted, And how afflictions followed and Ziusudra oddly was born.

**Ziusudra/Noah is born from an Igigi mating with his mother. Noah is described in the Bible at birth as snowy white in appearance, with red spots and glowing eyes, this is the same way that the Sumerians describe Anunnaki children at birth!**

One among them, Shamgaz his name was, their leader became. Even if none of you agrees, I alone the deed shall do! To the others he said. If a penalty for this sin shall be imposed, I alone for all of you shall it bear! One by one others in the plot joined together, by an oath together to do it they swore.

**Shamgaz is the leader of this fallen group as they swear an oath!**

The Earth by the Earthlings inherited will be! Enlil to Ninurta said.

***Did we inherit the Earth?***

In the Edin Lu-Mach was the workmaster, quotas to enforce was his duty, The Earthlings' rations to reduce was his task.

***The Sumerian (Egyptian) workmaster/taskmaster Lu-Mach reduces their rations. The Egyptians had them make brick with straw in the Biblical parallel. The use of straw was a substitute due to Earth changes in all probability.***

And when Lu-Mach to the domain of Marduk was summoned, To the household of Ninmah, in Shurubak, the Haven City, his spouse Batanash he brought, From the angry Earthling masses protected and safe to be.

***The Earthlings revolt!***

On the roof of a dwelling when Batanash was bathing Enki by her loins took hold, he kissed her, his semen into her womb he poured. With a child Batanash was, her belly was truly swelling; To Lu-Mach from Shurubak word was sent: To the Edin return, a son you have!

***Enki!***

White as the snow his skin was, the color of wool was his hair, Like the skies were his eyes, in a brilliance were his eyes shining. Amazed and frightened was Lu-Mach; to his father Matushal he hurried. A son unlike an Earthling to Batanash was born, by this birth greatly puzzled I am!

***Ziusudra/Noah is born.***

Matushal to Batanash came, the newborn boy he saw, by his likeness amazed he was. Is one of the Igigi the boy's father? Of Batanash Matushal the truth demanded;

To Lu-Mach your spouse whether this boy his son is, the truth reveal! None of the Igigi is the boy's father, of this upon my life I swear! So did Batanash him answer

***Batanash lies to Lu-Mach, even though an Igigi is not the father, she fails to tell him the whole truth. A lie of omission, is still a lie!***

Now this is the account of Earth's tribulations before the Deluge, And how the mysterious Galzu decisions of life and death in secret guided.

On the Sun's face black spots were appearing, from its face flames shot up;

***Solar flares (Sun Spots) began to stir things up.***

Kishar also was misbehaving, its host its footings lost, dizzying were their circuits.

***Saturn takes an irregular orbit as the gravity of its' satellites are perturbed.***

The Hammered Bracelet was by unseen netforces pulled and pushed, For reasons unfathomed, the Sun its family was upsetting;

***Gravitational disturbances are causing the asteroid belt to be upset, and they could not figure out why the Sun was upsetting its family.***

Angry is the Creator of All! Voices from amongst the people shouted.

*The people understand at this point that there is a Creator of All, that fashioned the Anunnaki as well.*

The snow-ice that the Whiteland covers to sliding has taken! So did they from Abzu's tip report.

*The iceshelf in Antartica is cracking as reported from the station in Africa (@ 12,000 BCE the Bolling Warming).*

The next time Nibiru the Sun shall be nearing, Earth to Nibiru's netforce exposed shall be,

*On Nibiru's next circuit the Earth will be exposed to Nibiru's gravitational pull (parabola/parabolic trajectory).*

Lahmu in its circuits on the Sun's other side shall a station take.

*Mars will be safe opposite the Sun.*

Kishar and its host agitated shall be, Lahamu shall also shake and wobble;

*Saturn and it's moons, along with Venus will be shaken.*

The next time Nibiru the closest to Earth shall approach, The snow-ice off the Whiteland's surface shall come a-sliding. A watery calamity it shall cause: By a huge wave, a Deluge, the Earth will be
overwhelmed!

*Nibiru's next approach will shake the iceshelf loose in Antartica causing the Great Flood!*

In Boats of Heaven in Earth's skies will we remain,

*The Anunnaki circle the skies to wait out the disaster. The meteors from Uranus do not fall to Earth during this disaster.*

Ishkur, Enlil's youngest, to remain on Earth with his father his decision made. Utu and Inanna, Nannar's children who on Earth were born, to stay declared. Enki and Ninki, to stay and Earth not abandon chose; proudly they so announced. The Igigi and Sarpanit I shall not desert! Marduk with anger stated. One by one Enki's other sons their choice to stay announced: Nergal and Gibil, Ninagal and Ningishzidda and Dumuzi too. All eyes to Ninmah then turned; with pride her choice to stay she declared: My lifework is here! The Earthlings, my created, I shall not abandon!

*The bulk of the Anunnaki choose to stay near their progeny durning the catastrophe.*

Let the Earthlings for the abominations perish; so did Enlil proclaim.

*Enlil (Yahweh, El, Toru-el,etc) is pleased to allow the Earthlings to perish, as he sees them as an abomination that should never have been created.*

That all leaders solemnly swear to let events unhindered occur, of all Enlil demanded.

*The Anunnaki swear an oath of secrecy to let mankind perish without knowledge of the catastrophe to come.*

The floodwaters I cannot arrest, the Earthling multitudes I cannot save,

*The Anunnaki are helpless.*

Let us tablets of records in Sippar, in the depths of the Earth, safely bury, Let what from one planet on another done in days to come uncovered be! Enki his brother's words with approving accepted. ME's and other tablets in golden chests they stored, In the depths of the Earth, in Sippar, for posterity they buried.

*Sounds like the Ark of the Covenant!*

Male and female essences and life-eggs they collected, Of each kind two by two, two by two they in Shurubak and the Abzu preserved, For safekeeping while in Earth circuit to be taken, thereafter the living kinds to recombine.

*The proverbial two of each kind to be stored on the Ark.*

**THE TENTH TABLET**

That the lord Enki, asleep in his quarters, had a dream-vision. In the dream-vision there appeared the image of a man, bright and shining like the heavens; And as the man Enki approached, Enki saw that the white-haired Galzu he was! In his right hand an engraver's stylus he was holding, And in his left hand a tablet of lapis lazuli, shining smooth, he held.

*This vision of Galzu is the prototype for the Man of Years, Wisdom of Years, and the symbol for Aquarius.*

Summon your son Ziusudra, without breaking the oath to him the coming calamity reveal. A boat that the watery avalanche can withstand, a submersible one, to build him tell,

*Noah/Ziusudra is the son of Enki!*

A boatguide who knows the waters, by me appointed, to you that day will come; On that day the boat you must enter, its hatch tightly close you must. An overwhelming Deluge, coming from the south, lands and life shall devastate;

*Ziusudra/Noah is warned by Enki of the Flood to come.*

My lord! My lord! He shouted. Your voice I heard, let me see your face! Not to you, Ziusudra, have I spoken, to the reed wall did I speak! So Enki said.

*This is the genesis of hearing the voice of the Lord God without seeing him, as Enki gets around his sworn oath by speaking to the wall of a hut.*

In the morning, to the townspeople he so announced: The lord Enlil with the Lord Enki, my master, angry has been,
On that account to me the lord Enlil is hostile. In this city I no longer reside can, nor in the Edin my foot anymore set;

*Ziusudra/Noah deceives his fellow humans into giving him help.*

Thereby the lord Enlil's anger will subside, hardships will end, Upon you the lord Enlil abundance henceforth will shower! The morning was not yet gone when the people about Ziusudra gathered, To speedily for him the boat build they each other encouraged. Timbers of boat-wood the elders were hauling, the little ones bitumen from the marshes carried. As woodworkers the planks together hammered, Ziusudra in a cauldron the bitumen
melted. With bitumen the boat he waterproofed inside and out,

*Ziusudra/Noah builds his covered vessel in same or similar fashion as the Biblical accounting.*

Any who to the abode of the lord Enki wish to go, let them too aboard come! So did Ziusudra to the gathered people announce. Envisioning Enlil's abundance, only some of the craftsmen the call heeded.

*Again Noah/Ziusudra deals craftily with his human counterparts.*

On the sixth day Ninagal, Lord of the Great Waters, to the boat came, A son of Enki he was, to be the boat's navigator he was selected. A box of cedarwood in his hands he held, by his side in the boat he kept it; The life essences and life eggs of living creatures it contains, by the lord Enki and Ninmah collected,

*Ninagal pilots the Ark for Noah/Ziusudra, as the DNA for repopulating the Earth is brought on board.*

In the station of the Constellation of the Lion was the avalanche looming.

*The Great Flood occurs during the Age of Leo which makes sense! The 3 stars in the Belt of Orion lineup with the Sphinx at around 10,500 BCE during the Age of Leo. The history books pickup during the Age of Taurus, as there are over 5,000 silent years on the records.*

For days before the Day of the Deluge the Earth was rumbling, groan as with pain it did; For nights before the calamity struck, in the heavens Nibiru as a glowing star was seen;

*The Earth moaned before Nibiru approached and it was seen glowing in the skies. This may account for the Hopi "Blue Star," of prophecy?*

Then there was darkness in daytime, and at night the Moon as though by a monster was swallowed.

*We have protracted darkness recorded.*

The Earth began to shake, by a netforce before unknown it was agitated. In the glow of dawn, a black cloud arose from the horizon, The morning's light to darkness changed, as though by death's shadow veiled. Then the sound of a rolling thunder boomed, lightnings the skies lit up.

*The Earth is shaken by gravitational disturbances, and darkness envelops the skies, as Nibiru causes plasma discharges.*

In Shurubak, eighteen leagues away, the bright eruptions by Ninagal were seen:

In the Whiteland, at the Earth's bottom, the Earth's foundations were shaking; Then with a roar to a thousand thunders equal, off its foundations the icesheet slipped, By Nibiru's unseen netforce it was pulled away, into the south sea crashing. One sheet of ice into another icesheet was smashing, The Whiteland's surface like a broken eggshell was crumbling. All at once a tidal wave arose, the very skies was the wall of waters reaching.

*The ice sheets in Antarctica begin to crash into the sea creating an extinction level tsunami.*

A storm, its ferocity never before seen, at the Earth's bottom began to howl, Its winds the wall of water were driving, the tidal wave northward was spreading;

*The storm winds begin to increase the height of the wall of water. This phenomenon has just been noted with winds helping to increase the height of what has been termed "rogue waves."*

Northward was the wall of waters onrushing, the Abzu lands it was reaching.

*The wall of water hits the African continent.*

The boat of Ziusudra the tidal wave from its moorings lifted, Tossed it about, like a watery abyss the boat it swallowed. Though completely submerged, the boat held firm, not a drop of water into it did enter.

*The Ark was water tight!*

The sluices of heaven opened, a downpour from the skies upon the Earth was unleashed. For seven days the waters from above with the waters of the Great Below were mingled;

*It rained for seven days (Ishtar's sacred number is 7).*

Then the wall of water, its limits reaching, its onslaught ceased, But the rains from the skies for forty more days and nights continued.

*It rains for forty more days! Enki's sacred number is 40!*

To check for dry land, for surviving vegetation to verify he sent them. He sent forth a swallow, he sent forth a raven; both to the boat returned. He sent forth a dove; with a twig from a tree to the boat it returned!

*We have the Biblical accounting as this is why the dove is a sacred icon to Israel.*

The lord Enki let us praise, to him thanks give! To them Ziusudra said. With his sons stones he gathered, with them an altar he built, Then a fire on the altar he lit, with aromatic incense he made a fire. A ewe-lamb, one without blemish, for a sacrifice he selected, And upon the altar to Enki the ewe-lamb as a sacrifice he offered.

*Just as in the Biblical account, we have a sacrifice right away.*

Let us in Whirlwinds from the celestial boats upon the peak of Arrata descend,

*Arrata – Mount Ararat*

Then Enlil by the whiffs of fire and roasting meat was puzzled. What is that? To his brother he shouted. Has anyone the Deluge survived?

*Enlil (Yahweh, El, Toru-el) smells the savory meat!*

Ninmah her necklace of crystals, a gift of Anu, touched and swore: On my oath, the annihilation of Mankind shall never be repeated!

*Ninmah (Earth) gives the declaration that she will never allow mankind to be destroyed again, similar to the Biblical story.*

Be fruitful and multiply, and the Earth replenish! Thus were the Olden Times ended.

*Sounds familiar?*

Lahmu by the passage of Nibiru was devastated! So did Marduk relate: Its atmosphere was sucked out, its waters thereafter evaporated, a place of dust storms it is!

*The atmosphere of Mars is totally destroyed after this last encounter.*

The Moon by itself life cannot sustain, only with Eagle masks is staying enabled!

*Space suits are now needed to exist on the Moon.*

To him as fruit cultivator Ziusudra's youngest son was assigned: The first fruit they found, the vine that by Ninmah was brought it was; Of its juice, as the Anunnaki's elixir renowned, Ziusudra took a sip. By one sip, then another and another, Ziusudra was overpowered, like a drunkard he fell asleep!

*Noah/Ziusudra gets drunk, but there's no molestation in this account.*

To Dumuzi the shepherding tasks Enki gave, in the task was Ziusudra's middle son
assisting.

*Dumuzi/Tammuz – The Good Shepherd=Bootes constellation*

Even Enlil, who the end of all flesh planned, was no longer angered.

*Enlil's (Jupiter) temper subsides.*

And the artificed twin mounts and how the image of the lion by Marduk was usurped.

*The face of the Sphinx.*

Let the heart of the plain the heavens reflect! So did Enlil to Enki suggest.

*The star charts from the layout of the pyramids in Egypt shows the direct correlation of this statement to their design!*

*Sphinx – aligned with the constellation of Leo around 10,500 BCE*
*Giza Pyramids – layout as the constellations of Orion, Sirius, and Alderbaran*
*Abusir Pyramids –layout as the 7 stars of the Pleiades constellation (Leg of the Sacred Bull) and Sun*
*Lower Egypt, Southern Pyramids – layout as the 7 stars of the Pleiades and the Andromeda constellation along the Milky way*

The Landing Path on the twin peaks of Arrata in the north were anchored; To demarcate the Landing Corridor Enlil

The dark-hued landmass that the Abzu included to Enki and his clan was for domains granted, The people of Ziusudra's middle son, Ham, to inhabit it were chosen. To make Marduk their lord, of their lands the master, Enki to appease his son suggested.

**Marduk is made lord over Africa.**

Slowly the Earth to teem with life returned; with the seeds of life by Enki preserved

***This must be the period between the Age of Leo to the Age of Taurus (silent period).***

Asar, unsuspecting, to **celebrate** with his **brother** also came.
A large **vessel**, mighty to look upon, with **elixired wine** he gave him.
Then by the **admixture** wine he was **overcome**, to the **ground** he **fell** down.
They **Asar** to another **chamber** carried, in a **coffin** they him laid,
The **coffin** with **tight** seals they **closed**, into the **sea** they threw it.

***This is similar to Joseph and his brothers in the Bible.***

Marduk his clothes rent, on his forehead he put ashes.

***Marduk exhibits the customary act of mourning, by renting his clothes and placing ashes on his forehead.***

By these twists of fate Asta was baffled; distraught, the rules to defy she was determined. Before the body of Asar was wrapped and in the shroud in a shrine preserved, From his phallus Asta the life seed of Asar extracted. With it Asta herself made conceive, an heir and avenger to Asar to be born.

***This is the "Immaculate Conception," concept.***

Among the river's bull rushes with the child she hid, the wrath of Satu she was avoiding; Horon she called the boy, to be his father's avenger she raised him.

***Moses was hid among the bulrushes in the Biblical tale. Innana and Utu were found in the reeds as well!***

In the dark-hued lands the child Horon by Earth's quick life cycles to a hero grew, By his great-uncle Gibil was Horon adopted, by him was he trained and instructed. For him Gibil winged sandals for soaring fashioned, to fly like a falcon he was able;

***Horon is Mercury! The legend of Mercury with winged sandals was fashioned from the story of Horon. Horon is Horus in the Egyptian pantheon, and is represented with the head of a Falcon.***

For him Gibil a divine harpoon made, its arrows bolts of missiles were.

***Gibil (old Mercury) gives Mercury (Horon) a harpoon, arrows, and missiles.***

Satu to Horon words of challenge sent: Between us two alone is the conflict, let us one on one in contest meet!

***Venus (Satu- became Saturn, Satan, etc.) and Mercury (Horon) go to do battle.***

When Horon toward him like a falcon skyward soared, A poisoned dart at him Satu shot, like a scorpion's sting it Horon felled.

***Satu (Venus) kills Horon (Mercury) with a plasma discharge.***

With magic powers Ningishzidda the poison to benevolent blood converted, By morning was Horon healed, from the dead was he returned.

*Horon (Mercury) rises from the dead as the morning returns him above the horizon.*

At first Horon's Fiery Pillar was hit, then with his harpoon Horon Satu smote. To the ground Satu crashing down came; by Horon in tethers he was bound.

*Venus (Satu) takes the worst in this exchange.*

The canals that the river's waters bore, red from blood became;

*The waters turn to blood just as in the Biblical account, and it's noted here that it was in the canals.*

Ishkur's brilliances the nights' darkness into flaming days converted

*Ishkur (Ishtar, Venus) is ablaze in the sky.*

Horon to defend his grandfather came; by her Brilliance was his right eye damaged.

*We have the legend of the Right Eye of Horon/Horus (Mercury) being damaged in celestial battle.*

Then Ninurta of the secret entrance learned, the swivel stone on the north side he found! Through a dark corridor Ninurta passed, the grand gallery he reached,

*A secret passage on the Great Pyramid of Giza.*

To a place where horned beasts are hunted with wife and son he went After Marduk had departed, Ninurta the Ekur through the shaft reentered,

*North America.*

How over Mankind lofty to remain, how to make the many the few obey and serve.

*This seems to still be the directive!*

**THE TWELFTH TABLET**

To come to Earth one more time Anu decided, with Antu his spouse he wished to come,

*The Chief Lord of all Anunnaki (Uranus and Neptune/Antu his wife) are coming to Earth for a visit.*

Above in a circle skyward pointing, the twelve constellations by their signs were marked out.

*The twelve constellations are reestablished from the new sky.*

Amid its people's dwellings and cattlefolds and stalls a sacred precinct was walled off. An abode for Enlil and Ninlil therein was built, in seven stages it arose; A stairway, rising as to heaven, to the topmost platform led.

*The Etemenanki AKA the Ziggurat of Ur!*

His Tablets of Destinies did Enlil there keep, with his weapons it was protected: The Lifted Eye that scans the lands, the Lifted Beam that penetrates all.
*Enlil holds the All Seeing Eye, and has the ability to look through matter.*

A pure white structure, the House of Anu, in its midst was built. Its exterior in seven stages rose; its interior like a king's quarters was.

A great banquet was for Anu and Antu prepared, for the sign in the heavens its start was awaiting.

*We have a lavish celebration on the entrance of the new Zodiac Age.*

For several Earth days and nights Anu and Antu slept; on the sixth day his two sons and daughter Anu summoned.

*And Anu (Uranus) rested for six days!*

To commemorate Anu's visit, a new count of time passage was introduced: By Earth years, not by Nibiru Shars, was what on Earth transpired to be counted. In the Age of the Bull, to Enlil dedicated, was the count of Earth years begun. When to the Edin the leaders returned, the place of the first civilized region,

*The Age and dating for Earth begins in the Age of Taurus!*

How to make bricks from mud the Anunnaki the Earthlings taught, therewith cities to build.

*The first Stone Masons!*

Therein the Anunnaki as Lofty Lords were served and worshiped, By number-ranks were they honored, the heirship to Mankind made known:

**Anu**, the heavenly, the rank of **sixty held**, Uranus – main deity/lord of the Anunnaki and mankind.

to **Enlil** the **fifty** rank was given, On **Ninurta** his foremost son did Enlil the same rank bestow.

*Enlil is represented by the Taurus constellation, also likened to Jupiter, Odin, El, and others.*

Next. In succession was the **lord Enki (Neptune)**, the rank of **forty** he held; *(Is mankinds sacred number as well!)*

To **Nannar**, the son of Enlil and Ninlil, the rank of **thirty** was assigned.

*Nannar was worshipped as the Mood God.*

To his son and successor, **Utu**, the rank of **twenty** was allotted;

*Utu was worshipped as the Sun God, aka Utu Shamash and Shamash.*

**Ten** as a number-rank to the other Anunnaki leaders' sons was granted.

Ranks by the **fives** between the **female** Anunnaki and spouses were shared.

Now this is the account of the first City of Men and of kingship on Earth, And how Marduk to build a tower schemed and wherefor Inanna the ME's stole.

*Marduk (Mars) has mankind build the Tower of Babel, and Venus (Inanna) steals the ME's (planet trajectory/orbit).*

Then to let the black-headed people a city of their own possess it was decided;

*The Babylonians are given their own land.*

Ninurta's glorious time it was, with the Constellation of the Archer he was honored.

*Ninurta represents the constellation of Sagittarius.*

When his followers at the place assembled, stones to build with they found not Marduk how to make bricks and burn them by fire, to serve as stone, to them he showed,

*Marduk (Mars) teaches mankind how to make fired bricks, and not with straw!*

Therewith a tower whose head the heavens can reach they were building. To thwart the plan Enlil to the place hurried, to placate Marduk with soothing words he tried; Marduk an unpermitted Gateway to Heaven is building, to Earthlings it he is entrusting! So did Enlil to his sons and grandchildren say. If this we allow to happen, no other matter of Mankind shall be unreached!

*Enlil (Jupiter) shows up to thwart Marduk (Mars) and mankind's plans.*

Henceforth their language I shall confound, that they each other's speech will not understand In each region and every land the people a different tongue he made to speak, A different form of writing thereafter to each was given, that one the other will not comprehend.

*Mankinds' speech and writing is chosen to be confused, just as in the Biblical accounting.*

But in the new domain, where Ningishzidda the Winged Serpent was called, a new count of its own began.

*The new calendar is created in the Americas for the Mayan and other civilizations.*

Marduk as Ra, the Bright One, was worshiped; Enki as Ptah, the Developer, was venerated. Ningishzidda as Tehuti, the Divine Measurer, was recalled;

*The seat of power moves to Egypt as the names now change to Ra (Mars), and Ptah (Neptune).*

To erase his memory Ra on the Stone Lion his image with that of his son Asar replaced.
*Asar is the face that we now see on the Sphinx.*

To count by tens, not by sixty, Ra the people made; the year he also by tens divided,

*The base system of ten counting begins. Anu's sacred number was 60, so the switch to a ten count system would have been done in opposition to Anu (Uranus).*

The watching of the Moon by the watching of the Sun he replaced.

*Marduk (Mars) turned the Egyptians into Moon (Nannar) worshippers versus the Sun.*

As a Great One of the Twelve Celestials, Ptah to Ra the constellation sign of the Ram
allotted.

*Ra (Marduk, Mars) rules over the Earth is to begin with the onset of the Age of Aries.*

Beforehand with her brother Utu the Station of the Twins she shared,

*The Constellation/Age of Gemini was from 6628 BCE to 4469 BCE before man reawoke during the Age of Taurus 4468 BCE.*

Henceforth, as a gift from Ninharsag, her Constellation of the Maiden to Inanna was
allotted;

*Innana (Venus) is one of the mothers of mankind, so she is given the constellation of Virgo to symbolize motherhood.*

**THE THIRTEENTH TABLET**

That in less than a third of one Shar a calamity unknown would befall, who could foretell?

*A Shar is 3,600 Nibiru years, so it would be 1,200 years before the disasters of the Exodus.*

By Inanna was the bitter end started, Marduk as Ra with Destiny tangled;

*Venus (Inanna) starts this war with Mars (Ra).*

The plant did the snake snatch from the sleeping Gilgamesh; with the plant it vanished.

*That evil snake deprives Gilgamesh of immortality.*

So did Ra in his, realm decree. The kings how to build tombs facing eastward he taught,

*Facing East toward the rising Sun to build their tombs and to pray!*

To the priest-scribes a long book he dictated, the Afterlife journey in detail in it was described. How to reach the Duat, the Place of the Celestial Boats, in the book was told,

*The Egyptian Book of the Dead.*

As his Rank of Thirty befitting, as the god of the Moon Nannar was worshiped;

*Nannar of the Moon.*

As the count of the Moon months in a year, twelve festivals each year he decreed, To each of the twelve great Anunnaki a month and its festival were dedicated.

*Monthly Moon festivals are established.*

In Cities of Man local rulers as Righteous Shepherds were designated;

*Have the Shepherds lost their way?*

To the people who in the upper plain of the two rivers dwelt Inanna took a liking; The sound of their tongue she found pleasant, to speak their language she learned. By the name of the planet Lahamu in their tongue Ishtar they called her,

*The Akkadians!*

Uruk her city Unug-ki they called, Dudu as Adad in their language they pronounced.

*We have two more names for Venus as Dudu and Adad in Akkadian.*

Sin, Lord of Oracles, her father Nannar they named; Urim-city by them Ur was called.

*Nannar is now being worshipped as "Sin," the Moon God.*

*Sin – Sinai?*

Shamash, Bright Sun, in their tongue Utu they called, him too they worshiped.

*Utu Shamash!*

*Shamash = Ash Sham = the Sun*

Enlil by them Father Elil was called, Nippur by them was Nibru-ki;

*Enlil, Elil, Elul, El, Jehovah, Yahweh, Jove, Bhrama, Toru El, El Toro, Zeus, and many more.*

Ki-Engi, Land of the Lofty Watchers, Shumer in their language was named.

**Shumeria.**

So did Marduk, as Ra, above all other gods himself emplace, Their powers and attributes to himself he by himself assigned; As Enlil I am for lordship and decrees, as Ninurta for the hoe and combat; As Adad for lightning and thunder, as Nannar for illuminating the night; As Utu I am Shamash, as Nergal over the Lower World I reign;
As Gibil the golden depths I know, whence copper and silver come I have found; As Ningishzidda numbers and their count I command, the heavens my glory bespeak!

**Marduk (Mars) has taken the attributes and deeds of the other Anunnaki, placing himself above all other gods.**

The Bull of Heaven, Enlil's constellation sign, by his own offspring was slain,

**The Great Flood occurred during the Age of Taurus (2344 BCE) thereby killing and changing the constellations.**

In the heavens the Age of the Ram, my age, is coming, unmistakable the omens are!

**Marduk (Mars) knows that his time of Aries is on the horizon.**

In his abode, in Eridu, the circle of the twelve constellations Enki examined, Still remote was the time of the Ram, the Age of the Bull of Enlil it still was! That the sun in the Constellation of the Bull was still rising to the people they showed.

**Enki checks for proof positive that they were still in the Age of Taurus.**

Babili, the Gateway of the Gods, Nabu in his father's honor named it,

**Babili (Babel, Bavel) was built to honor Marduk (Mars) the father of Nabu and Satu (Phobos & Deimos).**

Inanna's fury no boundary knew; with her weapons on Marduk's followers death she inflicted. The blood of people, as never before on Earth, like rivers flowed.

**Venus (Inanna/Ishtar) discharges plasma and catastrophe in her wake against the followers of Mars (Marduk).**

Amun, the Unseen One, in the Second Region was Ra henceforth called.

**Marduk to Ra – and now to Amun – the Unseen One**
**Amun – Amen = the Hidden One**

After Marduk Amun became, kingship in the Second Region disintegrated, disorder and
confusion reigned;

**The region of Egypt begins to decline under Ra (Mars).**

The image of a man to him appeared, bright and shining like the heavens he was; As he approached and by Enlil's bed stood, Enlil the white-haired Galzu recognized! In his left hand a tablet of lapis lazuli he was holding, the starry heavens on it were designed; By the twelve constellation signs were the heavens divided, to them with his left hand Galzu pointed.

**Galzu (Aquarius) visits Enlil (El, Elil, Elul, Toru-el, Yahweh) in a dream vision to inform him of the disaster to come, and that there will be a new constellation above.**

From the Bull to the Ram Galzu his pointing shifted; three times the pointing he repeated.

**Galzu lets Enlil know that the Age of Aries the Ram is here.**

In three celestial portions the Ram of Marduk the Bull of Enlil will replace,

*In 216 years, the Age of Aries will replace the Age of Taurus. This gives us a good time stamp on the dating of the text. The Age of Aries began in 2308 BCE, which means this document was authored around 2524 BCE. The disasters of the Exodus occurred 857 years later in 1487 BCE.*

One who himself as Supreme God has declared supremacy on Earth will seize.

*Marduk (Mars) declares himself the Supreme God during the period of the Exodus of Israel from Egypt!*

A calamity as has never before occurred, by Fate decreed, will happen!

*More people will die from the coming disaster (Exodus period) than during the Great Flood.*

The five cities of the valley he finished off, to desolation they were overturned. With fire and brimstones were they upheavaled, all that lived there to vapor was turned.

*I believe the five cities to be; Sodom, Gomorrah, Admah, Zeboiim, and Zoar/Bela.*

Swirling within a dark cloud, gloom from the skies an Evil Wind carried, As the day wore on, the Sun on the horizon with darkness it obliterated, At nighttime a dreaded brilliance skirted its edges, the Moon at its rising it made disappear.

*The Evil Wind I believe to be caused by effects that I will discuss in my conclusions. We have a period of extended sunlight which would correspond to a period of extended darkness on another side of the planet as has been recorded.*

When dawn the next morning came, from the west, from the Upper Sea, a stormwind began blowing, The dark brown cloud eastward it directed, toward the settled lands did the cloud spread; Wherever it reached, death to all that lives mercilessly it delivered;

*The Evil Wind swept from West to East as would be expected due to the rotation of the Earth.*

Stealthy was the death, like a ghost the fields and cities it attacked; The highest walls, the thickest walls, like floodwaters it passed, No door could shut it out, no bolt could turn it back. Those who behind locked doors hid inside their houses like flies were felled, Those who to the streets fled, in the streets were their corpses piled up.

*This is the same accounting that we receive in the Ten Plagues of Egypt. Stealthy, death, ghost, highest walls, thickest walls, passed, door, shut, bolt, turn, locked doors, flies, felled, streets, corpses, piled! The series of events match the accounts of the Biblical Passover to a tee!*

Cough and phlegm the chests filled, the mouths with spittle and foam filled up; As the Evil Wind the people unseen engulfed, their mouths were drenched with blood.

*The resulting cough, phlegm, spittle, foam, and blood coming from their mouths sounds similar to radiation sickness. In doses from 6 to over 30Gy, nausea and vomiting will be between 75-100%. The onset of symptoms at those doeses are anywhere from minutes to 48 hours, with the higher dose patients dying within 48 hours. The effects will range from; seizures, tremors, nausea, vomiting, disorientation, and diarrhea.*

Slowly over the lands the Evil Wind blew, from west to east over plains and mountains it traveled;

*We again have the trajectory as west to east, as it passes through the Arabian Peninsula to the Indus Valley region to points unknown.*

Babili, where Marduk supremacy declared, by the Evil Wind was spared.

*Babylon (Babili) was spared the Evil Wind.*

**THE FOURTEENTH TABLET**

All the lands south of Babili the Evil Wind devoured, the heart of the Second Region it also touched.

***Egypt was touched by the destruction of the Evil Wind.***

## Glossary Book of Enki Glossary

*Abael: The biblical Abel, killed by his brother Ka-in*
Abzu: Enki's gold-mining domain in southeast Africa
Adad: Akkadian name of Ishkur, Enlil's youngest son
*Adamu: The first successfully genetically engineered Primitive Worker, The Adam*
*Adapa: Son of Enki by an Earthling female, first Civilized Man; the biblical Adam*
Akkad: The northern lands added to Sumer under Sargon I Akkadian: The mother tongue of all Semitic languages
*Alalu: The deposed king of Nibiru who escaped to Earth and discovered gold; died on Mars; his image was carved on a rock that was his tomb*
*Amun: Egyptian name for the exiled god Ra*
An: First unity king an Nibiru; name of the planet we call Uranus
*Anak: The metal tin*
Annu: Sacred city in Egypt, the biblical On, Heliopolis in Greek
*Anshar: The fifth ruler on Nibiru of the unified dynasty; the planet we call Saturn*
*Antu: Spouse of An; spouse of Anu; early name of the planet we call Neptune*
*Anu: Nibiru's ruler when the Anunnaki came to Earth; also, the planet called Uranus*
*Anunnaki: "Those Who from Heaven to Earth Came" (from Nibiru to Earth) – Anu's meteorites!*
*Apsu: Primordial progenitor of the solar system, the Sun*
Arbakad: The biblical Arpakhshad (one of Shem's sons)
Arrata: The land and mountains of Ararat
Asar: The Egyptian god called Osiris
Asta: The Egyptian goddess called Isis, sister-wife of Asar
Awan: Sister-wife of Ka-in (the biblical Cain)
Aya: Spouse of Utu (the god called Shamash in Akkadian)
Azura: Spouse of Sati, mother of Enshi (the biblical Enosh)
Bab-Ili: "Gateway of the gods"; Babylon, Marduk's city in Mesopotamia
Bad-Tibira: Ninurta's city of smelting and refining gold
*Banda: Heroic ruler of Uruk (biblical Erech), father of Gilgamesh*
Baraka: Spouse of Irid (the biblical Jared)
Batanash: Spouse of Lu-Mach (biblical Lamech), mother of the hero of the Deluge
Beacon peaks: The two Great Pyramids of Giza; afterward, Mount Mashu in the Sinai
Ben-Ben: Conical upper part of Ra's celestial boat
Black-headed people: The Sumerian people
*Black land: The African domain of the god Dumuzi*
Boat of heaven: Aerial vehicle of various gods and goddesses
Bond Heaven-Earth: The complex instruments in Mission Control Center Branch of life essence: DNA-holding chromosome Bull of Heaven: Enlil's guardian of the Landing Place, symbol of his constellation
Burannu: The river Euphrates
Cedar forest: Location of the Landing Place (in present-day Lebanon)
Cedar Mountains: Location of Enlil's abode in the cedar forest
*Celestial Battle: The primordial collision between Nibiru and Tiamat*
Celestial chariots: Interplanetary spacecraft
*Celestial portions: The 7z-year period for 1° zodiacal shift due to Precession*
*Celestial stations: The twelve houses of the zodiacal constellations*
*Celestial Time: Time measured by the precessional shifts of zodiacal constellations*
Chariots' place: Spaceport
*Circuit: Orbit of a planet around the Sun*
Civilized Man: Homo sapiens-sapiens, of which Adapa was the first one
Count of Earth years: The count of years since Anu's visit to Earth, the Nippur calendar begun in 3760 B.C.
Creation Chamber: Genetic engineering and domestication facility on the Cedar Mountains
*Creator of All: The universal, cosmic God*
Damkina: Spouse of Enki, renamed Ninki; daughter of Alalu
*Dark-hued land: Africa*
*Dawn and Dusk: Earthling females impregnated by Enki, mothers of Adapa and Titi*
*Deluge: The Great Flood*

Destiny: Predetermined course (of events, of orbit) that is unchangeable
Duat: Egyptian name for the restricted zone of the spaceport in the Sinai
Dudu: Endearment name for the god Adad (Ishkur), Enlil's youngest son, Inanna's uncle
*Dumuzi: Enki's youngest son, in charge of shepherding in his Egyptian domain*
*E-A: "Whose home is water," the prototype Aquarius; firstborn son of Anu, half brother of Enlil; leader of the first group of Anunnaki to arrive on Earth; the fashioner of Mankind and its savior from the Deluge; given the epithets Nudimmud ("the Fashioner"), Ptah ("the Developer" in Egypt), Enki ("Lord Earth"); father of Marduk*
Edin: Location of the Anunnaki's first settlements, the biblical Eden, in southern Mesopotamia; later the area of Shumer
Edinni: Spouse of Enkime, mother of Matushal (the biblical Enoch and Methuselah)
Ednat: Spouse of Matushal, mother of Lumach (the biblical Lamech)
*Ekur: The tall structure in the pre-Diluvial Mission Control Center; the Great Pyramid (of Giza) after the Deluge*
Emitter: Instrument used together with Pulser to revive Inanna
Emzara: Spouse of Ziusudra (the biblical Noah) and mother of his three sons
*Endubsar: The scribe to whom Enki dictated his memoir*
*Enki: Ea's epithet-title after the division of duties and powers between him and his halfbrother and rival Enlil; father of Marduk by his spouse Damkina; failed to have a son by his half sister Ninmah, but fathered five other sons by concubines and also children by Earthling females*
*Enkidu: Artificially created companion of Gilgamesh – Constellation of Orion*
*Enkime: Taken heavenward and granted much knowledge; the biblical Enoch; father of Sarpanit, Marduk's spouse*
*Enlil: Son of Anu and his sister-spouse Antu and thus the Foremost Son entitled to the succession to Nibiru's throne ahead of the firstborn Ea; military commander and administrator, sent to Earth to organize wide-scale gold-obtainment operations; father of Ninurta by his half sister Ninmah, and of Nannar and Ishkur by his spouse Ninlil; opposed the fashioning of the Earthlings, sought Mankind's demise by the Deluge; authorized the use of nuclear weapons against Marduk*
Enshi: The biblical Enosh, the first to be taught rites and worship
Ereshkigal: Granddaughter of Enlil, mistress of the Lower World (southern Africa); spouse of Nergal; sister of Inanna
Eridu: The first settlement on Earth, established by Ea; his everlasting center and abode in Shumer
Esagil: Temple of Marduk in Babylon
Essence of life: The genetically encoded DNA
Etana: A king of Uruk who was carried heavenward but was too afraid to continue
*Evil serpent: Derogatory epithet for Marduk by his enemies*
*Evil Wind: The death-bearing nuclear cloud drifting eastward toward Shumer*
Fate: A course of events that is subject to free choice and is alterable
*Father of All Beginning: The universal Creator of All; the cosmic God*
Firmament: The Asteroid Belt, the remnant of the broken-up half of Tiamat
Gaga: The moon of Anshar (Saturn) that after Nibiru's passage became the planet Pluto
Gaida: Youngest son of Enkime (Enoch in the Bible)
*Galzu: A mysterious divine emissary who conveyed the messages in dreams and visions*
Gateway to heaven: The purpose of the launch tower built by Marduk in Babylon
*Gibil: A son of Enki, in charge of metallurgy, maker of magical artifacts*
*Gilgamesh: King in Uruk; being a son of a goddess, went in search of immortality Girsu: - Constellation Perseus*
Calamity: The devastation in the aftermath of the nuclear holocaust in 2024 B.C.
Great Deep: The Antarctic Ocean
Great Sea: The Mediterranean Sea; also called the Upper Sea
Gug Stone: Beam emitting crystal, transferred from the Great Pyramid to Mount Mashu
Guru: A lieutenant of Ea at the first landing
Ham: Second son of the hero of the Deluge, brother of Shem and Japhet
*Hammered Bracelet: The Asteroid Belt; also called the Firmament*
Hapi: The ancient Egyptian name for the Nile River
Harran: City in northwestern Mesopotamia (now in Turkey) that served as a twin city of Ur; sojourn place of Abraham; staging place of Marduk for usurpation of supremacy on Earth
Hem-Ta: Egyptian name for ancient Egypt
*Horon; The Egyptian god now called Horus*
House of Fashioning: Genetic laboratory in the cedar forest for crops and livestock
House of Healing: The medical-biological facilities of Ninmah in Shurubak
House of Life: The biogenetic facilities of Enki in the Abzu

*Ibru-Um (Ibruurn): Scion of a priestly royal family from Nippur and Ur, the biblical Abraham*
*Igigi: The three hundred Anunnaki assigned to shuttlecraft and the way station on Mars; abducted female Earthlings as wives; frequent rebels*
Imperishable Star: The Egyptian name for the planet from which Ra had come to Earth
*Inanna: Daughter of Nannar and Ningal, twin sister of Utu; was betrothed to Dumuzi; ferocious in war, lusty in lovemaking; mistress of Uruk and of the Third Region; known as Ishtar in Akkadian; associated with the planet we call Venus Ishkur: Youngest son of Enlil by his spouse Ninlil, the Akkadian god Adad*
*Ishtar: The Akkadian name for the goddess Inanna*
*Ka-in: The biblical Cain, who killed his brother Abael (Abel) and was banished*
Ki: "Firm Ground," the planet Earth
Ki-Engi: Shumer ("Land of Lofty Watchers"), the First Region of civilization
*Kingu: Tiamat's principal satellite; Earth's Moon after the Celestial Battle*
*Kishar: Spouse of Nibiru's fifth ruler; the planet we call Jupiter Kishargal: Spouse of Nibiru's fourth ruler*
Lahama: Spouse of Lahma
*Lahamu: The planet we call Venus*
Lahma: The eighth dynastic king on Nibiru
*Lahmu: The planet we call Mars*
Land Beyond the Seas: The Americas; settled by Ka-in's descendants, overseen by Ninurta
Land of the Two Narrows: The lands along the Nile River
Landing Place: The platform for skyships and rocketships in the Cedar Mountains
Law of the Seed: The rule giving succession precedence to a son by a half sister
Life seed: DNA extracted from semen
Lower Abzu: The southern tip of Africa, domain of Nergal and Ereshkigal
Lower Sea: The body of water now called the Persian Gulf
Lower World: The southern hemisphere, including southern Africa and Antarctica
Lugal: Literally, "Great Man"; epithet for a chosen king
*Lulu: The genetically engineered hybrid, the Primitive Worker*
*Lu-Mach: Son of Matushal and Ednat, the biblical Lamech Magan: Ancient Egypt*
Malalu: Son of Kunin and Mualit, the biblical Mahalalel
*Marduk: Firstborn son and legal heir of Enki and Damkina; worshiped as Ka in Egypt; jealous of his brothers, unsatisfied with Egypt alone as his domain, claimed and after exiles and wars attained supremacy on Earth from his city Babylon*
*Matushal: Son of Enkime and Edinni, the biblical Methuselah*
*ME: Tiny objects encoded with formulas for all aspects of science and civilization*
*Meluhha: Ancient Nubia*
Mena-Nefer: Egypt's first capital, Memphis
Mission Control Center: In Nibru-ki (Nippur) before the Deluge, on Mount Moriah after the Deluge
Mount of Salvation: The peaks of Ararat, where the ark rested after the Deluge
Mount of Showing the Way: Mount Moriah, site of post-Diluvial Mission Control Center
*Mushdammu: A lieutenant of Ea at the first landing*
Nabu: Son of Marduk and Sarpanit; organized human followers of Marduk
*Nannar: Son of Enlil and Ninlil, the first Anunnaki leader to be born on Earth; patron god of Urim (Ur) and Harran; associated with the Moon; known as Sin in Akkadian; father of Utu and Inanna*
Naram-Sin: Grandson of Sargon and a successor of his as King of Shumer and Akkad
*Navel of the Earth: Epithet for the location of Mission Control Center*
*Nergal: A son of Enki, ruler of the Lower Abzu with his spouse Ereshkigal; unleashed the nuclear weapons together with Ninurta*
Neteru: Egyptian word for gods meaning Guardian Watchers
*Nibiru: Home planet of the Anunnaki; its orbital period, a Shar, equals 3,600 Earth years; became the twelfth member of the solar system after the Celestial Battle – aka Phaeton, Destroyer, Blue Star, etc.*
Nibru-ki: The original Mission Control Center; Enlil's city in Shumer, called Nippur in Akkadian
Ninagal: A son of Enki, appointed by him to navigate the boat of the hero of the Deluge
Ningal: Spouse of Nannar (Sin), mother of Inanna and Utu
*Ningishzidda: Son of Enki, master of genetics and other sciences; called Tehuti (Thoth) in ancient Egypt; went with followers to the Americas after he was deposed by his brother Marduk*
Ninharsag: Epithet of Ninmah after she was granted an abode in the Sinai peninsula
Ninki: Title of Damkina, Ea's spouse, when he was entitled Enki ("Lord of Earth")
*Ninlil: Espoused by Enlil after she forgave his date rape; Mother of Nannar and Ishkur*

*Ninmah:* Half sister of Enki and Enlil, mother of Ninurta by Enlil; chief medical officer of the Anunnaki; helped Enki to genetically engineer the Primitive Worker; peacemaker among the rival and warring Anunnaki clans; renamed Ninharsag

Ninsun: The Anunnaki mother of Gilgamesh

*Ninurta:* Enlil's Foremost son, mothered by Enlil's half sister Ninmah, and his legal successor; battled with Anzu, who seized the Tablets of Destinies, and with Marduk; found the alternative sources for gold and established alternative space facilities in the Americas; patron-god of Lagash

Nippur: Akkadian name of Nibru-ki, where the calendar of Earth years was begun in 3760 B.C.; birthplace of Ibru-Um (Abraham)

Nudimmud: An epithet for Ea meaning He Who Fashions Things; the planet Neptune

Olden Times: The period that began with the first landing and ended with the Deluge

Place of Celestial Chariots: Spaceport of the Anunnaki

Plant of Being Young Again: The secret rejuvenation plant found by Gilgamesh

Plant of Life: Used by Enki's robotic emissaries to revive Inanna

Primitive Worker: The first genetically engineered Earthling

Primordial Begetter: "Apsu"-the Sun-in the creation cosmogony

Prior Times: The period of events on Nibiru before the missions to Earth

*Ptah:* Enki's name in Egypt; meaning "the Developer," it commemorates his deeds in raising the land from under the Flood's waters

Pulser: Instrument used, together with the Emitter, to revive the dead

*Ra:* The Egyptian name for Marduk, meaning the Bright One

Sarpanit: An Earthling, the spouse of Marduk, mother of Nabu

Sati: Third son of Adapa and Titi (the biblical Seth)

Satu: Son of Marduk and Sarpanit, the Egyptian god known as Seth

Seed of life: The genetic material encoding all life-forms, DNA

*Shamash:* Akkadian name for Utu Shamgaz: A leader of the Igigi and instigator of the abduction of Earthling females

Shar: One orbital period of Nibiru around the Sun, equal to 3,600 Earth years

Sharru-kin: The first king of unified Shumer and Akkad, the one we call Sargon I

Shem: The eldest son of the hero of the Deluge

Shumer: Land of the Watchers, the First Region of post-Diluvial civilization; Sumer

Shurubak: Healing center of Ninmah from before the Deluge and reestablished thereafter

*Sin:* The Akkadian name for Nannar (Moon!)

Sippar: The spaceport city in pre-Diluvial times commanded by Utu; his cult center after the Deluge

Skybirds: Aircraft of the Anunnaki for flying in Earth's skies

Snow-hued place: Antarctica

*Sud:* A nurse; also the epithet-name for Ninlil before she became Enlil's spouse – Sud-an, Sud –a-nese!

Tablets of Destinies: Devices used in Mission Control Center to track and control orbits and trajectories; later on, a record of unalterable decisions

*Tehuti:* Egyptian name for Ningishzidda as "Thoth," the god of science and knowledge

*Tiamat:* Primordial planet that broke up in the Celestial Battle, giving rise to the Asteroid Belt and to the Earth

*Ti-Amat:* Wife of Adamu; first Earthling female able to procreate

Tilmun: "Land of the Missiles," the Fourth Region in the Sinai peninsula

*Titi:* Spouse of the first Civilized Man, Adapa, mother of Ka-in and Abael

Unug-ki: City built for Anu's visit, granted by him to Inanna; later called Uruk (the biblical Erech); throne-city of Gilgamesh and other demigods

Upper Plain: Area in northern Mesopotamia where the descendants of Arpakad dwelt

Upper Sea: The Mediterranean Sea

Ur: Akkadian name for Urim; the rulers of Shumer and Akkad when the nuclear calamity happened are known as kings of the Third Dynasty of Ur; the biblical "Ur of the Chaldees" from which Abraham migrated to Harran

Urim: Nannar's city in Shumer and the land's capital three times (including at the time of the Great Calamity); a thriving center of culture, industry, and international trade

Uruk: Akkadian name for Unug-ki (the biblical Erech)

Utu: "Shamash" in Akkadian; twin brother of Inanna; commander of the Spaceport of Sippar in pre-Diluvial times and of the one in the Sinai after the Deluge; giver of laws from his cult center in Sippar after the Deluge; Godfather of Gilgamesh

Water of Life: Used to revive Inanna and bring her back from the dead

Water of Youth: Promised by Ra to his followers in an Afterlife

*Way of Anu:* The central band of the celestial sphere containing the zodiacal constellations; on Earth, the central band between the northern Way of Enlil and the southern Way of Enki

*Way of Enki: The celestial sphere below the 30<sup>th</sup> parallel south*
*Way of Enlil: The celestial sphere above the 30<sup>th</sup> parallel north*
Weapons of Terror: Nuclear weapons, used at first on Nibiru and then finally on Earth
Whirlwinds: Helicopter-like aerial vehicles of the Anunnaki
Whiteland: Antarctica
Winged Serpent: Epithet of Ningishzidda in the Americas
Ziusudra: Hero of the Deluge, a son of Enki by an Earthling (the biblical Noah)

# 40 Is The Number

We touched on the ongoing concept of the number 40 used in the Bible earlier in the book. I noted over 75 germane uses of the number 40 in the King James Version of the Bible, with over 100 occurences of that number in combination with others. Below are some very obvious use of this number in repetition throughout the Bible for various purposes.

Genesis 7:4 For yet seven days, and I will cause it to rain upon the earth _forty_ days and _forty_ nights; and every living substance that I have made will I destroy from off the face of the earth.

Genesis 50:3 And _forty_ days were fulfilled for him; for so are fulfilled the days of those which are embalmed : and the Egyptians mourned for him threescore and ten days.

Genesis 26:34 And Esau was _forty_ years old when he took to wife Judith the daughter of Beeri the Hittite, and Bashemath the daughter of Elon the Hittite

**Genesis 25:20** And Isaac was _forty_ years old when he took Rebekah to wife, the daughter of Bethuel the Syrian of Padanaram, the sister to Laban the Syrian

**Exodus 26:2** And their _forty_ sockets of silver; twosockets under one board, and two sockets under another board.

Exodus 34:28 And he was there with the LORD _forty_ days and _forty_ nights; he did neither ead bread nor drink water. And he wrote upon the tables the words of the covenant, the ten commandments.

Deuteronomy 25:3 _Forty_ stripes he may give him, and not exceed : lest, if he should exceed , and beat him above these with many stripes, then thybrother should seem vile unto thee.

Joshua 14:7  _Forty_ years old was I when Moses the servant of the LORD sent me from Kadeshbarnea to espy out theland; and I brought him word again as it was in mine heart.

Judges 3:11 And the land had rest _forty_ years. And Othniel the son of Kenaz died .

Judges 5:31 So let all thine enemies perish , O LORD: but let them that love him be as the sun when he goeth forth in his might. And the land had rest _forty_ years.

Judges 12:14  And he had _forty_ sons and thirty nephews , that rode on threescore and ten ass colts: and he judged Israel eight years.

Judges 13:1 And the children of Israel did evil again in the sight of the LORD; and the LORD delivered them into the hand of the Philistines _forty_ years.

1 Samuel 4:18 And it came to pass, when he made mention of the ark of God, that hefell from off the seat backward by the side of the gate, and his neck brake , and he died : for he was an old man, and heavy . And he had judged Israel _forty_ years.

2 Samuel 5:4  David was thirty years old when he began to reign , and he reigned _forty_ years.

1 Kings 6:17 And the house, that is, the temple before it, was _forty_ cubits long.

1 Kings 7:38 Then made he ten lavers of brass: one laver contained _forty_ baths: and every laver was four cubits: and upon every one of the ten bases one laver.

1 Kings 11:42 And the time that Solomon reigned in Jerusalem over all Israel was _forty_ years.

*2 Kings 12:1 In the seventh year of Jehu Jehoash began to reign ; and forty years reigned he in Jerusalem. And his mother's name was Zibiah of Beersheba.*

*Ezekiel 4:6 And when thou hast accomplished them, lie again on thy right side, and thou shalt bear the iniquity of the house of Judah forty days: I have appointed thee each day for a year.*

*Ezekiel 29:11 No foot of man shall pass through it, nor foot of beast shall pass through it, neither shall it be inhabited forty years.*

*Jonah 3:4 And Jonah began to enter into the city a day's journey, and he cried, and said, Yet forty days, and Nineveh shall be overthrown.*

*Acts 7:30 And when forty years were expired, there appeared to him in the wilderness of mount Sina an angel of the Lord in a flame of fire in a bush.*

*Acts 23:13 And they were more than forty which had made this conspiracy.*

## *7 Is The Number*

**We touched on the ongoing concept of the number 40 used in the Bible earlier in the book, and now we look at the number seven. There are over 300 hundred uses of the number 7 in the King James Version of the Bible**

Matthew 12:45 *Then he goes, and takes with himself* **seven** *other spirits more evil than he is, and they enter in and dwell there. The last state of that man becomes worse than the first. Even so will it be also to this evil generation."*

Matthew 15:34 *Jesus said to them, "How many* **loaves** *do you have?" They said, "***Seven***, and a few small* **fish***."*

Matthew 15:37 *They all ate, and were filled. They took up* **seven** *baskets full of the broken pieces that were left over.*

Matthew 16:10 *Nor the* **seven** *loaves for the* **four thousand***, and how many baskets you took up?*

Matthew 18:22 *Jesus said to him, "I don't tell you until* **seven** *times, but, until* **seventy** *times seven.*

**Matthew's number of FOUR just doesn't cut it, as he has to get to the supreme number of El's children/constellation at 70!**

Matthew 22:28 *In the resurrection therefore, whose wife will she be of the* **seven***? For they all had her."*

Mark 16:9 *Now when he had* **risen early** *on the* **first day of the week***, he appeared first to* **Mary Magdalene***, from whom he had cast out* **seven** *demons.*

**We see that Christ had risen (Sun) early on the first day of the week Sunday! This is clearly a solar reference to the Sun.**

Luke 2:36 *There was one Anna, a* **prophetess***, the daughter of* **Phanuel***, of the tribe of* **Asher** *(she was of a great age, having lived with a husband* **seven** *years from her virginity,*

Luke 11:26 *Then he goes, and takes* **seven** *other spirits more evil than himself, and they enter in and dwell there. The last state of that man becomes worse than the first."*

John 4:52 *So he inquired of them the hour when he began to get better. They said therefore to him, "Yesterday at the* **seventh** *hour, the fever left him."*

John 6:7 *"***Seven** *pounds' worth of bread," replied Philip, "is not enough for them all to get even a scanty meal."*

Acts 6:3 *Therefore select from among you, brothers,* **seven** *men of good report, full of the* **Holy Spirit** *and of wisdom, whom we may appoint over this business.*

Acts 13:19 *When he had destroyed* **seven** *nations in the land of* **Canaan***, he gave them their land for an inheritance, for about* **four hundred fifty years.**

Acts 19:14 *There were* **seven** *sons of one Sceva, a Jewish chief priest, who did this.*

Acts 20:6 *We sailed away from Philippi after the days of* **Unleavened Bread***, and came to them at Troas in* **five days***, where we stayed* **seven** *days.*

Hebrews 11:30 *By faith, the* **walls of Jericho fell down***, after they had been encircled for* **seven** *days.*

2 Peter 2:5 *and didn't spare the ancient world, but preserved Noah with* **seven** *others, a preacher of righteousness, when he brought a* **flood** *on the* **world** *of the* **ungodly***;*

*Revelation 1:4* John, to the **seven** assemblies that are in Asia: Grace to you and peace, from God, who is and who was and who is to come; and from the **seven Spirits** who are before his throne;

*Revelation 1:12* I turned to see the voice that spoke with me. Having turned, I saw **seven** golden lampstands.

*Revelation 1:13* And in the midst of the **seven** candlesticks one like unto the **Son of man**, clothed with a garment down to the foot, and girt about the paps with a golden girdle.

*Revelation 1:16* He had **seven** stars in his right hand. Out of his **mouth proceeded** a **sharp two-edged sword**. His face was like the **sun shining** at its **brightest**.

*Revelation 1:20* the mystery of the **seven** stars which you saw in my right hand, and the seven golden lampstands. The **seven stars** are the **angels** of the **seven assemblies**. The **seven lampstands** are **seven assemblies**.

*Revelation 2:1* "To the angel of the assembly in Ephesus write: "He who holds the **seven stars** in his right hand, he who walks among the **seven golden lampstands** says these things:

*Revelation 3:1* "And to the angel of the assembly in Sardis write: "He who has the **seven** Spirits of God, and the **seven stars** says these things: "I know your works, that you have a reputation of being alive, but you are dead.

*Revelation 4:5* Out of the throne proceed **lightnings, sounds, and thunders**. There were **seven** lamps of **fire** burning before his **throne**, which are the **seven Spirits of God.**

*Revelation 5:1* I saw, in the right hand of him who sat on the **throne**, a **book** written inside and outside, **sealed shut** with **seven** seals.

*Revelation 5:5* One of the elders said to me, "Don't weep. Behold, the **Lion** who is of the **tribe** of **Judah**, the **Root of David**, has overcome; he who opens the book and its **seven** seals."

*Revelation 5:6* I saw in the midst of the throne and of the **four living creatures**, and in the midst of the **elders**, a Lamb standing, as though it had been slain, having **seven** horns, and **seven eyes,** which are the **seven Spirits of God**, sent out **into** all the **earth**.

*Revelation 6:1* I saw that the Lamb opened one of the **seven** seals, and I heard one of the **four living creatures** saying, as with a voice of thunder, "Come and see!"

*Revelation 8:2* I saw the **seven** angels who stand before God, and **seven trumpets** were given to them.

*Revelation 8:6* The **seven** angels who had the seven trumpets prepared themselves to sound.

*Revelation 10:3* He cried with a loud voice, as a lion roars. When he cried, the **seven** thunders uttered their voices.

*Revelation 10:4* When the **seven** thunders sounded, I was about to write; but I heard a voice from the sky saying, "Seal up the things which the **seven thunders** said, and don't write them."

*Revelation 12:3* Another **sign** was **seen** in **heaven**. Behold, a **great red dragon**, having **seven heads** and **ten horns**, and on his heads **seven crowns**.

*Revelation 13:1* Then I stood on the sand of the sea. I saw a **beast** coming up out of the **sea**, having **ten horns** and **seven** heads. On his horns were **ten crowns**, and on his heads, blasphemous names.

*Revelation 15:1* I saw another great and marvelous **sign** in the **sky**: **seven angels** having the **seven last plagues**, for in them God's **wrath** is finished.

*Revelation 15:6* The **seven** angels who had the **seven plagues** came out, clothed with **pure, bright linen**, and wearing **golden sashes** around their breasts.

*Revelation 15:7* One of the **four living creatures** gave to the **seven** angels **seven golden bow**ls full of the wrath of God, who lives forever and ever.

*Revelation 15:8* The temple was filled with **smoke** from the glory of God, and from his power. No one was able to enter into the temple, until the **seven** plagues of the **seven angels** would be finished.

*Revelation 16:1* I heard a loud voice out of the temple, saying to the **seven** angels, "Go and pour out the seven bowls of the wrath of God on the earth!"

*Revelation 17:1* One of the **seven** angels who had the **seven** bowls came and spoke with me, saying, "Come here. I will show you the judgment of the **great prostitute** who sits on **many waters**,

*Revelation 17:3* He carried me away in the **Spirit** into a wilderness. I saw a woman sitting on a **scarlet-colored animal,** full of blasphemous names, having **seven heads** and **ten horns**.

*Revelation 17:7* The angel said to me, "Why do you wonder? I will tell you the mystery of the woman, and of the **beast** that carries her, which has the **seven heads** and the **ten horns**.

*Revelation 17:9* Here is the **mind** that has **wisdom**. The **seven** heads are **seven mountains**, on which the woman sits.

*Revelation 17:10* They are **seven** kings. **Five have fallen**, the **one is,** the other has **not yet** come. When **he comes**, he must **continue** a **little** while.

*Revelation 17:11* The beast that **was**, and is **not**, is himself also an **eighth**, and is of the **seven**; and he goes to **destruction**.

*Revelation 21:9* One of the **seven** angels who had the **seven bowls**, who were loaded with the **seven** last plagues came, and he spoke with me, saying, "Come here. I will show you **the wife, the Lamb's bride**."

*Genesis 4:24* If Cain will be avenged **seven** times, truly Lamech seventy-seven times."

*Genesis 7:2* You shall take **seven** pairs of every clean animal with you, the male and his female. Of the animals that are not clean, take two, the male and his female.

*Genesis 7:3* Also of the birds of the sky, **seven** and **seven**, male and female, to keep seed alive on the surface of all the earth.

*Genesis 7:4* In **seven** days, I will cause it to rain on the earth for forty days and forty nights. Every living thing that I have made, I will destroy from the surface of the ground."

*Genesis 8:10* He stayed yet another **seven** days; and again he sent forth the dove out of the ship.

*Genesis 21:28* Abraham set **seven** ewe lambs of the flock by themselves.

*Genesis 29:18* Jacob loved Rachel. He said, "I will serve you **seven** years for Rachel, your younger daughter."

*Genesis 31:23* He took his relatives with him, and pursued after him **seven** days' journey. He overtook him in the mountain of Gilead.

*Genesis 33:3* He himself passed over in front of them, and bowed himself to the ground **seven** times, until he came near to his brother.

*Genesis 41:2* Behold, there came up out of the river **seven** cattle, sleek and fat, and they fed in the marsh grass.

*Genesis 41:5* He slept and dreamed a second time: and behold, **seven** heads of grain came up on one stalk, healthy and good. Behold, **seven** heads of grain, thin and blasted with the east wind, sprung up after them.

*Genesis 46:25* These are the sons of Bilhah, whom Laban gave to Rachel, his daughter, and these she bore to Jacob: all the souls were **seven**.

*Exodus 2:16* Now the priest of Midian had **seven** daughters. They came and drew water, and filled the troughs to water their father's flock.

*Exodus 7:25* **Seven** days were fulfilled, after Yahweh had **struck the river.**

*Exodus 12:15* "'**Seven** days you shall eat **unleavened** bread; even the first day you shall put away **yeast** out of your houses, for whoever eats leavened bread from the first day until the **seventh day**, that soul shall be cut off from Israel.

*Exodus 22:30* You shall do likewise with your cattle and with your sheep. **Seven** days it shall be with its mother, then on the eighth day you shall give it to me.

*Exodus 25:37* You shall make its lamps **seven**, and they shall light its lamps to give light to the space in front of it.

*Exodus 29:30* **Seven** days shall the son who is priest in his place put them on, when he comes into the Tent of Meeting to minister in the holy place.

*Leviticus 4:6* The priest shall dip his **finger in the blood**, and sprinkle some of the **blood seven times** before Yahweh, before the veil of the sanctuary.

*Leviticus 13:4* If the bright spot is white in the skin of his body, and its appearance isn't deeper than the skin, and its hair hasn't turned white, then the priest shall isolate the infected person for **seven** days.

*Leviticus 13:5* The priest shall examine him on the **seventh** day, and, behold, if in his eyes the plague is arrested, and the plague hasn't spread in the skin, then the priest shall isolate him for **seven** more days.

**Leprosy has a two week period of contagion.**

*Leviticus 14:7* He shall sprinkle on him who is to be cleansed from the leprosy **seven** times, and shall pronounce him clean, and shall let the living bird go into the open field.

*Leviticus 23:6* On the **fifteenth day** of the same **month** is the **feast** of unleavened bread to **Yahweh**. **Seven** days you shall eat unleavened bread.

**The fifteenth being the ides of the month.**

*Leviticus 23:8* But you shall offer an offering made by fire to Yahweh **seven** days. In the **seventh** day is a holy convocation: you shall do no regular work.'"

**Sunday/Sun Day (Christian) and Saturday/Saturn Day (Hebrew)!**

*Leviticus 25:8* "'You shall count off **seven** Sabbaths of years, seven times seven years; and there shall be to you the days of seven Sabbaths of years, even forty-nine years.

**Hebrew Jubilee = 49 years          Mayan Jubilee = 52 years**

Numbers 8:2 "Speak to Aaron, and tell him,'When you **light the lamps**, the **seven** lamps shall give light in front of the **lampstand**.'"

Numbers 12:14 Yahweh said to Moses, "If her father had but spit in her face, shouldn't she be ashamed **seven** days? Let her be shut up outside of the camp seven days, and after that she shall be brought in again."

**It was okay to spit in Miriam's face!**

Numbers 13:22 They went up by the **South**, and came to Hebron; and **Ahiman, Sheshai, and Talmai**, the **children of Anak**, were there. (Now **Hebron** was built **seven** years before **Zoan aka Tanis** in Egypt.)

**The children of Anak are the Anakim, descendants of the Nephilim (fallen angels – meteorites) our Biblical giants.**

Numbers 23:1 Balaam said to Balak, "Build me here **seven** altars, and prepare me here **seven bulls** and **seven rams**."

Deuteronomy 7:1 When **Yahweh** your God shall bring you into the **land** where you go to **possess** it, and shall **cast out** many **nations** before you, the **Hittite**, and the **Girgashite**, and the **Amorite**, and the **Canaanite**, and the **Perizzite**, and the **Hivite**, and the **Jebusite**, **seven** nations greater and mightier than you;

Deuteronomy 15:1 At the end of every **seven** years you shall make a release.

Joshua 6:4 **Seven** priests shall bear **seven trumpets** of **rams' horns** before the **ark**. On the **seventh day**, you shall **march** around the **city seven times**, and the **priests** shall **blow** the **trumpets**.

**7 priests blowing for 7 days (7x7=49) is a Jubilee reference The ram's horns symbolize the solid shift into the Age of Aries.**

Joshua 18:2 **Seven** tribes remained among the children of Israel, which had not yet divided their inheritance.

Judges 6:1 The children of **Israel** did that which was **evil** in the **sight** of Yahweh: and **Yahweh delivered** them into the hand of **Midian seven** years.

**The captivity of the Children of Israel is always sin based versus political, racial, class, wars, or natural disasters!**

Judges 12:9 He had **thirty sons**; and **thirty daughters** he **sent abroad**, and thirty daughters he brought in from abroad for his sons. He judged Israel **seven** years.

**As sixty is the sacred number for the Sumerian Lord Enlil, we have thirty sons and thirty daughters.**

Judges 16:7 Samson said to her, "If they bind me with **seven** green cords that were never dried, then shall I become weak, and be as another man."

**Samson is representative of the Hercules constellation as the binding with cord speaks of zodiac binding!**

Judges 16:13 Delilah said to Samson, "Until now, you have mocked me and told me lies. Tell me with what you might be bound." He said to her, "If you weave the **seven** locks of my head with the web."

Ruth 4:15 He shall be to you a restorer of life, and sustain you in your old age, for your daughter-in-law, who loves you, who is better to you than **seven** sons, has borne him."

1 Samuel 2:5 Those who were full have hired themselves out for bread. Those who were hungry have ceased to hunger. Yes, the barren has borne **seven**. She who has many children languishes.

1 Samuel 6:1 The **ark of Yahweh** was in the country of the **Philistines seven months**.

*2 Samuel 21:9* He **delivered** them into the hands of the **Gibeonites**, and they **hanged** them in the **mountain** before **Yahweh**, and all **seven** of them fell together. They were put to **death in the days of harvest, in the first days, at the beginning of barley harvest**.

**We have seven men being hung in the mountain where the orbiting pillar/wheel in the sky orbited, and they were destroyed by its passage. We have what can definitely be considered a ritual human sacrifice as they were killed before Yahweh! The deaths happen to coincide with the barley festival!**

*2 Samuel 24:13* So Gad came to David, and told him, and said to him, "Shall **seven** years of famine come to you in your land? Or will you flee three months before your foes while they pursue you? Or shall there be **three days'** pestilence in your land? Now answer, and consider what answer I shall return to him who sent me."

*1 Kings 6:38* In the eleventh year, in the month **Bul**, which is the eighth month, was the house finished throughout all its parts, and according to all its fashion. So was he **seven** years in building it.

*2 Kings 3:9* So the king of Israel went, and the king of Judah, and the king of Edom; and they made a circuit of **seven** days' journey. There was no water for the army, nor for the animals that followed them.

*2 Kings 4:35* Then he returned, and walked in the house once back and forth; and went up, and stretched himself on him. Then the child sneezed **seven** times, and the child opened his eyes.

*2 Kings 11:21* Jehoash was **seven** years old when he began to reign.

*1 Chronicles 3:24* The sons of Elioenai: Hodaviah, and Eliashib, and Pelaiah, and Akkub, and Johanan, and Delaiah, and Anani, **seven**.

*1 Chronicles 11:23* He killed an Egyptian, a man of **great stature, five cubits high**; and in the Egyptian's hand was a spear like a weaver's beam; and he went down to him with a staff, and plucked the spear out of the Egyptian's hand, and killed him with his own spear.

**The Egyptian stood 7'6"  (David & Goliath)**

*Esther 1:10* On the **seventh** day, when the heart of the king was merry with wine, he commanded Mehuman, Biztha, Harbona, Bigtha, and Abagtha, Zethar, and Carcass, the **seven eunuchs** who served in the presence of Ahasuerus the king,

*Job 1:2* There were born to him **seven** sons and three daughters.

*Job 2:13* So they sat down with him on the ground **seven** days and **seven** nights, and none spoke a word to him, for they saw that his grief was very great.

*Psalms 12:6* The words of Yahweh are flawless words, as silver refined in a clay furnace, purified **seven** times.

*Proverbs 9:1* Wisdom has built her house. She has carved out her **seven** pillars. (WEB KJV JPS ASV BBE DBY WBS YLT NAS RSV NIV)

*Ecclesiastes 11:2* Give a **portion** to **seven**, yes, even to eight; for you don't know what evil will be on the earth.

*Isaiah 11:15* **Yahweh** will utterly **destroy** the **tongue** of the **Egyptian sea**; and with his **scorching wind** he will **wave** his hand over the **River**, and will **split** it into **seven** streams, and cause men to march over in sandals.

*Isaiah 30:26* Moreover the **light of the moon** will be **like** the **light of the sun**, and the **light of the sun will be seven times brighter**, like the **light of seven days**, in the **day** that **Yahweh binds** up the **fracture** of his people, and **heals** the **wound** they were **struck** with.

*This is one of the most revealing of Biblical passages as to some of what transpired during these periods. Isiah relays the Moon being as the Sun, and the Sun will be seven times greater. I feel that Isiah is relaying the increase (seven days of sunlight in one) in the Suns' size (sun spots/jaguars) and the Moon may have reflected the Suns' increased light at night and during the day. The Moon has typically been viewed in sackcloth (covered/darkened/mourning cloth) in these encounters. When Yahweh binds the zodiac constellations (stars/heavens) that have fractured the world and heals the heavens and Earth!*

Ezekiel 3:15 Then I came to them of the captivity at **Tel Aviv**, that lived by the **river Chebar**, and to where they lived; and I sat there overwhelmed among them **seven** days.

Ezekiel 40:22 The windows of it, and its arches, and the palm trees of it, were after the measure of the gate whose prospect is toward the east; and they went up to it by **seven** steps; and its arches were before them.

Ezekiel 41:3 Then went he inward, and measured each post of the entrance, two cubits; and the entrance, six cubits; and the breadth of the entrance, **seven** cubits.

Daniel 3:19 Then was Nebuchadnezzar full of fury, and the form of his visage was changed against Shadrach, Meshach, and Abednego: therefore he spoke, and commanded that they should heat the furnace **seven** times more than it was usually heated.

Daniel 4:16 let his heart be changed from man's, and let an animal's heart be given to him; and let **seven** times pass over him.

Micah 5:5 He will be our peace when Assyria invades our land, and when he marches through our fortresses, then we will raise against him **seven** shepherds, and eight leaders of men.

Zechariah 3:9 For, behold, the stone that I have set before Joshua; on one stone are **seven** eyes: behold, I will engrave its engraving,' says Yahweh of Armies,'and I will remove the iniquity of that land in one day.

Zechariah 4:2 He said to me, "What do you see?" I said, "I have seen, and behold, a lampstand all of gold, with its bowl on the top of it, and its **seven** lamps thereon; there are seven pipes to each of the lamps, which are on the top of it;

# Zodiac & Biblical Theology

## LEO

LEO – The Lion of Judah

    DECANS (3)

    a) Water Serpent (Hydra) – Hercules fought this many headed monster
    b) Cup (Crater) – The Cup of Wrath on the back of the Serpent
    c) Raven (Corvus) – On the back of the Serpent, and was invited to the Feast in Revelations

*Biblical Context:* The constellation of Leo has been important in the ages of mankind. The Tribe of Judah is represented by the Lion. The Sphinx in Egypt lines up with the 3 Kings (3 Wise Men/Magi) in Orion's belt at around 10,500 BCE. What was ancient man's fascination with an age that supposedly predates modern man on Earth. Hydra with her many heads rises from the waters with her Cup (Crater) of Wrath upon her back to spill upon the Earth. The Raven (Corvus) was also invited to the Feast at Revelations.

## CANCER

CANCER – The Crab

    DECANS (3)

    a) Little Bear (Ursa Minor)
    b) Big Bear (Ursa Major)
    c) Ship (Argo)

*Biblical Context:* This is yet another difficult group to read. We know that Jason used the ship Argo in his quest fro the Golden Fleece, but, little can be discerned at the moment.

## GEMINI

GEMINI – The Twins – Two Brothers

    DECANS (3)

    a) Hare (Lepus) – Under the foot of Orion and is considered evil
    b) Big Dog (Canis Major) – Chasing the Hase for Orion
    c) Little Dog (Canis Minor)

*Biblical Context:* This grouping is a puzzle? I believe that the Twins (Castor & Pollux) may also have come to stand for Romulus and Remus, of Rome. The Hare (Lepus) is considered to be evil.

## TAURUS

TAURUS – The Bull

    DECANS (3)

    a) Hunter (Orion)

b) River (Eridanus) – River of Fire
c) Charioteer (Auriga) – Portrayed as a man holding reins in one hand, and a goat with two kids in the other

*Biblical Context:* The Age of Taurus has been remembered fondly by many cultures. The Hindus venerate the bull, as do the Egyptians with the Apis Bull. The transition of the Age of Taurus to the Aryan (Aries) Age happened at a point of tremendous Earth upheaval. The 3 stars in the Belt of Orion (3 Kings) have played a pivotal part in makind's understanding of his place in Creation. Eridanus has been called the River of Fire, and Aurigia is the charioteer (Egyptian boatsman) of the heavens.

# ARIES

ARIES – The Ram

DECANS (3)

a) Queen (Cassiopeia)
b) Sea Monster (Cetus) – Attached to the bands
c) Hero/The Bridegroom (Perseus) – Rescues the Chained Princess

*Biblical Context:* The Age of Aries was represented by Moses during the Exodus of the Hebrews from Egypt. The Golden Fleece in the sky has come to represent Christ as well. The Queen of Heaven (Cassiopeia) sits near the Sea Monster (Cetus) with the Bands of Death, and await rescue from the Hero (Perseus).

# PISCES

PISCES – The Fishes – Represents the Christian Age

DECANS (3)

a) Bands – Ties the tail of the two fish
b) King (Cepheus) – A man often pictured holding ribbons
c) Chained Princess (Andromeda) – The Bride or Princess chained to a cliff and is being offered as a sacrifice

*Biblical Context:* Has come to stand for the Christian age. The Fish (Pisces) symbolizes mankind tied to the Bands of God (King). The Chained Princess (Andromeda) waits to be saved by the Hero (Perseus) from sacrifice upon the Altar (Ara).

# AQUARIUS

AQUARIUS – The Waterman / Water Bearer

DECANS (3)

a) Southern Fish (Pisces Austrinis)
b) Flying Horse (Pegasus)
c) Swan (Cygnus)

*Biblical Context:* Aquarius pours forth blessings onto the Southern Fish (Pisces Austrinis) with the Waters of Life. Pegasus is the winged horse of heaven, and the Swan (Cygnus) has been open to interpretation, bit it a very important star grouping. The constellation of Aquarius is the age to come, or that is underway according to the Zodiac Ages.

# CAPRICORN

**CAPRICORNUS – The Sea Goat**

*DECANS (3)*

a) Arrow (Sagitta)
b) Eagle (Aquila) – Invited to the Feast in Revelations
c) Dolphin (Dolphinus)

*Biblical Context: The Sea Goat (Capricorn) represents the sacrificial Scapegoat of the ancient Hebrews that wandered during the Exodus. The Arrow (Saggita) flies as the Sea Goat is the sacrifice. The Eagle (Aquila) flies across mid-heaven. The Dolphin (Dolphinus) symbolizes rebirth.*

# SAGITTARIUS

**SAGITTARIUS – The Archer**

*DECANS (3)*

a) Harp (Lyra) – Will lead the rejoice in heaven
b) Altar (Ara) – Where the Beast and the Sea Goat are to be sacrificed
c) Dragon (Draco) – Sits at the top of the sky and occupies 1/3 of the heavens

*Biblical Context: There will be great rejoicing (Lyra) in heaven when the Dragon (Draco) is slayed and placed upon Altar (Ara).*

# SCORPIO

**Scorpion (Scorpius) – Stung Dummuzi/Tammuz**

\* Scorpio is also represented in other charts by an Eagle

*DECANS (3)*

a) Serpent (Serpens) – encompasses 1/3 of the heavens
b) Serpent Bearer (Ophiuchus) – Man that wrestles with the Serpent
c) Hercules – Had to perform 13 labors just like Christ

*Biblical Context: The Serpent Bearer wrestles with the Serpent, and Hercules also as the Hero is in this banding.*

# LIBRA

**LIBRA – Balance or Scales**

*DECANS (3)*

a) Cross (Southern Crux or Cross) – This constellation was portrayed by the Persians as a man with a balance in one hand, and a lamb in the other
b) Beast (Lupus) – This is the Beast to be slayed by Centaurus and placed on the Altar (Ara) for sacrifice
c) Crown (Corno Borealis) – Known as the Crown in Heaven, and is often depicted as being worn by the Virgin

*Biblical Context: The Lamb (Southern Crux) that wears the Crown (Corona Borealis) and was crucified (Crux) on the Cross, and redeemed us for our sins (Libra-scales) by slaying the Beast (Lupus).*

# VIRGO

*VIRGO – The Maiden or The Virgin*

*DECANS (3)*

a) *Infant Prince – Portayed by the ancient Persians as an immaculate virgin sitting on a throne*
b) *Centaur (Centaurus) – Slays the Beast*
c) *Herdsman (Bootes) – Known as the Righteous Shepherd or Good Shepherd*

*Biblical Context: Virgin, Prince, and Shepherd! The Virgin (Virgo) gives birth to a Prince (Spica), known as the Good Shepherd (Bootes) that will vanquish the Beast (Lupus).*

## *Zodiac to the Left!*

*The binders of the zodiac constellation groupings used the left appendage on various characters to point to another star grouping as they overlap in the sky. Listed below are some curiosities;*

*Orion steps on the hare (Lupus) with his LEFT foot, while holding the head of the vanquished lion in his LEFT hand*

*The ram (Aries) touches the Bands of Pisces (fish) with its LEFT hoof*

*The Chained Princess (Andromeda) points to the LEFT wing of Pegasus (flying horse) with her LEFT hand*

*The Waterman (Aquarius) reaches back with his LEFT hand towards Capricornus (Capricorn)*

*Sagittarius (Archer) aims his bow with his LEFT arm towards the LEFT foot of Ophiuchus (Serpent Bearer)*

*Ophiuchus (Serpent Bearer) straddles Serpens (Serpent) with his LEFT leg as his LEFT arm is touched by the club of Hercules*

*Bootes (Good Sheperd) weilds his sickle with his LEFT arm*

| Event | Gregorian | Hebrew | Sacred Round | Venus | Other |
|---|---|---|---|---|---|
| Annunciation | Sun 13 Jun BCE | Firstfruits | | | 1 Jeshua (P) & Firstfruits (J) |
| Conception | Tue 15 Jun 2 BCE | 15 Sivan | | | |
| Baptist born | Wed 6 Oct 2 BCE | Atonement | 1 Monkey | | |
| Christ born | Wed 5 Apr 1 BCE | First Day Passover | 1 Reed | 1 Creation | 1 Creation (M) |
| Circumcision | Wed 12 Apr 1 BCE | Last Day Passover | | | Feast of Esther (EF) |
| To Temple | Sun 14 May 1 BCE | | 1 Grass | 1 Quick | Easter (EF, JF), 1 Birth (M), 1 Jeshua (P) |
| Wise Men | Sat 27 May 1 BCE | Firstfruits | 1 Serpent | | Firstfruits (E) |
| To Egypt | Wed 5 Jul 1 BCE | Mourning | 1 Dragon | 1 Birth | 1 Resurrection (M) |
| Herod's Death | @ Feb CE 1 | | | | |
| From Egypt | Thu 22 Mar CE 1 | Consecration | 1 Dragon | 1 Death | 1 Creation (M) |

This table shows how the events in the life of Christ coincide with holidays and events on several calendars. The Gregorian, Hebrew, Sacred Round, Jubilee, Jubilee Fixed, Enoch, Enoch Fixed, Priest, Mercury, and Venus calendars, all contain dates germane to events in the life of Christ.

The April 5th birth date of Christ put forth by several researchers has correlations to five of the listed calendars as days of Creation and Passover. This April 5th birth date are days of Creation on the Venus and Mercury calendars. On the Hebrew calendar the 5th is the first day of the Passover of the comet/Venus. The visit of the 3 Wise Men (Magi-Magician), coincide with the Feast of Firstfruits (Enoch) on the Hebrew and Enoch/Enki calendars. We know that the 3 stars in the Belt of Orion have been called the 3 Kings since antiquity. The Saturday the 27th date coincides with the Serpent (Venus) on the Sacred Round.

The trip to Egypt by Christ was a period of Mourning on the Hebrew calendar. On the Sacred Round it correlates to the Dragon (Venus). The Venus and Mercury calendars mark it as a day of Birth and Resurrection. The trip from Egypt is marked by the Consecration period on the Hebrew calendar. The Dragon represents this date on the Sacred Round. The trip from Egypt is Death on the Venus calendar as she left death and destruction each Jubilee orbit. On the Mercury calendar it represents Resurrection, as it would relate to dying in one portion of the heavens, and being REBORN in another.

# Angels & Demons

*Angels – Planets, Zodiac bindings, and Stars*

*Demons – Comets, Asteroids, and Meteors*

# What's in a Name?

*Curious?*

**Azazel & Azzael** – The **el** in their names indicate that they were followers of the **Canaanite God El**, thus, how could they be the **Devil** and Satan of the **God Yahweh (YHWH)**? In this tradition **Azazel (Venus)** was basically the number two to Yahweh and fell to **Earth** bringing **Sin (Moon)**.

**Baalzebub /Beelzebub** - The **Baal** in the Devil's name indicates that he was of the **God** or **Lord Baal**, thus, how could he be the Devil and Satan of the God **Yahweh**?

**Morning Star and Evening Star** – **Venus** has been called the **Morning** and **Evening Star** since her birth in our consciousness. **Jesus Christ** and **Quetzalcoatl** are also called the **Morning Star**.

**Visnu** – In **Hindi** appears to be an **anagram** for **Venus**. One need only substitute an **E** for the letter **I**.

**Vishnu** – The word means pervader in **Hindi**. This seems to intone that **Venus pervaded** its' way into the cosmos and the lives of **mankind**.

**Lucifer** – This is a very telling name for Venus, and the Vatican owned observatory!

**Babel** – The **el** in **Babel** denotes that they were **followers** of the **Canaanite God El**. The **tower** was being **built** by the **Children of the Sheep** in homage to the **Lord of the Sheep (Babel – Tower to God)**. The tower was destroyed and the languages confused by God, lest they do anything that they attempt to. The Children of Israel sojourned in this land for many centuries with an exchange of culture and deities.

**El** – is a **Northwest Semetic** word meaning **deity**, and has its roots in the **Canaanite** and **Levantine** religions. In Ugarit, **El**, is known as **Toru El (El Toro)**, or the Bull God! El has **consistently** been **identified** with **Yahweh**!

**EL** – The capital letters **EL** in the **Hebrew** language are pronounced **Beelzebub (Lord of Demon Flies)**! This is a direct relation of **Baal/Beel** and **El**, the **Canaanite Gods**.

| Breastplate Stone | Common Name | Hebrew Tribe/Month | Zodiac Stone/Sign |
|---|---|---|---|
| Oden (red) | Ruby | Reuvain | Garnet/Aquarius |
| Pitida (1/3 white, black, red) | Topaz | Shimon | Ruby/Capricorn |
| Bareket | Beryl | Levi | Amethyst/Pisces |
| Nofech | Turqoise | Judah | Onyx/Leo |
| Sapir | Sapphire | Isachar | Emerald/Cancer |
| Yahalom | Diamond | Zebulun | Bloodstone/Aries |

| Leshem | Jacinth | Dan | Beryl/Scorpio |
|---|---|---|---|
| Shvo | Agate | Naftali | Carnelia/Virgo |
| Ahlama | Jasper | Gad | Topaz/Sagittarius |
| Tarshish | Emerald | Asher | Peridot/Libra |
| Shoham | Onyx | Joseph | Sapphire/Taurus |
| Yashfe | Jade | Benjamin | Agate/Gemini |

The first century Jewish historian Josephus chronicled a direct connection between Aaron's breastplate and the twelve signs of the zodiac. The stones also clearly represent the Twelve Tribes of Israel, although that connection was omitted.

## Planet Names

| Enlgish | Sumerian | Babylonian | Akkadian | Greek | Egyptian | Sanskrit | Japanese | Latin |
|---|---|---|---|---|---|---|---|---|
| Sun | Apsu | Shamash | Shamash | Helios | Aten | Surya | | Sol |
| Moon | Kingu | Sin | Sin | Selene | Aah or Iah (Allah?) | Chandra | | Luna |
| Mercury | Mummu | Nabu | Nabu | Hermes | Sabgu | Buddha | Susei - Water Star | Mercurious |
| Venus | Lahamu | Ishtar | Ishtar | Aphrodite | Ba'ah or Seba-djal | Sukra | Kinsei - Metal Star | Venus |
| Mars | Lahmu | Nergal | Nergal | Ares | Heru-deshet | Mangala | Kasei – Fire Star | Mars |
| Jupiter | Kishar | Marduk | Marduk | Zeus | Her-wepes-tawy | Brhaspati | Makusei – Wood Star | Jupiter |
| Saturn | Anshar | Ninurta | Ninib | Kronos | | Sani | Dosei – Earth Star | Saturnus |
| Neptune | Antu | | | | | | | |
| Uranus | Anu | | | | | | | |
| Pluto | Gaga | | | | | | | |
| Earth | Tiamat/Ki | | | | | | | |

Ishtar = Astarte = Eastar/Easter = Venus

## Some Els in the Bible

Abel, Atel, Ishmael, Yisrael, Bethuel, Rachel, El wa Abirer, Bedsu' el, Ezekiel, Angel, Kokabel, Ezeqel, Araqiel, Shamsiel, Sariel, Michael, Uriel, Raphael, Gabriel, Dudael, Elohim, and El Shaddai.

Uriel – God (El) is my light     Michael – Who is like El (God)     Raguel – Friend of El (God)     Azazel – Strong Mountain of God (El)

El Shaddai – God (El) Almighty     Kokabel – Star of God (El)     Tamiel – Thunder of El (God)     Ramiel – Evening of God (El)

Salathiel – I asked El (God) for this child     Zerubbabel – The one sown of Babylon (El)     Abel – Breath of El/Herdsman of El (God)

Atel – El (God) has hearkened     Bethuel – House of El (God)     Gabriel – El (God) is my strength     Elohim – Gods (Els)


## Solomon's Archangels and Angels (Els)

| El Name | Meaning | Planet |
|---|---|---|
| Tzaphqiel - Archangel | Knowledge of El (God) | Saturn |
| Tzadiqel - Archangel | Righteousness of El (God) | Jupiter |
| Khaniel - Archangel | Enlightenment of El (God) | Mars |
| Raphael - Archangel | El Heals (God) | Sun |
| Haniel - Archangel | Grace of El (God) | Venus |
| Michael - Archangel | Who is like El? (God) | Mercury |
| Gabriel - Archangel | El (God) is my strength | Moon* |
| Cassiel - Angel | Time of El (**Father of Time?**) (God) | Saturn |
| Sachiel - Angel | Covering of El (God) | Jupiter |
| Zamael - Angel | Joy of El (God) | Mars |
| Michael - Angel | **Who is like El?** (God) | Sun |
| Anael - Angel | **Pleasure/Joy of El (God)** | **Venus (Ashera?)** |
| Raphael - Angel | El (God) heals | Mercury |
| Gabriel - Angel | El (God) is my strength | Moon* |

*\* The Moon is the only heavenly body that has one Archangel and Angel*

It is interesting to note that Solomon only knows of seven celestial bodies, excluding that of Earth. The Sumerians possibly knew of the existence of the outer planets long before any other civilization.

# A Few Biblical Word Frequencies

***Strong's Bible Concordance – King James Version***

*Signs – 53*

*Sign - 76*

*Gold – 417*

*Silver – 320*

*Master – 181*

*Servant – 502*

*Star – 15*

*Angel – 203*

*Satan – 56 (Natas, Tanas, Santa, and Sanat)*

*Yahweh – 0*

*Jehovah – 4*

*El – 0*

*Dagon (Gonad) – 13*

*Amen / Amun – 78 (Hidden One)*

*Lord – 7,970 (Baal, Beel – 104 references)*

*Love – 311*

*Hate – 85*

*Leprosy – 39*

*Gog – 11*

*Magog – 5*

*Orion – 3*

*Pleiades – 2*

## ZODIAC WHEELS AROUNG THE GLOBE

**Egyptian Zodiac Wheel**

**Mesopotamian Zodiac Wheel**

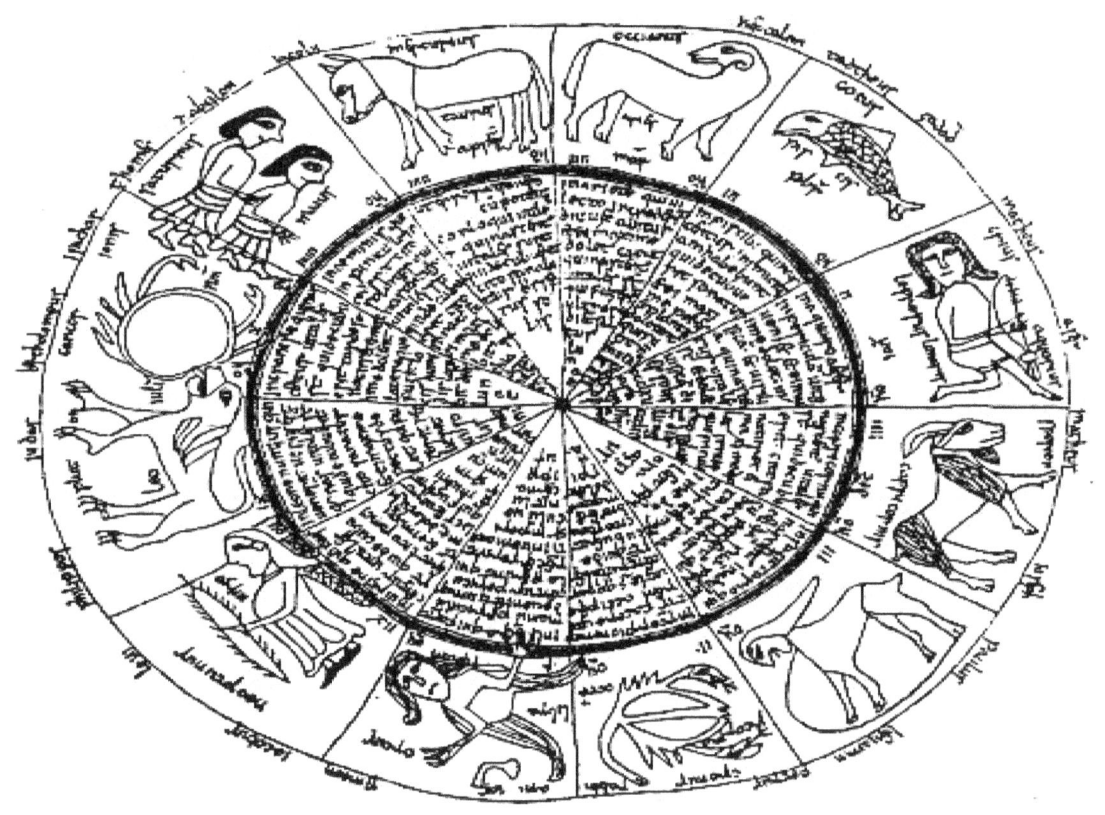

*Irish Zodiac Wheel*

*Ethiopean Zodiac Wheel*

# *Obelisks, Pillars, Steeples, Minarets, Spires, Jacob's Ladder, and Celestial Wheels in the Sky*

*Obelisk: Baal's Shaft AKA obeliskos in Greek. A tall four-sided, narrow tapering monument which ends in a pyramid shape at the top.*

*Steeple: A tall tower typically topped with a spire. Steeples are commonly found on Christian churches and cathedrals.*

*Minaret: From the Arabic "minarah" (Menorah) meaning lighthouse.*

*Jacob's Ladder: In the dream vision of the Biblical Jacob, he saw a ladder to heaven with flaming angels going up and down to the Earth.*

*Spires: A tapering conical or pyramidal structure on the top of a building, particularly a church.*

      Having lived in Maryland outside of Washington, D.C., for several years, I had the opportunity to consistently take advantage of the arts, culture, entertainment, and beautiful buildings in the city. I enjoyed wandering the museums and going to the top of the Washington Monument to marvel at the spectacular view. The layout and design of the city and structures have been greatly debated and theorized these past few years. It is noted that the Washington Monument is four-hundred and forty-four feet high (444'), with two-hundred and twenty-two feet (222') underground for a total of six-hundred sixty and six feet (666'). The architects in building these beautiful structures have been alleged to be paying homage to their Gods. These topics will be open to debate, until they are no longer open to debate.

      My seminal theory of what the obelisk represents came when I truly understood the word itself. Knowing that the word means Baal's shaft sparked my curiosity. Why would the ancient Egyptians, Sumerians, Israelites, Hindu, and modern man be so enraptured with the penis of God? Why did Jacob dream of a ladder to heaven where flaming angels went up and down? I began to look at the obelisks in Washington, New York, Egypt, England, Rome, Paris (Eiffel Tower), and so many other countries. This led me to look at the inordinate amount of large obelisks that serve as monuments in graveyards across the United States and the United Kingdom. I will show my discoveries in that area in another project. The fascination with the Egyptian obelisk made its way from Egypt to England, and then to the United States with the influx of immigrants. The obelisk craze for use as tombstones seemed to have ebbed in the 1940's, as they were expensive to make, and the wealthy were buried in some that rise twenty feet from the ground.

      Sacred texts from around the globe speak of the flaming wheel in the sky with an extended horn (shofur) or privy member. We begin to understand that the ancients in honor of what they were seeing in the sky created the oblesik! The penis in the sky that extended from the God that dripped the waters of life. This privy member often exploded God's life-giving semen over the Earth. This was actually debris that formed the manna from heaven. The horn in all probability ejected massive plasma discharges that destroyed mankind on occasion. The knowledge the people had that this was the object that weighed their sins and watched over them was a frightful period of existence.

      The shape of the horn in the sky changed from culture to culture, and from religion to religion. In the Christian/Catholic faith, the steeple of the church became representative of the horn. One can only notice the cross, sacred heart of Christ, and the parabrum being placed atop the steeple on many churches. The early builders placed a round glass circle in the roof known as a Holy Ghost Hole, to allow the Holy Spirit entrance to the congregation. In the Islamic world the horn is represented as a minaret. The Eiffel Tower and Washington Monuments in modern times have continued the representation of a phallus. The horn in the sky would appear to touch the pillar on Earth. This is also the Egyptian philosophy of As Above, So Below! I believe that this was the intentions of the ancients, and in all likelihood is what the Tower of Babel was built in imitation of and in homage to. When the structure was destroyed by God (Pillar) the ancients felt that they had angered God in their endeavors. It seems that the structure was a lightning rod for the horned wheel as it was the tallest thing on the Plain of Shinar!

*When civilization peeks its head out after these recurrent catastrophes, we come out the other side with far less knowledge of the prior times. To a people, that understood the catastrophe of the Great Flood, seeing this wheel that brought utter devastation with it engendered reverence. A cosmic event was misinterpreted as being a Divine presence that weighed the sins and iniquities of mankind. There is no doubt that documents, rites, and practices of prior times were discovered by some of the survivors, and when someone teaches or interprets without benefit of a teacher themselves, this can often be a problematic situation.*

*The theory that I have put forth, in regard to the wheel in the sky with horn being the object that we mimick with our structures and practices may be decried by theologians and scientist alike. There will be a section that rationally analyzes these theories, and will come to their own understanding of the subject. We continually feel that we have nothing left as mankind to learn of the past or of other concepts, and we are continually shown that we have a long way to go. A theory is just such, until it is proven or accepted to be fact!*

**Church with classic steeple and Parabrum of Christ**

*Sacred Heart of Quetzalcoatl*

*Sacred Heart drawing on house in ancient Egypt*

*Egyptian Sacred Heart – Luxor monument*

*Christian Sacred Heart of Christ*

  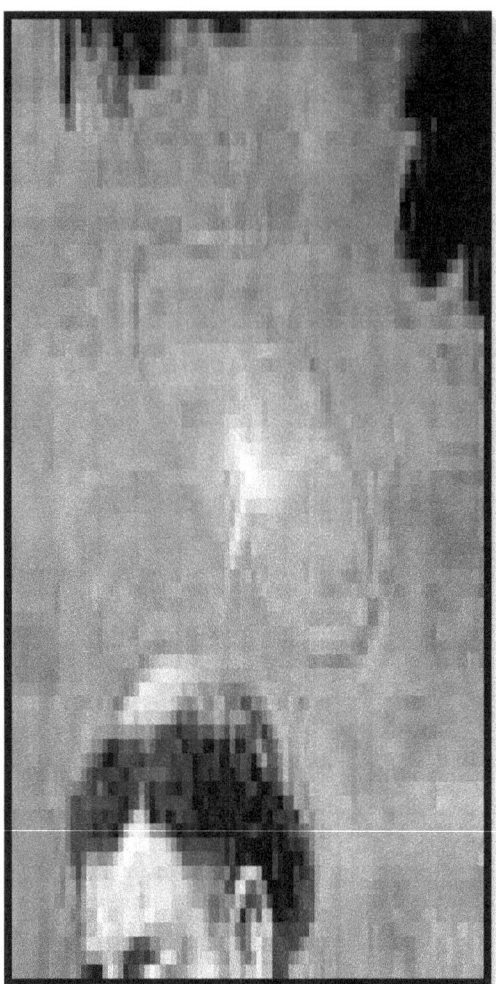

Naram Sin Victory Stele @ 2200 BCE          Tenochitlan Mexico @ 1450 CE          Medieval painting of a Saint with Privy Halo

*Left picture: Notice the wheel in the sky touches the pillar on Earth – "As above – So below." Naram Sin (Suen) was a grandson of Sargon of Akkad, and this stele commerates his victory over Satuni of Lullubi. Naram Sin claimed divinity for himself, as he is depicted ascending the mountain to the fiery wheel/pillar in the sky.*

*Middle picture: This recently discovered series of bas-relief (@ 1450 CE) on the floor of the Temple Mayor complex in Tenochitlan, Mexico, shows a series of celestial battles and human sacrifices. This relief shows the Wheel in the Sky with Privy Member extended toward the Earth. The site was demolished by conquistadors in the 16th century who said that it reeked like a slaughterhouse due to the ritual human sacrifices that took place at the site. The many stories and knowledge that these highly intelligent people left for posterity were destroyed due the hubris exhibited by a supposed more advanced civilization.*

*Right picture: The cropping of this Franciscan Saint with halo and privy member shows a clear association between the Wheel in the Sky and divinity. The artist fully understood what the church wanted depicted in the painting. The Wheel in the Sky was visible 400 to 500 years ago, and probably led to the European belief that the world was flat, as the disc in the sky was elliptical in shape.*

*There is a 3,600 year span between the Naram Sin stele of the Akkadian empire, and the bas-relief from the Temple Mayor in Mexico, meaning that the feature was long-lived in the skies of the Earth. There is 8,000 miles between the Middle East and Mexico, how did the cultures share an understanding? They both saw the same feature in the sky!*

## *Little Pyramids on Top*

*Egyptian obelisk – Washington, DC*

*Washington Monument – Washington, DC*

*Egyptian Obelisk – Vatican, St. Peter's Square*

*Karnak Egypt obelisk – Little pyramid on top*

*Flower of Life – Wheel of Death*

*Mycanae royal treasure*

**4-Flower Wheel from Mycanae treasure**

**Ancient 6-spoke Wheel coin**

**Venus clam shell coin with 4-spoke wheel**

**8-pointed Star of Ishtar (Venus)**

*Wheeled Coptic Equinox Cross/Halo with Zodiac – Very telling imagery (Leo-12, Scorpio-3, Aquarius-6, Taurus-9)*

# Aztec/Mayan World Suns

*In the Aztec religion there were 5 ages, or "5 suns". Every age had a different Sun god, and every age ended in disaster. Most religions and civilizations relate several world ages ended by destruction, and the Aztec tradition is very brief in relating the particular maladies associated with the destruction, they show a common relationship of cosmic disasters from the heavens with Gods waging war with the Earth being the ultimate victim of the conflict.*

**In the Beginning**

The dual-sexuality God Ometecuhtli/Omecihuatl had four children, which represent the four directions of north, south, east and west. The Gods were **Huizilopochtli** (south), **Quetzalcoatl** (east), **Tezcatlipoca** (west), and **Xipe Totec** (north).

*Huizilopochtli -* **Moon**

*Tezcatlipoca –* **Sun**

*Xipe Totec –* **Mars (Toltecs)**

*Quetzalcoatl –* **Venus (Smoking Star/Morning Star)**

**The first sun - Jaguar Sun (Nahui Ocelotl)**

*Tezcatlipoca managed to become half a sun making this first creation incomplete. During the first age, the gods created giants from ashes, and gave them acorns to eat. A fight began between Quetzalcoatl and Tezcatlipoca. The sun was knocked from the sky, and in anger Tezcatlipoca sent jaguars to destroy the giants.*

**We have the Sun embodied as Tezcatlipoca, who sees the Gods create giants during the 1st World. The giants were created from ashes (fire/naptha) and given acorns (micro-meteorites) to eat. The Sun (Tezcatlipoca) is knocked from the visible sky in a cosmic battle with Venus (Quetzalcoatl). Tezcatlipoca (Sun) sends jaguars (sun spots/coronal mass ejections) to destroy the giants. This overlooked scenario blends with Biblical, Egyptian, and Sumerian accounts for events during the time of Jared and Enoch/Enkime.**

> **Enoch 7:3** became pregnant, and they bare great giants, whose height was three thousand ells: Who consumed
> 
> **Genesis 6:4** There were giants in the earth in those days; and also after that, when the sons of God came in unto the daughters of men, and they bare children to them, the same became mighty men which were of old, men of renown.
> 
> **Numbers 13: 33** And there we saw the giants, the sons of Anak, which *come* of the giants: and we were in our own sight as grasshoppers, and so we were in their sight.
> 
> **Deut 2:11** Which also were accounted giants, as the Anakims; but the Moabites call them Emims.
> 
> **Lost Book of Enki:** On the Sun's face black spots were appearing, from its face flames shot up;

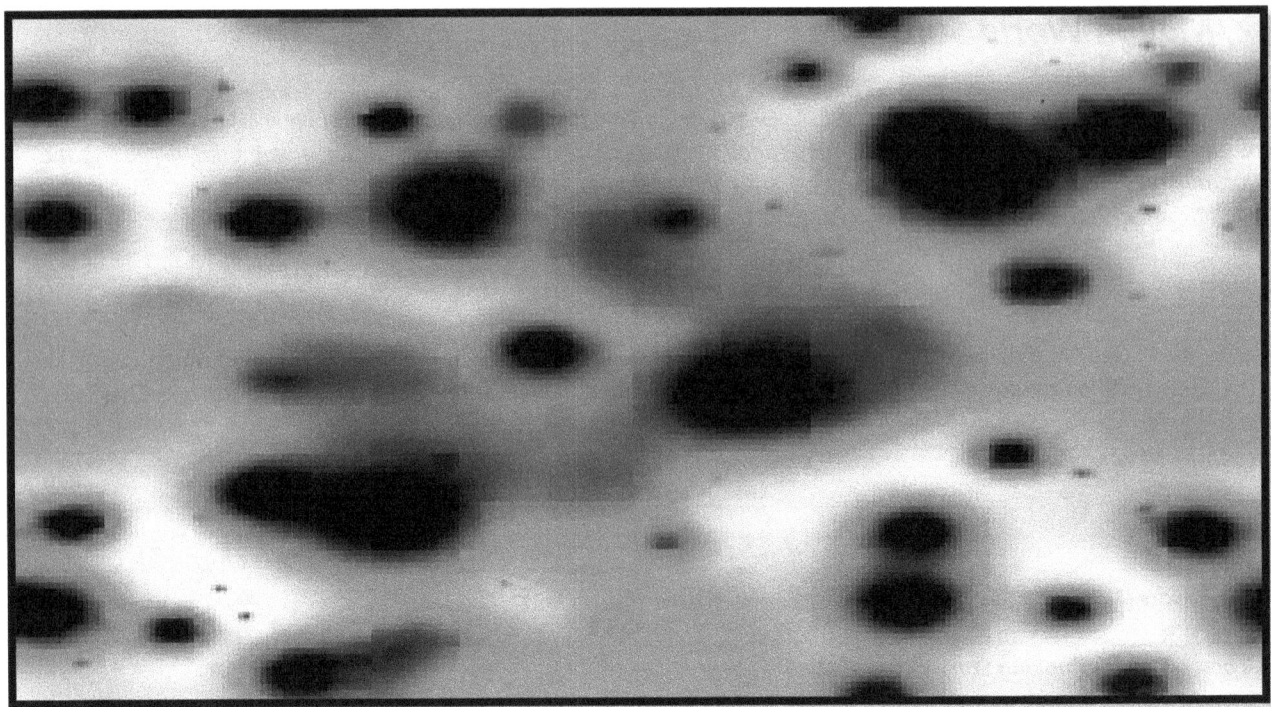

*Jaguar spots on the Sun*

**The second sun - Wind Sun (Nahui Ehecatl)**

*Quetzalcoatl took over for his brother as the Sun. Humans were created as they are now. The people became corrupt and out of revenge Tezcatlipoca turned them into monkeys. Quetzalcoatl sent a hurricane to blow the monkeys away.*

**Quetzalcoatl (Venus) shines as the Sun (2 Suns in the sky?), after a cosmic battle which elevates his/her stature around the globe as cults to Venus pop up. The effects of the celestial war may have changed man genetically (monkeys)? Quetzalcoatl (Venus) sends a hurricane (Hurakan/Evil Wind) to destroy the monkeys of the 2$^{nd}$ World.**

- **Jubilee 10:26** And YAHWEH sent a mighty wind against the tower and overthrew it upon the earth, and behold it was between Asshur and Babylon in the land of Shinar, and they called its name **'Overthrow'**.

- **Lost Book of Enki** - Swirling within a dark cloud, gloom from the skies an **Evil Wind** carried, As the day wore on, the Sun on the horizon with darkness it obliterated, At nighttime a dreaded brilliance skirted its edges, the Moon at its rising it made disappear *(sackcloth)*.

- **Job 1: 19** And, behold, there came a **great wind** from the wilderness, and smote the four corners of the house, and it fell upon the young men, and they are dead; and I only am escaped alone to tell thee.

**The third sun - Rain Sun (Nahui Quiahuitl)**

*Tlaloc (Tlaloc) was the god of rain and water, and became the next sun. Tezcatlipoca stole Tlaloc's wife (Xochiquetzal), and Tlaloc was grief-stricken. He shone as the sun but refused to send rain, drought swept the earth, and finally in a rage Tlaloc made it rain fire, burning away this world*

*Tlaloc may be the God of the Sun after the time of the Great Flood? The former Sun God, Tezcatlipoca, steals Tlaloc's wife Xochiquetzal (unknown?), causing the Sun (Tlaloc) to bring drought upon the Earth, and then it rained fire (fire & brimstone) destroying the 3rd world.*

> **Genesis 19: 24** Then the LORD rained upon Sodom and upon Gomorrah brimstone and fire from the LORD out of heaven;

> **Exodus 9:24** So there was hail and flaming fire mingled with hail; and the hail was very great, such as was not in Egypt, from the time there was a nation upon it.

**The fourth sun - Water Sun (Nahui Atl)**

> *The gods selected Tlaloc's sister to be the Sun, Calchiuhtlicue (Saturn?). Filled with jealousy, Tezcatlipoca and Quetzalcoatl struck down the Sun. As she fell, the sky opened up and water flooded the earth. All things were destroyed again. In the darkness between the Suns, Quetzalcoatl descended into the underworld to bring up the bones of the dead.*

*Calchiuhtlicue becomes the Sun God of the World, as Tezcatlipoca (old Sun) and Quetzalcoatl (Venus) continue their feud as they strike down the Sun (Calchiuhtlicue) and floods the Earth. The Earth is cast into darkness as Quetzalcoatl (Venus) descends (below the horizon for 3 days) to the underworld (Innana, Dummuzi, Christ) to bring up the bones of the dead (graves overturned). The descent of Quetzalcoatl (Venus) into the underworld was a concept readily understood by the Aztecs when Spanish Conquistadors and Missionaries arrived. The 4th World comes to an end.*

**The fifth sun - Earthquake Sun**

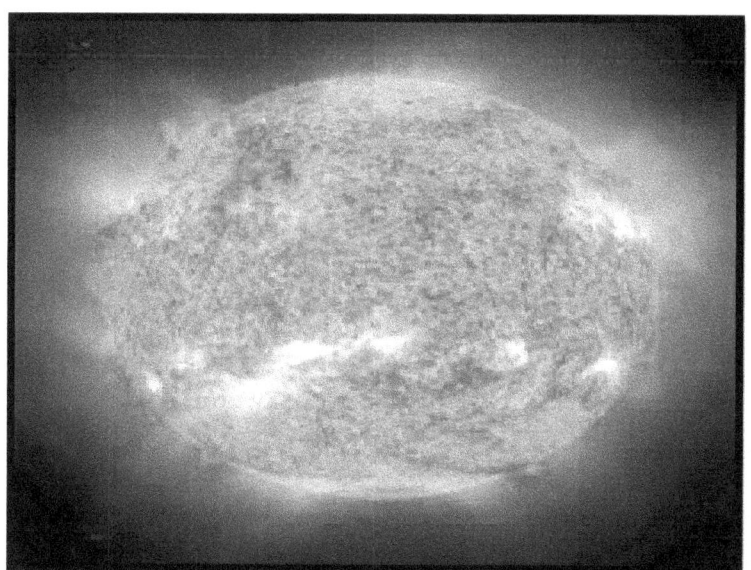

> *The gods gather to bring another Sun into being. The God Tecuciztecatl offered himself, but the other gods preferred the humble Nanahuatzin. A great fire was built, but Tecuciztecatl was afraid at the last minute to jump in. Nanahuatzin did jump. Filled with jealousy, Tecuciztecatl jumped after, followed by a brave eagle and jaguar. Two suns began to rise in the east. It was too bright the gods threw a rabbit into the face of Tecuciztecatl to dim the light, and he became the moon. But Nanahuatzin was weak. He was motionless, so the other gods gave their blood to give him the energy to rush across the sky. This is the world in which we now live.*

*Tecuciztecatl offers to be the new Sun God, but Nanahuatzin is chosen in his place. Tecuciztecatl lacks the courage to jump into the fire as Nanahuatzin jumps in followed by an eagle (Aquila constellation) and a jaguar (Sun spots). The overwhelming brightness caused the Gods to throw a rabbit (Hare-Lepus constellation) over Tecuciztecatl, dimming his glow, causing him to become the Moon. This covering of the Moon is a common theme in sacred texts and documents around the globe. The 5th Sun is the time that we currently live in.*

**Rev 6:12** And I beheld when he had opened the sixth seal, and, lo, there was a great earthquake; and the sun became black as sackcloth of hair, and the moon became as blood;

# Lord Krishna, Mahabharata, Ophiuchus, and Kali Yuga

In the Hindu epic, "The Mahabarata," there is a cosmic battle that takes place in the skies between the forces of millions led by Gods, like Lord Krishna. The hero of the classic tale is Arjuna, who Lord Krishna has been chosen by Yudisthira as the driver of Arjuna's chariot in the heavens during the battle for the Pandavas. Lord Krishna was chosen versus wielding a special weapon which went to the Kauravas. The story of the battle is one of the most well written and visual works of classic literature, with constant moral, ethical, and philosophical overtones. I will touch on some things that I have discovered within the context of this epic, as this book is too extensive to present at this point.

Lord Krishna, who is the reincarnation of Vishnu, 36 years (1/2 a celestial portion) after the epic battle is seated practicing his yoga in the forest, when the curse uttered by Gandhari 36 years earlier is fulfilled. A hunter named Jara came near the spot and saw the partially visible left foot of Lord Krishna and mistook it for a deer. Jara let the arrow fly and pierced Lord Krishna's foot, as he approached and saw the Lord he touched his feet and begged for forgiveness. Arjuna cremated Lord Krishna and his wives! Upon his death the women of Dvarka (Krishna's mythic city) became ascetics and nuns, as the people of Dvarka abandoned the city before the sea engulfed it leaving no trace. To understand just these few passages, we must understand Kali Yuga. The typical Kali Yuga is thought to last for 432,000 years. The Kali Yuga that we live in is a special 10,000 year age, and this began on 3102 BCE. The chart below shows the full special Kali Yuga age in comparison to the corresponding Zodiac Age.

| *Zodiac Age* | *Start* | *End* |
|---|---|---|
| Taurus – Bull, Brahma | 4469 BCE | 2309 BCE |
| **KALI YUGA – begins (Maya 3114 BCE)** | **3102 BCE** | |
| Aries | 2308 BCE | 149 BCE |
| Pisces | 148 BCE | 2012 CE |
| Aquarius | 2013 CE | 4173 CE |
| Capricorn | 4174 CE | 6334 CE |
| Sagittarius | 6335 CE | |
| **KALI YUGA – ends (ecliptic equinox)** | **6898 CE** | |
| Sagittarius | | 8494 CE |
| Scorpio | 8495 CE | 10,655 CE |

We see from the charting that Kali Yuga begins in the constellation of Taurus (Brahma) and passes through Aries, Pisces, Aquarius, Capricorn, Sagittarius, and finally to Scorpio during its 10,000 year voyage across the cosmos. The Age of Sagittarius begins in 6332 CE, and 656 years later the Kali Yuga comes to an end in 6898 CE. This end date is all-telling when we look at the heavens in the round. Sagittarius the Archer (Arjuna-Bowman) stands poised with his bow flexed pointing toward Scorpio, who happens to be in the process of being stepped upon by Ophiuchus (Serpent Bearer – Lord Krishna) with his LEFT FOOT! The arrow is pointing in the general direction of the left foot of Ophiuchus. Krishna (Ophicuchus) drives the chariot of Arjuna (Sagittarius) across the heavens in their celestial battle. Lord Krishna is relating that his death will come in the sky when Sagittarius passes into Scorpio. Balarama, an avatar for Vishnu speaks of the serpent on which the Lord Vishnu sleeps. Ophiuchus the Serpent Bearer straddles the serpent, and could be said to rest upon it. The author of the Mahabharata has done what was typical of writers during the period by relating cosmic events with Gods and men, comingled with theology.

The constellation of Scorpio is where Dumuzi/Tammuz stepped on the scorpion and was killed (they weep for Tammuz). Ophiuchus wrestles with the Serpent as the Hero, and Hercules wields his mighty club. The thing that we must remember is that the larger portion of the populace during these times were illiterate in that only the elite were educated, and the poor's education came in lessons told in the stars. In the usual multiple names and symbolism that is used for deities, Lord Krishna has a multitude of names. I will share a few revealing names, as Krishna is a reincarnation of the God Visnu, and Visnu is an anagram for Venus! This underpins the correlation between the Lord Krishna and Jesus Christ, as they both are representative of the planet Venus.

**Vishnu** – The maintainer or preserver      **Shiva** – Destroyer or Transformer      **Visnu** – to enter into or pervade

**Balarama (Vishnu Avatar) – Serpent** on which the supreme **Lord Vishnu** sleeps      **Kalki** – Destroyer of time or Destroyer of foulness

**Anirudha** – The one that cannot be stopped      **Vishal** – The Unstoppable One      **Vasudeva** – All Pervading God

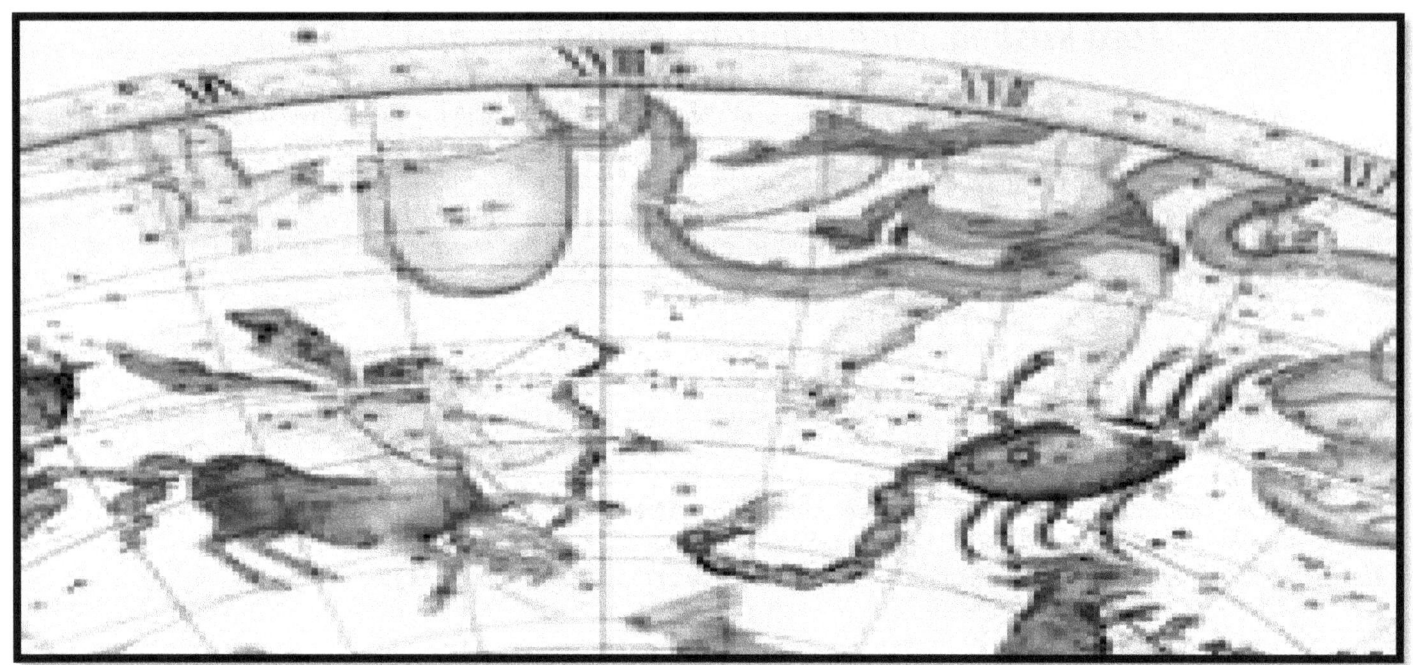

*The bow of Sagittarius (Arjuna, Jara) is set to unleash his arrow towards the left heel of Ophiuchus (Lord Krishna, Dummuzi, Tammuz)*

*I maintain that Truth is a pathless land, and you cannot approach it by any path whatsoever, by any religion, by any sect.*
**Jiddu Krishnamurti**

BELOW: At the Zodiac Equinox in 6988 CE Kali Yuga ends with an arrow to Lord Krishna's (Ophiuchus-Serpent Bearer) left heel

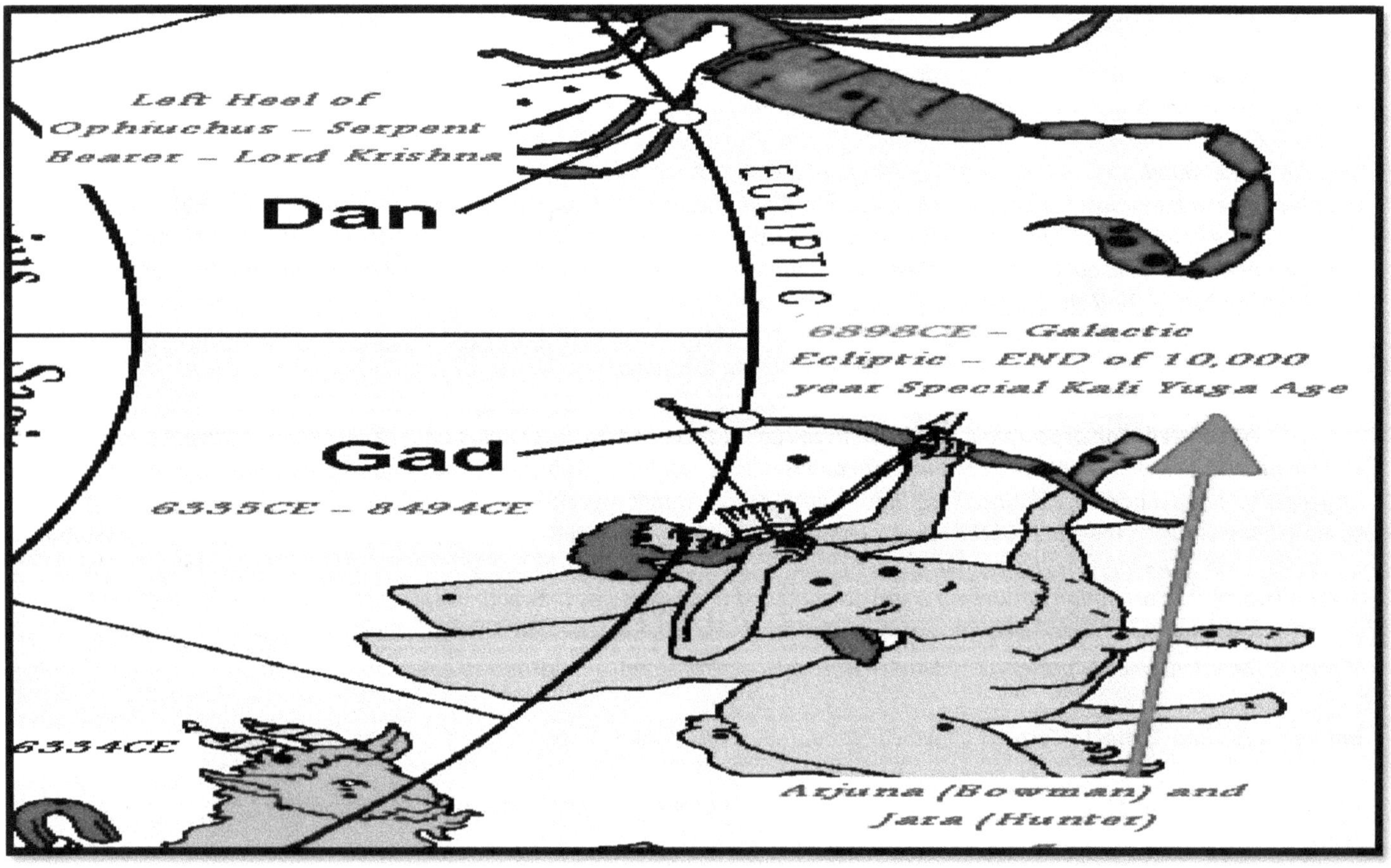

## Egyptian Kings List of Note

| Period | Dynasty | Pharaoh (# of) | Dynasty Start | Dynasty End | Total/Avg. Years |
|---|---|---|---|---|---|
| Early Dynastic | 0 | Several noted (Kings) (4) | 3250 | 3050 | 200 |
| Late Dynastic | 1 | Horus Aha<br><br>10 Pharaohs named Horus (10) | 3050 | 2857 | 193 (19.3) |
|  | 2 | Horus Hetepsekhemwy<br><br>7 Pharoahs named Horus (10) | 2857 | 2705 | 152 (15.2) |
| Old Kingdom | 3 | Horus Nekhtza<br><br>5 Pharaohs named Horus (5) | 2705 | 2630 | 75 (15) |
|  | 4 | Snefru (8) - Djoser | 2630 | 2524 | 106 (13.25) |
|  | 5 | Userkaf (9) | 2524 | 2400 | 124 (13.7) |
|  | 6 | **Teti (8)**<br><br>**Unas – 2375 to 2345 BCE Pharaoh of the Great Flood**<br><br>**Teti – 2345 to 2333 Pharaoh after the Great Flood 2344 BCE** | 2400 | 2250 | 150 (18.75) |
|  | 7 | (10) Listed<br><br>*Period of turmoil* | 2250 | 2230 | 20 (2) |
|  | 8 | *Qakare Ibi (4)* | 2230 | 2213 | 17 (4.25) |
| 1st Intermediate | 9 | Meryibre Akhtoy (2) | 2213 | 2175 | 38 (19) |
|  | 10 | Nebkaure Akhtoy (6) | 2175? | 2035 | 140 (28) |
|  | 11 | Horus Tepi-'o (12)<br><br>8 Pharaohs named Horus | 2134? | 1991 | 143 (11.92) |
| Middle Kingdom | 12 | Amenemhat 1 (8)<br><br>4 Paharaohs with "Amen" | 1991 | 1784 | 207 (25.875)<br><br>Hebrews @ 1917 |
|  | 13 | *Khutawyre Wegaf (38)* | 1784 | 1668 | 116 (3.05) |
| 2nd Intermediate | 14 | *Nehsi (17)* | 1720 | 1665 | 55 (3.44) |
|  | 15 | Sekhaenre Shalik (8) | 1668 | 1560 | 108 (13.5) |

| | 16 | Saket (6) | 1665 | 1565 | 100 (16.66) |
|---|---|---|---|---|---|
| | 17 | *Nubkheperre Inyotef V (14)* | 1668 | 1570 | 98 (7) |
| New Kingdom | 18 | (14) Ahmose 1<br><br>Noted: Amenhotep 1, 2, 3, 4, Tuthmosis 1, 2, 3, Amenhotep 4th / Akhenaten*, Hasphepsut, and Tutankhamun, 5 Amen/Amun, 5 Mose/Mosis<br><br>Who was Pharaoh of the Exodus 1487 – 1447? Tuthmosis 3rd 1504 – 1450, Queen Hatshepsut 1498 – 1483, or Amenhotep 2nd 1453 – 1419 | 1570 | 1293 | 277 (19.78) |
| | 19 | (9) Ramesses 1, 2, Seti 1 and 2 | 1293 | 1185 | 108 (13.5) |
| | 20 | (10) Ramesses 3, 4, 5, 6, 7, 8, 9, 10, and 11 | 1185 | 1070 | 115 (11.5) |
| 3rd Intermediate | to | Upheaval period | 1070 | 656 | 414 |
| Late Period | 31 | Saite, Persian, Macedonian, and Ptolemaic | 685 | 30 | 655 |
| | | **Roman Era Ends as the Dark Ages begin!** | 30 | 395 CE | 425 |

*The Egyptian Kings list offers us an excellent window into the global and regional disasters that affected Kingship, religious, cultural, and historical continuity. From the Early Dynastic Period to the 3rd Dynasty, the focus was on worship to Horus (Mercury), as witnessed by twenty-two of the early Pharaohs assuming the title of Horus (Hours). The planet Mercury is anthropomorphized as the hawk God Horus. The association with this planet from the onset of their society testifies to their belief in this heavenly body.*

*The 6th Dynasty gives us the period of Teti and Pepi 1st twice! Pepi 2nd reigned from 2355 – 2261 BCE, the Great Flood occurred possibly during the reign of Unas (2375 – 2345 BCE) on 2344 - 2343 BCE. Teti 1st took over as pharaoh in 2345 to 2333 BCE, which may show the toll that the event took on the previous kingdoms, as this turmoil leads to the New Kingdom. These timelines in antiquity can be considered a movable feast based on inaccurate dating methods. Pepi 2nd (disputed) reigned for the extremely long period of ninety-four years which would span that possible period for the disaster of the Great Flood.*

*We move forward 680 years to 1570 BCE, and we find ourselves in the New Kingdom in the 18th Dynasty. We see a shift in the worship to Amen aka Amun, as five Pharaohs use this in their names. Amen had not been used for over 300 years in a Pharaohs name, as this shift picked up pace pre-Exodus and continued onward. The God was worshipped as "Amun/Amen," or the "Hidden one," and as "Ra," as "Revealed Divinity." I feel that the onset of the disasters as recorded by the books of the Exodus and Ipuwer Papyrus led to the elevation of Ra (Sun) that continues today. The use of Mosis was prevalent for the Pharaohs as well during this dynasty and has lived on in our common lexicon. The Exodus could have occurred during the reign of Tuthmosis 1st in 1524 BCE up to Amenhotep 2nd in 1453 BCE. The timeline of events leads us to conclude that Tuthmosis 3rd was the Pharaoh that reigned during the Exodus, but, we are presented with an interesting conundrum! Tuthmosis 3rd could not be the Pharaoh that drowned in the parted waters with his army, as we have his mummified body on display, and those of his predecessors and successors! This problem has plagued researchers as to the exact identity of the Exodus Pharaoh, if all accounts are accurate.*

*The Roman conquest of Egypt in 30 BCE brought an end to the Dynastic period. The Romans conquered a land that had passed through the hands of the Macedonians, Persians, and the Ptolemaics. All civilizations in the region had been in a downward spiral for a millennia or more. The Romans had Egypt until 395 CE before ceding control. Our Judeo-Christian concepts and beliefs were inextricably enmeshed in Egyptian culture from its conception. The Children of Israel did not found their own writing system until @ 1000 BCE a full 2000 years after the civilizations that they spent these millennia amongst.*

*The length of rule as Pharaoh varied by disaster periods. The Old Kingdom Pharaohs reigns averaged a little over 11 years. The Pharaohs of the Middle Kingdom averaged a one term reign of 4.62 years. Taking into account the first three Dynasties of the New Kingdom the average reign lasted for 15 years. The pageantry and lavish lifestyle of the Pharaohs seem to pale in comparison to their short lifespan upon becoming ruler.*

<u>*CURIOUS:*</u>

*34 – Pharaohs named Horus (Mercury) – Hours = Horus!*

*17 – Pharaohs named Amen/Amun (Hidden/Unseen One)*

*5 – Pharaohs named Mosis*

*12 – Pharaohs named Ramesses*

**\* There are several different Egyptian Kings List with disputed dates; Turin, Oxford, and more\***

# *Conclusions*

It has become quite clear that the language used by the ancients to portray what was transpiring in the heavens above was synthesized with their theology. To a citizenry coming out of several extinction level events, reacquainting themselves with a familiar heaven above in order to regain a semblance of a normal existence was essential. This was of primary importance for farming, establishing time, festivals, and more. The fear and terror that the survivors endured has haunted us through the millennia. Carl Jung has tied many of our archetypal dream images to repressed trauma. Immanuel Velikofsky has stated that we are a people withcollective amnesia. This amnesia would result from mankind narrowly escaping through the bottleneck several times. Each successive disaster took more knowledge of the previous life with it. When mankind came out the other side of these catastrophes, teachers were lost, scribes were decimated, those that studied the stars now rested among them, and those that gave theology to the people were gone. When the ruling and educational arms perished, these civilizations began anew with less knowledgeable persons in possession of sacred texts, spells, and knowledge. Theology may have been accidentally or intentionally mixed with the astronomy. The skies were the cathedrals for the early theology as the stories were told in the stars.

It is believed that the zodiac was begun in the Age of Leo around 10,949 to 8790 BCE as our fondness for the Lion has been exhibited by all cultures. One can only wonder why we think back to this age with adoration, but the books on the next two ages of Cancer 8789 BCE to 6630 BCE and Gemini 6629 to 4470 BCE are totally silent. Modern man pops up during the Age of Taurus 4469 to 2309 BCE at around 4000 BCE with the tale of the birth of Adam. Within 600 years of modern mans existence he is faced with near total destruction. There will be those that say that time began for us with the birth of Adam, but curiously, the three stars (3 Kings) in the Belt of Orion lineup with the three pyramids of Giza at @ 10,500 BCE. Why would the ancients line their pyramids up so precisely with a sky that no longer existed? This answer is quite simple in that it was built during that time in homage to that sky and their patron stars.

There has been a complete synthesis of events, deities, disasters, cultures, theology, technology, astronomy, astrology, parables, prophecies, and superstitions. When these ancient documents and sacred texts are examined side by side, we begin to understand how this synthesis began to occur. The earliest known civilization started in Sumeria, as these people left the first known writing, moral, legal, and belief systems. Starting with Sumeria as the seat of known knowledge it moves up to Egypt after the Great Flood of Noah/ziusudra. With the change of locale and culture, the same systems undergo a morphing into new deities and beliefs, but the same principals are at the core of the beliefs. The Hebrews live among the Egyptians and take from their system what seems favorable to their current beliefs. The disasters during the period of the Exodus allow the Children of Israel (Isis/Ra/El) to migrate to what is at that point being called Babylon (Sumeria). The Children of Israel live among these people for some time and undergo another exchange in cultures, as their belief system begins to solidify. The Hebrew names of their calendar months are taken from the Babylonian calendar. (ex: Tammuz) during this era. Yet another disaster scatters the people of Israel to wander into other lands. The spread of Judaism based monotheism becomes popularized into the Catholic and Christian churches as their core foundations.

The Toltecs and the Mayan of South America worshipped Mars and Venus respectively. These two cultures waged war based on what transpired in the heavens. I believe these selfsame planets were chosen as Saint or Demon based on the people doing the choosing. The Sumerians/Babylonians were followers of Mars (Marduk) and the Hebrews living among them worshipped Venus. The Hebrews initiated their Venus worship while living among the Egyptians who worshipped Mercury (Horus), Ra (Sun), and Isis (Venus). This fear and worship of the heavenly bodies became mixed with their theology.

There have been several collisions and near misses that have occurred in the Earth's known history. The exact culprit in each encounter is not easily discernible, but the texts show us that Venus either began as a comet, or took on cometary elements from a collision. Mars has been involved in collisions with Venus which depleted its atmosphere almost completely, leaving it a barren waste. The moon has been destroyed and rings like a bell, because her inards lay in the asteroid belt. There are many unsettling questions as to the possible age of the Moon being older than that of the Earth and Sun! The ancient Sumerian texts say that the Moon was the last satellite to stay with Earth after a cosmic encounter, and the Aztecs speak of a former Sun becoming the Moon. The Sun has also wielded its mighty hand at times with massive coronal ejections, sun spots, and solar flares that disturbed the balance in her neighborhood. The other planets such as Mercury, Jupiter, Saturn, Uranus, and their moons have been *involved in these wars in the heavens as well. There may be a comet of legend known as; The Destroyer, Nibiru, The Blue Star, Typhon, Phaeton, and more, that has initiated cosmic upheaval and celestial battles that may reappear one day. We seem to be in a period of relative calm in the neighborhood, but we never know when a jolt to our reality may appear from the heavens. I believe that when we live in knowledge, we are able to approach even the most dire of situations with a lower level of fear and with a higher intellectual response.*

*I have come to have so much fear and respect for Venus than I ever could have imagined. Venus has shown herself to be the primary culprit in the rape and decimation of mankind. The Flood of Noah/Ziusudra may have been precipitated by issues with the Sun or Venus. I believe that Venus passed in close proximity causing the iceshelf in Antartica to dislodge a massive amount of ice into the Southern Sea. The Bible tells us that during the time of Jared a man could walk from sea to sea, suggesting a one continent land mass. The sacred and biblical texts from around the world are accurate on lots of accounts, the key is to figure out fact from fabulation. Noah/Ziusudra cried out to Enoch/Enkime that the Earth had sunken down! This shows a clear knowledge of a the magnetic poles, precession of the equinoxes, and the axis of the Earth. This happened seventy-five years prior to the Great Flood. If this magnitude flood occurred the tsunami would wash back and forth over most of that landmass, and may well account for the large distribution of marine life and whale skeletons high atop places like the Andes. This flood would have taken decades to fully recede, and for civilization to begin anew. The knowledge that mankind had of exactly who destroyed them was seered into their souls. The ancient scribes wrote down in their fashion what happened and who the destroyer was. The modern literacy rate in the world is at an all-time high, what we must remember is that only the privileged and ruling class learned to read and write during these epochs. This process helped to reinforce a caste system that was almost inescapable.*

*The lifespan of man prior to the disaster of Noah/Ziusudra was almost a thousand years according to Biblical genealogy. Once the comet/Venus stole the Earth's innocence we began to age at an alarming rate. The flybys and Passovers that Velikofsky and others have postulated occurred every forty-nine to fifty years according to the Passover and Jubilee traditions. The predeluge Earth must have provided a stronger atmosphere, pristine lands, and pure waters. The Great Flood ushered in the Bronze Age as it happened at the end of the zodiac Age of Taurus, and on the onset of the Age of Aries. The meteors, naptha, and toxic gases began to kill the planet and its' inhabitants. Mankind begins to have never seen before diseases like leprosy, which is noted to result from arsenic in the water table. There were other survivors across the continent that recall the story of the Flood in their ancient texts. The lifespan of men begin almost immediately after the flood to bottom out. At the time of Noah/Ziusudra's death (950 yrs old), he had outlived several of his great grandchildren. The children of Noah/Ziusudra begin to die sooner like Shem (600 yrs old), and their children like Rue (239 yrs old) and Terah (Tehran?) at 205 years old. I believe the dropoff in length of life from father to son to be the most profound. This loss of life expectancy for Shem, Ham, and Japeth, did not result genetically. Noah/Ziusudra had the pre-flood life total, where one-third of the sons lives were already cut short. The next generations lives were half of Noah's, and each successive generation was lowered to the century mark. The evidence will not always be found in the soil layers, they're often found in what our ancestors are telling us in those texts.*

| TEXT/EVENT | DATE | RELIGION/CULTURE |
|---|---|---|
| End of Ice Age | 9500 BCE | |
| Sinking of Atlantis - Plato | 9500 BCE | Greek |
| NO RECORDS | | NO RECORDS |
| Earliest Sumerian writing | @ 3500-4000 BCE | Sumerian |
| Earliest Egyptian writing | @ 3400 BCE | Egyptian |
| Start of Maya time | 3114 BCE | Maya |

| | | |
|---|---|---|
| *Kali Yuga Age Begins* | 3102 BCE | Hindu |
| *Pyramid Texts* | 3100 BCE | Egyptian |
| **GREAT FLOOD** | **2344 BCE** | **GLOBAL** |
| *Enuma Elish (Creation story)* | 1800 BCE | Sumerian |
| *Code of Hammurabi – 1<sup>st</sup> documented law codes (commandments)* | 1792 BCE | Sumerian |
| *Epic of Gilgamesh* | 1760 BCE | Sumerian |
| *Indus Valley civilization collapses* | 1750 BCE | Hindu |
| *Egyptian Book of the Dead* | 1600 BCE | Egyptian |
| **Volcanic destruction of Thera in Greece** | @ 1500 BCE | Greek |
| **City of Dwarka near Gjarat submerged under water** | @ 1500 BCE | Hindu |
| ***\* 2 Flood stories, 1 sacred book, first legal & moral code, and two cultures decimated*** | 1800-1500 BCE | 4 Cultures |

    We flash forward six or seven hundred years and the wars in the heavens continue as we get repeated dustings, and orbital disruptions from Venus and Mars. The Earth is in upheaval with massive earthquakes and meteor storms from periodic Passovers. The meteors have deposited naptha and iron that man has learned to fashion, create oil products and cosmetics. There are droughts and famine in the Pangean continent that proliferate wars and enslavement. I believe that we still speak one tongue (Semetic?), and write in one glyph (Cuneiform) at this period in our existence. Men cry out for help to their Gods for help as the comet/Venus strikes the Earth with plasma discharges that viciously seperates the land masses in a moment in an hour the globe is changed! I posit this as a possible reason why cultures in the Americas show so many parallels to those on the other continents at a time when man was supposed to be incapable of traversing the oceans. This may account for why older rock strata lay atop younger and fossils layers are jumbled. The continent that was Atlantis may have sat in a small sea, but it now dropped into a bottomless abyss of the newly expanded Atlantic Ocean. Volcanoes around the globe become active during this era, on the Island of Santorini with the eruption of Thera being one of the major volcanic events in recorded history. The bulk of the worlds' exposed (without ice) deserts lay within a certain line of latitude. This area runs from 10° N to 50° N, with the Tropic of Cancer intersecting this area. The major civilizations that have recorded the phenomenal destruction of the past are residents of the area such as; Egypt, Sumeria, Israel, China, India, Pakistan, Iran, Meso-America, and the Americas.

    The Sumerians speak of a nuclear explosion and an Evil Wind in some of their epics. The cause of this has been posited to be advanced lifeforms, volcanic, or seismic activity. Another possibility came to mind recently. There is a natural uranium mine in Oklo, Gabon, that was found to be completely spent of its Uranium-235 potency. How could ancient man have depleted a uranium mine? A plasma strike or internal upheaval of the Earth may have set off a chain reaction of nuclear fission. Uranium-235 has a *half-life of 700 million years. Scientists believe the depletion was caused by natural forces over billions of years based upon the decay of the material. Uranium is a substance that is known to be pyrophoric, meaning that it ignites with air. Pyrophorics are often water reactive as well and will ignite when they contact water or humid air. Meteors contain iron sulfide which is a pyrophoric solid, and are often found in oil and gas facilities. Here is a short list of some pyrophoric solids; iron, aluminum, magnesium, uranium, titanium, plutonium, and yellow and white phosphorus. Believe me when I say that I am no expert on fissile or nuclear material. The more that we know, the less we seem to understand. I feel that the natural uranium mine became active, and may have channeled these nuclear explosions and gases underground over thousands of miles. The escape of these gases through vents may have allowed the nuclear winds to tear across the surface in different regions. These are just some possibilities posited as gases and Evil Winds have been destroyers in the Biblical, Mayan, and Sumerian texts.*

*Below are 12 cities and 3 civilizations in a similar path around the globe in that region with close latitudes (below 30° North) that may have been decimated as a result of a planetary passover. The cities in the Indus Valley have been found to have radiation levels in skeletons and structures with those on par with Hiroshima and Nagasaki:*

*Sodom (Babe dh-Dhra), Gommorha (Numeira), Admah (Adam), Zeboiim, and Bela – Dead Sea/Valley of Siddim Middle East – the dead cease being buried in these cities after 2200 BCE*

*Dvarka, Harrapa, Mohenjo-Daro, and Lothal – India/Pakistan*

*Aztecs and the Maya – Central America*

*Tower of Babel, Sumer, and Ur – Babylon*

*The Children of the Exodus begin their journey under the spectre of death, and under the Wheel in the Sky with privy member. The Israelites lived among the Sumerians and the Egyptians for over a thousand years. There was a large exchange of culture, arts, entertainment, marriages, lifestyle, and religion. The ruling class in a society has their laws, religions, culture, and other factors in the forefront of their civilization. Some cultures allowed others to worship the deity of their choosing, while others did not allow the people to choose.*

| EXODUS DISASTERS | 1487 BCE – 1447 BCE | GLOBAL |
|---|---|---|
| Bharata battle fought | 1424 BCE | Hindu |
| The fall of Troy | 1194 BCE | Greek |
| Rise of the Mayan culture | 1100 BCE | Mayans |
| Time of Solomon | 1000 BCE | Hebrew |
| Earliest Hebrew writing | @ 1000 BCE | Hebrew |
| Atharva Veda | 1000 BCE | Persian |
| *2 Sacred disasters (40-80yrs apart), 1 culture falls, 1 culture rises, 2 sacred stories | 1487-1000 BCE | 4 Cultures |
| Homer's Odyssey & The Iliad | @ 800 BCE | Greek |

|  |  |  |
|---|---|---|
| Rome Founded | @ 753 BCE | Roman |
| Books of Deuteronomy, Joshua, & Samuel | 700 BCE | Hebrew |
| Egyptian Book of the Dead | 664 BCE | Egyptian |
| Zoroaster & Zarathustra | 628 BCE | Persian |
| Buddha | 563 BCE | Asian |
| The Mahabharata | 540 BCE | Hindu |
| Books of Proverbs & Job | 400 BCE | Hebrew |
| The Critias by Plato | 360 BCE | Greek |
| Septuagint | 300 BCE | Greek |
| *4 Epic battles recorded, 7 Sacred books recorded, 3 New religions rise | 800-300 BCE | 6 Cultures |
| Apocryphal Book of Enoch | @ 300-160 BCE | Hebrew |
| Roman Rule of Egypt | 30 BCE – 641 CE | Egyptian |
| Jesus | @ 5 BCE | Hebrew |
| New Testament | 30-96 CE | Christian |
| Revelation to St. John | 81-96 CE | Christian |
| Nag Hammadi Scriptures | 100 CE | Greek |
| Zohar | 100 CE | Hebrew |
| Popul Vuh | 200 CE | Mayan |
| Jewish Talmud | 350 CE | Hebrew |
| Babylonian Talmud | 400 CE | Hebrew/Babylonian |
| Guttenberg Bible | 1456 CE | Christian |
| Darwin's Origin of Species | 1859 CE | |

| | | |
|---|---|---|
| *No more extinction level events (hopefully) | 1487 BCE – 2012 CE years | 3499 |

     *I feel that I have shown a common genesis and link to all of the sacred books and texts within this manuscript. The Sumerian texts link to the Exodus and to the Book of Ezekiel. The Book of Revelations and the Essene's Revelations were taken from Enoch. The books of the Exodus, Revelations, Essene Revelations, and Jubilees, were all crafted from the Book of Enoch. It was always curious to this researcher and others why the Book of Enoch was never included in the Bible or Torah. After all he was considered a prophet to the early church, and established a calendar for mankind. I believe that Enoch was the victim of plagiarism and copyright violations. Enoch tells a parable of, "The Bull that becomes a man," and this is clearly the story of Noah/Ziusudra and the Great Flood. The next story that was lifted from Enoch and reworked was the founding of the, "Twelve Tribes of Israel," and "The Twelve Sheep." The parable of, "That Sheep (Moses)," leading the sheep from among the wolves to the already parted waters could not be included as it changes the Torah and Biblical accounts. I believe the biggest change and source of discord is the parable of the, "Lofty Tower (Babel)," to the Lord of the Sheep (Yahweh). Enoch tells a decidedly different story, as the Children of the Sheep (Israel) have their Tower (Babel) destroyed by the Lord of the Sheep (Yahweh) that they are building with the Wolves (Babylonians) in the Pleasant Land (Promised Land) after their Exodus from the Wolves (Egypt). These stories are diametrically opposed to how we have been taught that these events transpired. Could the people of Babylon have been the victims of the ultimate slander campaign? Did the Children of Israel help to build the Tower of Babel? I believe there are those that have the answers!*

SIZE IMPROBABILITIES:

*Enoch's Giants – 4,500' height – .85 miles – In the atmosphere*

*Tower of Babel – Height: 5,433' (1.028 miles) Wall 1: 7,800' (1.47 miles) Wall 2: 18,600' (3.52 miles)*

*Ezekiel's Temple/Observatory: 6 cubits (8') in height with no ceiling*

     *Enoch seems to have been the first person with the modern concept of being raptured. Enoch lived 65 years, walked with God 300 years, and was no more. The disappearance of Enoch got me to wondering if Enoch (Enkime) ever existed as a man? The Book of Enoch was dictated to his son Methusaleh, who was the second man said to have learned writing. Enoch (Enkime) gives his son a 364 day calendar, the paths of the sun, the moon, the working of the lightnings (comets), and the names of the heavenly angels (planets). The language that Enoch uses in this portion speaks totally of astronomy, such as; windows, intercalary, chambers, portals, arches, binding, houses, and parabolic meaning (trajectory/Kepler Orbit). The parabolic reference is a telling statement to this portion of the book. Translators of the text have felt that Enoch meant parable, when he clearly meant parabolic. The previous forty (Enki's Sacred number) chapters were an exhaustive astronomy lesson.*

     *After Enoch/Enkime is raptured to heaven, he is called upon by Methusaleh to ensure his son Lamech that the child born to his wife truly was his, and not the son of a Watcher (Warner/Fallen Angel/Igigi). Enoch/Enkime tells him that the child is meant to start the world anew after a disaster. The child Noah/Ziusudra was born glowing with white skin and a red spot. I feel the glow and white skin symbolized the comet/Venus to come, and the red spot either for the Sun or Mars. This would denote the disaster to come, as it was almost six-hundred years from Noah/Ziusudra until the Great Flood. Understanding the seasons and signs in the sky to come was of primary Importance. The last time that Enoch/Enkime is noted in scripture is when his great grandson Noah/Ziusudra that never met him, cries in woe to heaven for Enoch/Enkime who returns to calm his fears.*

*Enoch: 4 Voices (planets) – John 4 Angels & 9 Messengers (planets & satellites)*

*Enoch: 4 Presences – John 4 Horsemen*

*Enoch: Bulls: Red, Black, White, and White – John: Horses: Red, Black, White, and Pale (White)*

*These are just a few examples of John borrowing Enoch's/Enkime's imagery. I will return to the Book of Revelations later in the paragraph. The next imagery borrowed by John and Ezekiel is strictly the description of an astronomical observatory. Once I understood that Enoch/Enkime was talking of astronomy, it was clear from the language what he was describing. Enoch/Enkime speaks of the portals of heaven and describes an astronomical observatory. This was further detailed by later writers such as Ezekiel (wheel within a wheel- Mayan calendar) and John, giving great detail and building instructions. We have an ancient observatory such as Stonehenge and the Great Medicine Wheel as examples of what Enoch/Enkime, Ezekiel, and John were describing in their texts. The first person to divide New Testament chapters into verses was Italian Dominican biblical scholar Santi Pagnini (1470–1541), but his system was never widely adopted. Robert Estienne (1503-1559) created an alternate numbering in his 1551 edition of the Greek New Testament which was also used in his 1553 publication of the Bible in French. Estienne's system of division was widely adopted, and it is this system which is found in almost all modern bibles. The Mayan timeline was conjoined with the Gregorian Calendar during this period, as it would be a little more than one Baktun (1618CE -2012CE) until the Second Coming at th end of the Great Age. We have been stumbling over the obvious since these books were written. I do not know if the mix of astronomy and theology was intentional, accidental, or necessary to maintain order and rule amongst the people. It's my hope that we are at a point of collective intellect and understanding to approach this subject matter with a calm and rational mind.*

*The early Chrisitan church followers were firm believers in the "close, or end of Age," and that world ending changes were soon to follow. The many cosmic and astrological references in our sacred texts have been misinterpreted on an ongoing basis. The Book of Revelations has been the most misunderstood and feared book of any canonized or sacred text. A cottage industry of fear has encapsulated and debilitated humanity with this manipulation of those horrors. This fear keeps us in a perpetual cycle of hate, bias, murder, war, famine, plague, ignorance, false claims, and sins against creation. There are those that write books that speak of "Rapture to Heaven," as our reward for being truly faithful. This plays on our primal fears of being left behind on that Day of Judgment (Tribulation) has led humanity further down the fear factor road. No one wants to be left behind from all of the people that we love, and even the ones that we do not kow. I truly do not think that the manipulation was intentional on the part of most clergy, scribes, writers, researchers, educators, or leadership. People consistently say that they can't wait to get to heaven and away from these burdens, or that we are living in the End Times. I hear so few people speak of loving and enjoying the wonderful transitional existence and test that we are in. This planet Earth is ours to shape her future and ours, for better or for worse.*

*There are various reasons why people look forward to the "End of the world as we know it (TEOTWAKI)." The problems that we face in our daily lives, the visions of violence that stream 24-hours a day from our media centers, and with the impending sense that only God or some other deity can resolve our problems. We have lived in, been encapsulated by, and had the end of the world as we know it promoted for thousands of years. The participants in the pantheon of this prognostication continues to grow daily from misunderstood documents, texts, and teachings. Dread and doom has been the consistent prophecy even before the time of the Christians. Here is a short list of some failed TEOTWAKI prophecies in the recent epoch of time.*

*Prophet Hen of Leeds, England, 1806 – A hen began laying egss with "Jesus is coming," written on them. This drew widespread attention in the Second Coming, until it was discovered to be a hoax.*

*The Millerites, April 23, 1843 – New England farmer William Miller after several years of Bible study concluded God's return to be between March 21, 1843 and March 21, 1944. Many of his followers (Millerites) became disenchanted when the time came and passed with no event, and formed an offshoot group known as The Seventh Day Adventist.*

*Mormon Armegeddon @ 1891 – The founder of the Mormon Church, Joseph Smith, has a meeting with God, and during their discourse learns that Jesus will return in 56 years. The prophesized return never transpired.*

*Pat Robertson, 1982 – Christian Coalition founder Pat Robertson prophesied on his 700 Club show that Judgment on the world would take place in 1982. The prophesized return never transpired.*

*Harold Camping, May 21, 2011 – Brought billboards and sent caravans of followers issuing the prophecy of doom on October 21, 2011. Mr. Camping's time passed as did his failed 1994 prophecy. The news media eagerly followed his story, and those of anyone prophesying doom. The prophesized return never transpired.*

*\* The prophecy dates are typically on the monthly transition from sign to sign 21$^{st}$ to the 23rd*

*John has pulled from older texts and documents, still having lived in a time of disasters he was expectant of more upheaval to come. How could John know that the comet/Venus and others in the neighborhood would settle in and play nice for a period of time. My feeling is that John's Apocalypse occurred in antiquity, and he had a foreboding of doom to come based on archival documents, timelines of disasters, and teachings. One cannot say if we will undergo a catastrophe in the near future as so many prophets of doom declare, but I feel that John is relaying past events used as prophetic vision. This misunderstanding in the text and use of prior prophecy has crippled us for far too long. I am not here to belittle or decry anyone's faith or tenets, as I know that religion and faith has provided some stability and order to a struggling world. Every eon and epoch has its signifigance, and I believe that we are in an age of expansion, reawakening, and enlightenment. I cannot, and will not, tell any man or woman what to believe, whom to worship, or their place in existence. I do know without a doubt that we spring from one source. I am thankful for all of the beautiful souls that I have had the pleasure to encounter, and for all of those that I have yet to encounter. I hope that one and all begin to see that we have to make a fundamental change.*

## DIVINE TRINITY

| The Way of Enlil - 30°N to 90°N | The Way of Anu - 30°N to 30°S | The Way of Enki - 30°S to 90°S |
|---|---|---|

The bulk of the world's deserts lay between 50°N to 10°N – The Sumerians have the world divided between their Trinity of Gods. The cosmic devastation wrought by comets, meteors, and planets over the millennia has destroyed countless civilizations:

1-Mesoamerica; Aztec, Maya, Toltec, Olmec, and Hopi

2-Valley of Siddim/Dead Sea/Sea of Gallilee; Sodom, Ghommorah, Admah, Zeboiim, and Zoar/Bela

3-Babylon; Tower of Babel, Sumer, Ur, and the Euphrates River

4-India/Pakistan; Lothal, Harrapa, Mohenjodaro, and Dvarka

Enlil=Heaven

Anu=Heaven/Earth

Enki=Hell

## Rift Theory

The Jordan Rift Valley runs from the Gulf of Aqqaba (Red Sea crossing?) through the Valley of Siddim, on to the Dead Sea, the Sea of Galilee, and up to the mountains of Lebanon. The 5 cities (and Jericho) that were burned to cinders in Biblical and sacred texts lay in an exact line with the rift fault line. Scientists date the fault line from 5-28 million years ago, but I feel that it played a major part in the destructions of the Bible and other Sacred documents.

| Valley of Siddim | Sea of Galilee |
|---|---|
| Sits in the middle of the Jordan-Gihon Rift which is a highly seismic fault line. | Lowest freshwater lake on the planet (702' below sea level) and the 2$^{nd}$ lowest body of water that happens to be 103.7 miles from the lowest body of water on the planet (Dead Sea). |
| **5 Destroyed Cities of the Dead Sea Area** | **Mount Hermon** |
| Sodom (Bab edh-dra), Gomorrah (Numeira), Admah, Zeboiim, and Zoar/Bela | Sits at the end of the rift and is mentioned as the place where the fallen angels swore an oath |

The Jordan-Gihon Rift runs from the Gulf of Aqqaba all the way up to Lebanon

The journey of Gilgamesh in the Sumerian classic from Uruk to the Cedars of Lebanon

The route of Abraham (Brahma) from Ur to Haran and then down the fault area

## GREAT RIFTS

*East African Rift*

*Jordan Rift*

*Albertine Rift*

*Great Rift – Kenya/Ethiopia*

*X – Oklo, Gabon depleted natural Uranium-235 mine sits near the Prime Meridian and Equator - 0° 23' 0"N, 9° 27' 0" E*

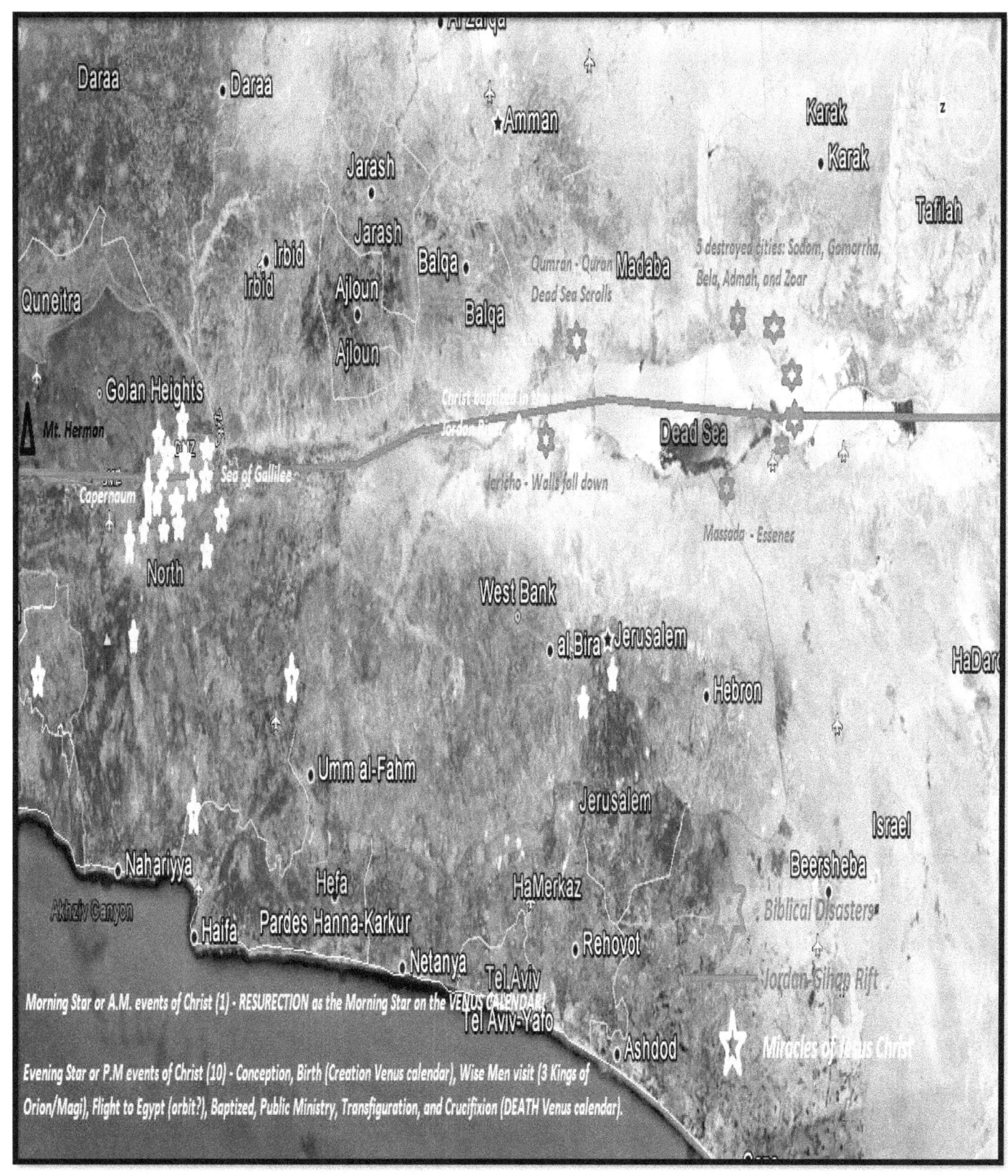

*Clustr map locations of the bulk of miracles associated with Jesus Christ, and the location of most Biblical disasters run along the Jordan-Gihon Rift!*

During the course of research I noticed an interesting parallel between Biblical disasters and miracles within numerous locations in the Jordan-Gihon Rift (seismic fault line). The Jordan-Gihon Rift runs from the Gulf of Aqqaba all the way up to Lebanon in an almost straight line that intersects with the large bulk of Biblical miracles and disasters. I believe this almost undeniable parallel supports the theory of a large planetary sized object causing disaster and distrurbances on a frequent basis in antiquity. The Sea of Galilelee or port cities of that sea, are associated with at least twenty miracles of Jesus Christ. The disasters and miracles that transpired during this period of chaos have been anthropomorphized into deeds of the historical figure of Jesus Christ. The majority of miracles associated with Jesus Christ transpired at Capernaum, which rests along the fault line at the start of the Sea of Galilee. The Red Sea did part, but not because the historical figure Moses brought this about. The apocryphal book of Enoch tells us that the waters were already parted when they arrived, which speaks to a massive gravitational disturbance caused by a passing planetary sized body. Mount Hermon lays at the end of the Jordan-Gihon Rift, and is where the meteorites (Fallen Angels) came to Earth and caused genetic anomalies in mankind. The walls of Jericho fell due to continued earthquakes and being burned by naphtha from the skies as it sits right along the Jordan Rift. The Essenes in the mountain fortress of Masada wanted to be closer to God next to the Dead Sea. The Dead Sea Scrolls were found in a cave in Qumran (Quran?) by the Dead Sea. The 5 cities of the Valley of Siddim(Sodom, Gomorrha, Zoar, Bela, and Admah) were destroyed at the southern part of the Dead Sea. The Sea of Galilee was continually disturbed by the cycles of Venus/comet on a regular basis that brought miracles and disasters in its wake. The Sea of Galilee is the $2^{nd}$ lowest body of fresh water on the Earth and sits 100 miles away from the $2^{nd}$ lowest body of salt water on the planet. These two interesting contradictions shows how the Dead Sea was decimated totally by the passage of Venus and sulfur dioxide that is the main composition of her atmosphere. Theology must not place constraints on science, and science must learn not to stand on rigid empiricals. We are at a crossroads in understanding the past in order to see where we must go for a brighter future as humanity.

| Miracle | Disaster | Location | Water/Mountain/City | Body Part |
|---|---|---|---|---|
| Water to wine<br>John 2:1-11 | Iron Sulfide? (uncovered water vessels?) | Cana – Galilee | Water/City | |
| Fever<br>John 4:46-54 | | Capernaum | City by Sea of Galilee | Body |
| Possessed<br>Mark 1:21-28<br>Luke 4:33-37 | | Capernaum | City by Sea of Galilee | Body |
| Fever<br>Matt 8:14-15<br>Mark 1:29-31<br>Luke 4:38-39 | | Capernaum | City by Sea of Galilee | Body |
| Multpile illnesses<br>Matt 8:16<br>Mark 1:32<br>Luke 4:40-41 | | Evening Capernaum | City by Sea of Galilee<br>*Evening Star? | Various |
| Large number of fish caught<br>Luke 5:3-10 | Planetary Passover | Sea of Galilee | Sea of Galilee | |

| | | | | |
|---|---|---|---|---|
| Leper healed (which type?)<br>Matt 8:1-3<br>Mark 1:40-42 | | Capernaum | City by Sea of Galilee | Body |
| Centurion's Servant<br>Matt 8:5-13<br>Mark 1:2-12<br>Luke 5:18-26 | | Capernaum | City by Sea of Galilee | Body |
| Withered hand<br>Matt 12:9-15<br>Mark 3:1-6 | | Capernaum | City by Sea of Galilee | Hand |
| Paralytic healed<br>Matt 9:1-8<br>Mark 2:1-12<br>Luke 5:18-26 | | Capernaum | City by Sea of Galilee | Body |
| Widow's Son resurrected 3-days<br>Luke 7:11-17 | 3-day Venus cycle below ecliptic | Nain | City near Sea of Galilee | Body |
| Calms the Seas<br>Matt 8:23-27<br>Mark 4:35-41<br>Luke 8:22-25 | Planetary Passover | Sea of Galilee | Sea of Galilee | |
| Possession<br>Matt 8:28-32<br>Mark 5:1-13<br>Luke 8:26-33 | | Gerasene | City by Sea of Galilee | Body |
| Internal bleeding<br>Matt 9:20-22<br>Mark 5:24-34<br>Luke 8:43-48 | | Gerasene | City by Sea of Galilee | Body (Hemophilliac/Lupus?) |
| Resurrection<br>Matt 9:18-19 and 23-25<br>Mark 5:22-24 and 35-43<br>Luke 8:41-42 and 49-56 | | Gerasene | City by Sea of Galilee | Body |
| Vision restored<br>Matt 9:27-31 | Planetary Passover | ? | ? | Eyes |
| Possession<br>Matt 9:32-33 | | ? | ? | Body |
| Invalid helead<br>John 5:5-17 | | Bethesda | City by Sea of Galilee | Body |
| 5,000 Fed<br>Matt 14:16-21<br>Mark 6:35-44<br>Luke 9:12-17<br>John 6:5-17 | Planetary Passover | Shore of Galilee | Sea of Galilee | |
| Walking on Water | Planetary Passover | Sea of Galilee | Sea of Galilee | |

| | | | | |
|---|---|---|---|---|
| Matt 14:22-23<br>Mark 6:45-52<br>John 6:16-21 | | | | |
| Healings<br>Matt 14:34-36<br>Mark 6:53-56 | | Gennesaret | City by Sea of Galilee | Various |
| Possession<br>Matt 15:21-28<br>Mark 7:24-30 | | Tyre | Port City | Body |
| Hearing & Speech restored<br>Mark 7:31-37 | | Tyre | Port City | Ears & Throat |
| Vision restored<br>Mark 8:22-26 | Planetary Passover | Bethsaida | City by Sea of Galilee | Eyes |
| 4,000 Fed (3-day cycle)<br>Matt 15:29-39<br>Mark 8:1-10 | Planetary Passover | Sea of Galilee & Mountain | Mountain near Sea of Galilee | |
| Vision restored<br>John 9:1-41 | Planetary Passover | Siloam | Pool | Eyes |
| Fish with coin<br>Matt 17:24-27 | | Capernaum | City by Sea of Galilee | |
| Resurrection (3-day cycle)<br>John 11:1-44 | Planetary Passover | Bethany | Lazarus | Body |
| Vision restored<br>Mark 10:46-52 | Planetary Passover | Jericho | City by Jordan River | Eyes |
| Resurrection (3-day cycle)<br>1 Cor15<br>Matt 28<br>Mark 16<br>Luke 24<br>John 20 | Planetary Passover | Jerusalem | Jesus Christ | Morning/Evening Star |
| Large number of fish caught<br>John 21:4-11 | Planetary Passover | Sea of Galilee | Disciples – Jesus Christ post resurrection | |
| Ascension<br>Acts 1:1-11 | Planetary Passover | Heavens | Jesus Christ 40 days after death | Continued use of the number 40 |
| Walls of Jericho fall down | Earthquake | Jordan River fault line | Land near water | Jordan-Gihon Rift |
| Sodom | Planetary Passover | Naphtha & meteorites | Fire & brimstone | Jordan-Gihon Rift |
| Gomorrah | Planetary Passover | Naphtha & meteorites | Fire & brimstone | Jordan-Gihon Rift |
| Zoar | Planetary Passover | Naphtha & meteorites | Fire & brimstone | Jordan-Gihon Rift |
| Bela | Planetary Passover | Naphtha & meteorites | Fire & brimstone | Jordan-Gihon Rift |

| Admah | Planetary Passover | Naphtha & meteorites | Fire & brimstone | Jordan-Gihon Rift |
| Red Sea Crossing (Burned Mountains) | Planetary Passover | Gulf of Aqqaba | Water diverted | Jordan-Gihon Rift |
| Mount Hermon (Burned Mountains) | Planetary Passover | Meteorites | Fallen angels swear an oath | Jordan-Gihon Rift |

*Morning Star / Evening Star*

*Evening Star or P.M events of Christ (10) - Conception, Birth (Creation Venus calendar), Wise Men visit (3 Kings of Orion/Magi), Flight to Egypt (orbit?), Baptized, Public Ministry, Transfiguration, and Crucifixion (DEATH Venus calendar).*

*Morning Star or A.M. events of Christ (1) - RESURRECTION as the Morning Star on the VENUS CALENDAR!*

**CONCEPTION, CRUCIFIXION, AND RESURRECTION = CREATION, DEATH and RESURRECTION = VENUS**

"*Phaeton first it veered too high, so that the earth grew chill. Then it dipped too close, and the vegetation dried and burned. He accidentally turned most of Africa into desert; bringing the blood of the Ethiopians to the surface of their skin, turning it black*"

*Ovid*

# ADDENDUM I

## "The Celestial Vault of Alessandro Farnese aka Pope Paul III"

*Pope Paul III with his grandsons, Cardinal Alessandro Farnese (14), and Cardinal Ottavio Farnese, Duke of Parma (22) in 1534.*

**Pope Paul III** *(29 February 1468 – 10 November 1549), born* **Alessandro Farnese**, *was Pope of the Roman Catholic Church from 1534 to his death in 1549. During his reign, and in the spirit of the Counter-Reformation, new Catholic religious orders and societies, such as the Jesuits, the Theatines, the Barnabites and the Congregation of the Oratory, attracted a popular following and he convened the Council of Trent in 1545. He was a significant patron of the arts and employed nepotism to advance the power and fortunes of his family.*

*The Farnese family had prospered over the centuries but it was Alessandro's ascendency to the papacy and his dedication to furthering family interests which saw the vastly significant increase in the family's wealth and power. Pope Alexander's mistress, Giulia, was Farnese's sister; and he was sometimes mockingly referred to as the "Borgia brother-in-law." Under Pope Clement VII (1523–34) he became Cardinal Bishop of Ostia and dean of the College of Cardinals, and on the death of Clement VII in 1534, was elected as Pope Paul III.*

*One of various popes to have fathered children before his election, he had four illegitimate offspring. By Silvia Ruffini, he fathered Pier Luigi Farnese, whom he created Duke of Parma; others included Ranuccio Farnese and Costanza Farnese. His first action, on 18 December 1534, was to appoint his grandsons as* cardinals. At the time, Alessandro Farnese and Guido Ascanio Sforza were aged fourteen and sixteen years respectively. One of the most significant artistic works of his reign was the depiction of the Last Judgement by Michelangelo in the Sistine Chapel of the Vatican Palace. Although the work was commissioned by Paul's predecessor, it was finished in 1541. The military fortifications in Rome and the Papal States were strengthened during his reign. He had Michelangelo relocate the ancient bronze of the Emperor Marcus Aurelius to the Capitoline Hill, where it became the centerpiece to the Piazza del Campidoglio.

Paul III had many personal reasons to trust Astrology because one of the most important Italian astrologers, Luca Gaurico, had foreseen his election many years before, when Alessandro was just a noble from a small town, of restless temperament and uncertain faith who succeeded in becoming a cardinal more for the beauty of his sister Giulia the Beautiful, fondly loved by the Pope Alexander VI, than because his religious ardour.

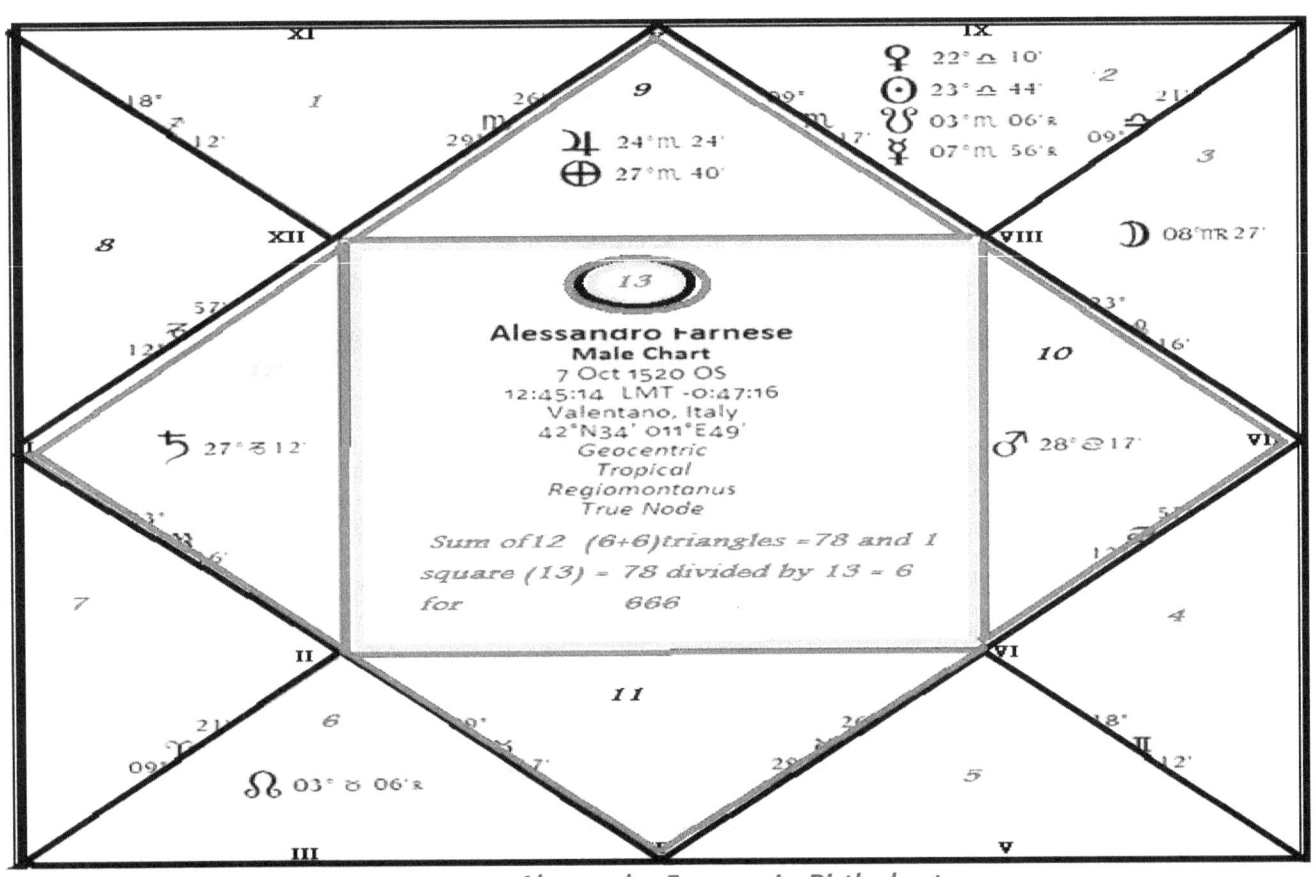

Alessandro Farnese Jr. Birth chart

After the death of Paul III, when works were resumed, the famous architect Jacopo Vignola turned the military fortress in a wonderful representation of celestial order building inside the pentagonal walls of the fortress an unusual round porch—the circle inside the pentagon- according his peculiar architectural system based on Pythagoras' musical harmony, the same on which Ptolemy based his planetary theory. In order to highlight the idea of Caprarola as a symbol of the Universe, Vignola built a long straight road departing from the entrance of the Villa and crossing all the town, an axis mundi, the world axis around all the Universe turns around.

*Against a bright blue background are shown the 48 Ptolemaic constellations, the stars painted according their magnitude, the line of ecliptic (with the zodiacal signs from Gemini to Taurus from left to right), the tropics of Cancer and Capricorn, the axis of Poles. The most evident divergence is the presence of Jupiter with his Eagle in the top-left corner while throwing his thunderbolts against Phaeton, who is falling into the river Eridanus. Jupiter is a planet and not one of the forty-eight constellations, and if so prominently featured should be very important and meaningful for Alessandro- in fact it was one of his own* imprese, *chosen by his grandfather because God himself who gave him the power to the Pope, and with his thunderbolts he, God on Earth, could destroy the sin of heresy and pride (as Phaeton was destroyed for his own sins).*

*Frescoes in the walls shows signs in this order:*
**PISCES-ARIES- TAURUS: (Western wall)**
**Pisces:** *Venus and her son turning themselves into Fishes in order to escape Typhon;*
**Aries:** *Phrixus saved by the Ram and Helle with Neptune;*
**Taurus:** *Europa and Jupiter disguised under the form of the Bull;*

**LEO-GEMINI-CANCER: (Eastern wall)**
**Leo:** *Hercules killing the Nemean Lion;*
**Gemini:** *Neptune presenting the reins of his horses as a gift to the Twins;*
**Cancer:** *Hercules with the Hydra;*
**VIRGO-LIBRA-SCORPIO (Southern wall)**
**Virgo:** *Astrea rising to the sky with the Spike in her hand (the star Spica);*
**Libra:** *An imperial Eagle carries the Balance heavenwards while Virgo and Scorpio are receding at the sides of the fresco.*

**Scorpio:** *Diana and Orion, and the Scorpio sent by Jupiter;*
**SAGITTARIUS-CAPRICORN-AQUARIUS (Northern wall)**
**Sagittarius:** *Some centaurs engaged in combat with male figures;*
**Capricorn:** *A male goat pouring water and she-goat suckling an infant;*
**Aquarius:** *Ganymede who is pouring water from a vase and people in despair (Aquarius is linked with Deluge too).*
- **Capricorn** *is his rising sign, with its ruler Saturn dignified in the first house;*
- **Libra** *is on the cusp of his ninth house, the God house, strictly connected to his hopes, so near to become true during the years this room was frescoed.*
- **Aries** *was a recurring sign in Farnese group, a warrior family well signified by Mars, the sign ruler.*
 **Gemini** *could be referred to the special link, like in the story of Castor and Pollux*

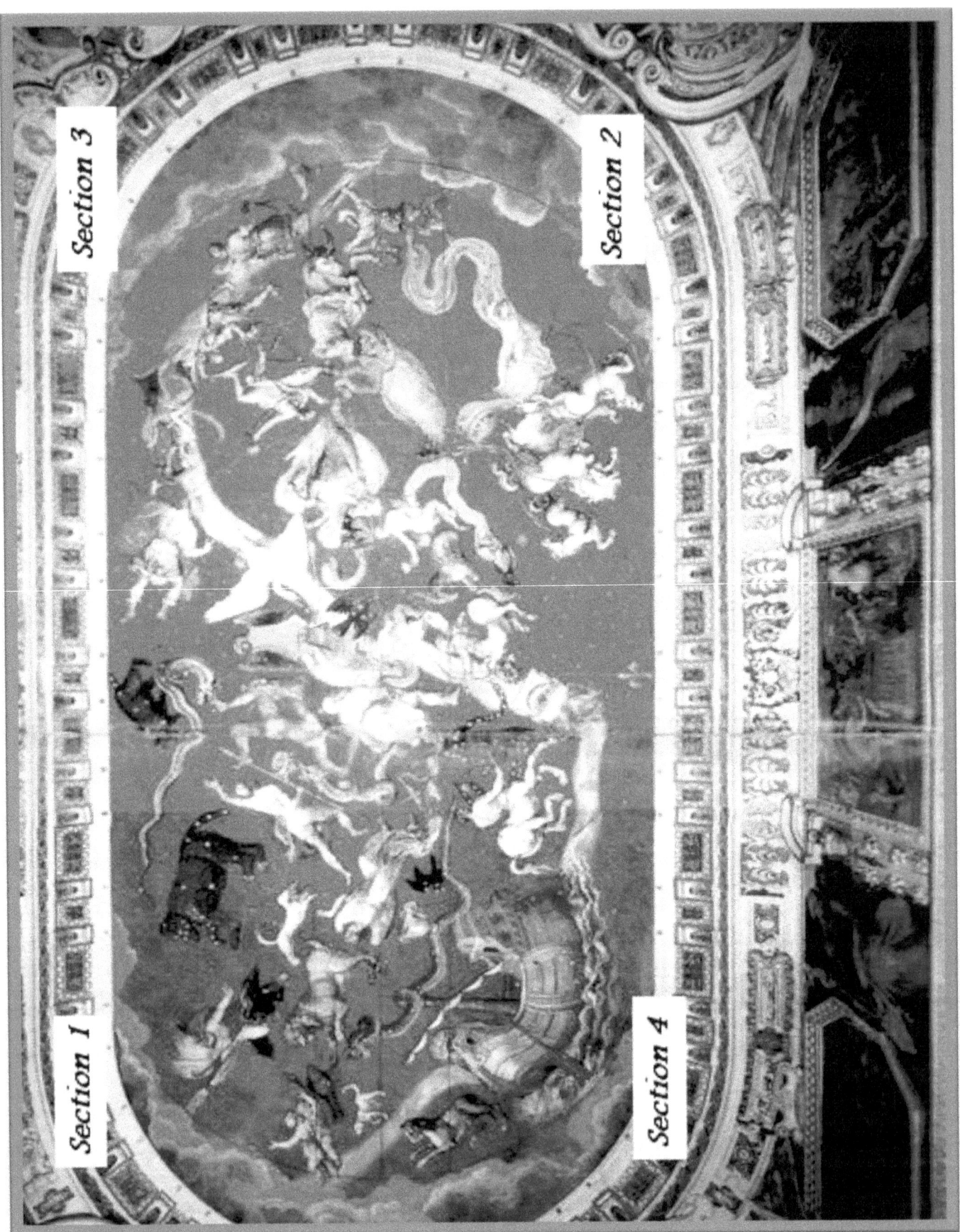

### Section 1 – Planet Jupiter

We see the planet/god Jupiter as he sits astride the black eagle, set to unleash his mighty lightning bolt. What is the planet/god Jupiter doing pictured with the zodiac constellations? I chose to show Jupiter first as he is the catalyst to the whole series of events in the heavens that bring about catastrophe. The lightning bolt that Jupiter wields has been postulated by Mr. Velikofsky to be that of a plasma discharge. Section 1 shows Gemini(Twins), Cancer (Crab), Leo (Lion), Canis Minor (Little Dog), Canis Major (Big Dog), Virgo (Virgin), Bootes (Good Shepherd), Ursa Major (Big Bear), Ursa Minor (Little Bear), Hercules (Laborer), Ophiuchus (Serpent Bearer), Corona Borealis (Crown), Serpens (Serpent), and Draco(Dragon) constellations in their general accepted locale.

### Section 2 – Phaeton Falls from the Celestial Chariot

The lightning bolt that Jupiter is set to release is headed towards Phaeton. In Greek mythology Phaeton was the son of Helios (Sun) and the Oceanid Clymene. Phaeton seeks assurance that his mother, Clymenē, is telling the truth that his father is the sun god Helios (as her husband is Merops, a mortal king). When Phaeton obtains his father's promise to drive the sun chariot as proof, he fails to control it and the Earth is in danger of burning up when Phaeton is killed by a thunderbolt from Zeus to prevent further disaster. The name "Phaëton", which means "shining", is also an epithet of Eosphoros, the **Morning Star Venus**. Phaethon is also the name of another minor Greek deity, the god of the wandering star Dios (the planet Jupiter).

We see Phaeton (Venus) begins to cause catastrophe in the Age of Taurus (4469 BCE – 2309 BCE) with the Orion constellation facing off with the Bull as he steps on the Lepus (Hare) constellation in the Eridanus (River of Fire) constellation. There is a notable absence of several zodiac constellations in this cropping! Where is Cetus (Sea Monster) constellation? Where is Aries (Ram) constellation? Why is the Pegasus (Winged Horse) constellation in a blurred turmoil? The Age of Aries follows the Age of Taurus, and preceeds the Age of Pisces, yet is clearly missing and not depicted! The second fish of Pisces is clouded in the mass with Pegasus as the Bands constellation blurs into the celestial morass. The artist *Giovanni Vanosino knew what the Farnese family wanted depicted as the more illumined class understood the celestial battles that had come to an end, but assigned their theology through anthropomorphism to these heavenly bodies and battles.*

The stolen chariot of Phaeton (Venus) falls from the sky during the Age of Pisces (148 BCE – 2012 CE) as this depiction is from 1530's CE. This knowledge of catastrophe and cosmic upheaval had ceased after the Dark to Middle Ages, but the knowledge was passed down through closed circles.

Section 2 shows us Taurus (Bull), Orion (Hunter), Eridanus (River of Fire), Lepus (Hare), Pisces (Fish), Aquarius (Waterman), Capricorn (Sea Goat), Sagittarius (Archer), Southern Crux/Cross (Fleur-de-lis), Summer Triangle (Cygnus, Lyra, Aquila), and Pegasus (Winged Horse – blurred) constellations.

### Section 3 – Disorder in the Heavens"

Section 3 is in general turmoil as are most of the constellations noted. The two major areas of note are the Cygnus (Swan) and Pegasus? (Winged Horse) constellations. Cygnus seems to be flowing on a mist in the direction of the disruption. Although the Summer Triangle (Aquila, Lyra, and Cygnus) constellation is pictured, it is Cygnus that seems to be in the midst of the fray as well. What appears to be the Pegasus constellation may be embroiled with the missing Aries (Ram) and Dolphinus (Dolphin) constellations?

Section 3 features; Taurus (Bull), Cygnus (Swan),Summer Triangle (Cygnus, Lyra, Aquila), Eagle (Aquila), Perseus (Hero), Andromeda (Chained Princess), Virgo (Virgin), Infant Prince (Infant & Mother), Bootes (Good Shepherd), Hercules,Ophiuchus (Serpent Bearer), Serpens (Serpent), Auriga (Charioteer),Ursa Mnior (Little Bear), Draco (Dragon), and Lyra (Harp) constellations.

### Section 4- "What happened to Lupus?"

Section 4 brings the celestial chaos to a completion as the Lupus (Beast) constellation is usually portrayed as being speared by Centaurus (Centaur). Notice that Lupus is just a link of stars of undefined shape near the Altar (Ara) constellation.

Section 4 shows; Argo (Ship), Hydra (Water Serpent), Crater (Cup), Corvus (Raven), Centaurus (Centaur), Lupus (Beast), Ara (Altar), and Libra (Scales) constellations

**CONCLUSIONS:**

It's clear that Pope Paul III and the Farnese family had secret knowledge as to the nature of the destruction from Phaeton, and this clearly blended with their theology. The zodiac constellations are in chaos as they are flowing clockwise, and not counter clockwise as it does in our sky. The disturbance during the Age of Taurus, Aries, and ending during Pisces shows the worldwide catastrophe that was suffered during these epochs. The zodiac constellations are set up in a left hand (toe, horn, hoof, etc.) manner in passing off from age to age. I will show in a future project how Ovid recorded these cosmic observation in his work, "The Metamorphoses," and their decoding into modern understanding. The Farnese family used the most famous artists of their time, and would not be paying them lucrative amounts for a myth, but for a portrayal of their strong belief in astrology and astronomy!

# ADDENDUM II

## Earth's Gobal Geomagnetic Field 12,000 BCE to 2012 CE

I will attempt to show my belief that a heavenly body such as Venus (Phaeton/comet/Mars/etc) disturbed and increased the Earth's geomagnetic field during various periods. These periodic catastrophes saw the fall and rise of civilizations, the genesis and death of Gods, and the destruction and rebirth of our planet.

The weak periods of the geomagnetic field correlate directly with many global disasters in the low range 7 to >8 from 12,000 BCE to around 1500 BCE. The geomagnetic field begins to increase sharply from >8 to a high of 11 around 0 AD. This high geomagnetic field corresponds with the sharp rise in theologies, and monotheisim in particular. From 0 CE to 500 CE we peak at a level of 11 for this epoch. The high geomagnetic field shows a rise in theology as this object took a geosynchronous orbit around the planet for 1500 years. Venus (Phaeton, etc.) was no longer the threat it had formerly been, but shown in the sky twenty-four hours a day. The famous "Wheel in the Sky," finally faded into mystery as explorers like Columbus finally chanced going out to voyage the oceans as things had settled down. We see in 1530 CE, Pope Paul III has the scene of turmoil emblazoned in his Celestial Vault. The Maya now forsee the coming of visitors to their shores! The loss of this celestial body from a geosynchronous orbit probably weakened the geomagnetic field of the planet as it went down to 10 during the 1800's.

In the period of roughly 200 years, up to today, we have gone from 10 to 9! This is a massive dropoff in a short period of time. I feel that I have shown how our geomagnetic field has been either positively or negatively affected by these events. One cannot say if industry, nuclear testing, and other unfriendly activities that we have undertaken are to blame. There are currently almost 8 billion humans on the planet, and our governments are unable to save all of humanity in the event of a catastrophe. I believe that our best and brightest minds are actively seeking a solution, but, to tell you of the true status may be to alarm you falsely or too soon! It is my belief that all people should be allowed to live and die, in truth and honesty. Woe to the man that has his brother help to build his ark, while being none the wiser of catastrophe to come!

| Date | Geomagnetic Field | Event |
|---|---|---|
| 9500 BCE | >8 | End of Ice Age, Plato's destruction of Atlantis, Gobekli Tepe (12,000 BCE) |
| 8500 BCE | 7 | SILENCE 9500 BCE to 4000 BCE |
| 7500 BCE | >8 | |
| 6500 BCE | >8 | |
| 5500 BCE | >7 | |
| 4500 BCE | <8 | |
| 3500 BCE | 7 | |
| 2300 BCE | >8 | Global Flood(2344 BCE), Egyptian writing, Sumerian writing, start of Maya time, start of Kali Yuga |
| 1500 BCE | 9 | Global Exodus disasters(1487-1447 BCE), Enuma Elish, Epic of Gilgamesh, Indus Valley Collapse, Santorini erupts, Dwarka falls into the sea, Bharata Battle |

| | | |
|---|---|---|
| 1000 BCE | 11 | Fall of Troy, Maya Rise, Rome founded, Atharva Veda, Deuteronomy, Samuel, Joshua, Egyptian Book of the Dead, Zoroastrianism, Zarathusra, Buddha, Mahabharata, Book of Enoch |
| 0 CE | 11 | Jesus Christ, New Testament, Revelations, Nag Hammadi, Zohar, Popul Vuh, Jewish Talmud, Babylonian Talmud |
| 750 CE | <11 | **DARK AGES** |
| 1500 CE | >11 | **MIDDLE AGES** – Columbus discovers (rediscovers) the New World, Guttenberg Bible |
| 1800 CE | >10 | Darwin's Origin of Species |
| 2000 CE | 9 | Nuclear testing - 2012 Present Day |

RED = >7 to <7 (EXTINCTION LEVEL)   = >8 to <8 (ONSET LEVEL)

ORANGE = >9 to <9 (CAUTION LEVEL)   GREEN = 10> (POSITIVE LEVEL)

| | 12,000 BCE | 10,000 BCE | 8000 BCE | 6000 BCE | 4000 BCE | 2000 BCE | BCE = 0 = CE | 2000 CE | 4000 CE | |
|---|---|---|---|---|---|---|---|---|---|---|
| | | | | | | | | | | 12 |
| | | | | | | | | * | * | |
| | | | | | | | * * | * | * | 10 |
| | | | | | | | * | | * | |
| | | * | | * | * | | * | | | 8 |
| | | * | | | * | * * | | | | |
| | | | | | | | | | | 6 |
| | | | | | | | | | | |
| | | | | | | | | | | |
| | | | | | | | | | | 4 |
| | | | | | | | | | | |
| | | | | | | | | | | 2 |
| | | | | | | | | | | |
| | 12,000 BCE | 10,000 BCE | 8000 BCE | 6000 BCE | 4000 BCE | 2000 BCE | BCE = 0 = CE | 2000 CE | 4000 CE | 0 |

# ADDENDUM III

## *Ezekiel the Prophet – Tammuz*

**Ezekiel 8:13**  He said also unto me, **Turn** thee yet **again**, and thou shalt see **greater abominations** that they do.
**Ezekiel 8:14** Then he brought me to the **door** of the **gate** of the **LORD's house** which was **toward** the **north**; and, behold, there **sat women weeping for Tammuz.**

This is yet another statement of astronomy mingled with theology, as Ezekiel has been shown the North, West, South, and East gates of the Kingdom of God. These statements show the often repeated use of the four cardinal points in relating cosmic events. The The sun's path through the sky is similarly farther north in June and farther south in December. In late March and late September (at the "equinoxes"), the sun's path follows the celestial equator. It then rises directly east and sets directly west. The exact dates of the equinoxes vary from year to year, but are always near March 20 and September 22. After the March equinox, the sun's path gradually drifts northward. By the June solstice (usually June 21), the sun rises considerably north of due east and sets considerably north of due west. For mid-northern observers, the noon sun is still toward the south, but much higher in the sky than at the equinoxes. After the June solstice, the sun's path gradually drifts southward. By the September equinox, its path is again along the celestial equator. The southward drift then continues until the December solstice (usually December 21), when the sun rises considerably south of due east and sets considerably south of due west. For mid-northern observers, the noon sun is quite low in the southern sky. After the December solstice, the sun's path drifts northward again, returning to the celestial equator by the March equinox. As you travel southward in the northern hemisphere, the noon sun gets higher and higher. The first qualitative change occurs at 23.5° latitude, where the noon sun on the June solstice passes directly overhead. This latitude is called the Tropic of Cancer. Farther south, in the so-called tropics, the noon sun will appear in the northern sky for a period of time around the June solstice. At the equator, the noon sun is straight overhead on the equinoxes. And after you pass 23.5° south latitude (the Tropic of Capricorn), the noon sun is always in the north.

Tammuz/Dumizid was a Sumerian king/Sheperd god that reigned for 360,000 years. This is another reference to the 360°'s of the chariots that the constellations take in the heavens. In Babylonia the month Tammuz (June/July) was established in his honor. Starting with the summer solstice began a time of mourning in the ancient Near East; the Babylonians marked the decline in daylight hours and the onset of brutal summer heat and drought with a 6-day funeral for the god, as they "Weep for Tammuz." Tammuz is an annual life-death rebirth god as he is revived for 6-months, and his sister Gestinanna takes over for the other 6-months of the year. In one version Tammuz steps on a scorpion as he flees through the desert at night. This scenario correlates with the celestial configuration of the Ophiuchus constellation (Serpent Bearer) who steps on the Scorpio constellation with his left foot. Ophiuchus (Lord Krishna) happens to be the lost 13$^{th}$ zodiac constellation. Tammuz was also likened to the Sun as a celestial being.

The Hebrew calendar and the Torah were formed during the captivity period in Babylon. The Hebrew use of the name of Tammuz for their calendar and festival shows a clear borrowing of Sumerian/Babylonian customs and practices. The Hebrew celebration of Tammuz takes place in the same time period yearly, but is dedicated to the breaching of the walls of Jerusalem by King Nebuchadnezzar. I feel it safe to say that Tammmuz was anthropomorphized as a man, and only existed through the imaginings of mankind.

**Tammuz/Dumuzid – Harvest god**
**Sun – Tammuz**

**Inanna/Ishtar – Venus**
**Venus - Inanna**

**Gestinanna – Tammuz's sister**
**Sun – Gestinanna**

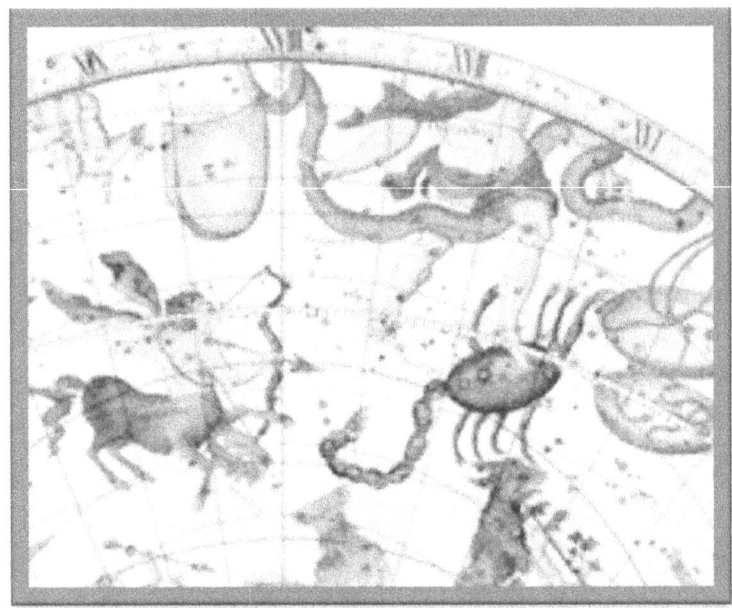
**Ophiuchus Constellation – Serpent Bearer -13$^{th}$ zodiac sign**

**Bootes Constellation – Good Shepherd**

*\* Stonehenge, United Kingdom*

*Every year hundreds of thousands of people make a pilgrimage to Stonehenge, on the Salisbury Plains in the United Kingdom. This is done to observe the celestial majesty that is the rising of the sun, on the day of the summer solstice, which is usually June 21$^{st}$. The day that the sun dies yearly is marked by its' rise in direct alignment with the heel stone as this signals the head towards colder weather. This is celebrated as the death of Tammuz/Dumuzi and many others in legend. Tammuz is reborn on December 25$^{th}$ as is celebrated in many cultures and religions. Noted researcher Bert Janssen, has shown how the sun sets there on June 21$^{st}$ the day of the summer solstice at directly 103.5 degrees, which in Pythagorean, Archemides, and Masonic terminology is squaring the circle!*

*Wailing Wall, Jerusalem*

# Contest Extra

This is a lost text recently discovered. The task is to figure out the disaster that the scribe is relating to the reader using his terminology mixed with theology. The incident being related and the text must be deciphered line by line, as close as possible to the incident being related. One must see through the language to decode the tragedy. The winner will be announced one year from the date of book publication. All submissions must be by e-mail only, with text copied and pasted, no attachments will be accepted. The earliest correct submission will be certified by their e-mail date and time received. Full content details will be found on the website listed below:

*Verse 1* – The Advesary came at the end of Hel' emmelek, on the equinox of Mel' ejal borne on the wings of the Advesary, twelve was the number of the Beast as from ten it came. The Evil Wind was forming to judge the sins and iniquities of the Saints.

*Verse 2* – The seal was broken after two days while the angel of the Lord sounded the trumpet. God has passed His Judgment against the land that worships Shamash, the fallen Saints, and their federates. Yea, not since the days of Noah and Moses has such a Judgment befallen man. Men in their boats laughed in defiance of God, and perished in their pride as they were sent to the dark abyss of Baalzebub.

*Verse 3* – The Sinners and Saints laughed mightily as the prayers to their gods had seemed to ease the tempest to come. This one day of calm was all in God's plans to give the wicked time to come to Him in supplication. As He passed through the Land of the Shamash worshippers the gulf widened as the trumpet sounded and the number one opened the seal.

*Verse 4* – As the tempest roared once more, those in the Halls of Leadership began to fear our God. The lawmakers found no relief in their Gods, soldiers, services, or statutes. The Red Bull was the leader of the Sinner Saints and roared orders for the other Bulls that they should do.

*Verse 5* – Before the Sun made its ascent on that day, the angel opened the third seal and the trumpet roared; woe, woe, woe, in the heavens! The Saints and Sinners in their congregations and parishes were ordered to flee before the face of the Almighty. None could stand before the face of the tempest of the Lord, as that Evil Wind swirled and washed away them in their low houses.

*Verse 6* – Then the Black Bull enforced the order of the Red Bull to flee in three score hours. The coffers of the toll collectors went without. The Children of the Lord that heard His word late were sent to the Temple of Saints where God Almighty would shelter them from the Evil Wind still to land. God led the Black Bull to order all to lay down their arms upon entrance to the New House of Saints as the Advesary caused man to war with man. That the people should shelter with food to sustain them for a time. Fifteen times a thousand new Saints there did shelter was the plan.

*Verse 7* – The Red Bull sends an emissary to the White Bull with a plea for aid from the Judgment that has been decreed.

*Verse 8* – The old White Bull decreed by an Act that the Red Bull should receive help.

*Verse 9* – Thereby the old White Bull one-thousand seven hundred and one foot soldiers, with nine-hundred and thirty-two and two eagles to the tempest that they may try to alter the Judgment of God.

*Verse 10* – The Black Bull and the Red Bull were informed of the rage of God's tempest as it grew. The Black Bull wept and cried to heaven as the trumpet roared; woe, woe, woe!

*Verse 11* – The Sabbath arrived with the opening of the fourth seal. The sound of the third trumpet had barely faded as the fifth seal was opened and thereupon Judgment was final. Twenty-thousand of His New Children sheltered at the Temple of the Saints, as wolves made their way into the midst of His Lambs. The wolves began to usurp the means of His Children, and thereby did do them harm.

*Verse 12* – The tempest raged as the Beast name they knew! Their land did it walk to and fro three times. The Evil Wind fueled the sails of the Beast, as poisoned waters heaped in piles upon the land as in the days of Noah. The breech was severe as the tempest *opened an abyss upon the land. The Sinners and Saints that still worshipped Shamash fled in their yellow beasts, as their soldiers failed in their mission, and many of the sinners began to perish.*

**Verse 13** – *The seventh day drew to an end as the Beast's fury was now sated, His Judgment executed, and the number of His Judgment claimed. Sinner and Saint, man and woman, beast and fowl, were scattered to the federacies that their brethren may house them to hear His gospel. The land was to be left fallow for four seasons was His decree, before the return of His faithful to rebuild anew. Many were still to answer among their brethren for their chosen God, but, the Beast name shall resonate, and His Judgment Divine!*

# *Reference Material*

**Apocryphal Book of Enoch**

*The Apocyrphal & Pseudoepigripha of the Old Testament – RH Charles*

*A Modern Enlgish Translation of the Ethiopean Book of Enoch*

**Book of the Exodus**

*Septuagint Book of the Exodus – Benton*

**Ipuwer Papyrus**

*Leidin Papyrus 344 – National Archelogical Museum – Leiden, Netherlands*

**Lament for Sumer & Urim**

**Book of Jubilees**

**Book of Job**

*King James Bible – American Version*

**Book of Ezekiel**

*King James Bible – American Version*

**Apocalypse of Peter**

*King James Bible – American Version, The Akhmin Fragment – Greek*

**Apocalypse of Paul**

*King James Bible – American Version*

**Book of Revelations**

*King James Bible – American Version*

**Revelations of the Essenes**

*Dead Sea Scrolls – EB Szekely*

**Lost Book of Enki**

*Sumerian cylinder seals & tablets – Zecharia Sitchin*

In the picture above we have several clear examples of planetary adoration and worship within our theologies. The Temple Mount complex in Jerusalem is the most fought over piece of real estate on the face of the Earth, and sits on top of a much older site. Several events tied to the lives of Solomon, Jesus Christ and the Prophet Muhammad occurred at this complex. Looking at the current layout of the complex, the reason for all of the hub bub becomes transparent. The golden dome represents the Sun, as the much smaller black domed chapel represents the Moon. Veneration of the Sun was first observed in Egypt and Sumeria, and was antrhropomorphized as Ra and Shamash respectively. Egyptians and Sumerians showed their adoration by holding their arms skyward with palms facing the rays of the Sun, just as modern day Christians. The reverse of the Christian palms forward, would be the Islamic practice of palms facing the supplicant. We have the Sun vernerated forward, and the Moon worshipped in reverse!

Sun = Shamash/Ash Sham = Sol     Moon = Luna/Sin/aah/lah     Solomon = Sol/Sun & Omon/Moon

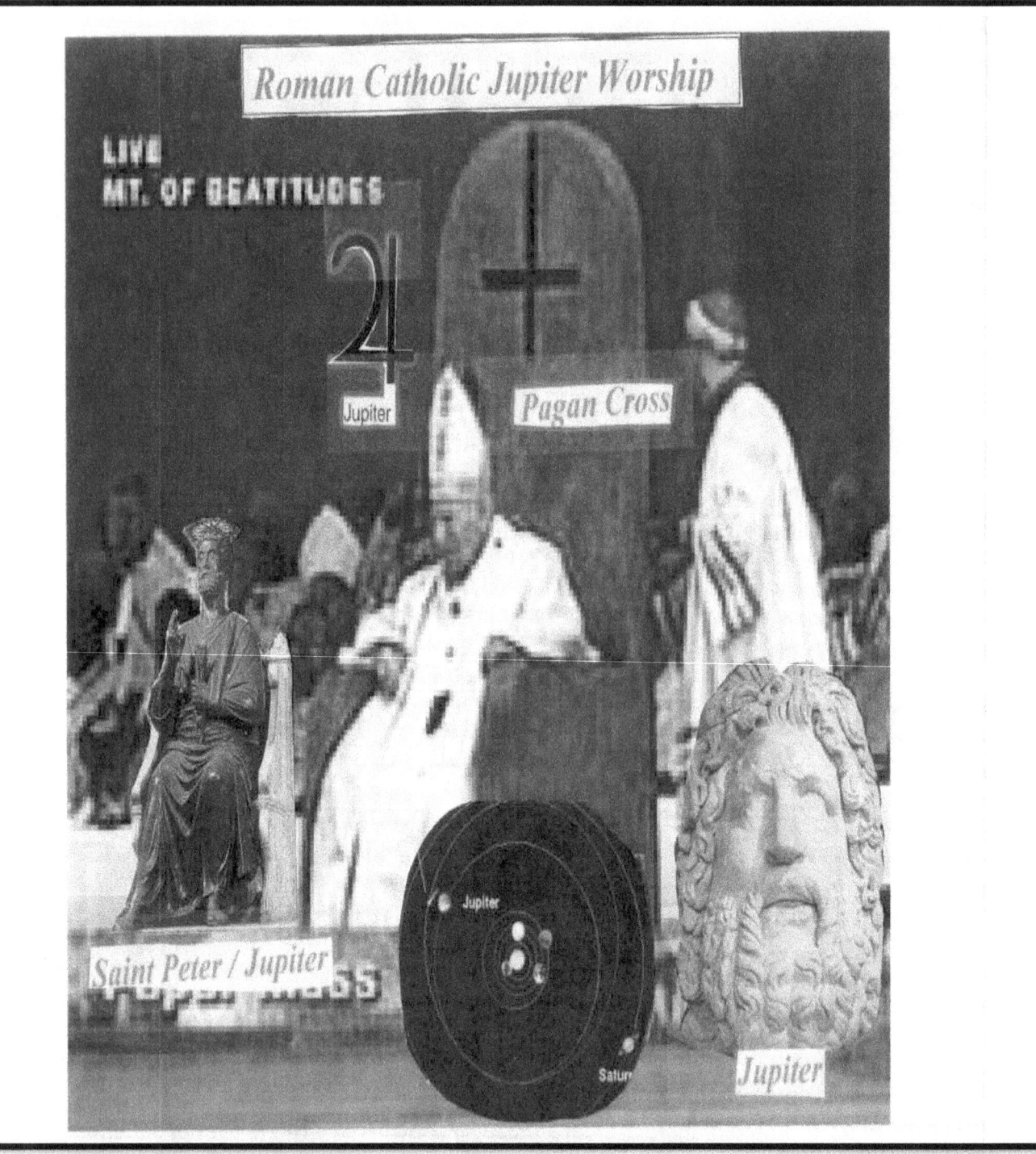

*The Romans were long known to worship the God Jupiter, as well as a large pantheon of Gods and demigods. The planet Jupiter is anthropomorphized as ruling over the Universe from on high, wielding a mighty lightning bolt. The chair chosen by the late Pope John Paul II for certain ceremonies caused many to wonder about the pagan signifigance of the inverted cross. The astrological symbol for Jupiter is an inverted cross and sickle. The sickle has just been removed, and adopted as a separate item of veneration. The statue of St. Peter has long been suspected of being that of Jupiter, having been removed from a pagan temple and rededicated in his name. We see that the correlation between them may have been correct!*

The Cross of Saturn has been used in Chrisitanity and Catholicism as a symbol of Jesus Christ's suffering. The use of the cross as a symbol predates this modern use, and traces its roots back to Egypt (Horus) and Sumeria (Tammuz). The Roman festival of Saturnalia was combined with that of the Christians by Emperor Constantine to become what we know today as Christmas. The planet Saturn has been anthropomorphized as Cronos who ate his children (planets), but his son Zeus/Jupiter leads the Titans (Jupiter's moons) to kill Cronos/Saturn. The planet Saturn is associated with the Black Cube, and symbolizes time and confinement!

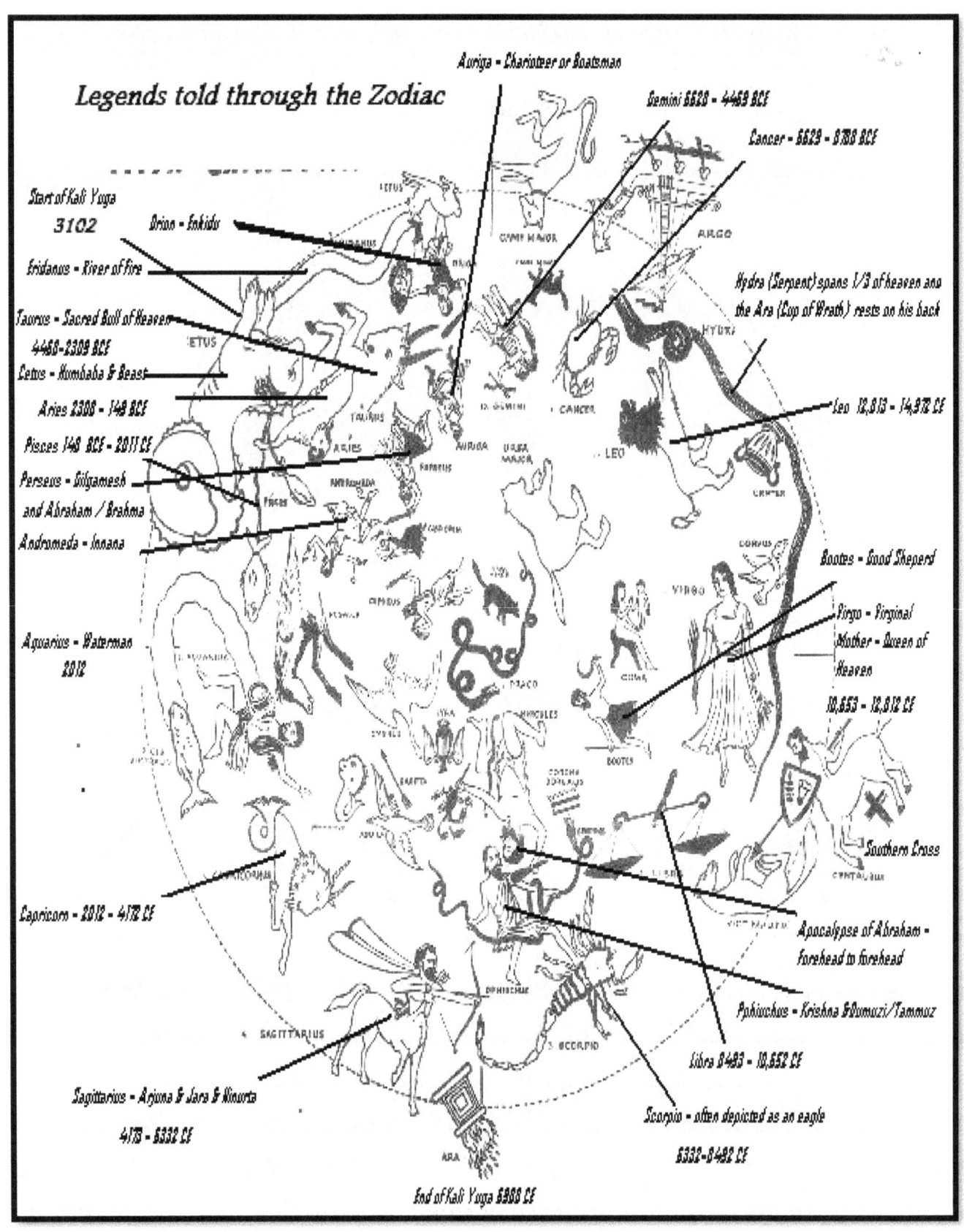

**It's time to re-examine the basis for our religious teachings!**

*"Those things which are sacred are to be imparted only to sacred persons; and it is not lawful to impart them to the profane until they have been initiated into the mysteries of science."*

**Law of Hippocrates – Hippocratic Oath**

*"It's no measure of health to be well adjusted to a profoundly sick society."*
**Jiddu Krishnamurti**

*"for they had no adequate faith in their divinity to keep them from changing them, nor had they any sufficient understanding of them, either, as still being at that time under veil – even obscure to the Jews themselves, whose peculiar possession they seemed to be."*

**Ovid – Christianity versus the philosophers**

**Velikofsky vindicated!**

**Rest in peace Sir**

www.ingramcontent.com/pod-product-compliance
Lightning Source LLC
Chambersburg PA
CBHW080533170426
43195CB00016B/2550